BODIES OF MEMORY

BODIES OF MEMORY

NARRATIVES OF WAR IN
POSTWAR JAPANESE CULTURE, 1945–1970

Yoshikuni Igarashi

PRINCETON UNIVERSITY PRESS, PRINCETON AND OXFORD

Library of Congress Cataloging-in-Publication Data

Igarashi, Yoshikuni, 1960-
Bodies of memeory: narratives of war in postwar Japanese culture,
1945-1970/Yoshikuni Igarashi.
      p. cm.
Includes bibliographical references and index.
ISBN 0-691-04911-4 (cloth: alk. paper)—
ISBN 0-691-04912-2 (pbk.: alk. paper)
1. Japan—Civilization—1945- I. Title.
DS822.5 .I33 2000
952.04—dc21   99-088263

This book has been composed in Sabon

The paper used in this publication meets the minimum
requirements of ANSI/NISO Z39.48-1992 (R1997)
(*Permanence of Paper*)

www.pup.princeton.edu

Printed in the United States of America

(Pbk.)
10 9 8 7 6 5 4 3 2 1

10 9 8 7 6 5 4 3 2 1

For My Parents —————————————————

IGARASHI KURAZŌ AND KUNIKO

Contents

Acknowledgments _____

THIS BOOK is a personal endeavor to make sense of Japan's postwar history. Yet it is obvious that the project would not have been completed (or even begun) without the encouragement and support of various people. Their help often came at the most opportune moments.

I would like to express my gratitude to those who guided me at various stages of my intellectual training. I am indebted to William Steele, who first introduced me to the rigor of historical thinking and encouraged me to pursue scholarship in the United States. Bill Haver, Marilyn Ivy, Tetsuo Najita, and Harry Harootunian taught me, through their own exciting practices of cultural criticism, the manners of critical discourse. Bill Sibley opened my eyes to the depth of postwar Japanese literature.

Noriko Aso, Michael Bess, Joyce Chaplin, Alan Christy, Jim Epstein, Gerald Figal, Joel Harrington, Susan Hegeman, Leslie Pincus, Helmut Smith, Anne Walthall, and Mark Wollaeger read the manuscript of this book, either in its entirety or in its parts. Their comments were extremely helpful to me in thinking about the larger implications of my argument as well as the lacunae within it. The comments of the two anonymous reviewers for the Princeton University Press were enormously useful in fine-tuning my discussions. I am particularly grateful to Noriko Aso, who painstakingly proofread the manuscript and transformed it into a more readable form. Rory Dicker was also helpful in making stylistic changes.

I would like to thank Lisa Yoneyama and Mark Abé Nornes for kindly sharing information with me from their ongoing projects. Tom Looser provided me an opportunity to test the ideas from this book with an audience at Emory University. Wesley Sasaki-Uemura inspired the title of this book. Akio Igarashi's generous help enabled me to conduct research in Japan. I was also privileged to work with Deborah Malmud, my editor at the Princeton University Press, whose encouragement and support were crucial to the completion of this work. I also want to thank Marilyn Pilley, Jim Toplon, and the other staff at Vanderbilt University Interlibrary Loan Office for handling numerous requests from me in an unfamiliar language.

I would like to extend my gratitude to various institutions for their financial and institutional support. The leave that Vanderbilt University granted and a Fellowship for University Teachers from the National Endowment for the Humanities allowed me to focus on my research and writing during the academic year 1996–97. Harvard-Yenching Library provided a travel grant at a critical stage of my research. The Faculty of

Law and Politics at Rikkyo University warmly welcomed me as a research associate for extended periods. A Vanderbilt University Research Council summer stipend supported the preliminary research for the project in the summer of 1995. As a member of the faculty seminar, "Questions of Culture," sponsored by the Robert Penn Warren Center for the Humanities at Vanderbilt University during the year 1996–97, I benefited from lively seminar discussions and a generous stipend. The Department of History at Vanderbilt University has been a great base for my intellectual activities.

This book is about the period of history that my parents personally experienced. I have benefited from the fruit of their hard work in the postwar years and am grateful that I was given the opportunities that they never had. For that, I dedicate this book to my parents. My daughter, Maya, was born as I was revising this book. Although I was intensely involved in writing, I knew my priority was you, Maya, when I misspelled *disappear* as *diaper* in the manuscript. Your enthusiasm for life is so contagious. Finally, my thanks to Teresa Goddu for her unfailing belief in me. You make everything enjoyable.

An earlier version of chapter 1 appeared as "The Bomb, Hirohito, and History: The Foundational Narrative of United States–Japan Postwar Relations," in *Positions: East Asia Cultures Critique* 6, no. 2 (1998): 261–302.

Throughout the book, Japanese names appear in the Japanese order, that is, family name first. However, I have reversed the order for those who have primarily or extensively published in English, excluding translations (e.g., my own name).

BODIES OF MEMORY

Introduction _____

> Remembering is never a quiet act of introspection
> or retrospection. It is a painful remembering, a
> putting together of the dismembered past to
> make sense of the trauma of the present.
>   *Homi K. Bhabha,* "Interrogating Identity"

THE IMAGE reproduced on this book's cover and as figure 1 was painted by the artist Ōgai Yatarō. Ōgai completed this painting of a young Japanese pilot in 1944 and died two years later from tuberculosis.[1] Ōgai's works have been forgotten by postwar Japanese society. Never publicly displayed, this piece deteriorated while stored by his bereaved family for more than a half-century. In 1997, however, Ōgai's painting was restored and brought before the public for the first time at Mugonkan, a museum dedicated to young aspiring artists who died either during the Asia Pacific War or shortly after.[2] The image of the young pilot is one of the first sights a visitor to Mugonkan encounters; framed by a spotlight, the pilot quietly gazes into the museum's dark space.

Even after being restored, the painting shows the wear of more than fifty years. The paint has cracked into minute fragments, and almost half of the painting is lost. The cardboard paper that Ōgai used as a canvas peaks through large cracks in the paint. The bottom portion of the pilot's face is obliterated, and his left arm is barely visible. The pilot's uniform appears threadbare, and his once proud expression is reduced to an empty gaze. The fifty-some years of postwar history have scarred the surface of this painting, which stands on the brink of total disappearance. Yet the pilot and the artist insist upon their existence through the remaining fragments of paint. It is this tension between the process of the image's disappearance and its insistence on its presence that gives the painting a powerful appeal.

Like the image of the pilot, postwar Japan's relation to its past is filled with tension. This book is an attempt to read the absent presence of the country's war memories. Its goal is not to reconstruct an original image of past events but to examine how the past is signified and forgotten through the mediation of history. Japanese society rendered its traumatic experiences of the war comprehensible through narrative devices that downplayed their disruptive effects on Japan's history. These narratives, however, made it more difficult to discuss the impact of experiences of

Figure 1. Portrait of a young Japanese pilot by Ōgai Yatarō, 1944. Courtesy of Ōgai Haruko.

war. Rather than dismiss these narrative strategies as mere obstacles to historical inquiry, the book reads them along with particular counternarratives that attempted to register the original impact of the war. It is through examining the tension between the repression and expression of the trauma of the war that I contemplate the impact of the war and Japan's defeat on postwar society. In order to provide a critical perspective on present discussions of the war's legacy, this study focuses on how memories of the war were transformed in the first twenty-five years of the postwar period. Just as its scars from the past half-century are integral to the present meaning of Ōgai's painting, so too are the fading traces of war trauma to postwar Japanese history.

In its effort to examine the specific example of postwar Japan, this book also participates in the larger scholarly discussion of memory, which has gained momentum since the early 1980s.[3] Humanists and social scientists have deployed the concept of memory as part of their continuing efforts to expand the horizons of history. Memory connotes what is personal and emotional in an individual's relation to the past—the elements that often disrupt the common narratives of history. However, memory does not exist outside of the boundaries of history. Socially constructed historical narratives often define the shape of individual memories. This book is not a celebration of memory: it does not attempt to liberate memory from hegemonic historical narratives, but problematizes the concept of history by claiming memory as an integral part of historical production. By revealing cultural desires and anxieties—elements that have been traditionally attributed to memory—this study aspires to conceive of ways in which to intervene in the process of historical construction.

The title of this book, *Bodies of Memory*, signifies how Japan after the war remembered the past: its memories were discursively constructed through bodily tropes. Postwar Japan inherited this discursive practice from the wartime regulatory regime that aspired to create a healthy national body (*kokutai*). Furthermore, in the immediate aftermath of the war, many Japanese discovered their bodies as the entities that survived destruction and thus embodied historical continuity. Their bodies became sites for national rehabilitation, thus overcoming the historical crisis that Japan's defeat created. The title also calls the reader's attention to the materiality of memory: the production of both bodily tropes and memories was deeply embedded in the material conditions of postwar Japan. Just as Ōgai's painting's physical condition—its scarred surface—is essential to the past it invokes, the material conditions in which Japanese bodies existed deeply affected wartime memories in postwar society. Hence, the project of this book is to examine both the discursive and the material conditions of postwar Japan for its memory and historical production.

The Voiceless Museum

Ōgai's painting serves as a useful site to explore postwar Japan's struggle
with its own past. In order to consider the ghastly presence of the past in
his painting, I need to discuss at length the museum that houses it. Named
Mugonkan (Voiceless Museum) by its owner, Kuboshima Sei'ichirō, this
small, private art museum opened at Ueda, Nagano, in May 1997. Mugonkan's austere thirty-one-hundred-square-foot building houses an un-
conventional collection that includes the works of young artists who died
during or shortly after the Asia Pacific War. The paintings of the young
artists line the walls, and personal effects left by the deceased—letters,
diaries, and other art objects—are displayed in glass cases. Most of the
works in the museum have never appeared in public; the majority of them
had been stored by the artists' families. After numerous trips to those
families over a period of two and a half years, Kuboshima managed to
acquire the collection and bring it before the public.

Kuboshima's museum is an imaginative response to the desperate need
to deal with memories of the war. Kuboshima seeks to demonstrate
throughout the Mugonkan collection the contradictory nature of the past:
its simultaneous presence and absence. "Re-membering"—an effort "to
make sense of the trauma of the present" in Homi Bhabha's definition—
requires a recognition of loss. Like Ōgai's painting, the reassembled fragments of the past inevitably reveal cracks and missing pieces; and the
cracks and absent pieces are central to understandings of the past. "To
make sense of the trauma of the present," one must comprehend how
traumatic loss in the past defines one's present. Japanese society successfully mitigated the devastating loss it suffered in the war; yet memories
of loss were fundamental to the postwar construction of Japan's cultural
identity. Against postwar practices that rendered the absence invisible,
Mugonkan strives to re-present the losses of war within Japanese society.
In the present volume, I try to articulate the centrality of loss in remembering the past by tracing various attempts to reconstruct the past in the
cultural discourses of postwar Japan.

In his *"Mugonkan" e no tabi* (The journey to Mugonkan), Kuboshima
offers the history of the museum from its inception to its opening, along
with his own thoughts on what motivated him to carry out this project.[4]
Kuboshima maintains that his meeting with the artist Nomiyama Gyōji
was instrumental in the materialization of his museum. Nomiyama was
recruited into the army immediately after he graduated from the Tokyo
College of Arts (Tokyo Bijutsu gakkō, the predecessor of the Tokyo National University of Fine Arts and Music) in 1942. Although he was sent
to the Manchurian front, he was eventually discharged from the army

due to illness. However, many graduates of the Tokyo College of Arts were not as fortunate as Nomiyama and did not live to witness the post-war period. In 1977, with two collaborators, Nomiyama traveled throughout Japan to visit the families of schoolmates who died in the war and published their works posthumously in the book *Inori no gashū*.[5] Although Kuboshima saw this collection when it came out, he did not pay much attention to it. Indeed, he resisted a connection between the war and the aesthetic qualities of art; the collection receded from his consciousness over the next few years. It took the next nineteen years and a personal discussion with Nomiyama for him to realize the value of Nomiyama's project.

When Kuboshima met Nomiyama in 1994, Nomiyama discussed his desire to create a museum for the artworks to which he paid homage in 1977. This museum would not attempt to reify the aesthetic quality of the collection—Nomiyama himself recognized the immaturity of these works—but would instead bring them together in order to let them collectively express the artists' desire to live and paint. Although the individual works were somewhat clumsy, they nonetheless illustrated both the artists' pleasure in producing art and their desire to keep painting. When displayed together, Nomiyama explained, these pieces could work much like orchestral music to produce a larger effect on those who see them. The museum that he envisioned is a site where individual works are displayed together to create a solemn music. Nomiyama's vision moved Kuboshima to action; they began visiting the families of the artists, and Kuboshima continued to visit the artists' relatives on his own even after Nomiyama withdrew from the project. After struggling for three years to raise money, Kuboshima finally managed to create the museum.

Halfway through the project, Nomiyama stopped accompanying Kuboshima but did not explain the reasons for this decision. Kuboshima could only speculate how Nomiyama felt in visiting the bereaved families for the second time in twenty years. When Nomiyama first visited the artists' relatives in 1977, the parents of the deceased artists were still alive. The memories of the war and the artists' lives remained with their parents; Nomiyama's visits reawakened the memories buried within their daily lives. Kuboshima remembers one such episode in *Inori no gashū*. When Nomiyama was about to leave a family's house, a mother touched his shoulder and quietly muttered: "You are young. . . . If my son were alive, he would have been exactly the same age as you are."[6] By facing the parents of the deceased, Nomiyama burdened himself with an unanswerable question: why had he survived the war when they had not? He was guilty both of surviving the war and of leaving his schoolmates behind. Yet, within the emotionally charged meetings with his schoolmates' parents and his own feelings of guilt, Nomiyama found a path that led him back to the past. For Nomiyama, the project recovered his ties to the war dead, however temporarily, and enabled him to act as one of them. By the mid-1990s, however, even that narrow path had disappeared. The artists' parents were all dead, and their siblings did not meet Nomiyama with the same emotional intensity. When he realized that he could not reproduce the effects of his 1977 visits, he asked Kuboshima to visit the families by himself.[7]

Nomiyama, however, did continue to help raise money for the project by soliciting donations; his vision and assistance were crucial to the materialization of the museum. Yet the museum belongs to Kuboshima not only because he personally shouldered the financial responsibility—from the construction costs to the operating expenses—but also because the museum directly reflects Kuboshima's own efforts to confront his war memories. The fact that he named the museum Mugonkan signals a departure from Nomiyama's original desire to recover the past. The murmurs of the young artists may collectively create a grand music; yet that music remains inaudible to Kuboshima and to those who visit the museum. For Kuboshima, a simple recovery of the voices of the deceased is an impossible project, and Mugonkan stands as an enigmatic place where visitors listen to silence.

When Nomiyama decided to entrust the project to Kuboshima, Kuboshima was relieved that he would no longer have to pretend he belonged to Nomiyama's generation. Kuboshima expressed his discomfort at being without firsthand war experiences. Born in 1941, his memories of wartime Japan were fragmentary. In the early stage of visiting the bereaved families with Nomiyama, Kuboshima was acutely aware of his outsider status. While Nomiyama and the families immediately struck up conversations about their commonly shared war experiences, Kuboshima felt as if he were an impostor who should not be there at all. For Kuboshima, the project began with his somber realization that it was impossible for him to have privileged access to the experiences of the deceased: he would be an eternal outsider to his own project.

When he faced the bereaved families without Nomiyama's mediation, Kuboshima needed to signify the project in his own terms. Nomiyama's absence relieved Kuboshima from a search for authentic experiences; instead, his reflections on the project led him to the shadow of the war in his own life. Although he was not privy to the war experiences of the artist-soldiers, his life in the postwar years had been deeply affected by the Asia Pacific War. Yet Kuboshima had been reluctant to recognize the effects of the war on himself until he became involved in the project. In collecting the works of the artist-soldiers, for the first time Kuboshima began contemplating what he had long turned away from—the loss he suffered in the war. This was also the beginning of his struggle to make sense of his life in the postwar period.

Kuboshima painfully realized how deeply the war affected his personal life. Before they lost everything in the war, his foster parents used to lead a modest life running a shoe repair shop in Tokyo. Their shop was destroyed by the American air raids in April 1945, and they never recovered from the damage. Returning home from Sendai, the city where they took refuge, the family found their neighborhood leveled; there was nothing but dirt and debris in the area where their house used to stand. On a hot summer day among the ruins, Kuboshima began the postwar period. In the immediate postwar years, Kuboshima's family lived in a tiny shack of three tatami mats (about fifty-five square feet), and his foster parents struggled for the family's survival. As Kuboshima became conscious of the state of his family, he began to resent his foster parents for their inability to take him out of extreme poverty. Kuboshima remembers the deep shame he felt when he saw them, covered with leather scraps, fixing college students' shoes.

Kuboshima knew he was adopted, and his resentment toward his foster parents increased when they refused to reveal the identity of his biological parents. He desired to escape his parents' condition by becoming rich. He dropped out of high school and pursued material wealth. After attaining the comfort of middle-class life, he even symbolically divorced himself from his foster parents by locating his biological parents himself. To his surprise, Kuboshima discovered that the writer Minakami Tsutomu was his biological father, and his reunion with the esteemed author in August 1977 attracted wide media attention. Father and son quickly established close ties. However, his relations with his foster parents deteriorated as quickly as his affection for his father increased. At one point, Kuboshima and his foster parents ceased talking to each other, even though they continued to live together.

Kuboshima's postwar peregrination resembles the path that the larger society followed—from destruction to economic prosperity. Kuboshima and postwar Japan opted not to face the memories of their war loss and instead attempted to displace it with material wealth. Once Kuboshima attained modest economic success in the 1970s, however, he was not satisfied with what he attained. Even then, Kuboshima's life reflected larger social conditions. Just as Japanese society finally reached a point where it could afford cultural consumption, Kuboshima began collecting paintings to find spiritual satisfaction to relieve him from his mind-numbing days of moneymaking. However, he soon grew so engulfed by the excitement of art collecting that he decided to make it his living: he closed his successful business and taught himself to be an art dealer. His affection for his art collection, however, escalated to the point where he eventually

opened his own private art museum in the early 1980s. Kuboshima's decision to create his own museum rather than to trade art marks his move
toward distancing himself from postwar society and toward reflecting on
his postwar life.

The journey to collect art for his new museum became his process of
self-reflection on his own postwar life. Kuboshima argues that the artworks of Mugonkan are messages from fifty years ago; the museum signifies his attempt to assemble the dismembered past to the present audience.
Almost fifty years after the defeat of Japan, Kuboshima began the process
of understanding the effects of the war on his postwar life. Bringing together the dismembered bodies of artworks, Kuboshima began his efforts
to make sense of his present—the postwar period.

Kuboshima is aware that remembering is paired with the process of
forgetting. Postwar Japan has naturalized the absence and silence of the
past by erasing its own struggle to deal with its memories. It may appear
that postwar society readily left its experiences behind in the pursuit of
economic success. However, the actual process of forgetting the loss was
not an easy one: it involved a constant struggle to render memories of
war into a benign, nostalgic form. However, Japanese society eventually
managed to conceal the postwar struggle to forget. When the historical
process of forgetting itself became erased, the experiences and loss in war
were buried within postwar society. In order to remember the past, this
process of forgetting has to be brought to consciousness. The paintings
of Mugonkan, for instance, are restored only minimally in order to mark
the processes of deterioration and forgetting. Kuboshima does not try to
reverse the process by forcefully intervening in it; he only wishes to reveal
the process of forgetting by temporarily slowing it down. By marking the
process of forgetting, the collection at Mugonkan urges the viewer to
begin the process of remembering and to make sense of what necessitated
the forgetting in the postwar Japanese society.

The museum has attracted a fair amount of attention; the media favor-
ably reported Kuboshima's efforts, and the museum had sixty thousand
visitors in its first year. Yet Kuboshima recognizes that the silence that his
museum re-presents is open to each visitor's interpretation. Although the
museum attempts to problematize the ways in which postwar society has
represented its loss, the collection still exists within the larger discourse
of the war. The collection can easily be construed as a nostalgic project
within a nationalistic discourse. By featuring aspiring young artists—a
group with a nonaggressive image—the museum can be read as endorsing
the ideological position that portrays the Japanese as victims. Indeed, visiting the museum on one Sunday in May 1998, I heard laments of "ka-
waisō" (what a pity) uttered with a sympathetic tone that barely disguised
its underlying cheerfulness. When someone says this word, the utterance

tacitly confirms his or her privileged status as a person enjoying life, in contrast to the denied future of the artists. The museum could easily become a tool through which to validate what the viewers have, rather than what they have lost.

However, Kuboshima cannot do much to counter such nostalgic responses since he understands that he cannot offer a proper reading of the silence; the silence should not be filled with his utterance. Kuboshima tries to undermine the nationalistic sentiments within such nostalgia by diversifying the collection and incorporating works beyond the present national boundaries of Japan. The museum currently displays only works by Japanese artists, mostly graduates of the Tokyo College of the Arts. Kuboshima has already begun to collect paintings by artists with no affiliation with that institution, and he also hopes to include artworks produced by art students from outside of Japan who died in the war, from both Japan's former colonies and the countries against which Japan fought. Kuboshima also presents Mugonkan not as a war memorial but as an art museum; appreciating its collection as art pieces rather than as remains of the war is perhaps the best way to problematize the young artists' absence in postwar Japanese society. Viewers are invited to read the art, not through Kuboshima's commentaries, but through their own appreciation. Kuboshima hopes his visitors will discover their own relation to the art displayed at the museum by contemplating the conditions under which these works were produced and have deteriorated.

At Mugonkan, diverse individual experiences, including Kuboshima's own, are assembled through the artworks of the deceased artists to constitute a mosaic image of postwar Japan. The parts that have been permanently lost in this mosaic are just as expressive as the parts that remain. Yet the collection remains silent about the meaning of this image. The dilapidated mosaic embodies the paradoxical process of forgetting and remembering and urges visitors to complicate their relation to postwar Japanese society. It is this dual process of forgetting and remembering in postwar Japan that this book attempts to excavate.

Nation, Body, and Culture

This book critically documents what necessitated and naturalized the process of forgetting in the postwar years. It also traces the genealogy of cultural discourses that countered the process of forgetting by re-presenting the war loss in Japanese society. As a nation, Japan survived its devastating defeat in 1945 by reinventing itself as a peaceful nation that attained economic prosperity in the following decades. Yet the process of recovery and the construction of a new Japan were not easy: memories of loss haunted postwar society. Kuboshima's museum attests to the fact that the tension between the nation's contradictory desires—its desire to forget and its desire to remember the past—still persists fifty years after defeat. The tension between these desires has shaped the cultural productions of postwar Japanese society and constitutes the focus of this study.

This book pays particular attention to the narrative strategies employed to create a continuity that masked the historical disjunction of defeat. Japan desperately sought narratives of historical continuity that could encompass and transcend the loss that it had endured. Narrative explanations of defeat enabled Japan to claim its identity despite, and because of, the radical historical changes the nation had endured. Loss was transformed through narrative representations into a sacrifice needed for Japan's future betterment. By explaining loss as a precondition for postwar society, many narratives of the war simultaneously expressed and repressed this loss.

This study comprises readings of various narrative strategies deployed in Japanese culture to make sense of the war's trauma. The readings do not promise to reveal any deeper, more essential meaning of the loss; rather, they demonstrate how extensively postwar society was related to the sense of loss and how in turn this sense motivated its cultural productions. Most of the cultural expressions and phenomena discussed in this book are familiar to those who lived in Japan during the first twenty-five years after the war. They have perhaps seemed too familiar to be discussed against a historical background; often they have often received dismissive treatment as peculiarities of postwar history. However, by positing a deep desire to signify loss, we can reveal how deeply embedded in social conditions are cultural forms that have hitherto appeared nonsensical and trivial.

While this book focuses on a range of cultural forms from the high- to the lowbrow, it is particularly concerned with popular forms of cultural productions because they provided the broad basis against which nationalist sentiments were expressed in postwar Japan. Japan's defeat was a national event: as a nation, it could no longer exist as it had, and its members were forced to reconsider its very foundation. However, after Japan's nationhood was literally blasted by the atomic bomb, the process of reassembling the fragments of the nation could not be conducted through political discourse. The nation's disavowal of its militaristic past along with its negative associations with militarism made the political expression of nationalism extremely difficult in postwar Japan. Nevertheless, Japan's nationalist sentiments did not disappear from postwar social consciousness. Its nationhood survived the devastating defeat, and many in Japan in the postwar period sought to produce a new national identity that could encompass the memories of loss and devastation through the realm of everyday culture rather than through abstract political discourse. The chapters in this book examine the nation's image as expressed in such cultural productions as literature, sports events, radio, film, and television. Moreover, by situating such authors as Ōe Kenzaburō and Maruyama Masao within the discourse of Japanese hybridity, the book demonstrates how cultural discourses normally regarded as highbrow emerged from the nexus of desire and anxiety that motivated the production of popular culture after the war.

In discussing the process of forgetting and remembering the past within specific cases of postwar Japanese popular culture, the arguments in this book revolve around two other primary points, the first of which is Japan's relation to the United States. In the postwar period, the United States was a defining factor in Japan's self-invention. The surrender of Japan to the Allied nations in the Asia Pacific War largely registered in postwar Japan as its defeat by U.S. forces. The fact that the United States had a virtual monopoly on the Allied nations' occupation policies in Japan also helped postwar Japanese society to focus exclusively on its relations to the United States. Japan's colonial ambitions were concealed by its articulation of its war experiences as a conflict with the United States; moreover, Japan's defeat itself was reconfigured as a necessary condition for its postwar peace and prosperity under U.S. hegemony. Once adversaries during the Asia Pacific War, the two countries transformed themselves into close allies after the war; both countries' attempts to smooth over this radical disjunction of history together produced the official narrative that forged the historical continuity from the war to the postwar period. This narrative cast Japan's defeat as a drama of rescue and conversion: the United States rescued Japan from the menace of its militarists, and Japan was converted into a peaceful, democratic country under U.S. tutelage.

Second, the discursively constructed body becomes the central site for the reconfiguration of Japan's national image. Japanese bodies had already been at the heart of nationalist discourse before 1945; ideological configurations of nationhood emphasized Japan's organic unity and often resorted to metaphorical representations of the political entity through bodily images. The wartime regime subjected Japanese bodies to rigid regulations: it attempted to create obedient, nationalist bodies by forging ties between nationalist ideology and bodily functions. Even after the disappearance of the wartime regulatory regime, Japanese bodies remained at the juncture of various social discourses. The official narrative of the war, complicitly produced by American occupation forces and the Japanese government, expressed the new alliance between the United States and Japan through images of hygienic, democratic bodies. In contrast, war-scarred bodies were admitted into the discursive space of postwar

Japan as signifiers of war experiences only insofar as they confirmed the official narrative. The many bodily images produced in the postwar Japanese cultural media must be read against the official narrative's impulse to construct an ahistorical body.

Bodily images also attest to the dual process of the expression and repression of the past in postwar cultural discourse. The healthy body of the nation was dismembered as imperial Japan experienced a radical transformation, and these dismembered bodily images were assembled again in the postwar period in order to articulate the new nationhood. Body parts were metaphorically sutured together to regain the nation's organic unity and to overcome its trauma; yet the suture left on the discursive body's surface served as a constant reminder of the trauma. Japan's loss was concealed and simultaneously inscribed as a visible sign on the body's surface. This contradictory function of suturing demonstrates that the act of remembering is far from a simple recovery of the past. Even those attempts to make sense of the trauma could reinforce rather than defy the official silence; on the other hand, efforts to conceal the loss could also unintentionally reveal it. Tropes of the body in postwar Japanese cultural discourse accommodated the contradictory nature of remembering/forgetting and remain a fertile ground for a historical inquiry into the ways in which Japanese society dealt with its war memories.

The book's inquiry into Japan's struggle to deal with its past begins with the production of the official narrative, which I call the foundational narrative of the postwar period. The first chapter, "The Bomb, Hirohito, and History: The Foundational Narrative of Postwar Relations between Japan and the United States," discusses the role that the atomic bomb and the emperor played in creating the official narrative of the war's end. The two countries' leadership complicitly constructed a narrative that explicated the sudden realignment of U.S.-Japanese relations (from enemies to allies) by sexualizing the two countries' alliance. Images of postwar Japanese bodies not only were the site of Japan's reinvention but also were gendered and reflected the power relations between the two countries. In relation to its colonies, Japan occupied the position of the dominant male. Yet as Japan accepted U.S. authority, this male-female relation was replicated in the relation between the United States and Japan. Japan's subjugation to U.S. hegemony cast Japan in a feminized role. Moreover, the two countries' relations were often naturalized in sexually charged terms. The two nations established the foundation of their postwar relations in the desire for each other and the acceptance of the other's desire. At the core of this sexualized relationship was the emperor's feminized body, which metonymically represented Japan's nationhood. It was through the emperor's feminine image that Japan disavowed its colonialist legacy.

Both Japan and the United States eagerly consumed and circulated this narrative, which provided the standard framework within which each country articulated its war memories. The chapter discusses the historical process through which this narrative was produced and reinforced and how it powerfully defined the process of forgetting and remembering in postwar Japanese society.

The second chapter, "The Age of the Body," focuses on the celebration of the bodily senses after the collapse of the wartime regime. This chapter looks both at how the body reentered Japan's social consciousness and became a symbol of its liberation and at how the body was immediately placed under the regulatory regime of U.S. occupation forces. Despite the drastic change in political conditions from wartime to the postwar period, bodily images remained central to Japan's conceptualization of its nationhood. The chapter offers readings of Maruyama Masao's medicalized social scientific discourse and Tamura Taijirō's so-called literature of the flesh. These writings offer contrasting responses to the bodily images that postwar popular culture produced. Maruyama and Tamura seemed to have stood at opposite poles in their evaluations of the body's radical possibilities: Tamura posited the body as the site for radical social change, while Maruyama severely criticized such optimism. Yet their writings ironically attest to their shared desire to transcend the historical conditions in which Japanese bodies were deeply embedded.

The third chapter, "A Nation That Never Is: Cultural Discourse on Japanese Uniqueness," focuses on hybrid identities that were expressed through sexualized Japanese bodies in 1950s literary works and argues for hybrid identities' affinity to a larger cultural discourse that ultimately denied the impact of Japan's defeat. The concept of hybridity was deployed in the 1950s as an ideological apology for defeat and its effect on Japanese society: because Japan was always already hybrid, the presence of the enemy within itself announced little change. Japan's hybrid identity supposedly embraced the other within itself and made it impossible to recognize past conflictual relations with the "other"—either Asia or the United States. The chapter discusses how the writers Kojima Nobuo and Ōe Kenzaburō problematize this ideological concept through the hybrid characters in their short stories.

Japanese nationalism also returned to postwar Japan in a grotesque form through monstrous bodies in the Japanese media. The fourth chapter, "Naming the Unnameable," focuses on war memories expressed in the mass media of radio, television, and film immediately before and after Japan regained its independence in 1952. The end of the American occupation caused memories of the war to resurface in the popular consciousness, and these memories were made visible through these media. This chapter looks at three sites of cultural production. The first site is the popular radio show *Kimi no nawa* (Your name is. . . ?), which concerns a missed encounter with the past. The repeated attempts and failures of the two protagonists to locate each other and to be united figuratively articulate their ambiguous relation to the past. Second, the chapter focuses on the 1950s movie series *Godzilla* in order to trace the wartime memory that haunted postwar Japan. Godzilla's monstrous body stood in for the memories of war and loss that could not be recuperated by the resurgent Japanese nationalism of the 1950s. The final segment of the chapter reads the bodily performance of nationhood staged by the professional wrestler Rikidōzan. A radio show, a monster, and professional wrestling matches offered their contemporary audiences three distinctively different narrative strategies to make sense of the loss that Japan had suffered. *Kimi no nawa* ultimately confirms the foundational narrative by offering a way to reconcile with the past; *Godzilla* rejects the foundational narrative by destroying postwar recovery; and Rikidōzan turns the foundational narrative upside down by beating American wrestlers.

The fifth chapter, "From the Anti–Security Treaty Movement to the Tokyo Olympics," shifts the book's focus to 1960s Japan. The popular protest movement against the United States–Japan Security Treaty of 1960 provided an opportunity for millions of participants to reencounter their memories of the war and their nationalist feelings. The movement began as a direct challenge to the legacy of Japan's defeat, U.S. hegemony within Japan and East Asia. However, when it gained a mass basis, it transformed the nature of the movement to a defense of the postwar democratic social order—the legacy of American occupation policies. Once this popular political movement was defeated with the renewal of the Security Treaty, postwar society shifted its focus to its economic growth. The enormous investments made for the 1964 Tokyo Olympics were instrumental to Japan's economic transformation. Furthermore, the spectacular sports event of the Olympics provided an opportunity for postwar Japanese society to reconfigure and sanitize its memories of the war through athletic bodies and cityscapes. The images of healthier Japanese bodies and cleaner Japanese cities metaphorically announced postwar Japan's departure from its problem-ridden past. Memories of the war were still with postwar society; yet they were discursively transformed into a necessary condition for Japan's postwar prosperity.

The final chapter, "Re-presenting Trauma in Late-1960s Japan," concludes the book by discussing two Japanese writers' attempts to represent their war memories in late-1960s Japan. Within a society that was eager to leave the memories of war behind, Nosaka Akiyuki and Mishima Yukio struggled to articulate the meaning of Japan's loss in 1945 through bodily images. The body for them returns as a locus of conflicting desires:

a nostalgia for and a simultaneous repudiation of the past. Nosaka's and Mishima's bodies were caught between these contradictory desires and oscillated between the past and the present, repeating that which they simultaneously yearned for and dreaded—their bodily memories of the past. Although the protagonist in Nosaka's story persistently returns to his teenage years seeking a release from his memories of loss, he invariably ends up re-presenting the loss through his bodily acts. Similarly Mishima attempts to represent the loss in postwar Japanese society through symbolically dismembering his own body; yet his suicide ironically demonstrated the extent to which forgetting the loss was naturalized in postwar Japan.

The six chapters of this book document the process of remembering the past against the historical background of postwar Japan, beginning in 1945 and ending in the late 1960s. While the book moves forward in history, it also traces a narrative progression: remembering the war became increasingly difficult in postwar Japanese society. The book ends with a discussion of how that society managed to naturalize the process of forgetting—how it reached the point where the loss itself was lost—after the first twenty-five years of the postwar period. The material conditions of prosperity provided closure to the popular narrative of the war that claimed Japan's defeat and loss were necessary for its peace and prosperity. Against this erasure, Japanese bodies nonetheless remained a central site for remembering. As the social conditions that supported Japanese bodies drastically changed, new sets of bodily images became necessary; as a result, the body remained a site for cultural signification. Yet, despite the efforts to represent loss within the prosperity of the late 1960s, Japanese society steadily erased the process of forgetting by positing the loss as the basis of the narrative of Japan's postwar progress.

Japan's struggle to deal with its war memories came to a temporary resolution with the prosperity of its high growth economy in the late 1960s. This timing coincided with the height of the Cold War. By embracing the U.S. hegemony in East Asia, Japanese society managed to insulate itself from the haunting memories of the war. However, through the shift in the Cold War political paradigm that began in the early 1970s and culminated in that paradigm's collapse in the late 1980s, the foundational narrative weakened its hold on Japanese society. Because of these political changes, there has been a renewed interest since the early 1970s in representing the past, which has generated a series of controversies. Memories of the war have most insistently returned through images of suffering Asian bodies. The conclusion of the book looks at how the struggle to forget and to remember the past through an encounter with the bodies of the Japanese colonial past continues in Japanese society.

Much like Ōgai Yatarō's painting of the young pilot, images of war mediated through the various postwar narratives appear disfigured. Many fragments of the disembodied past are forever lost, yet these absent pieces are just as constitutive as the remaining part of the portrait of how postwar Japan dealt with its past. The goal of this book is not to restore the "original" experiences of the war but to read what is absent through the layers of postwar narrative signification. Such a reading practice, I believe, is an indispensable part of our current moment's renewed efforts to remember Japan's past.

1

The Bomb, Hirohito, and History:
The Foundational Narrative of Postwar
Relations between Japan and the United States

Japan is like a woman that he can't live with, and
can't live without, you know.
Michael Crichton, Rising Sun

WAR IS PEACE.
George Orwell, 1984

THE EMOTIONALLY charged discussions on both sides of the Pacific over the Smithsonian Institution's attempt to represent the atomic bomb in a larger historical context demonstrate how deeply American and Japanese societies are still invested in memories of World War II.[1] Each country's "orthodox" history surrounding the use of the bomb presents a diametrically opposing view: as the Smithsonian Institution's drastic scaling down of its exhibit suggests, the prevalent view among Americans is that the use of the bomb was justified and that the bomb brought peace. Many Japanese, on the other hand, argue that the bomb was a cruel weapon that should never have been used: peace could have been attained without it. Each side's characterization of the bomb, however, is ultimately vested in a moral judgment that condemns the two countries to conflicting relations.

Memories of World War II may still linger in the two countries' perceptions of each other; however, their actual postwar relations have easily overcome the mutual animosity fostered throughout the war years.[2] Immediately after the war, Japan and the United States, the two most adversarial enemies in the Pacific, became the two closest allies. In the Cold War world order, the United States–Japan alliance provided the basis for U.S. policies against Communist regimes in Asia. Moreover, material assistance from the United States and access to the American market enabled Japan to make a remarkable economic recovery during the postwar years. This chimerical change in the international alliance between Japan and the United States in the immediate postwar years created a difficult situation for Japanese national identity because the survival of Japan depended upon the hegemony of its former enemy. I argue in this chapter that the sequence of events leading to the conclusion of the two countries' conflict—the attacks on Hiroshima and Nagasaki and the emperor's so-called divine decision to terminate the war—provided the grounds upon which the Japanese wartime leadership would found a narrative that could explain away the tension created by its acceptance of defeat. This narrative managed to cloak Japan's defeat in the guise of strategic necessity and concern for humanity at large; moreover, in the immediate postwar years, U.S. leadership participated in the reinforcement of this narrative through its support of the emperor.

In the ideological remapping of the immediate postwar period, any history between the United States and Japan that was incongruous with the political necessity of the Cold War was soon repressed in the United States as well as in Japan. For both countries, yesterday's foe became today's friend. The demonstration of the unprecedented power of the nuclear weapons detonated in Hiroshima and Nagasaki provided the impetus for the United States and Japan to reconfigure their collective memories. At the end of the war, the United States and Japan cast themselves in a melodrama, so to speak, that culminated in the demonstration of the atomic bomb's unprecedented power.[3] Through the bomb, the United States, gendered as male, rescued and converted Japan, figured as a desperate woman. Hirohito's so-called divine decision to end the war participated in this drama by accepting the superior power of the United States. Despite its hyperbole, this popular narrative was effective in defining the two countries' perception of the war and how it ended.

I call this narrative the "foundational narrative" of U.S.-Japanese postwar relations. I will trace the creation of the foundational narrative and examine what this narrative managed to mask in the two countries' postwar relations. The foundational narrative was generated by the two countries' efforts to render understandable the experiences of the atomic bomb and the ensuing transformation of their relationship. The United States unilaterally used the atomic bomb against Japan; yet both the United States and Japan were complicit in the maintenance of the narrative that subsequently encoded the bomb and the conclusion of the conflict through the figure of the emperor. The two countries' contradictory orientations in encoding the war's conclusion notwithstanding, many people in both countries found popular representations of the historical events convincing. Popular narratives in both countries offered various narrative devices—the great man theory, the melodrama of conversion and rescue, the contradictory image of a good enemy—as a means to comprehend the series of events that took place in August 1945 and the following few months; all of these devices coalesced into the foundational narrative.

The foundational narrative powerfully captured the popular imagination of the two countries and defined the discussions of their mutual relations until the 1980s, when the Cold War political paradigm began to dissolve. With less emphasis on the importance of nuclear capability in the strategic planning of the post–Cold War period, Japan appears to be freeing itself from its prescribed role in the foundational narrative.[4] Yet, the strong opposition to attempts to rethink history in either country—the *Enola Gay* controversy and the Japanese controversy over the Diet resolution admitting Japan's war responsibility[5]—demonstrates the degree to which many Americans and Japanese are still invested in the foundational narrative of the postwar period even fifty years after the conclusion of the conflict.[6] The structure of the foundational narrative is not only intact but also regenerated each time the two countries attempt to face their war memories.

This chapter revisits the popular sites from which the foundational narrative was assembled. By tracing the genealogy of the foundational narrative and discussing its components, I will explore the possible means to untangle the complex web created between the bomb's explosion and Hirohito's so-called divine decision. The discursivity of these events—how history is constructed through narrative—is the primary focus of my discussion. While the narrative, which defined the tone of relations between the United States and Japan in the immediate postwar years, was no doubt more foundational to Japanese society because of the asymmetry in the two countries' power relations, it informed the ways in which each country defined the other's image in their postwar relations.

The Production of the Foundational Narrative

The United States and Japan stand miles apart from each other over the use of the atomic bomb at the end of World War II. The majority of U.S. citizens still feel that the bombing of Hiroshima and Nagasaki was justifiable, while a large number of Japanese feel moral repugnance toward the use of the bombs.[7] However, despite their contrary responses to historical events, the narratives accepted in the two countries concerning how the war ended show a remarkable structural resemblance: in both versions, history is propelled by the decisions of great men and events.

The story widely accepted in both the United States and Japan concerning how the war ended is illuminated by a series of heroic decisions.[8] On July 26, 1945, the United States, Great Britain, and the Soviet Union demanded in the Potsdam Declaration "the unconditional surrender of all Japanese armed forces." Although the inner circle of the Japanese government held a meeting concerning this declaration, it was rejected two days later. Faced with this rejection, the American government had no recourse other than to drop atomic bombs on the selected cities of Hiroshima and Nagasaki (the latter of which was substituted for the originally chosen city of Kokura because of weather conditions). Realizing the enormous power of the new weapon, the emperor expressed his desire to bring the conflict to a conclusion. The Supreme Council was convened in the emperor's presence, but their prolonged meeting reached a deadlock. Three members—Baron Hiranuma Ki'ichirō; Tōgō Shigenori, the minister of foreign affairs; and Admiral Yonai Mitsumasa—insisted on the immediate acceptance of the Potsdam Declaration, with the single condition that the imperial institution would be retained. The other three—the war minister, Anami Korechika, and the two chiefs of staff—insisted on three more conditions: "if Japan were to surrender, she must insist on acceptance of her four conditions guaranteeing not only the integrity of the Imperial structure but also Japan's right to disarm her own soldiers, conduct her own war trials, and limit the forces of occupation."[9] It is important to note that the members of the Supreme Council were not debating whether they should accept the unconditional surrender. They were debating what kind of conditions they should place on their acceptance of the Potsdam Declaration. The deadlock was ended by the emperor's "divine" intervention. Hirohito finally broke away from the apolitical, monarchical role he had established for himself when he acceded to the throne and decided how Japan would surrender. He made clear his preference for the immediate acceptance of the Potsdam Declaration with a single proviso: the retention of the imperial institution.

Despite the fact that Hirohito was more concerned with the fate of the imperial institution than with the devastation of the country, this narrative lauds him as an enlightened yet reticent sovereign who made a crucial decision to save Japan as well as all human beings. At this critical historical juncture, Hirohito for the first and last time managed to intervene in the historical process. The narrative's corollary is that much of Japan's prosperity today is the result of his "divine decision," which saved Japan from total destruction. Facing uncertainty as to his own fate, the emperor supposedly said, "I do not care about what may happen to me. I cannot continue the war any longer, for I cannot bear to see the suffering of the people."[10] However, this statement, often quoted to illustrate Hirohito's humanistic concerns at the end of the war, has to be placed in a political context: the future of the imperial institution was secured.

In a similar manner, the American popular narrative characterizes President Harry S. Truman's decision to use the bomb as a sacred moment in American history—a moment that allows no challenges: the bomb was a benevolent weapon that ultimately saved millions of lives. The years of developing the weapon and the process involved in deciding to use the bomb are reduced to Truman's decision; his is the single human agency that corresponds to the singular event of the bomb's explosion. In this equation of Truman and the bomb, the complex bureaucratic organization of the U.S. government is erased. History is simplified to a great man's deed.

The American and Japanese narratives seem to contradict each other with their seemingly separate emphases: Truman's decision and Hirohito's intervention. In fact, however, they nicely dovetail. Their differences function as the subplots of a larger narrative in which Truman and Hirohito mirror each other, and in which their decisions are construed as benevolent lifesaving acts. According to this narrative, Hirohito's intervention was just as crucial as Truman's decision in terminating the two countries' conflict; the blast of the atomic bomb is centrally located between these two men's acts. The unprecedented power of the bomb was encoded through the acts of human agents.

Both governments were complicit in giving signifying power to the explosion of the bomb: through the decision of the emperor, this unprecedented experience was rendered comprehensible as Japan's defeat. On August 10, the Allied governments were informed of the Japanese government's intention to surrender: "The Japanese Government are ready to accept the terms enumerated in the Joint Declaration which was issued at Potsdam on July 26, 1945, by the heads of the Governments of the United States, Great Britain, and China, and later subscribed to by the Soviet Government, with the understanding that the said Declaration does not comprise any demand which prejudices the prerogatives of His Majesty as a sovereign ruler."[11] This message implies that the Japanese government would have kept fighting if the Allies had rejected Japan's terms. The government was indeed ready to sacrifice the Japanese people for its last demand—the maintenance of the imperial institution. After the transmission of this message, the emperor made that commitment clear in the meeting held with other members of the imperial family on August 12. Hirohito answered "Of course" to the question asked by Prince Asaka as to whether he would continue the war if the national polity, namely the imperial institution, could not be maintained.[12]

Receiving this response from the Japanese government, Truman was totally baffled. He wondered whether it could really be called an unconditional surrender, given such a huge proviso. Truman's memoirs read:

> Were we to treat this message from Tokyo as an acceptance of the Potsdam Declaration? There had been many in this country who felt that the Emperor was an integral part of that Japanese system which we were pledged to destroy.

Could we continue the Emperor and yet expect to eliminate the warlike spirit in Japan? Could we even consider a message with so large a "but" as the kind of unconditional surrender we had fought for?[13]

Despite Truman's claim of surprise, the members of the early Truman administration, including the president himself, had already been discussing a possible modification to the "unconditional surrender" demand—namely, an assurance that the imperial institution would remain—to make it more acceptable to the Japanese government.[14] The authority of the emperor had been recognized by U.S. officials as a useful tool to carry out the terms of the surrender, and the U.S. media had widely discussed the issue of possible conditions.[15] Although Tokyo's expedient response caught the U.S. government by surprise,[16] its contents were not unexpected; a compromise was quickly struck between the two countries when the U.S. government implicitly accepted the Japanese condition to the unconditional surrender. The response written by the secretary of state, James F. Byrnes, and jointly issued with Great Britain, China, and the Soviet Union on August 11 included a crucial clause that implicitly acquiesced to the Japanese terms: "From the moment of surrender the authority of the Emperor and the Japanese Government to rule the state shall be subject to the Supreme Commander of the Allied Powers who will take such steps as he deems proper to effectuate the surrender terms."[17]

It was no secret that the Allies struck a compromise with Japan at the conclusion of the conflict: the condition was again widely discussed in the American news media.[18] Yet, the drama of great men's decisions satisfied the American public; strong objections to the condition that the American government conceded to Tokyo were not loudly articulated in the American media. Ironically, as Michael Sherry claims, "the use of the bomb allowed the United States to offer surrender terms it previously withheld, giving the bomb as decisive an impact in Washington as in Tokyo."[19] In short, the abstract power of the bomb was made comprehensible to U.S. leaders through the emperor's initiative. Accepting the disciplinary power of the weapon, Japan surrendered. The emperor served as the prophet who deciphered the oracle of the atomic bomb. The total destruction of Japan and the imperial institution would have left no means to render the miraculous effects of the bomb comprehensible—the atomic bomb would have remained a huge explosive devise without a narrative. It was not the destructive power of the bomb per se but rather the narrative that "the bomb ended the war" that brought the war to its denouement; the emperor offered this narrative for the citizens of both the United States and Japan.

The narrative of how the war ended also established a circular referential relationship between the bomb and the emperor: the bomb was special because it shocked the emperor into accepting the terms of surrender; the emperor accepted the peace because he realized the bomb was special. Within this circle, the bomb's detonation and the emperor's decision refer only to each other, and they are separated from any other factors that happened before or after. Hence, the hermeneutic nature of the explanation as to how the bomb (Truman's decision) and the emperor (Hirohito's intervention) ended the war makes it impossible to establish any dialogue between the supporters and opponents of the bomb's use. One either believes the explanation or not: there can be no middle ground as long as one assumes the mutual referentiality of the bomb and the emperor.

The final step in the peace process, the United States' acceptance of Japan's condition, confirmed the referential relationship between the atomic bomb and the emperor. In this referential relationship, the bomb and the emperor became the sole bases of mutual signification. The impressive power of the atomic bombs awoke the great liberal mind of Japan—Hirohito. Hirohito exploded like the bomb. Moreover, the bombs, like Hirohito, stayed apolitical up until 1945 because they were hidden from the public eye. However, they were brought to the public's attention at a crucial moment in order to intervene in the political process and to achieve peace in Japan. The bomb and Hirohito mirror each other's image in their singular political impact. This was the first and the last intervention they made. Since these "explosions," they have remained political symbols never to be used again. The bombs ushered the United States into the Cold War paradigm, and the emperor's decision transformed Japan into one of the United States' closest allies during the Cold War.[20]

Hirohito and the bomb also became paired through their paradoxical nature: the destructive power of the bomb brought peace to the Pacific, while the autocratic power of the emperor was the key to that peace. The narrative of great men's interventions and the circle of mutual reference trap the bomb and the emperor at the moment of a radical shift from a negative to a positive effect. August 1945 becomes the privileged moment of this transformation. Therefore, as long as this contradiction remains intact, revelations about the negative force of the bomb and the emperor cannot challenge their value as the ultimate peacemakers. Negative revelations only dramatize the positive outcome of the transformation—it was awful, but it was necessary. The images of charred bodies in Hiroshima and Nagasaki and the dictatorial figure of Hirohito become the necessary conditions for peace. The more destructive or autocratic these images, the more dramatic the moment of conversion becomes. The radical contradiction between the negative and positive qualities of the bomb and Hirohito becomes the prerequisite for the postwar drama between the United States and Japan.

This narrative of conversion has been used by conservative voices in Japan to deny the emperor's responsibility in the Asia Pacific War. As the Japanese wartime government leaders prepared the drama of Hirohito's intervention, they added a subplot to the narrative: the autocratic power of the emperor was attributed to the Japanese militarists.[21] The government issued an imperial rescript on August 15, 1945, declaring the end of the war in Hirohito's name. After the American acceptance of the Japanese condition, the Japanese cabinet became confident that they could maintain the national polity. On August 14, the emperor resorted to his second "divine decision" by accepting the Allied response in an imperial meeting. The only thing left for the cabinet was to separate itself from the military by blaming everything on the militarists and to convince the Japanese people that it was necessary to terminate the conflict. For this purpose, the government fully utilized the authority of the emperor. First, the government leaders created and circulated a myth that the decision to end the war was due solely to Hirohito's divine decision.[22] Second, the emperor read the rescript announcing the conclusion of the conflict on radio. This was the first time in history his voice was heard on the radio, and this unprecedented announcement highlighted Hirohito's active involvement in the final decision making.[23]

The philosopher Washida Koyata makes the following four points about the rescript: First, it presented the emperor as the agency that ended the war; according to the rescript, this was not a defeat because it was the emperor's conscious act. A corollary was that nobody was responsible for the defeat, let alone for the war itself. Second, the rescript declared that the government would accept the Potsdam Declaration, but nowhere did it mention the content of this declaration.[24] Furthermore, it defined the war only in relation to the European powers and the United States and neglected Japanese aggression against other Asian countries. Thus, according to the rescript, the war began after Pearl Harbor. The attitude of those who wrote the rescript was that the war in Asia was necessary to bring peace and stability to Asia and was not an act of colonization, and that even if there had been aggression and colonization, they were carried out against Hirohito's will. It was the military that was responsible. Third, the rescript noted that innocent civilians had been killed by brutal weapons (atomic bombs). If the government did not stop the war, the Japanese people and human civilization would be made extinct, it said. The logic was that the Japanese people were the victims of the war and the emperor risked his life to protect them. Fourth, the rescript insisted that it was the emperor who would lead the Japanese people into the future.[25]

The operative logic of the rescript was rather simple: by defining Hirohito as apolitical and ahistorical, the government managed to absolve

him from his actual political actions, and by extension, the leaders of the
government who were faithfully following Hirohito could be similarly
exonerated from their political responsibility. This logic also applies to
the general populace, since their will was just an extension of the emper-
or's will. If the emperor was not responsible, then they were not responsible either. According to this reasoning, the militarists were the ones who
should be blamed; the emperor was kept captive in the hands of the military leaders against his desire to keep the peace. In this way, the emperor
separated himself from the political conditions of the 1930s and the first
half of the 1940s and exonerated himself from the implication that he
was responsible for the act of war. If he was not responsible, nobody in
Japan could be responsible because the war had been fought in his name.[26]
The emperor was responsible only for his attempt to bring peace to Japan.
Similarly, for many ordinary Japanese, the emperor was a useful instrument through whom they could suppress the history of the war and slide
into the postwar period absolved of responsibility.

The postwar Japanese political system was only too eager to reconfirm
the fiction that the rescript offered. The Shidehara administration passed
a resolution on November 5, 1945, that included the following characterizations of the war and the emperor's role in it:

1. The Japanese Empire could not help but start the Great East Asian
War, given the surrounding circumstances;
2. The emperor wished to see the American negotiations reach a
peaceful compromise;
3. In accordance with the established precedents in observing the
Constitution, the emperor never rejected the decision of the imperial
government and the Imperial General Headquarters to start the conflict
and to execute plans.[27]

With the help of postwar administrations, the image of the peace-loving
sovereign portrayed in the imperial rescript steadily seeped into the Japanese popular imagination.[28]

The accounts of the period recorded by the very people who suffered
from the atomic bomb attest to the persuasive power of the narrative of
Hirohito's "divine intervention." The blast of the bomb managed to instill
a sense of fear and dismay among the residents of Hiroshima and Nagasaki; yet, these instinctive responses did not necessarily translate into a
desire to terminate the conflict.[29] Hachiya Michihiko, a doctor who experienced the Hiroshima atomic bomb, recorded in his diary's August 15
entry: "Many who had been strong advocates of peace and others who
had lost their taste for war following the pika [the blast of the atomic
bomb] were now shouting for the war to continue."[30] To many who resolved to keep fighting even after the blast, the emperor's announcement

to accept the surrender terms was more shocking. Hachiya continues: "The one word—surrender—had produced a greater shock than the bombing of our city."[31]

Tanimoto Kiyoshi, who also lived through the bomb in Hiroshima and whom John Hersey interviewed for his journalistic piece *Hiroshima*, experienced a similar shock after learning of Japan's surrender. However, his sense of devastation was healed as he learned how the emperor made his decision. He recalls:

> Afterward, as the process through which and the reason for which the emperor decreed the imperial rescript accepting the end of the war was published in the newspapers, we found hope to live. The emperor could not endure to witness his subjects suffer in the war any longer and accepted the terms the four nations presented "by enduring the unendurable and suffering what is insufferable" in order to save his subjects and the human beings of the world from the destruction of war. The sacrifice in Hiroshima became the basis "to pave the way for a grand peace for all the generations to come."[32]

Tanimoto's account, with quotations from the imperial rescript, demonstrates how the experiences of Hiroshima became an integral part of the foundational narrative of postwar Japan. In his recollection, the cruelty of the war and the atomic bomb only served to enhance the benevolence of the emperor's "sacrifice."

The narrative devices of Hirohito's "divine decision" and "sacrifice" supported the myth that the unprecedented power of the atomic bomb ended the war. The governmental decision expressed in the rescript rendered the power of the bomb comprehensible to those both inside and outside of Hiroshima. Through reading the implicit message in the U.S. government's response correctly and actively producing the narrative of conversion—that is, the conversion of Japan from a militarist state to a peaceful one—the Japanese government prepared the stage for the drama that would solidify Japan's relations with the United States in the postwar world.

MacArthur and Hirohito—the Rendezvous

With the implicit assurance that the imperial institution would remain, the American government also participated in the production of this foundational narrative based in part on the deeds of great men. However, since the relationship between the two countries was far from stable, there was a need for other explanatory devices to stabilize the foundational narrative. Immediately after the defeat of Japan, the United States and Japan recast their relationship in terms of a melodrama of rescue and conversion. According to this melodrama, the United States rescues a good enemy, Hirohito, from the deleterious elements in the enemy country, and the good enemy becomes converted into a representative of U.S. values. Hirohito emerges as a desirable object in the drama to explain why he deserves to be rescued; both countries' relations are expressed through a drama that features an entanglement of desires for the other.

The relationship between the United States and Japan in the postwar melodrama is highly sexualized. The drama casts the United States as a male and Hirohito and Japan as a docile female, who unconditionally accepts the United States' desire for self-assurance. As a good enemy that is also constructed as a docile woman, Japan provides the United States with a reflection of its own power. However, Japan's female character also encompasses the obverse image of the enemy: the dangerous woman. Thus, Japan's role as the good enemy both enacts and threatens to transgress its prescribed role in the melodrama. The narrative of great men unfolds in the postwar period as a melodrama between Hirohito, a feminized Japan, and the new male protagonist, Douglas MacArthur.

On September 27, 1945, Emperor Hirohito visited General Douglas MacArthur, the supreme commander for the Allied powers, for the first time at the American Embassy. This meeting was carefully prepared by Japanese officials.[33] MacArthur describes the scene of his meeting with Hirohito in an overly theatrical fashion:

> He was nervous and the stress of the past months showed plainly. I dismissed everyone but his own interpreter, and we sat down before an open fire at one end of the long reception hall. I offered him an American cigarette, which he took with thanks. I noticed how his hands shook as I lighted it for him. I tried to make it as easy for him as I could, but I knew how deep and dreadful must be his agony of humiliation.

Hirohito is transformed into a feminine character in MacArthur's description. In the domestic atmosphere in front of a hearth, MacArthur offers Hirohito an American cigarette. Accepting this American object par excellence, Hirohito communicates his nervousness through his shaking hands. His "agony of humiliation" renders him a helpless and emasculated figure, worthy of MacArthur's pity and aid. MacArthur continues:

> I had an uneasy feeling he might plead his own cause against indictment as a war criminal. There had been considerable outcry from some of the Allies, notably the Russians and the British, to include him in this category. Indeed, the initial list of those proposed by them was headed by the Emperor's name. Realizing the tragic consequences that would follow such an unjust action, I had stoutly resisted such efforts. When Washington seemed to be veering toward the British point of view, I had advised that I would need at least one million reinforcements should such action be taken.[34]

Appearing docile, Hirohito still represents a potential danger to the American commander. Indeed, in MacArthur's mind, one million soldiers will be necessary to contain Hirohito's danger. Moreover, once again Hirohito and the bomb are equated, this time through the magic number one million. MacArthur claims that the emperor equals at least one million American reinforcements, while Henry Stimson maintained in 1947 that the atomic bomb saved over one million American lives;[35] the emperor and the bomb are represented as prerequisites for peace through the same number of soldiers they can replace. MacArthur's equation insists on the contradictory value of the emperor: he is dangerous yet necessary.

The emperor's announcement of his war responsibility and his self-sacrifice, however, helped to reinforce his docile image. MacArthur describes his surprise at the emperor's acceptance of his defeat as follows:

> But my fears were groundless. What he said was this: "I come to you General MacArthur, to offer myself to the judgment of the powers you represent as the one to bear sole responsibility for every political and military decision made and action taken by people in the conduct of war." A tremendous impression swept me. This courageous assumption of a responsibility implicit with death, a responsibility clearly belied by facts of which I was fully aware, moved me to the very marrow of my bones.[36]

The meeting was a drama staged for MacArthur's personal consumption; it contained the necessary ingredients for a melodrama—humiliation and the heroic acceptance of humiliation. MacArthur emphasizes the sense of humiliation born by the emperor, which only enhances the heroic quality of Hirohito's total conversion. Although the emperor was probably less articulate and heroic in the actual scene, his speech fulfilled the drama of conversion enough to move MacArthur to "the very marrow of my bones."[37] According to an account of Shigemitsu Mamoru, who met MacArthur ten years later in Washington, D.C., MacArthur was then so moved that he wanted to kiss Hirohito on the cheek.[38] MacArthur found Hirohito's act worthy of American rescue; hence, the emperor's affinity with American values had to be highlighted. MacArthur claimed in *Reminiscences* that, through their subsequent meetings, he "found he [the emperor] had a more thorough grasp of the democratic concept than almost any Japanese with whom I talked."[39] The union of Japan and the United States was not strange since Hirohito demonstrated a natural affinity for American principles.

Written eighteen years after their actual meetings, MacArthur's descriptions contain a series of errors. For example, no list of war criminals "headed by the Emperor's name" was ever presented by other allied nations; MacArthur's famous warning of the potential need for one million reinforcements was not telegraphed to Washington until January 1946;

and Hirohito was also well known for his dislike of smoking.[40] MacArthur's misremembering notwithstanding, his dramatized account is valuable for showing how easily the leader of the American occupation forces accepted the narrative of rescue and conversion.

This narrative was useful to both MacArthur and Hirohito. The historian Toyoshita Narahiko argues that, although MacArthur was later perceived by many Japanese to be a powerful autocratic leader of the occupation forces, his authority as supreme commander for the Allied powers was precarious at the beginning of the American occupation.[41] MacArthur found himself in the midst of a power struggle between the United States and the Soviet Union over Japan. The U.S. government did not desire to grant undefined autonomous power to MacArthur because it did not want to address directly the Soviet challenge to American control over Japan. Under these circumstances, the emperor's complete cooperation with the occupation policy was a fortuitous gift for MacArthur, who was seeking to fortify his position as supreme commander. On the other hand, the emperor was in desperate need of support from the occupation leadership: his personal fate was not assured in the absence of a clear occupation policy toward the throne. Hence, MacArthur and Hirohito entered into a covenant that fulfilled each other's needs.

MacArthur and Hirohito were destined to find each other, as is often the case in a melodrama. Together, they were able to stave off the other Allied nations' attempts to interfere with the American occupation policy and to indict the emperor for war crimes; together, they embodied the melodrama of rescue and conversion to a liberal American creed: the emperor was rescued by the Americans from the evil hands of the Japanese militarists. A picture taken by an American photographer prior to MacArthur and Hirohito's meeting represents the happy union of the two countries (fig. 2). Newspaper articles on the emperor's visit with MacArthur first appeared the next day, and the photo appeared on the front pages on September 29. MacArthur towers over the emperor in a relaxed posture with his hand on his own buttocks. Meanwhile, the stiff figure of the emperor, dressed in formal wear, stands gazing straight into the camera. In the sexualized power relations of the two countries, it is only appropriate for Douglas Lummis to call this picture their "wedding photo."[42]

To many Japanese, this photograph was material evidence that the authority of the U.S. occupation forces had displaced that of imperial Japan. The minister of the interior banned the circulation of newspapers carrying the photo, finding the contrast between the two figures demeaning to the emperor. Yet, MacArthur's General Headquarters (GHQ) immediately intervened to enforce the freedom of the press and had the Japanese government lift its ban the very same day.[43] The stark contrast of the two figures in the photo reminds the viewer of the kind of power relation

Figure 2. General Douglas MacArthur and Emperor Hirohito, September 27, 1945. Courtesy of the MacArthur Memorial.

that existed between the United States and Japan at the beginning of the postwar period. The meaning of the loss of the war was negatively embodied by the emperor, while the power and the material wealth that defeated Japan was represented by the towering figure of Douglas MacArthur.

Many Japanese writers who lived through the immediate postwar period articulated their encounter with the United States in purely physical terms. For instance, Toshio the protagonist in Nosaka Akiyuki's semiautobiographical story "American *Hijiki*" ("Amerika hijiki") (1967), recollects his social studies teacher's theory of the correlation between physical strength and national power: "Look at the Americans. Their average height is five feet, ten inches. For us, it's only five three. This difference of seven inches figures in everything, and I believe that's why we lost the

War. A basic difference in physical strength is invariably manifested in national strength."[44] Toshio does not have to hear this theory from his teacher; he already knows it. In Toshio's memories, the image of "MacArthur with the Emperor just up to his shoulders"[45] is meshed with other fragmentary impressions of the United States' material wealth; moreover, the physical strength of American soldiers translates into sexual prowess in Toshio's memories of the immediate postwar period when GIs walked around with Japanese prostitutes clinging to their arms.[46]

To Ide Magoroku, who turned fourteen on September 29, 1945, the memories of his first encounter with GIs are wrapped in the homoerotic images evoked by the corporeality of the victors: "The GIs riding in a few jeeps were almost unarmed, except for a pistol each of them had, and they threw candies from the rear pockets of their pants to the emaciated snotty kids standing on the street. I even heard a mysterious humming. That was the first jazz I ever heard. The bursting buttocks that bounced [burun burun to yureru] to every rhythmic move—that was the body that displayed the victor."[47] In Ide's recollection of the immediate postwar period, the description of the GIs' buttocks leads to a paragraph in which he recalls the surprise of seeing the photograph of the emperor and MacArthur on his birthday: "Yet, the grave shock on that day [the day he saw the GIs for the first time] came when I glanced at a newspaper on the table after returning home from school. The huge photo showed 'The Emperor Visiting the Supreme Commander for the Allied Powers.' In contrast to the tall general full of pride, the figure of the emperor's worn-out body wrapped in morning dress was nothing but the evidence of defeat to the patriotic boy in the second year of middle school."[48]

In spite of these negative readings of the picture, ultimately the visual image of the photograph insisted upon the emperor's sacrifice. The image of the emperor as an unimpressive figure in contrast to MacArthur's powerful physique embodied the meaning of the sacrifice that the emperor made for Japan. If people could identify with the emperor as a human being in the postwar period, as Ueno Kōshi claims, that identification was facilitated through the myth that the emperor sacrificed himself for the future of his country.[49] The photograph vividly demonstrates what happened to the emperor who supposedly insisted: "I do not care about what may happen to me." The shabbier the image of the emperor in the photo, the easier it was to perceive his sacrifice. Many Japanese transposed their own fate in Japan after the defeat onto this figure of Hirohito.

The photo was not only a reminder of the power imbalance between the United States and Japan but also a representation of how the two countries resolved their conflict. At the core of the foundational narrative lay the destructive force of nuclear weapons. The narrative suggested that the United States managed to rescue and convert Japan through a show of power. As Douglas Lummis claims, peace and democracy materialized from the destruction wrought by the nuclear weapon.[50] The creation of the new Japanese constitution shows how the postwar peace was entangled with the destructive power of the bomb.

Realizing the Japanese government's unwillingness to depart from the conservative Meiji Constitution, on February 3, 1946, Douglas MacArthur directed Courtney Whitney, chief of the Government Section of GHQ, to prepare a draft of a new Japanese constitution. With the help of his staff of lawyers and members of the Government Section, Whitney managed to produce a draft in a week. On February 13, copies of the draft were handed over to Japanese officials, namely Matsumoto Jōji, the chairman of the Constitution Revision Committee of the cabinet; Yoshida Shigeru, the foreign minister; Shirasu Jirō, the assistant to the Foreign Minister; and Hasegawa Motoyoshi, who served as an interpreter.[51] The three GHQ staff members who accompanied Whitney to the meeting documented the scene:

> General Whitney sat with his back to the sun, affording [the] best light on the countenances of the Japanese present who sat opposite him. . . . General Whitney at once throttled any discussion of the Matsumoto draft by saying slowly, weighing every word: "The draft of constitution revision, which you submitted to us the other day, is wholly unacceptable to the Supreme Commander as a document of freedom and democracy. The Supreme Commander, however, being fully conscious of the desperate need of the people of Japan for a liberal and enlightened Constitution that will defend them from the injustices and the arbitrary controls of the past, has approved this document and directed that I present it to you as one embodying the principles which in his opinion the situation in Japan demands."[52]

Whitney intentionally sits "with his back to the sun" so that the Japanese delegates have the sun in their eyes. The sun's blinding effect symbolizes the United States' power to define the two countries' relations. Whitney acts out the narrative of rescue and conversion. He will save Japan by offering her a path to conversion—a liberal and enlightened constitution. Moreover, he goes on to remind the Japanese of the connection between their conversion and the United States' nuclear capability:

> At 10:10 o'clock General Whitney and the undersigned left the porch and went out into the sunshine of the garden as an American plane passed over the house. After about fifteen minutes Mr. Shirasu joined us, whereupon General Whitney quietly observed to him: "We are out here enjoying the warmth of atomic energy."[53]

According to Mark Gayn, a journalist who was stationed in Japan at the time, "Just about then, a U.S. bomber buzzed the house. It was a well-

timed incident, even if General Whitney insisted that it had been unsched-
uled."[54] The idyllic garden scene is interrupted by the sound of a U.S.
bomber. If Mark Gayn is right, the plane was a B-29 bomber, the same
type as those that released the atomic bombs. Because of these perfectly
performed theatrics, Whitney needed few words to remind the Japanese
officials of the way the two countries' conflict had been concluded. The
metaphor of the sun projects the image of a benevolent American power
that rescues Japan from the brink of its own self-destruction. The sun's
power forces the Japanese leaders to accept a democratic constitution
and hence become converted to the postwar paradigm. General Whitney's
statement concerning the atomic sunshine reminds the Japanese delegates
that Japan's future issues from the bomb's destructive power: the United
States has the power both to foster the garden's growth and to destroy it.

Japan as the Colonial Other

So as not to privilege the moment of conversion in August 1945, it is
necessary to show that the melodrama of the two countries was hack-
neyed even as it was being played out, having already been rehearsed
in Japan's relations with other Asian countries. Then, however, Japan
performed the male role, while Asia was often cast as the heroine. After
its defeat, Japan's status as occupier was easily translated into that of the
occupied through the familiar tropes of colonial power relations; once the
United States displaced Japan and Japan took up the position of Asia in
the drama, Asia was squeezed out. With its defeat in the war, Japan lost
not only its former colonies but also the memories of its colonial enterprises. By displacing Japan's role as colonizer with that of the United
States, the United States–Japan melodrama assisted in concealing Japan's
historical connection with Asia in postwar Japanese social discourse.

Immediately after the defeat, many Japanese anticipated their encounter with the arriving Americans in sexual terms: Japanese womanhood
was in peril of being violated by American troops. People hid valuables
and young women, and some local governments encouraged women to
leave city areas. The poet Kaneko Mitsuharu reports that in the village
where he and his family took refuge during the war, even elderly women
infested with lice fled to the mountains in fear of rape upon hearing the
rumor that "the Americans are beasts."[55] On an official level, as early
as August 18, 1945, the Japanese government began setting up "sexual
comfort stations" to alleviate the American soldiers' libido and to reduce
rape incidents.[56] When many Japanese gave up the idea of fighting with
bamboo spears—and hence the masculine defense of their community—
they were ready to accept the feminine role into which Japan was cast.[57]

A feminized Japan surreptitiously moved into the position of the occupied, a position that used to be held by other Asian countries in wartime Japanese propaganda films. Postwar relations between the United States and Japan replicated the earlier power relations between Japan and Asia. Hence, the narrative of rescue and conversion in the melodrama of August 1945 had its precursors in wartime Japanese propaganda films that were distributed throughout Asia. A desirable colonial relationship between Japan and its colonies was often portrayed through the figures of two lovers in these films. The narrative often followed a similar pattern: Japan's altruistic intention, initially misunderstood, prevails in the end. *Shina no yoru* (China night, 1940) provides an exemplary case of this melodramatic narrative. Its justification of violence against the Chinese heroine probably added to its popularity in Japan.[58] The drama in *Shina no yoru* is a precursor to the actual melodrama that later unfolded between the United States and Japan. However, the difference between the film's diagesis and the foundational narrative of the postwar period is the fact that it was China, not Japan, that was rescued by its enemy in the film.

The plot of the film is as follows: a young Chinese heroine who nurses an intense hatred of Japan because her family was destroyed in the war against Japan falls in love with a Japanese sailor—an idealist who embodies official Japanese ideology. She loses all of her anti-Japanese feelings once she realizes the earnestness of her lover as well as the sincerity of his Japanese friends. The heroine first appears on the screen with a dirty face and in a ragged dress; however, after she is rescued from destitution by the sailor and taken to his residential hotel, she emerges from the hotel's communal bathroom as a shining beauty. Despite the goodwill of the sailor and the Japanese who are staying at the hotel, the Chinese heroine remains resentful toward Japan and does not hesitate to show it. Finally, after enduring the unendurable, the sailor gives her a slap in the face. With this slap, the rebellious heroine turns into an obedient woman who fully understands the true intentions of the male protagonist.[59] The slap also consummates the romantic relationship between the sailor and the heroine. The story thus resolves the entanglement of sexual desire between the two protagonists through the conflict of love and hate. It is through violence that the heroine realizes her desire for the sailor; her hatred turns out to be a sign of her desire. Her vengeful gaze disappears and is replaced with an adoring look. The slap on the face awakens the female protagonist to the true intentions and sincerity of the sailor. The slap is not desirable, but it is administered to wake her to her own unreasonableness and to his sincerity: in other words, violence is necessitated by an act of goodwill. However, despite her conversion, the heroine con-

tinues to be in contact with a harmful element—a clandestine anti-Japanese group organized by her cousin. Her associates in the organization
refuse to go away and use her as a decoy to trap the sailor, from whom
they want an ammunition-shipping schedule. With her help, the sailor
manages both to escape and to rescue her. Her innocence and conversion
are proven after the rescue when she is found handcuffed.

The atomic attack on Hiroshima and Nagasaki in August 1945 was a
slap in Japan's face; with this slap, Japan's vengeful gaze toward the
United States was transformed into an adoring look. By moving into the
feminine position that Asia had occupied, Japan easily assumed the role
of victim. Hirohito played the role of the heroine who first recognizes the
didactic values of the slap. According to the foundational narrative, the
United States rescued a longing for liberalism in Japan: though (s)he initially resisted, (s)he eventually succumbed to America's allure. Facing inevitable defeat in World War II, the Japanese leadership produced a drama
of rescue—the rescue of Hirohito from the corrupt militarists—in an attempt to rationalize the defeat. Just as the Japanese sailor saves the heroine from the underground anti-Japanese organization, the United States
rescues Hirohito from coercion by the militarists. By retaining Hirohito
on the throne, the American government not only accepted this narrative
of a rescue, but it also used it to consolidate the bilateral relations (holy
matrimony) of the two countries in the postwar period.

Perhaps it is no coincidence that the Chinese heroine in *Shina no yoru*
(fig. 3) was actually played by Ri Kō-ran (pronounced "Li Xiang-lan" in
Chinese), a Japanese actress who passed as Chinese because she grew up
in Manchuria and spoke fluent Chinese.[60] Thus, the good enemy (a Chinese in this case) rescued by the Japanese sailor was an extension of Japan
after all. After the war, Ri Kō-ran resumed her career as the Japanese
actress Yamaguchi Yoshiko; yet, her life and her pursuit of a new identity
were once again caught in the power relations of two countries—the
United States and Japan this time. In the early 1950s, Yamaguchi studied
acting in New York, where she met her first husband, the Japanese American artist Isamu Noguchi; she appeared as Shirley Yamaguchi in two Hollywood films, *Japanese War Bride* (1952) and *House of Bamboo* (1955).[61]
In these postwar films, Yamaguchi fulfilled the American male fantasy of
what Japanese women were—obedient and dedicated to their masters or
to their American husbands.[62] The conjugal relations of the United States
and Japan were figuratively told through her roles.

Ri Kō-ran's career reveals the adaptability of the narrative of rescue
and conversion. Even before August 1945, Japan was playing out a drama
of desire with Asia. Because Japan was already consuming this narrative,
it was ready to see its relationship with the United States in similar terms.

Figure 3. Ri Kō-ran and Hasegawa Kazuo in *Sina no Yoru*. Courtesy of the Ka-wakita Memorial Foundation.

The narrative of rescue and conversion that Japan propagated during the war with Asia returned to postwar Japan with its roles recast.

No longer the male aggressor, Japan assumed the identity of the woman in need of rescue. By switching roles, Japan managed to sustain the drama and conceal the rupture of defeat that initiated the postwar period.

American Hirohito

Hirohito ardently fulfilled the role of rescued and converted enemy in the melodrama by ventriloquizing the United States' desire as his own. He was well aware of the United States' role in shielding him from the Tokyo Trial (International Military Tribunal for the Far East). Thanks to the protection provided by MacArthur as well Japanese collaborators, Emperor Hirohito was neither indicted nor subpoenaed in the trial.[63] In the absence of material evidence—many key documents were destroyed prior to the arrival of the American occupation forces—it was not hard to corroborate the theory that the emperor had been a peace-loving constitutional monarch, a puppet figure for the Japanese military. The fact that the emperor was not subpoenaed by the court provided political legitimacy to the claim that he was innocent and that responsibility for the war rested elsewhere. The emperor metonymically proved the innocence of Japan; as many scholars have claimed, the exemption of the emperor from the trial has effectively preempted discussions of Japan's involvement and responsibility in the Asia Pacific War.[64]

The emperor was appreciative of American assistance in shielding him from the trial and eager to perform his assigned role as the supporter of the United States' policy in Asia. In 1979, the international relations scholar Shindō Ei'ichi discovered two important U.S. documents, both authored by William J. Sebald, the diplomatic section chief of GHQ; dated September 1947, they were addressed to Douglas MacArthur and to Secretary of State George C. Marshall respectively.[65] According to the memoranda, the emperor had sent his interpreter, Terasaki Hidenari, to deliver a message to Sebald. In the message, the emperor expressed his wish to see the long-term U.S. occupation of the Ryukyu Islands as a defense against the Russian threat. The emperor's message directly challenges both the perception that he was a passive sovereign and the new definition of the monarch as "the symbol of the state" in the postwar constitution. The emperor felt compelled to rearticulate U.S. interests in East Asia as Japan's own security concern in order to accept his deference to U.S. political authority.

The emperor was later rewarded for his efforts with a warm welcome by Americans when he visited the United States for the first time in October 1975. The American media greeted him with generous coverage, replicating all the official explanations for his noninvolvement in politics. One of the United States' most hated enemies during World War II was described thirty years later by a *New York Times* article as the person who "has a shy charm and conveys to those who meet him a sense of almost painful honesty, sincerity and kindness."[66] The figure of the frail old man appeared on television screens and newspapers in the United States as a symbol of reconciliation between the two countries. Two days after Hirohito's visit to the Tomb of the Unknown Soldier, an editorial in the *Washington Post* stated: "The visit here by Emperor Hirohito is the kind of symbolic ceremony by which nations acknowledge the large silent changes in the world's affairs. It is not the recollection of World War II that is being marked here, but the long succession of other events that have pushed it back in memory."[67] The postwar political order surrounding the United States and Japan necessitated the repression of memories of World War II. As long as this political order remained as "silent changes," there was no way to articulate what it had repressed. Even when a political protest was made against Hirohito, the message—"Emperor Hirohito: Please Save Our Whales" on a streamer attached to a small aircraft—had less to do with his past political function than his new identity as a marine biologist, an identity that foregrounded his apolitical existence in the postwar period.

In Los Angeles, he was welcomed by conservative Hollywood figures such as John Wayne, Charlton Heston, Robert Goulet, and Carol Lawrence at a banquet at the Los Angeles Music Center. A UPI report in the *Atlanta Constitution* describes the meeting with John Wayne as reminiscent of Hirohito's meeting with Douglas MacArthur: "The lanky Wayne, star of many a picture showing him fighting the Japanese in World War II, towered over the tiny Emperor as they met at the reception."[68] One such movie was the 1958 financial flop *The Barbarian and a Geisha*, in which John Wayne played Townsend Harris: Harris successfully negotiates a treaty to open Japanese ports to the United States; during his mission, he finds the unconditional love of a "geisha" (played by Andō Eiko).[69] The towering figure of John Wayne and his popular association with U.S. masculinity once again evoked Japan's defeat through Hirohito's feminized form—his diminutive figure and his shy charm.

During this trip, the emperor also was portrayed as a representative of American values, appearing happily in the media alongside American popular icons. He visited Disneyland, where Mickey Mouse greeted him along with Snow White, the Seven Dwarves, Goofy, and other Disney characters; he also watched a New York Jets–New England Patriots game at Shea Stadium. Disneyland and American football—perhaps no two symbols could have demonstrated his affinity for American culture better.

Hirohito's sojourn in the United States was a success compared to his trip to Western Europe four years earlier. In that 1971 visit, protest signs underscored the fact that a brutal war had been fought in Hirohito's name, and his car was physically attacked in Holland. The *London Times* reported that "some householders flew Dutch flags at half-mast, Japanese flags were burned and the Emperor was booed in Amsterdam."[70] According to *Asahi shinbun*, someone cut down the trees in London that the emperor planted to commemorate his visit, and there were no Japanese flags flying in the Hague or Amsterdam to welcome the royal couple.[71] On the official level, to the extent that the leaders of the Western European countries embraced U.S. Cold War policy, they welcomed the Japanese monarchy. Yet these incidents demonstrate that memories of the war still affected popular perceptions of Japan and the Japanese monarchy in Europe. Largely excluded from the U.S. occupation policies of Japan, European countries remained outside of the foundational narrative that the United States and Japan coproduced and maintained.

War Is Peace

The foundational narrative that confines Japan to the ambivalent category of good enemy/loser masks the most fundamental element in post–

World War II international relations—that the two enemy countries became the two closest allies in the Pacific. Yet the narrative's readings diverge in the two countries. What has been repressed in the United States is not past memories of the conflict between the two counties but the present alliance between the two countries that the narrative of conversion and rescue carefully masks. The trope of the good enemy/loser freezes the relations of the United States and Japan at the contradictory moment of the conflict's resolution: August 1945. As shown in the controversy over the planning of the *Enola Gay* exhibit at the Smithsonian Institution, discussions of the atomic bomb in the postwar United States have often linked the destructive power of the bomb to the miraculous moment of conversion, the conversion of the entire Japanese nation led by Hirohito. For instance, after reiterating the foundational narrative—the bomb helped to convert the emperor and Japan—James R. Van de Velde, a dean of Yale University, declared with a tone of finality: "it is historically accurate to state that the two atomic bombs helped hasten this terrible war's end—period. And that was unambiguously good."[72] This emphatic insistence on conversion haunts and traps Japan in the duality of the good enemy/loser. Although the transformation of Japan into a good enemy/loser signals a détente between the two countries, a belligerency must remain to maintain the category of enemy: a model enemy is still an enemy, not to be fully trusted. The loser always conjures up memories of the original condition of a conflict; hence, discussions of the atomic bombing are often paired with memories of Pearl Harbor. As long as Japan is identified as a good enemy/loser, it is caught in the moment of the conversion from an enemy to an ally.

On the other hand, by repressing its memories of the conflict in the postwar period, Japan accentuated its alliance with the United States. By accepting the role of model loser, Japan managed to enter into intimate relations with the United States: a model loser deserves rescue and conversion by the United States. By privileging its close relations with the United States, Japanese postwar popular discourse managed to repress the memories of Japan's past conflict with the United States as well as with other countries; according to this logic, because Japan is presently a friend, it always was one.

It is the image of the good loser that has haunted postwar Japanese discussions of Japan's role in World War II. On the level of official discourse, Japan's representation of the bomb supplements the American government's stance toward its use by mimicking the U.S. government's justification for bombing Hiroshima and Nagasaki: the bomb was necessary to conclude the conflict between the two countries.[73] With the show of overwhelming American power, Japan transformed itself into a model, desirable loser for the United States. At the level of popular discourse, the bomb's impressive power became a lightning rod that attracted much of the discussion of the war in Japan; the bomb has come to metonymically represent all memories of the war.[74] The story of the rescue and conversion of Japan privileges bilateral relations with the United States and represses the memories of Japan's conflicts with other countries. The war, fought over a period of fourteen years beginning in late 1931 and involving other Asian and European countries, is reduced to the United States' bombing of Japan (with incendiary bombs and particularly with the atomic bombs).

In *1984*, his caricature of the Cold War world, George Orwell deftly characterizes the logic of contradiction that defines international relations after 1945: the constant realignments of alliances between three states—Oceania, Eurasia, and Eastasia—necessitates a constant rewriting of history. The protagonist, Winston Smith, lives in London, a city in Oceania, and begins questioning the authority of Big Brother, the Ministry of Truth, and the Party—the authorities that repress and rewrite history. In the constant shift of alliances between Eurasia and Eastasia, memories of a past alliance with a present enemy and a past adversarial relationship with a present ally are obliterated through various ideological conditionings. One central method to overcome the contradictions in history is "doublethink," a practice all the members of Oceania have to adhere to. The contradiction between goodness and destruction is embodied by the Party's ubiquitous slogan: "WAR IS PEACE / FREEDOM IS SLAVERY / IGNORANCE IS STRENGTH." One of the characteristics of doublethink is "to hold simultaneously two opinions . . . , knowing them to be contradictory and believing in both of them."[75]

It is easy to detect the process of doublethink in the American popular discourse of the bombs. In the midst of the recent *Enola Gay* controversy, the Senate passed Resolution 257, which reads: "the role of the *Enola Gay* during World War II was momentous in helping to bring World War II to *a merciful end*, which resulted in saving lives of Americans and Japanese" (emphasis added).[76] It is precisely the destructiveness of the weapon that brings good: the slap had to be serious enough to wake the heroine. In *1984*, the use of doublethink constitutes the means to suspend people's critical thinking and to repress memories; in the postwar foundational narrative, doublethink, which posits that the atomic bomb (and the emperor) brought peace, naturalizes the destructive nature of the nuclear weapons.

One is also required to doublethink the existence of Japan in the postwar U.S. hegemony: Japan is an ally and an enemy simultaneously. It is precisely this ambivalence that both enables and ironically destabilizes the narrative that smoothes over the drastic and arbitrary historical transformation in U.S.-Japanese relations in the postwar period. The chasm in the historical narrative has been sutured through the construction of Japan as a good enemy/loser; yet the suture functions as a constant reminder of the chasm itself—the sudden realignment of alliances. As long as Japan stays in this category of a good enemy—an enemy that submits to U.S. might—the semblance of peace can be maintained. However, once Japan steps outside, or is perceived to step outside, of its prescribed role in the drama, the good enemy simply slides back into the category of enemy. It is no surprise that Japan once again emerged as a threat to U.S. national security in the fervor of "Japan bashing" in the late 1980s by the U.S. media, a response to numerous trade conflicts between the two countries in the postwar period. The postwar foundational narrative's power has been constantly challenged by the ever changing power dynamics of the two countries, and to each challenge, the narrative responds with its basic theme of the popular representations of the two countries' relations— rescue and conversion.

In recent criticisms of Japan and its economic practices, Japan emerged once again as a contradictory entity; moreover, the popular discourse that emphasized Japan's economic threat to U.S. interests was expressed in the form of sexual anxiety. In a May 1989 article, the Washington-based journalist James Fallows advocated the necessity of dealing with the Japanese economic threat. Although Fallows's article did not offer new insights into the state of Japan's economy, his rhetoric, along with the article's accompanying illustrations, revealed not only the deep-seated narrative structure of the good enemy in recent attempts to explain Japan but also the ease with which tropes of nuclear containment inform the discussion of U.S.-Japanese relations. Fallows argued that "there is a basic conflict between Japanese and American interests—notwithstanding that the two countries need each other as friends."[77] If Japan's "adversarial trade" practices were not contained, they would harm the United States and the rest of the world. This containment was symbolically depicted in one of the article's illustrations: a smiling globe—its face on the Atlantic and North America—offers a corset to an oversized sumo wrestler (fig. 4). The smooth and hairless body of the sumo wrestler announces its gender trouble: Japan, pictured as an aggressive male figure because of its economic power, must be forced back inside a corset and into the image of a good, effeminate, and docile enemy.

One finds a similar sentiment expressed in Michael Crichton's 1992 novel *Rising Sun* (Crichton actually includes Fallows's article in his bibliography). Crichton's novel opens with the discovery of the murder of a young Caucasian female at the Nakamoto Building, the U.S. headquarters of a Japanese corporation. Detective Smith, the novel's protagonist, learns that the Japanese economy is taking over the United States. The United States and Japan are in an economic war that most Americans are un-

Figure 4. Art by Robert Grossman. *The Atlantic*, May 1989, 46–47.

aware of, and Japan is winning. Japan emerges in the story as an aggressive male, as the mystery unfolds around two main themes: the deviant sexual behavior of the Japanese male and Japan's aggressive trading practices. The chastity of white womanhood is juxtaposed to American security, both of which have to be protected from aggressive Japanese (male) behavior. Crichton's writing appears to be a simple extension of American wartime propaganda, which often invoked white womanhood in need of defense (fig. 5). Yet there are curious parallels in the story between postwar U.S.-Japanese relations and the domestic conflicts that Detective Smith experiences in *Rising Sun*. It is his wife's ambition to be a successful lawyer that destroys their family life: the couple was divorced because she was not satisfied with her domestic role as a mother. Her career success is a threat to Smith much in the same way as Japan's economic might is a danger to American security. Japan and Smith's wife become threats once they overstep their assigned roles in Crichton's misogynist world.

Detective Smith indulges in a sense of anxiety after the case comes to its conclusion, a conclusion that is far from the usual denouement of a mystery novel. A dark chasm of anxiety begins to erode the foundation of his daily life, which has hitherto appeared solid. He ruminates over the uneasy feeling in his heart as he watches his daughter sleep in her crib:

> I thought of the way she slept, so trustingly, lying on her back, her arms thrown over her head. I thought of the way she trusted me to make her world for her now. And I thought of the world that she would grow into. And as I started to make her bed, I felt uneasy in my heart.[78]

Figure 5. One of two hundred war posters displayed at the Museum of Modern Art in 1942. *Life*, December 21, 1942, p.53.

Smith sees the future of American womanhood in his daughter, and he is not sure whether he will be able to protect it. It used to be that the destructive power of nuclear weapons was the main threat to U.S. security and an anxious obsession of the American people. Here, Smith's fear is less clearly definable and more insidious. Ironically, he fears that the very principle the United States fought the Cold War for—the principle of a free economy—may now allow American women and Japan to transgress their docile feminine roles.

Crichton and Fallows are fearful that the two nations may be breaking out of the roles prescribed by the foundational narrative of the postwar period. Japan should simply adhere to the role of good enemy. At one point in Crichton's novel, a character states, "You know I have colleagues who say sooner or later we're going to have to drop another bomb. They think it'll come to that."[79] Ultimately, the atomic bomb recalls the memories of the two countries' conflict and the narrative of rescue and conversion. For Crichton, the boundaries need to be re-marked: the United States should reassert its male role, and Japan should be reminded of its role as a good, feminized enemy.

Crichton's character imagines the bomb as an option in dealing with the shifting historical conditions between the United States and Japan, at the risk of annihilating the entire human population. However, I would like to suggest a more modest measure. We should return to the postwar history of the two countries, where the foundational narrative has been produced, repeated, negotiated, distorted, exaggerated, denied, and accepted. The narrative may have confined the historical imagination; yet the process through which the narrative has exerted itself has not been uniform. The power of the foundational narrative derives from its contradictory claims; hence, it requires constant maintenance. We must attend to these processes in our search for alternative paths in history. By excavating the historical processes that produced and sustained the foundational narrative in both countries and by realizing the United States' and Japan's shared space in history we can start to imagine new narratives for U.S.-Japanese relations. The following chapters focus on the processes through which postwar Japanese society recuperated war-scarred Japan's nationhood within this shared space. In chapter 2, I return to the immediate postwar period to examine strategies for restoring the health of the national body.

2

The Age of the Body

"Thought" today attempts to threaten and
oppress us from above. Among the Japanese
people, "thought" has maintained a despotic
hold—tinged with tyranny—on the Japanese.
[But] now the body is clearly rebelling. The
Japanese people thoroughly distrust thought.
We believe in nothing other than our own bodies.
The body is the truth. The pain of the body,
desire of the body, anger of the body, ecstasy of
the body, confusion of the body, sleep of the
body—these are the only truths.
> *Tamura Taijirō, "Nikutai no bungaku"*

AFTER THE COLLAPSE of the pre-1945 regulatory regime, the bodies that
stood among the ruins of the cities were celebrated as signs of the new
life in Japan. Most Japanese cities had been destroyed by American incendiary bombing, and there was little to block the view in these urban
spaces. For many survivors of the war, their bodies were the only material
objects they managed to rescue from the destruction of the air raids. As
Hirohito began actively traveling through the war-torn country and min-
gling with the Japanese people, the image of the emperor standing in the
urban ruins metaphorically represented the state of Japanese bodies in the
immediate postwar period.[1] The emperor's body, which had been subjected to a rigid bureaucratic system and kept away from the general population's gaze, reappeared before the people. Shiba Ryōtarō, who covered
the emperor's trip to Kyoto in 1950 as a newspaper journalist, later
claimed that the image of the emperor was produced in the course of his
trips through the ruined country: "There was a feeling that, in a Japan
that had nothing, the emperor alone existed, and the rest was ruins. His
[postwar] image was created when he made trips to different regions in
such a time."[2] To the eyes of many Japanese the figure of the emperor was
humanized and liberated from the constraints of the pre-1945 regime, just
as were their own bodies in the postwar period.

Japanese bodies had been at the heart of nationalist discourse before
1945. The wartime regime subjected Japanese bodies to rigid regulations,

attempting to create obedient, patriotic bodies by forging ties between nationalist ideology and bodily functions. All the functions of people's bodies had to be dedicated to the nation's war efforts, whether these efforts were ideological, biological, or economic in nature. With the defeat of Japan, the wartime government's rigid regulatory practice collapsed, giving rise to a sense of liberation in the immediate postwar period. Black markets that appeared in the ruins of the cities became privileged sites for such celebrations, places where many contemporary Japanese writers discovered the raw, erotic energy of Japanese bodies.

Yet, even after the disappearance of the wartime regime, Japanese bodies remained at the juncture of various social discourses in postwar society. Bodies were soon subjugated to a new American medical discourse that sought their normalization. It was not nationalistic jingoism but the concept of democracy that the American authorities sought to instill in Japanese bodies through their normalization and sanitization. As displaced objects of nationhood, these bodies were feminized, cleansed, normalized, and democratized by the victors' hands. Scientific discourse and the American use of medical technology assisted in naturalizing Japan's trauma. In this chapter, I will examine how the sanitization of bodies and the universal developmental scheme of science helped to transform Japan's defeat into a necessary condition for an eventual return to the international community.

In postwar Japan, both the American occupation authorities and Japanese society deployed bodily images as tropes for radically shifting social configurations. Bodies emerged in the immediate postwar period as ambivalent entities that represented both the liberation and the subjugation of Japan. This chapter foregrounds the interplay between the discourse of liberation and the practice of subjugation, both of which sought to redefine Japanese bodies and Japan's nationhood.

The Body under the Wartime Regulatory Regime

As Japanese leadership increased its war efforts against China in the late 1930s, Japanese bodies became subject to increasingly tight regulation. The production of healthy bodies had been a national concern even prior to the full-blown invasion of China in 1937. Yet, as the nation sank deeper into the quagmire of war against China and entered into conflict with the Allies, the government steadfastly increased its hold on the nation's population through a strict national regulation and mobilization system. The body gained official attention not only as the basis of national production and reproduction but also as the medium through which the official ideology for the nation could be materialized.

In 1929, the University of Tokyo professor and nationalist ideologue Kakei Katsuhiko devised a calisthenics that fixed the body as the site of ideological struggle.[3] Aiming at instilling a nationalist spirit, Kakei imbricated each move in his exercise with mythological interpretations: through physical movements, Kakei believed, bodies could return to the mythological origin of the nation and thus embrace its uncontaminated spirit. The mythological explanations that Kakei attached to his exercises seem rather excessive. The link between calisthenics and ideological indoctrination was similarly identified in the series of exercises devised in the latter half of the 1930s by the Zen Nihon Taisō Renmei (All Japan Federation of Calisthenics). For instance, the aim of the 1937 *kenkoku taisō* (nation-building calisthenics) was to realize a loyal Japanese spirit through the training of one's own body.[4] The 1939 *Kô-A taisô* (advancing Asia calisthenics) were devised to produce physical-education personnel to serve as the driving force in advancing Asia.[5] Toward the end of the Asia Pacific War, participants in a popular radio calisthenics show exercised to the jingoistic slogan, "Bei-Ei-geki-metsu" (destroy, perish America and England).[6] As the historian Tanaka Satoshi argues, the strategy that Kakei adopted in his ideological effort—using physical exercise as a means to convey nationalist ideology—was not exceptional.[7] Indeed, regulations for Japanese bodies constituted one of the concerns of official propaganda.

The distance between mind and body was collapsed in wartime efforts to create a nationalist body. What was regarded as "unhealthy"—unproductive and unreproductive—was branded as threatening national interests. With much the same zeal that the government demonstrated in policing thought crimes in the 1920s and 1930s, the government in the 1940s caught bodies in a matrix of surveillance. First identified through physical examinations, "unhealthy" elements became targets of repression. In 1940, the government issued two pieces of regulation—the National Physical Strength Law (Kokumin tairyoku hō) and the National Eugenic Law (Kokumin yūsei hō)—which aimed at monitoring and improving the Japanese body. Under the National Physical Strength Law, everyone under the age of twenty had to get a physical examination and receive documentation of its results.[8] In addition to recording people's physical measurements, examiners also checked for tubercular diseases, venereal diseases, leprosy, mental illness, trachoma, parasites, beriberi, malnutrition, and tooth decay. In 1942, the National Physical Strength Law was revised so that the physical examination came to include the testing of motor skills—vital for military purposes.[9]

On the other hand, the National Eugenic Law allowed the government to order operations to be performed on those suffering from hereditary illness, and these orders could be extended to apply to those related in the fourth degree. The law listed five subcategories of illness under its jurisdiction: hereditary mental illness, hereditary mental retardation, extreme and malign cases of hereditary pathological character, extreme and malign cases of hereditary physical ailment, and extreme cases of hereditary physical deformity.[10] Although the actual number of eugenic operations administered was relatively small, the exclusionary strategy of the law enhanced the wartime regime's regulation of bodies.[11] Once eugenic policy had been established as a bulwark against unsound elements in the population, the government issued an "Outline for a Policy Establishing Population Growth" in 1941 in an attempt to increase the population from seventy-three million to one hundred million in twenty years.[12] This "Outline" encouraged women to marry early in their lives and to have at least five children and thus defined reproduction as a national project.

Unsound bodies were subjected not only to the state's possible eugenic intervention but also to other practices of exclusion from society. Leprosy and mental illness, for instance, received particular official scrutiny under the National Physical Strength and the National Eugenic laws. Throughout the 1930s the government increased its efforts to corral into national leprosariums those who suffered from leprosy. With the assistance of nongovernmental organizations, the state managed to promote the exclusion of leprosy patients from society.[13] In 1936, the Japan Association for Leprosy Studies not only accepted the Home Ministry's ten-year plan to quarantine leprosy patients but also urged the ministry to reduce the timetable to five years in order to coincide with the 1940 celebration of the twenty-six hundredth year of imperial rule.[14] Moreover, the imperial household donated a large sum of money for the care of leprosy patients in order to underscore the beneficence of the imperial family.[15] As a result, patients were obliged to appreciate their own exclusion as the expression of the state's and the imperial institution's paternalistic care. However, despite such imperial charity, the living conditions of patients at the medical facilities worsened as the nation began to suffer from general shortages toward the end of the war.[16] A lack of basic food items and medical supplies in particular resulted in high death rates at the leprosarium. At two of the nine national facilities on the Japanese mainland (excluding the two facilities in Okinawa), the death rate exceeded 20 percent in 1945.[17]

Those who were in mental hospitals fared even worse. At the Matsuzawa Hospital in Tokyo, 41 percent of the patients died in 1945, while the death rate at its branch facility was as high as 53 percent.[18] According to the records of the mental ward of the Kyoto Imperial University Hospital, patient deaths constituted 34 percent of its "discharge" cases. Many patients steadily lost weight, sometimes as much as a kilogram a week, had chronic diarrhea, and finally died. To Tsukazaki Naoki, who authored a critical history of the state of medical service at this hospital during the war years, the patients' diarrhea appeared to be the only means left for them to communicate their suffering in the dire conditions of the hospital.[19] In sum, members of Japanese society were ordered to adjust their bodies and thought to accord with state requirements. When this was not possible, their bodies were mercilessly discarded.

Medical facilities were not the only institutions that strove to normalize bodies. The regulatory regime of wartime Japan manifested itself most harshly within the military. The photographer Fukushima Kikujirō, known for pictures that recorded militarist legacies in postwar society, was a young patriot during the war who managed to control his bodily symptoms to stay alive. When drafted into the army in 1944, he was suffering from acute jaundice and could not even eat thin rice gruel. A sense of duty to serve his country caused Fukushima to disregard his doctor's advice to postpone his enlistment. A believer in jingoist nationalism, Fukushima ignored his bodily ailments in order to serve the country. However, his naive belief in the Japanese military was immediately shattered when he saw men who could not recite the "Imperial Rescript to Soldiers and Sailors" beaten to a bloody pulp; this brutality was the reality of the Japanese army. In spite of his ailing body, Fukushima had to jump into this hell and somehow survive:

> My stomach, which was weakened to its limit, did not accept the military meals, which contained soy beans. Extreme diarrhea persisted—what I ate came out in its original shape—I let it go in my pants while I was in training sessions.
>
> Yet this private second class covered with shit did not die. Miraculously, he recovered his physical strength in a half month and began to be treated as a model soldier in the platoon. However, the few soldiers who were slow in their motions and memorization continued to be beaten up [as they had] since the beginning of their enlistment. Three of them escaped one night: one of them was found as a mutilated corpse run over by a train, while the two others were pulled out of the well in the military compound, bloated like rubber balls. The officers and platoon leaders who rushed to the scene kept kicking the bodies until the bellies were ruptured and internal organs burst out, shouting, "Those traitors" all the while.[20]

As Fukushima indicates, unfit bodies were unpatriotic bodies. The army was an institution that aspired to produce ideologically sound bodies through its vigorous training. Regulating body functions and daily activities down to the most minute details was a sine qua non for the production of loyal imperial soldiers, and success in physical training was proof of loyalty. Bodies that failed to pass muster were marked and subjected to further brutal treatments. Fukushima's account of his experiences shows in extreme form the state of the bodies in the Japanese military toward the end of the war.

As material support diminished, the production of nationalist bodies within the military reached the bankrupt stage. For example, the army demanded that soldiers fit their feet to the shoes they received by ignoring pain, yet, as the war came to a close, there were no shoes to distribute among the soldiers. Fukushima was enlisted as a soldier for the second time in 1945 in a unit comprised mostly of those in their forties and fifties. Utterly unfit for military service and lacking provisions such as shoes, rifles, and even water bottles, such bodies were useful only as sacrifices for the nation's war efforts. Bodies unfit for sustained fighting could undertake only short-term missions requiring minimum provisions. Day in and day out, they were trained to execute suicide missions against U.S. tanks, to carry bombs on their backs, and to throw themselves underneath enemy vehicles.[21]

The state further expanded its surveillance over Japanese bodies through neighborhood and village associations (*chōnaikai and burakukai*). By controlling the material needs to support bodily functions, the state forcefully created docile, nationalistic bodies, not only through such institutions as the military, but also through such instruments of surveillance as neighborhood and village associations. In 1940, the Home Ministry mandated the creation of these associations throughout the nation, and these associations were further subdivided into neighbor groups (*tonarigumi*). Recognizing such groups as administrative units in 1943, the state located them centrally in quotidian lives by defining them as the basis for ration distribution. Individuals had to belong to an association in order to receive their rations of food and clothing. The wartime regime not only encouraged mutual policing among neighbors but also forced conformity through placing individuals at the mercy of associations.

The Defeat of Japan, or the Liberation of the Body

It is then of little surprise that on August 15, 1945, ordinary citizens celebrated the end of the war as the liberation of their bodies. Immediately after hearing the emperor's voice on the radio, Kuwana Sadako, who had evacuated to Niigata with her husband, found smoke rising from the smokestack of a public bathhouse. To her surprise, it was open for business, as if nothing had happened. During the war, dire shortages of fuel had limited the business days and hours of bathhouses, which were accordingly always crowded.[22] On this day, the owner had opened the baths early in the afternoon, as if to recover the normalcy of daily life. Kuwana immediately walked in and enjoyed a sense of liberation in the bath, where she was the sole customer.[23] For Kuwana, the postwar period began with cleansing of her own body.

For others as well, the defeat was an opportunity to reclaim their bodily senses. That night Totsuka Fumiko, who was working as a magazine editor, had a "wild party" with her coworkers at a restaurant in Nagano, the evacuation site for their office. They lit all the lights, sang all the jazz songs they knew, and drank. Feeling angry and desperate, she showed her defiance by wearing a red dress and lipstick, luxury items prohibited during the war.[24] Meanwhile, after hearing the news of Japan's defeat, future cartoonist Tezuka Osamu took a deserted train from Takarazuka to Osaka. As soon as he stepped off the train at the end of the line, he was greeted with the sight of Osaka's dark sky illuminated by lights:

> Inside the station building, the lobbies of department stores and Midō Street were all flooded with lights. The scene was so spectacular that one wondered where in the devastated town those many lights came from. I was overjoyed and stood there for half an hour. They moved me so much that they shattered the bitter sense of defeat.[25]

Under the regulatory regime, Japanese bodies had been forced to endure the deprivation of sensory stimuli. On the night of August 15, 1945, Totsuka, Tezuka, and all those who decided to light up the town of Osaka took their first steps into the postwar period by celebrating their bodily senses.[26]

Many remembered the war's end as liberation from the wartime regulation of bodies. However, celebration was not the only response at the end of the war; many struggled to meet basic needs in the cities where the infrastructure had been destroyed by incendiary bombing. People needed to procure food and shelter for themselves and their families. The food shortages that characterized the war grew even worse immediately after, forcing people to scramble for basic food items. The production of staple foods drastically declined in 1945: rice production declined to an estimated 5.85 million tons from the previous year's 8.78 million tons, and the production of barley similarly decreased to an estimated 0.74 million tons from 1.08 million tons.[27] Meanwhile, in 1945 and 1946, five million Japanese returned from overseas. The rationed food distributed through neighborhood associations was chronically delayed and utterly insufficient to needs.[28] One simply had to find food outside of the official distribution system. A Tokyo District Court judge was reported to have died from malnutrition at the age of thirty-five in October 1947 because he tried to be faithful to the legal system by living on nothing more than his official food rations.[29] His much publicized death was a testimony to the insufficiency of the official ration system.[30]

Those who were living in the cities took trains into the countryside and bartered their belongings for food. They also paid exorbitant sums for essentials in black markets. Eating was the central component of daily life: food-related expenses were as high as 68 percent of household expenses in April 1946.[31] Although the government attempted to control the skyrocketing prices of everyday items by issuing the Imperial Edict on Price Control (Bukka tōseirei) in March 1946, the edict only encouraged the black market through its stranglehold on the legal market.[32] Resources were creatively recycled and merchandised in black markets in the immediate postwar years. Iron helmets as well as duralumin stocked for airplane production were converted into pots and pans.[33] Industrial alcohol found its way into the black markets as intoxicants—many lost their sight and even lives by drinking methyl alcohol. Garbage from American military facilities' mess halls was also a valuable resource, cooked and served in black markets. Stew made out of such garbage was a popular item, selling out in no time.[34]

Nosaka Akiyuki was fifteen years old at the end of the war, his adolescent years marked by experiences with black markets. He constantly returned to scenes of war devastation in his literary work, later claiming that his writing belonged to the "school nurtured in fire ruins and black markets" [yakeato yamiichi ha]. For Nosaka, the realization that the war was over hit him only when he tasted the sweetness of diluted starch syrup at Sannomiya.[35] Recalling the general change in atmosphere of Japanese society from 1945 to 1946, Nosaka wrote:

> 1945 was still much the same. It was in 1946 that the old mores were really overturned. Things became dreadful once people, at least those who had been disheartened, managed to convince themselves that they could do whatever they wanted from then on: it was okay even to sell one's own parents and suck the blood out of one's own children so long as it lined one's pockets.[36]

Nosaka himself soon came to practice petty theft to feed himself. He even learned to ruminate the food in his stomach (a fact whose historical significance I will discuss in the book's final chapter.) Whether or not he was on the brink of starvation, eating became his obsession out of severe fear.

In the struggle for survival in postwar society, the act of eating deeply resonated with sexual desire. Kurumizawa Kōshi's experience at a POW camp in Mongolia attests to the intricate relations between hunger and sexual desire. The chronic shortages of food at their camp—much worse than those experienced by Japanese at home—caused Kurumizawa and other POWs to think constantly about food. One day his unit was told that each prisoner would receive a weeklong break from work and a loaf of white bread if the unit finished its work quota earlier than scheduled. Kurumizawa immediately knew that it was an empty promise intended to motivate the POWs in their work: only high-ranking Mongol officials could eat white bread. Although the camp supervisors only conjured up the idea of food, it was enough to set the imaginations of the POWs in motion:

> White bread two months from now was too far away. Yet the others were ex-cited for the first time in a long while and could not fall asleep. Among those on active duty, some felt blood concentrate in their penises and experienced their first erections in six months and spontaneously held their crotches with their hands all the while thinking about the day when they would be able to eat a whole loaf of white bread. The sweetness of imaginary pleasure—softness chewed in the mouth—led to unconscious motions of the hand. Although they were in dire need of nutrition, youth is a strange thing: they ejaculated while dreaming of swallowing. This was the first sexual impulse they had had since they entered this country.[37]

In the extreme deprivation of bodily comfort, sexual desire becomes equal to one's will to survive. Kurumizawa himself later learned to masturbate while thinking about the dishes he had eaten in Japan.[38]

The struggle for survival in the immediate postwar years was also a process to recover the bodily senses, and particularly sexuality in its keen-est form.[39] Sexual enjoyment marked the postwar liberation of Japanese bodies and expressed defiance of the regulatory regime that demanded bodily sacrifices. That the state could not curtail black markets despite a series of attempts only confirmed the state's inability to control bodies in everyday life. Attentive care for bodily functions and senses was a means of moving beyond the state's regulatory mandates. The postwar culture emerging out of black-market experiences celebrated sexuality as the em-bodiment of bodily senses.

Body Literature

When Tamura Taijirō published a story entitled "Nikutai no mon" (The gateway of the flesh) in March 1947, it sparked a sensation. In August 1947, the story was produced as a play, which had a run of nearly one thousand performances over three years.[40] Based on the success of this story and two other stories Tamura wrote in this period, his work was called "literature of the flesh" (*nikutai bungaku*), and he himself was nick-named "body writer" (*nikutai sakka*).[41] Tamura explained his intention to write stories that emphasized the physical dimension of human existence as a critique of the wartime "thought" that alienated the body and was useless in preventing war.[42] Tamura expressed his belief in the body as follows:

> "Thought" today attempts to threaten and oppress us from above. Among the Japanese people, "thought" has maintained a despotic hold—tinged with tyranny—on the Japanese. [But] now the body is clearly rebelling. The Japanese people thoroughly distrust thought. We believe in nothing other than our own bodies. The body is the truth. The pain of the body, desire of the body, anger of the body, ecstasy of the body, confusion of the body, sleep of the body—these are the only truths.[43]

Although Tamura's absolute opposition of body and "thought" appears rather naive, he privileged the immediacy of the body in order to resist the forces of both the "thought" that mobilized Japanese people into the war and the "thought" that concealed the fact of Japan's defeat.

The body was to Tamura the basis for a critical understanding of history. The "lie" that Japanese writers and thinkers embraced during wartime had to be demolished by the body. In arguing for the importance of facing Japan's defeat, Tamura wrote that

> Japanese "thinkers" and writers are irredeemable chronic liars. Their lying is so habitual that they don't even notice that they are liars. Above all, they don't even realize Japan's defeat. Literature in Japan needs to be more like the literature of a defeated country: it needs to be more confused, more absurd, more erotic, and more raucous. Japanese literature should naturally be thus since Japan is a defeated country. The fact that it is not points to deception being practiced somewhere.[44]

Tamura claims the body is the sole site where one can encounter the historical reality of defeat and confusion. That is, Japan's defeat and subsequent social confusion made survival—the maintenance of the body—the central concern for the majority of Japanese. Survival in the chaos of postwar Japan was, in other words, an object lesson through which one could come to understand the repressive nature of "thought" and what it brought to Japan: defeat. The bodies that Tamura rediscovered in the immediate postwar period declare the bankruptcy of "thought."

Although Tamura identifies the radical possibilities of the body, the binary of body and thought in his argument replicates the postwar ideological justification of Japan's position: the Japanese people were somehow duped by the wartime leaders. For Tamura, "thought" was the tool that served the leaders' ideological manipulations, while the body itself remained a neutral substance on which wartime ideologies had been inscribed. Now that wartime ideology had disappeared, the body reemerged as chaos, the final shape of which remained to be determined. The Japanese were left only with their bodies, and only in their bodies lay possibilities for the future.

The body provided the basis for radical social change for Tamura; hence, care for the body was essential for his ideological battle. Tamura asserted that "we have to fatten up Japanese bodies. Japanese people must have bodies that embrace eroticism and still have strength left over. On the basis of these bodies, we have to create a magnificent, solid humanity."[45] In the end, Tamura expresses his belief in fundamental ties between humanity and the body: "we have to become true humans [*ningenrashii ningen*]. To achieve this, we have to liberate bodies from the restrictions that formerly tied them down, to let them breathe naturally like babies, to explore them."[46] In following a normative developmental scheme beginning with the infant stage, the Japanese would attain a higher level of humanity. A universal conception of humanity could at last rescue the Japanese from their particular history, which had forced them to experience the misery of war.

Although Tamura did not target the wartime regulatory regime per se in this criticism, he saw the possibility of postwar social confusion as directly stemming from the lapse of state control over Japanese bodies. The liberation of bodies from all ideological strictures constituted the basis of Tamura's liberal vision in his "literature of the flesh."

Tamura's position on the critical importance of postwar social confusion had, however, already been articulated by Sakaguchi Ango, who made use of similar language. In his essay of 1946, "Zoku darakuron" (A sequel to the thesis on depravity), Sakaguchi encouraged Japanese to "rip off the various veils of deception such as the emperor system, *bushidō*, the spirit of endurance, and the virtue of cutting prices from fifty sen to thirty sen, in order to start fresh as naked human beings."[47] Although he was not nearly as optimistic about humanity as Tamura, Sakaguchi similarly posited the body as the key element in contemplating postwar Japanese society. In another essay published the same year, Sakaguchi claimed with regard to the philosophical and ethical possibilities of the body: "In the history of our ethics, the spirit [always] contemplated the body. People forgot, did not know, or did not even think that the body itself can also think and speak, or that there should even be such a stance."[48] Radical possibilities lay in the language of the body, and only through this language could one begin to approach the question of morals in postwar society.[49]

Postwar Japanese society did elevate the body as a symbol of liberation from the former regime of repression, and Tamura and Sakaguchi provided literary justification for this privileging of the body. However, the body that received attention in occupied Japan was gendered: female bodies and sexuality became the focus of celebration and commodifica-

tion in postwar culture. The body was already subjected to market demands: it was impossible to conceive of the body in a form uncontaminated by social forces. However, images of sexually active women
dominated postwar society: numerous short-lived magazines featured
sexually charged stories,[50] and striptease became a popular form of male
entertainment.[51] Even Tamura's play *Nikutai no mon* was consumed
largely as a striptease: its popularity stemmed from the climax scene,
where the female protagonist is stripped naked and beaten by other prostitutes. Female bodies may have been freed from the strict pre-1945 dress
codes that prohibited female dancers from exposing their thighs onstage,
but they were immediately caught up in market forces that offered them
to male desire at a price.

Furthermore, the female body served as a metonym for Japanese
society, which was liberated from the wartime regime but immediately
reenveloped by the victor's political order. Women as whores—tens of
thousands of Japanese women worked as prostitutes (*pan pan*) for GIs—
were ambivalent symbols of both the liberation and subjugation of Japanese sexuality by the former enemy country. In "Nikutai no mon," Tamura attempts to transcend this ambivalence by locating autonomous
agency in a prostitute.

In Tamura's story, a group of prostitutes refuse either to engage emotionally with anyone or to have sex for pleasure. The condition for joining
their group, this refusal constitutes a psychological defense against the
degradation of their work: they may sell their bodies, but not their souls.
When the prostitutes beat Omachi for breaking the rules, Komasa no Sen,
the leader of the group, castigates her: "Omachi, do you ever think about
your deceased husband? How could you do such a disgusting thing while
thinking about your husband who died at Iwo Jima?" Tamura immediately annotates what Komasa actually meant to say: "For these women,
who do not know sexual ecstasy yet, selling their bodies itself is not a sin.
It is just a business transaction. The sin is to experience a secret joy of the
body not even receiving money. For a widow, this is too imprudent and
unfaithful."[52] In this formulation, the female body is the final line of defense against the ideological constraints of the wartime regime. Although
the prostitutes lost their families to the war's destruction, they re-created
familial ties and adhered to old social mores. Despite their appearance of
freedom, their real liberation is not complete yet and will not come until
they experience corporeal pleasure.

"Nikutai no mon" is a story about the enlightenment that sexual pleasure brings to a female character. Present at Omachi's beating, Borneo
Maya feels at the time a mixture of "fear and reverence" toward Omachi's
body, which knows the life that Maya has not experienced yet. Soon after,
Maya, too, liberates herself by experiencing sexual pleasure, yet it has to

be granted to her by the Japanese male character. Her newly discovered
carnal pleasure also rescues Maya from the past in which she is trapped
(she has acquired her nickname because she always talked about Borneo,
where her brother died). Maya initiates a sexual act with Ibuki Shintarō,
the male character who one day wanders into their hideout and decides
to stay. Since Maya is drunk, her sexual provocation takes a violent form:

> Maya bit into Ibuki's shoulder. "Umm, it hurts." Ibuki tried to stand up. Maya's
> jaws, however, bit into the man's shoulder and would not let it go. "Hey, what
> are you doing!" "I'm gonna kill you and I'll die too." Ibuki saw two drab pupils
> that burn like phosphorus in the dark. "Shin-chan, please die, die with me."
> Maya climbed onto the man's body and choked his neck. She thought she had
> gone out of her mind. There was no shame, no hesitation, nothing. "Damn it,"
> she swore and bit into the man's body. Anger welled up from the bottom of his
> heart. In his intoxicated head, hatred and lust flared up.[53]

Maya did not know how to express her intense sexual desire for him
except as the desire to annihilate his body. Ibuki responds to Maya's provocation with violence:

> Looking at her [lying on the floor in an awkward position], Ibuki felt his instinc-
> tual thirst grow. He grabbed her legs suddenly, pushed them open, and tried to
> tear them apart like ripping a frog into pieces. Yet Maya's joyful moan irritated
> him further. Ibuki knew by intuition that his hatred wouldn't subside unless he
> tortured this sassy girl through and through. He then felt an old feeling return
> to him, a sense of the fulfilled life he had when operating a machine gun at the
> front, he felt so intense with desire to fight and instinctive fear that he had
> almost fainted. The moan of pleasure that Maya's body emanated poured oil
> onto Ibuki's burning hatred. Borneo Maya was completely transformed into a
> white animal. She writhed, groaned, and howled for her body's almost sorrow-
> ful seduction, pleasure, and pain. She felt her loins burn, melt, and flow like
> wax. She experienced a fulfilled feeling for the first time since her birth—no,
> she felt as if she had been born into this world for the first time.[54]

While Borneo Maya has to be punished for displaying her sexual desire,
only in punishment by the male character can she find sexual satisfaction.
Only as a result of Ibuki's uncontrollable anger and his desire to dominate
her does Maya reach ecstasy. Thus, the scene that Tamura describes caters
to a male fantasy of women under male sexual tutelage. In their sexual
act, Ibuki sinks into his memories of war: he reexperiences both the excitement of killing and the fear of death. On the other hand, Maya is "born
into this world for the first time" and is liberated from the past.

The female protagonists in the story are burdened with the task of transcending the past through discovering carnal pleasure, while the male
character can safely return to the past and recover enjoyment experienced

during the war. Male sexuality was augmented with the war experiences; Japanese men resided within their memories of the past. Just as his war experiences help Ibuki to survive postwar society, his combat experiences give him the authority to take a condescending attitude toward the prostitutes. Tamura, on the other hand, demands that the female protagonists transcend their past—the repressive regime of pre-1945 Japan—to be reborn through their bodies. For the prostitutes, the war had a solely negative impact on their lives, an impact that needed to be overcome, and they had to rely on Japanese men in this task. In rescuing female sexuality from the weight of history, Japanese men enable women to leave the position of victim and to join male members of society in celebrating the rejuvenation of Japanese society. By constituting female subjectivity though sexual enjoyment, men could safely erase the aspects of war that created numerous victims and proudly look back on what they experienced during the war as a sign of their virility. Japanese male subjectivity thereby used female bodies to confirm its historical continuity from wartime into the postwar period.

Borneo Maya finally experiences sexual pleasure and thus liberates herself from the fetters of the past. However, the final scene of the story complicates our reading of male and female subjectivity. Immediately sensing that Maya had experienced sexual enjoyment, Komasa hangs Maya from her bound wrists. Despite the pain, Maya

> swore to herself that, even if she sank down to hell, she would not let this pleasure of the body go. As she gradually lost consciousness, she knew her new birth was beginning.
>
> Suspended in the darkness of the underground, Borneo Maya's body was magnificent, like that of the prophet on the cross, enwrapped in a halo of faintly white light.[55]

The sudden invocation of Christ at the very end of the story intimates that the ultimate salvation of female subjectivity does not belong to Japanese males.[56] It belongs to Japan's other, the Christian culture of Europe and the United States: it is a process of identifying with the other, the process of becoming something else at the expense of historical memories. The body and its sexual enjoyment are not ends in themselves. They are vehicles for the powerless, war-devastated country to transcend its historical condition altogether. Tamura's interest lies in the universal principle that transcends local and particular concerns. The sinful—in other words, the local and particular—Japanese female bodies must ultimately be rescued by the transcendental West. Hence, despite his polemics, Tamura's work ultimately relegates the body to a secondary position. The body here and now is significant to his writing only insofar as it serves as a condition for future salvation—a salvation to be found through identification with the victors.

Sixteen years later, Tamura explained the source of salvation and called it the "modern." In a 1963 essay, he described how he arrived at the title "Nikutai no mon":

> I gave the story the title thinking that the enfeebled and, in a way, medievalistic Japanese, saddled with a long spiritual tradition, had to go through the gate of body at least once in order to modernize themselves as human beings. In short, to me, "the gate of body" means "the gate to the modern."[57]

To Tamura, the return of the body in postwar society heralded the arrival of a new era, and his celebration of the body was intended as a preparation for the modernization of the Japanese people. By participating in the universal process of modernization, Japan managed to shed its particularistic—that is, its enfeebled and medievalistic—past, a past associated with war experiences.

Tamura's literary works were perhaps prophetic as they prefigured the trajectory of postwar Japanese history by locating spiritual salvation in the materiality of the body. Once it placed itself on the track of economic recovery, Japanese society focused its energy on modernization as if the production of material culture were a prerequisite for salvation. Tamura's writings told readers that it was acceptable to enjoy the feminized Japanese body. In such enjoyment, they could reconcile their past war experiences and a future salvation in a universal principle of progress.[58]

Postwar history, which I continue to discuss in the chapters that follow, demonstrates that the transformation of bodily images remained the crucial focus within Japanese society in the immediate postwar years. I focus on the medicalized discourses that enwrapped Japanese bodies at this period: they were diagnosed, sanitized, and treated with antibiotics as part of the efforts to democratize Japan.

The Illness unto Itself

There was a curious reversal in Tamura's emphasis on the importance of the body. The body ironically ceased to be the prime cause in his "literature of the flesh." One is ultimately responsible for the decision whether or not to use one's own body and how to use it. The postwar writings of Maruyama Masao present us with another reversal, this time a reversal in the opposite direction. Although the political scientist Maruyama emphasized the importance of the subjective position of spirit over the body, the body and its symptoms emerged as the determining factor in his discussions of Japan's modern history. Maruyama was irritated by the "literature of the flesh" because it intimated the possibility that the body and its symptoms belonged to individuals' subjective domain. However, despite his hatred of the literature of the flesh, the bodily images in Maruyama's own writing render a similar message as Tamura's: Japan retained its essential qualities even after defeat.

Maruyama vehemently rejected the literature of the flesh on the grounds that it lacked the literary imagination to transcend quotidian experience. In his 1949 essay, "Nikutai bungaku kara nikutai seiji made," Maruyama criticized the fetishization of bodily dimensions in Japanese literature.[59] The essay takes the form of a dialogue in which one person is more outspoken than the other in his criticisms of Japanese literature. By the end of the conversation, however, they show a remarkable degree of agreement in their assessment of Japanese literature and politics. The dialogue starts off on the topic of literature but eventually offers parallels between the fields of literature and politics.

Maruyama claims that, in the literary tradition of Japan, writers simply present "individual sensual experiences as a bundle" and there is "no internal integrity as fiction."[60] For Maruyama, bodily functions are natural conditions that need to be integrated by the spirit. The more outspoken participant in the conversation declares:

> Even realism is a method of creation. Copying sensory objects simply as they are cannot be called realism. Reality can be called a "work" (fiction) when it emerges, not as immediate reality, but as reality mediated by the active intervention of the human spirit. Therefore, what is decisive is the integrating power of spirit. However, in places like Japan where spirit has not gained independence from sensory nature—nature, of course, includes human bodies—the intervention of spirit is correspondingly weak. Thus, fiction does not have its own internal integrity, and it is dragged around by unintegrated sensory experiences.[61]

Maruyama does not hide his irritation at modern Japanese literature as a genre that, he believes, is all " 'body' literature in that writers' spirits cling like oysters to sensory—natural—conditions, lacking truly free flights of imagination."[62]

Once the conversation moves to politics, the discussants eagerly point out that no political spirit exists in Japanese society and that such a spirit is needed to transcend premodern social relations. Social relations in Japan have been trapped in sensory modes unmediated by the political spirit; this condition is best attested to by the often used bodily metaphors describing Japanese social interactions. For example, Maruyama argues (through the voice of a discussant) that such terms as *kao* (face) and *hara* (stomach), the bodily metaphors often used to describe the importance of pseudofamilial relations, represent the premodern character of Japanese social relations.[63] Maruyama coined the term "body politics"—politics based on premodern conditions—to describe what he saw as the obstacle to modern Japanese political institutions. According to Maruyama, body had to be overcome by the cultivation of independent political spirit. Bodily experiences had to be elevated in modern literature and politics through the intervention of the spirit. For Maruyama, the Japanese body was the factor hampering the integration by the spirit. The body had to be normalized in order for Japanese society to have a modern political subjectivity. The body becomes a symbol of premodern social conditions and thus has to be overcome.

Maruyama's position is particularly apparent in his designation in "Nikutai" of Japan's family system as the "private parts" (*chibu*, which literally means shameful part) of Japanese society.[64] In his writings, bodily metaphors were used to describe the negative conditions of Japanese politics. Similarly, his 1947 essay on political science stressed "the infertility of our country's political science."[65] Maruyama was eager to diagnose the "social pathology" of society during his time, which contrasted with the "healthy nature" (*kenkōsei*) of Meiji society.[66]

Maruyama's image of an ailing Japanese body and his focus on social pathology constituted a counterdiscourse against the rather naïve understanding of the postwar period as the liberation of Japan, a view held by people such as Tamura and Sakaguchi. According to Maruyama, premodern social conditions persisted, and, as a result, Japanese society maintained deep continuities with the pre-1945 era. Maruyama insisted on the study of the historical conditions that gave rise to the fascistic regime of pre-1945 Japan; and, according to his diagnosis, Japanese bodies and politics had not yet reached a healthy stage due to inherent developmental impediment. That is, Maruyama refused to privilege 1945 as a radical turning point in Japan's history.

The shock of Japan's defeat in the Asia Pacific War had already been absorbed in Maruyama's scholarship: the defeat was part of Japan's chronic condition. Locating the incomplete production of Japanese political subjectivity in the Tokugawa period, Maruyama prefigured the defeat of Japan in this intellectual history. Maruyama discovered the historical possibility of a construction of political agency in Ogyū Sorai's logic of invention. However, due to the limitations imposed on the nascent bourgeois class in Tokugawa society, Ogyū's logic managed only to introduce an incomplete form of political subjectivity. The merchant class was too dependent on political authority, and this dependency hampered development of the political subjectivity of the bourgeois class. This incomplete development thereby deprived modern Japanese society of fully autonomous political agency. Maruyama's argument is rather deterministic: the development of political agency was and has always been incomplete. Modern Japanese society has been trapped in a vicious circle: Japan never possessed historical conditions favorable for the production of autonomous political agency, and this lack of agency meant that the nation never could produce such conditions.[67]

Maruyama had thus theorized the ground for Japan's inevitable defeat in the war and did not feel an emotional letdown when he heard the news of Japan's surrender. All he said to his army fellows concerning the end of the war was, "It is hard to look sad."[68] The defeat of Japan could be no shock if the causes of the defeat were inherent attributes of Japanese society. For Maruyama, Japanese society did not change overnight in 1945 and would not change in the near future. Maruyama's use of bodily metaphors posited Japan as an organic whole, with an emphasis on the unremediable nature, the timeless continuity, of illness in Japanese politics and society. Japanese society was ailing in Maruyama's appraisal, but this illness was precisely what made Japanese society uniquely Japanese throughout time.

Maruyama's early postwar writings, which articulated the nation as bodily symptoms, gained enthusiastic support in Japan. Maruyama's discourse was enormously popular in postwar society for two main reasons. First, it presented the historical continuity of the nation beyond its devastating defeat. Japan managed to maintain a unique quality that resisted easy identification with Japan's other—the United States and Europe. Second, Maruyama in effect exonerated actual Japanese people from responsibility in both the Asia Pacific War and Japan's defeat. If it was indeed an illness beyond cure, then nobody was really responsible for the illness. The only blame one should accept was that one happened to be Japanese and thus sick. The negative characterization of Japanese society offered by Maruyama diffused a sense of loss in Japan's modern history. The loss that Japan suffered in August 1945 was only a symptom of Japan's chronic illness. Hence, the deeper his pessimism and critical discourse reached into Japanese society, the less guilt was attached to each individual who participated in the war.

Maruyama's thesis of the hampered development of political subjectivity in Japan provided the basis for his argument during the 1950s, which emphasized Japan's unique quality against Europe and the United States. I will pursue the logical consequence of Maruyama's characterizations of Japan in the following chapter. However, I will remain in 1940s Japan in the following section in order to discuss other forms of medicalized discourses that surrounded Japanese bodies.

The Production of Clean, Democratic Bodies

Maruyama's critical discourse constructed historical continuity within Japanese society by emphasizing the chronic nature of its illness. However, Maruyama's discourse also nicely complemented the medical and hygienic practices of the American occupation forces in Japan, practices that aspired to produce a democratic Japanese body. In the language of the American occupation forces, slippage between medical and social science discourses occurred in the opposite direction as it did in Maruyama's. GHQ posited ailing Japanese bodies suffering from malnutrition and infectious diseases as a threat to its program of democratizing the Japanese and to the personnel of the American forces. However, the material wealth of the United States afforded the occupation forces a means to suppress infectious diseases without drastically transforming Japan's hygienic infrastructure.

New medical developments enabled GHQ to intervene in the spread of infectious diseases at a relatively low cost. Mass-produced DDT (dichloro-diphenyl-trichloro-ethane) and antibiotics provided a relatively inexpensive way to deal with the health problems of occupied Japan. In the occupation forces' medical and social discourses, the production of healthy bodies became a prerequisite for the construction of a democratic society. Maruyama's dire diagnosis of Japan's illness could not be too threatening if the disease turned out to be curable. While postwar Japanese society celebrated the liberation of Japanese bodies from the wartime regime's regulatory practices, these bodies were soon subjugated to a new regulatory regime that aspired to produce clean, democratic bodies out of the Japanese.[69]

Echoing Maruyama's medicalized discourse, the production of healthy bodies by the occupation forces constituted a symbolic eradication of Japanese illness. Crawford F. Sams's memoir, which recalls his duties as the head of the Section of Public Health and Welfare (SPHW) within GHQ, provides a valuable firsthand account of the occupation authorities' health and hygiene policies in occupied Japan. Sams's summary of the activities of the "medic" reveals the inherent connections that he saw between the health and hygiene policies of the United States and the democratization of developing countries. Sams maintains that

> most underdeveloped nations are underdeveloped for many reasons, but one of the reasons is that the bulk of the population is sick, chronically infested with diseases that may cause mental retardation, loss of physical stamina, and many other things. If we desire to improve the standard of living of some undeveloped nations as a policy in our foreign relations, hoping thereby that they will under-

stand our version of democracy and the worth of the individual, then the place
to start is in the health and welfare field, which is fundamental to the success
of any such improvement.[70]

According to Sams, it is essential to have a material basis—a healthy
body—to implement democratic values successfully in developing nations. That is, the democratic principle that "each individual has value"
has to be accompanied by care for each individual's body.

The healthy, democratic bodies that Sams envisioned also needed to be
nonthreatening to American military personnel. On August 22, 1945, the
State-War-Navy Coordinating Committee (SWNCC) issued a two-point
U.S. occupation policy statement, outlining the U.S. government's initial
postsurrender goals in Japan. The first of the two ultimate objectives outlined by the SWNCC document was "to insure that Japan will not again
become a menace to the United States or to the peace and security of the
world."[71] If we juxtapose this passage with the "Basic Plan for Operations," a document issued on August 31 by the Section of Public Services
(the predecessor of the SPHW), we can observe an intriguing slippage.
The Section of Public Services aspired to support the U.S. occupation policies through its health and sanitary measures. The first of the three goals
of public health policies in occupied Japan was "to so control health and
sanitary conditions as to prevent the Japanese people from becoming a
menace to the Occupation Forces."[72] Thus, the language of the "Basic
Plan" equated the boundaries of each individual Japanese body with national boundaries: the production of clean, healthy bodies was a sine qua
non for making Japan democratic and, thus, less of "a menace to the
Occupation Forces."

For the Japanese to acquire democratic bodies, however, they were in
dire need of adequate nutrition; the average caloric intake in the major
cites dropped to 1,570 calories in 1946—and with the nonexistent health
infrastructure in many of the urban areas many malnourished Japanese
were at increased risk of contracting lethal diseases.[73] In 1946, such diseases as cholera, dysentery, typhus fever, smallpox, and malaria spread
throughout the country.[74] However, food assistance from GHQ and the
American government in the form of flour, soy beans, corn, and dry milk
alleviated the most acute food shortages.[75]

Meanwhile, the SPHW managed to reduce the number of diseased patients through a combination of large-scale vaccination programs and extensive use of DDT. On the one hand, the production system of serum,
vaccine, and antibiotics that the SPHW established in Japan provided a
basis for fighting diseases on the immunological level.[76] On the other
hand, DDT was an essential tool in preventing epidemics spread by insects
carrying infectious diseases. The American forces were already using

DDT in various regions by the end of the war.[77] As an extension of this use of DDT, the occupation forces sprayed DDT from the air twenty-four hours prior to their actual landing at Yokosuka.[78] Similarly, before they moved into the city of Tachikawa, the occupation forces notified the local government of their use of DDT.[79] GHQ continued to spray DDT from airplanes in rather large targeted areas during the first months of 1946.[80] After mid-1946, however, DDT was sprayed on the ground in the targeted areas with the assistance of the Japanese health personnel whom GHQ helped to train.[81] Although DDT was imported from the United States during the initial stage of occupation, Japanese production, which began under the aegis of GHQ, satisfied the needs of both Japan and Korea by the end of occupation.[82]

Encounters with DDT were rather humiliating experiences for many Japanese. At schools and major stations in 1946, GIs and Japanese health workers indiscriminately covered people with DDT powder.[83] Nosaka Akiyuki recalls the misery of being powdered with DDT:

> When powdered with DDT on my head, it stuck to my skin forever since I could rarely take a bath. My skin looked like it was infected with ringworm. It was particularly awful when powder was injected into my pants with a dispenser which looked like a horse's penis.
>
> With the taste of diluted starch syrup, I felt glad the war was over. But, with DDT, I really understood Japan's defeat.[84]

DDT sprayed in the ruins of Japanese cities was material proof of Japan's humiliation; moreover, Nosaka implies that the submission of Japanese bodies was sexually charged. The act of injecting DDT, a white substance, into his pants with "a dispenser which looked like a horse's penis" was a sexual act. One might even call it a symbolic rape that emasculated the teenager, Nosaka. DDT became another symbol linking Japan's humiliating defeat with sexual submission to American virility.

The following recollection by a journalist similarly suggests that the sanitization of Japanese bodies was a means of producing docile bodies.

> One day [in 1946] toward evening, two American GIs with DDT dispensers showed up at the editorial room of the *Mainichi shinbun*. We all understood that they were there for lice extermination to prevent the spread of typhus fever. Thus, all of the reporters received white powder, even inside their clothes, enduring the feeling of humiliation without saying anything. When one female employee ran away to escape from the approaching GIs, one of them ran after her in order to prevent this.
>
> After a while, she returned [to the editorial room] crying, with white powder covering even her hair—a point of female pride.
>
> I remember I had no words to soothe her.[85]

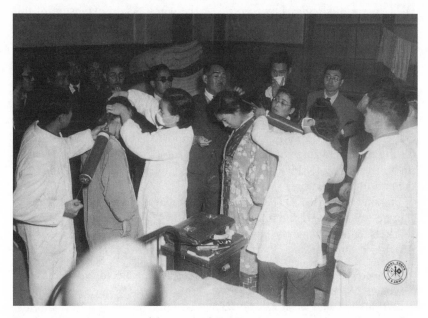

Figure 6. Demonstration of dusting with DDT at Komagome Hospital, December 1946. Women's hair was the target. National Archives, SC-287308.

DDT represented in visible form the authority of the American occupation forces. It was a treatment that, as a resident of the defeated nation, one had to accept silently in the name of hygiene (fig. 6). There were no words of comfort for the woman at the *Mainichi shinbun* because the author had already managed to repress his humiliation with the rationale that they needed DDT for health reasons. The ailing body that Maruyama described in his postwar writings needed a treatment; the American occupation authority provided DDT as a cure for its chronic illness, and a means of democratization.

Watanabe Naoko recalls not only her teacher's lessons regarding DDT but also her own feelings of humiliation when powdered with DDT at school. On days when the health workers sprayed DDT on the students, her teacher "eagerly" taught them about communicable diseases and the curative effects of DDT. The DDT song—emphasizing the effectiveness of DDT against typhus fever—was part of this lesson. She recalls: "After the lesson, we all sang the DDT song while dancing. Then we made a single line while still singing the song, heading toward the DDT dispensing station at the corner of the schoolyard."[86] Pupils had to swallow their sense of humiliation for the sake of both their health and their normalization. Not only their bodies but also their minds were subjected to DDT treatment.

DDT meant more than just hygienic conditions to the Japanese people. To Sakurai Tsunao, a doctor who worked for a mental hospital during the war, DDT served as a retroactive explanation for Japan's defeat:

> The occupation forces were very sensitive about lice. The medical officer who came to inspect the hospital saw [that the hospital was infested with lice] and immediately arranged to send DDT in large quantities. With DDT, the lice were exterminated right away. With this illustration [of American scientific power], we thought it only natural that Japan lost the war. A problem about which we could do nothing was instantaneously solved by the occupation forces.[87]

DDT eloquently demonstrated the United States' scientific superiority, a power that defeated Japan's militarism.

Murakami Yōichirō similarly recalls that DDT embodied the "power" of the United States, which produced and deployed on such a massive scale effective means of suppressing infectious diseases.[88] Murakami's impression was not limited to what he saw of DDT. Around 1948, when he first saw a bottle of penicillin covered with a protective crown, it "shone too modern, and appeared as if it were a magic trick."[89] Superior medicine of the United States derived from a material power that Japan aspired to emulate in the postwar period. Young Murakami, like his contemporaries, was mesmerized by the allure of the material power of the victors. He continues: "The story that penicillin had saved Churchill's life during the war spread to Japan; penicillin was understood [in postwar Japan] as an almost magical medicine."[90] Although this information was not accurate and a sulfa drug was actually used for Churchill's illness, this misinformation helped Japanese medical researchers convince the wartime Japanese regime of penicillin's effects.[91] In occupied Japan, people contrasted the United States and England, the places from which such medicine came, with their own impoverished lives and looked up to these places as if they constituted the ideal worlds.[92] The miraculous effects of DDT powder and bottled penicillin minted the image of victors to Murakami and many other Japanese in the abstract form of scientific knowledge.

One finds echoes of this understanding of American material power in a statement that the newly appointed education minister Maeda Tamon made less than two weeks after the atomic attacks on Hiroshima and Nagasaki. A newspaper report indicates the way in which Maeda hoped to rebuild Japan's culture: "We were defeated by the enemy's science. This fact is proven by one atomic bomb dropped on the city of Hiroshima. The new education minister Maeda at his inauguration spoke of his sincere desire for rebuilding culture in a broad sense, including science, and founding the nation on scientific knowledge."[93] This focus on American scientific power transformed Japan's enemy into an abstract image. In the name of science, Maeda and many others endured the humiliation of defeat.

The intended effects of DDT on Japanese bodies were contrary to those of the atomic bombs. The white powder was used to restore smooth surfaces and to erase damage inflicted by the war, whereas the white flash of the atomic bombs scorched the skin. Yet, there was striking agreement between what Murakami saw in DDT and what the education minister saw in the atomic bombs. The presumed neutrality and universality of scientific knowledge made it easier for Japanese to swallow the experience of loss. Scientific knowledge was supposed to transcend local and national boundaries. Although Japan was defeated in the war, this defeat was not the end, but the beginning of history.[94] Postwar Japan, too, would be able to participate in a new competition.

Although medical and scientific knowledge was supposedly unaffected by local conditions, its actual application in the postwar Japanese society was shaped not only by social conditions but also the power dynamics of United States–Japan relations. GHQ was highly concerned about the health of the American soldiers stationed in Japan—particularly with regard to the spread of venereal disease among them. American officials resorted to rather high-handed methods in their battle against such diseases. As the "Basic Plan" of the Section of Public Services claimed, the "health and sanitary conditions" of occupied Japan had to be controlled "to prevent the Japanese people from becoming a menace to the Occupation Forces." Under GHQ command, in November 1945 the Japanese government issued a law that ordered those who had contracted venereal disease to report to the Japanese health authority. The law also both prohibited prostitution by those who failed to pass examinations and mandated the hospitalization of prostitutes with sexually transmitted diseases.[95] Meanwhile, in the Tokyo and Yokohama areas, the American military police forcibly rounded up all women on the streets after a certain hour, transported them to an area surrounded by barbed wire, and subjected them to physical examinations. Telephone operators, women working for GHQ, and even one female member of the Diet were subjected to such random roundups.[96]

Facing an uproar in Japan protesting its coercive tactics, GHQ shifted the burden of responsibility onto the Japanese government. From January 1946, Japanese police began rounding up women on streets. However, despite the efforts of both GHQ and the Japanese government to monitor the hygienic conditions of prostitutes, it was ultimately the expanded production of penicillin that suppressed the number of cases of sexually transmitted diseases.[97] GHQ encouraged the Japanese pharmacological industry to produce better-quality penicillin in larger quantities. For this purpose, GHQ made the production technologies of penicillin—reputed to have cost 20 million dollars to perfect —available to potential Japanese producers.[98] The first batch of penicillin produced in Japan was used at the Yoshiwara Hospital, which was located in one of Tokyo's red-light districts, and at the clinic attached to the RAA (Recreation and Amusement Association) facility, a comfort station established by Japanese entertainment and restaurant associations for American solders.[99] By 1950, penicillin was widely used in Japan to fight pneumonia and various infectious diseases. According to Crawford Sams's memoirs, widespread treatment in Japan with antibiotics "reduced the reservoir of infected cases who could spread the disease"; at the same time, the prophylactic effects of antibiotics on sexually transmitted diseases unexpectedly prevented "the occurrence of venereal disease."[100] Thanks to the policies of the American occupation forces, which encouraged the widespread use of DDT and penicillin, Japanese bodies became so clean that even venereal diseases could not infect them.

Although postwar society celebrated the liberation of Japanese bodies from the wartime regulatory regime, Japanese bodies were immediately captured and regulated by the new medical regime of the American occupation forces. The wartime production of healthy, nationalistic bodies was displaced by the production of clean, democratic bodies in the postwar period. Many Japanese justified their subjugation to the new regulatory regime by stating that it was necessary to improve their own health.

American medical technology was also an object lesson to the defeated country. The material basis that supported that technology amply demonstrated to postwar Japan what had separated the victor from the vanquished. Furthermore, the scientific grounding of the American hygienic policies reduced the humiliation of the defeat: the neutrality and universality of scientific knowledge supposedly transcended the local conflict between Japan and the United States. Japan was in the end subjected to an authority larger than the United States. In the postwar period, the willingness to overlook the American and the postwar Japanese regulatory practices underscored the postwar celebration of the "liberation" of Japanese bodies.[101] Japanese bodies did not escape from the regulatory forces that sought to produce docile bodies out of them. As long as the presence of the United States and its political practices were naturalized as a "necessity," the cause that brought Americans to Japan—the defeat of Japan—remained invisible. Thus, by accepting the sanitization of their own bodies as a necessary practice, many Japanese managed to sanitize their memories as well.

Vulnerable bodies stood both as the symbols of Japan's humiliating position in relation to the United States and as sources of hope. During this "age of the body," bodies returned to Japanese consciousness as ambivalent entities: bodies represented the optimism of liberation as well as Japan's subjugation to the power of the victor. Although the universal image of scientific knowledge alleviated the pain of defeat and loss in occupied Japan, the fundamental ambivalence of Japanese bodies did not disappear. Bodies remained sites that retained traces of loss. In the following chapters, I will examine how this "embodied" ambivalence motivated the cultural discourses of the 1950s and 1960s. Between liberation from the past and subjugation to the present, many producers and consumers of postwar culture sought to reconcile the past and the present in the different images of Japanese bodies.

3

A Nation That Never Is: Cultural Discourse on Japanese Uniqueness

IN THIS CHAPTER, I discuss cultural discourse in 1950s Japan in order to trace the effects of the foundational narrative of postwar United States–Japan relations on postwar Japanese nationalism and also to examine how cultural discourse transformed images of Japanese bodies. Many Japanese emphasized culture but not politics in their attempt to construct new images of a nation against the political reality of the postwar period. Politically speaking, Japan's subordination to the United States was obvious: expressing nationalistic sentiments in political terms—asserting Japan's political sovereignty in international politics—required its members to face what the foundational narrative managed to conceal: the traumatic reality of Japan's defeat. Hence, culture became the dominant area of nationalistic discourse in postwar Japan. Culture, or tradition, was a convenient medium through which to project continuity with Japan's past in order to mask the historical disjuncture of Japan's movement from a former enemy to ally of the United States. By positing Japan as an always already desirable cultural object to the United States, many Japanese and Americans managed to turn away from memories of the conflict.

The suppression of history has been an important aspect of postwar cultural discourse. *Nihonjinron*, the enormously popular discourse on Japanese uniqueness in the 1970s and 1980s, instantiates the ideological construction of Japan, in the worst sense of the ideology. Although this chapter primarily focuses on cultural discourse of 1950s Japan, it is nonetheless useful to take a moment to look at later examples of *nihonjinron* in order to illustrate its full ideological ramifications. *Nihonjinron* makes totalizing, essentialist claims regarding the unique quality of Japanese culture and distinguishes the Japanese from all other peoples. The logic is reductive: supposedly ahistorical categories, such as biology or ethnicity, are employed as essentialist sources of Japanese uniqueness. Indeed, Japan is purportedly so unique that others cannot possibly comprehend it. Japan's cultural uniqueness functions as an ideological device to assure the superior status of Japan in relations with other countries.

Revealing the ideological underpinnings of *nihonjinron* is crucial to an exploration of postwar Japanese nationalism. Critical appraisals of the discourse began to appear in the 1980s, and were widespread by the

1990s. It has today become almost obligatory both in the United States and Japan to disavow any claim of Japanese uniqueness if one wishes to claim a critical stance in the study of Japan. Indeed, many critics have successfully demonstrated the historical construction of Japanese culture and tradition in their studies: examinations of historical specificity render totalization of Japanese culture unattainable. Such ideological debunking is effective both in dismantling the deductive form of knowledge exemplified in *nihonjinron* and in reducing the normative pressure transmitted in its imperative form: behave like a Japanese if you are one. The effectiveness of empirico-historical criticism of the ideological form of knowledge resides in the fact that such criticism affords the observer a critical distance from the ideological claims of *nihonjinron*. By offering knowledge of cultural and ethical diversity in Japan's past, such studies have demonstrated why the ideology of *nihonjinron* does not provide an adequate account of Japanese history.

Debunking is perhaps a necessary step in criticizing seductive ideologies like *nihonjinron*. Empirical historical knowledge creates a critical distance from ideology. This distance in turn empowers observers in their analyses of ideologies. Consequently, in the terrain of polymorphous historical reality, ideology is stripped of its magical power and confined in the category of "ideological." At such point, a given ideology simply appears ridiculous, not worth serious inquiry. However, its critical function notwithstanding, ideological debunking begs the crucial questions of why *nihonjinron* indeed worked, and why it still works. The answer to such questions cannot be found in empirical historical knowledge itself since this form of historical criticism strives to reveal the chasm between ideology and history: ideology by definition exists outside of history. In other words, the empiricist critique posits ideology as false consciousness to be overcome with concrete historical knowledge. It is precisely a lack of historical knowledge that constitutes the condition for the acceptance of ideology: one can be duped when one possesses inadequate historical knowledge. The more correct information one has, the less likely one is to believe in ideology.

Moreover, production and consumption of *nihonjinron* largely fall outside of the empirical historicist critique of ideology, since this line of debunking cannot in the end deal with the historicity of an ideology itself. To posit an ideology as historical requires the conceptualization of history as an ideological space and abandoning an external location from which to criticize the said ideology: without such distance from the object of inquiry, an empirical historicist critique cannot maintain its transparency.

Thus, rather than adopting an empirical historicist approach, I propose an analytical framework in which ideology is seen as a form of historical reality, not as a false consciousness. *Nihonjinron* dominated the postwar historical landscape for those who were emotionally invested in the category of "Japan." Studies of such affective investment must take into account the historicity of *nihonjinron* itself. This chapter traces the genealogy of *nihonjinron* back to 1950s Japan, where the new political reality desperately called for a new discursive formation of the nation.

Since bilateral relations with the United States had a profound impact on Japan's national identity, postwar ideological production must be analyzed in terms of an economy of desire between the two countries. A critique of such ideological production leads us to return to the foundational narrative through which the destinies of the two countries were tightly interlocked, and then to excavate the cultural aspects of the narrative's production process.

In the following section, I will begin my genealogy of *nihonjinron* by looking at Japanese cultural discourses of the 1950s that emphasize the hybrid, in-between quality of Japanese culture. The tropes of hybridity and in-betweenness ultimately serve as the ideological tool that masks the historical disjunctures in U.S.-Japanese relations. By claiming the essential form of Japan and Japanese culture in a reverse form—Japan as a fragmentary entity—the cultural discourse of the 1950s preempted the drastic changes that the war's defeat brought to Japan.

In critically reviewing the intellectual milieu of this period in Japan, I examine the literary representations of "in between" people (*chūkansha*) in two short stories by Kojima Nobuo and another story by Ōe Kenzaburō from the 1950s. Kojima and Ōe are not satisfied with a simple debunking of postwar cultural discourse; these authors also seek to discern how and why tropes of in-betweenness work. It was the conflicting desires of fascination and revulsion toward the former enemy that motivated the ideological construction of Japan's nationhood in cultural discourse of the 1950s. Kojima and Ōe untangle the web of desires in their writing not to criticize ideological production from a safe distance but to find a critical purchase within such production. Their writings in the mid-1950s presented the critical voices that articulated the conditions that naturalized the foundational narrative within contemporary Japanese society.

Japan as Always Already Hybrid

Japan in the 1950s was steadily recovering from the devastating effects of the war. In 1952, the occupation of Japan formally ended when the Treaty of Peace with Japan, concluded between Japan and forty-eight other countries, went into effect. In 1955, the Japanese economy had returned to its pre-1945 levels. Thus, in 1956, the government's *Economic*

Whitepaper proudly repeated the claim of the social critic Nakano Yo-shio: "It is no longer the postwar" [mohaya sengodewa nai], on the basis that the Japanese economy was no longer recovery-oriented.

Nevertheless, Japan regained its formal independence only through its close alliance with and dependence on the United States. The clearly inter-locked nature of Japan's peace and security was illustrated by the fact that a few hours after Japan and delegates from forty-eight countries signed the peace treaty in San Francisco, Prime Minister Yoshida Shigeru went to the headquarters of the U.S. Sixth Army in the same city and signed the United States–Japan Security Treaty (both the peace treaty and the Security Treaty were implemented on April 28, 1952). The conditions that the treaty warranted to the two countries were at best unequal.[1] In practical terms, the U.S. government had a far greater latitude in its mili-tary decisions than its treaty partner. The language used in the text of the treaty attests to the inequitable relations of the two countries: for exam-ple, the preamble specifies that "Japan desires" the presence of U.S. forces and that "the United States is willing" to grant Japan's request. Article 1 speaks euphemistically of the two countries' unequal relations:

> Japan grants, and the United States of America accepts, the right, upon the coming into force of the treaty of peace and of this treaty, to dispose United States land, air and sea forces in and about Japan. Such forces may be utilized to contribute to the maintenance of international peace and security in the Far East and to the security of Japan against armed attack from without, *including assistance given at the express request of the Japanese Government to put down large-scale internal riots and disturbances in Japan, caused through instigation or intervention by an outside Power or Powers.*[2]

According to this treaty, the U.S. government may intervene in Japanese domestic disturbances, yet the United States was not obliged to use its armed forces in a crisis situation. Moreover, there was no specific limita-tion placed on the effective term of the treaty agreement, nor was the U.S. government obliged to consult with the Japanese government prior to the activation of the U.S. forces stationed in Japan.

The text of the Security Treaty was fairly short and consisted only of a preamble and five articles. The actual details of the treaty's terms were specified in the Administrative Agreement signed by both coun-tries, which, being nothing more than an administrative agreement, did not have to be ratified by the legislative body of either country. According to the initial agreement, U.S. jurisdiction in Japan was far larger than was the case in other NATO countries. For instance, the Agreement granted U.S. military personnel extraterritoriality in Japan. According to Article XVII, the United States service courts and authorities shall have the right to exercise within Japan exclusive jurisdiction over all offenses which may be committed in Japan by members of the United States armed forces, the civilian component, and their dependents, excluding their dependents who have only Japanese nationality. Such jurisdiction may in any case be waived by the United States.[3]

The Americans in Japan serving under the treaty would not be submitted to the Japanese justice system.

This particular imbalance concerning American jurisdiction in the Agreement was amended by a 1953 protocol signed by both countries.[4] Furthermore, the Security Treaty of 1960 obliged the United States to take action in case of "armed attack against" Japan in order "to meet the common danger." The Status of Forces Agreement, which displaced the Administrative Agreement, also dictated that the U.S. government consult the Japanese government prior to mobilization of its forces in Japan.[5] The new treaty could be terminated by either party at any point after ten years of its implementation; a year after such notification of termination, the treaty would cease to be in effect.

Despite such later changes, the Security Treaty of 1951 established the fundamental power relationship between the two countries: Japan was militarily dependent on the United States. With the conclusion of this treaty, the U.S. military bases became permanent fixtures in Japan's political as well as physical landscape. The United States–Japan joint committee determined "the facilities and areas in Japan that are required for the use of the United States" (Administrative Agreement, Article XXVI), and, by the end of January 1953, seven hundred facilities and 346,000 acres of land (0.4 percent of all Japanese territories) were requisitioned for U.S. military use.[6] Although the number of U.S. soldiers has steadily decreased since 1953 as the size of Japan's Self-Defense Forces has grown, 150,000 Americans were stationed in Japan in 1955. Japan was firmly planted in American strategic planning as an important outpost in East Asia.[7] Although the Liberal Democratic Party (LDP), the product of a merger between two conservative parties in 1955, struggled to gain a larger degree of independence from Washington's policies, its party leadership in the second half of the 1950s had clearly confirmed the basic framework of U.S.-Japanese relations laid out through the security treaty. The overarching goal of the LDP in 1950s was to create a more autocratic government with a larger military in Japan, an anti-Communist regime vital for the U.S. strategic planning in East Asia.[8]

Even Japan's economic recovery in the early 1950s attested to dependence on the American military presence in East Asia. The Korean War, which broke out in 1950, revived the recessed Japanese economy: the "special procurements" on the part of the U.S. military for fighting in the Korean War injected much-needed dollars into the Japanese economy.[9] A total of more than one billion dollars was spent in Japan by the end of the conflict; special procurements in 1953 reached 64 percent of Japan's export total of that year. Even after the 1953 armistice, special procurements continued until 1955.[10] Furthermore, in April 1949, the exchange ratio for currency was set by Washington at 360 yen for the dollar, undervaluing the yen in order to encourage Japanese exports.[11] The Japanese economy grew even more closely linked to the U.S. economy as Japanese industries became increasingly dependent on American corporations for technology and energy resources.

Japan experienced economic prosperity within the political and economical structure largely defined by American strategic interests. Reliance on the U.S. forces kept Japan's military expenditures lower than was the case for many European countries, while relatively unrestricted access to the American market contributed greatly to the postwar growth of Japanese industry. Along with such economic growth, U.S. consumer culture seeped further into everyday life in Japan. As the economic historian Nakaoka Tetsurō argues, the desire for material wealth represented by American culture was the foundation for the self-sustained economic development of postwar Japan.[12] The desire to consume grew strong in the immediate postwar years, as many Japanese turned an envious gaze toward the material wealth of American society portrayed in various media. For instance, the short textbook for English conversation *Nichibei kaiwa techō* (1945) was an early bestseller, thereby suggesting that the United States had swiftly returned to Japanese popular consciousness.[13]

Many Japanese were fascinated by the signs of the material wealth of American society, particularly household appliances. These signs were conveyed in various ways. The comic strip *Blondie* and *Readers' Digest* portrayed American daily life through idyllic images.[14] Another important source for such images were the films circulated by the Civil Information and Education Section of General MacArthur's headquarters. Though intended to promote American values, these films presented American material wealth, and such a spectacle often impressed Japanese viewers.[15] Numerous Japanese were employed at either American bases or resident areas, and closely witnessed the use of appliances in households. Washington Heights, a U.S. military residential area in downtown Tokyo, functioned as a showcase of American household life in Japan.[16] Radio station reports and department store exhibitions were often venues for presenting the American way of life.[17]

In the 1950s, Japanese consumers were eager to replicate the American dream, and Japanese manufacturers responded by producing smaller Japanese versions of American household appliances. Refrigerators, washing machines, and black-and-white televisions were all introduced to the Japanese market in the 1950s, immediately becoming the ultimate objects of consumer desire. Called the *sanshu no jingi*, or "three imperial regalia," these household appliances were equated with the symbols of imperial legitimacy in the popular media. It is ironic that the cultural legitimacy that the imperial family used to represent in pre-1945 Japan diffused into postwar middle-class households in the form of such consumer goods.[18] Urban residents were also eager to move into the functional, yet small space of *danchi*, the residential units of modern public apartment complexes.[19] Japan's economy grew dependent upon the Pax Americana, and everyday life in Japan began to reproduce the lifestyle of the former enemy. It is no coincidence, then, that the second half of 1950s was marked by cultural discussions of in-between, hybrid Japan. Indeed, these articulations must be read against the political conditions surrounding and within Japan.[20] As Katō Norihiro points out, the use of *chū* (middle, in between) as a trope became widespread in 1950s Japan.[21] For example, the cultural critic Katō Shūichi emphasized the hybridity of Japanese culture in articles published in 1955, while the sociologist Katō Hidetoshi forwarded "the thesis of the in-between [*chūkan*] culture" in 1957. Similarly, between 1957 and 1959, Maruyama Masao also published four articles that argued, albeit in a critical fashion, that the Japanese intellectual tradition was best characterized as fragmentary in nature, as embracing fragments of foreign traditions ad infinitum.[22]

Tropes of in-betweenness and hybridity were deployed to confirm the unique position of Japanese culture and Japan in relation to other nations, with Japan conceptualized as a third term that defied the very premise of the binary opposition. This emphasis on uniqueness in turn served to alleviate the acute sense of dislocation in the postwar period. Japan was already hybrid even before the arrival of American occupation forces: Japan did not lose its own unique identity since Japan had always already been saturated with elements of European and American culture. Furthermore, by evacuating Japan from the East, tropes of in-betweenness helped to mask Japan's wartime aspiration to be the leader of Asia. Thus, tropes of in-betweenness and hybridity satisfied a desire to transcend the particular historical conditions of postwar Japan.

Even political discourse during this period deployed *chū* as a trope. Neutrality (*chūritsu*) was an attractive position to many liberal intellectuals who were opposed to the "partial" peace treaty, which excluded the Communist regimes. Their argument was as follows: the neutrality of Japan was a sine qua non for peace, which was threatened by the emergence of two rival blocks during the Cold War. Japan had to maintain its distance from both the United States and the USSR, which meant not relying on the United States for its recovery. This call for Japan's neutrality embraced the desire to transcend the historical reality of the Cold War and to critique Japan's tacit acceptance of the United States' East Asian policies. Even after the peace and security treaties were signed and Japan had been established as a supporter of the Pax Americana, the appeal of "neutrality" to liberal intellectuals did not diminish. Indeed, the appeal of neutrality was heightened by the challenge of the USSR to American hegemony. The success of *Sputnik* in October 1957 implied that nuclear weapons could be delivered anywhere in the world by powerful missiles. The somber realization that Japan could not stay out of the threat of nuclear war shifted the Socialist Party's official stance from one that called for a revision of the Security Treaty to one of unarmed neutrality.[23]

Katō Shūichi's well-known thesis of the hybridity (*zasshusei*) of Japanese culture stands as a preeminent example of intellectual responses to the new political conditions surrounding late-occupation and postoccupation Japan. During an extended stay in Europe in the early 1950s, Katō began to locate the essential characteristics of Japanese culture in its close intertwining with Western culture, despite his initial desire to locate the pure form of Japanese culture. Katō posits Western and Asian cultures as the pure forms of cultures, against which he measures Japanese culture's hybrid quality. According to Katō, English and French cultures retained their pure forms as the pinnacle of the West, while India and China have only been superficially affected by European influence.[24] As a result of Katō's dichotomization of the West and Asia, Japan is placed in a unique position as a hybrid, exterior to both cultural traditions. In this hybridity, Katō finds generative possibilities.

Katō, for instance, privileges the experiences of postwar Japan without giving consideration to the actual historical conditions of other geographical regions:

> What will happen when Western culture encounters a completely different culture beyond Christian borders? This is the fundamental problem for Japanese culture [in the postwar period]. Singapore and Hong Kong have not faced this problem, or even if they have, it has not had the impact it had in Japan. This problem presently exists only in Japan; it has never existed outside of Japan.[25]

Katō argues that Japan is unique in offering a space where an encounter between the West and the non-West can take place, and with surprising ease, he dismisses any commonalties among Japan, Singapore, and Hong Kong. Furthermore, although Katō sees Japan as unique on the global stage, encounters between the West and the non-West were not historically unique to Japanese culture, which had already embraced Western cultural elements at a deep level. Katō was thus able to preserve historical consistency in Japanese culture, while finding uniqueness in the spatial coexistence of different cultural traditions within Japan. Katō's thesis regarding hybridity also served as a critique of the linear developmental scheme of modernization (*kindaishugi*) in which Western European countries were posited as models for Japan. As long as Japanese people face Japan's unique problem, "the West's modern civil society is not a goal to be achieved, but simply a reference point for our [Japan's] project, a point of comparison for Japanese society."[26] Japan could and should assume its own historical trajectory on the basis of its unique spatial condition of hybridity.

By defining Japanese culture as a third term and by complicating the binary opposition of East and West, Katō attempted to reconstruct Japan's cultural uniqueness. Katō's thesis also affirmed a popular desire for the other, the West, expressed in the realm of cultural consumption, even as it claimed the globally unique status of Japanese culture. The simplicity and optimism of his thesis had strong appeal in mid-1950s Japan, which was experiencing a continuing wave of American culture. Although American material culture was the most visible example of foreign cultural infiltration in postwar Japan, Katō offered only a generic image of the West. Historical and geographical specificities were lost in his general categories of the West, the non-West, the hybrid. His claim of historical relativism ideologically liberated Japan from the negative implications of its hybridity.

Although Maruyama Masao broached the question of hybridity, he responded to Katō's thesis rather negatively. According to Maruyama, eclectic acceptance of foreign traditions only reveals the lack of an integral subjective position in the Japanese intellectual tradition. Instead of the generative possibilities of hybrid culture, Maruyama emphasized the infertility of the intellectual climate of Japan, where various imported European traditions merely coexisted.[27] Yet Maruyama's presentation of the intellectual climate of Japan in *Nihon no shisō* (1961) strikingly resembles Katō's vision of Japanese culture in terms of an emphasis on eclecticism. While Katō sees cultural possibilities in hybridity, Maruyama emphasizes what he perceives as a negative aspect of eclecticism in the Japanese intellectual tradition.

The constant theme in Maruyama's writings bespeaks their own historical nature and their relation to *nihonjinron*. In *Nihon seiji shisōshi kenkyū* (Studies in the intellectual history of Tokugawa Japan), a collection of his wartime writings, Maruyama portrayed Japan as a contradictory entity located at the juncture of the eternal stagnancy of Asia and the historicity of Europe; in so doing, he condemned Japan to an eternal inbetweenness.[28] During the war, Maruyama tried to find the possibility of historical development in Japan's in-betweenness, while in the postwar period he searched for the cause of the hampered development of modern Japanese society. Throughout his career, Maruyama was trapped between his own contradictory desires to locate possibility and impossibility in Japan's in-betweenness. By the early 1970s, Maruyama located a transhistorical negativity in Japanese culture: Japan and the Japanese had always suffered from a lack of integral historical agency.[29] Throughout his career, Maruyama advocated Japan's unique historical problem on the basis of his negative assessment of Japan's in-between character.

Hence, despite their disagreement, what the texts of Katō and Maruyama demonstrate is that 1950s Japan was no longer defined in simple oppositional terms with the West or the United States. According to Katō and Maruyama, Japan had become a third term outside the binary opposition of East and West. Although the conceptualization of Japan as hybrid has been presented since before the war, it found a wide acceptance in postwar society. The 1970s discourse on Japanese uniqueness emphasized Japan's ability to understand the West and the West's inability to understand Japan. This asymmetrical flow of knowledge stems from the categorization of Japan as a hybrid of West and East. Although the West might be able to understand the East through analogy—for example, Confucianism in the image of Christianity—the West had no way to understand the hybrid Japanese culture that defied such analogies. However, Japan, as a hybrid of both, could easily understand both West and East.

In other words, during the 1950s, cultural discourse along these lines surreptitiously removed Japan from an association with the East and located it in a position between the East and the West. This move reflected Japan's actual position in the 1950s: Japan became dependent for its security on U.S. military power and U.S. markets. Against this politico-economic backdrop, such claims of Japanese cultural hybridity had the highly ideological function of confirming the status quo. Through this ideological construction of Japan, memories of past conflicts with the United States and Europe as well as the colonization of fellow Asian countries received little attention, let alone critical discussion. The Japan that had aspired to represent the East against the West was abandoned in discussions of Japan's hybrid culture: Japan had always been hybrid and imbued with the West.

Revulsion and Desire for the Other

Tropes of in-betweenness and hybridity were important elements of the foundational narrative in the 1950s. By placing the Japanese and their culture at the halfway point, this cultural discourse about Japan managed to reconcile two seemingly contradictory desires: fascination with, and revulsion for, the other. Japan had assimilated the alterity of the other, the United States, while maintaining a certain distance. The historical rupture of 1945 seems to have been nicely sutured with these tropes. Nevertheless, this suturing left traces of a forceful, if not awkward, ideological operation on the surface of the nation's cultural discourse, thereby revealing the conflicting desires beneath the restored surface.

The writers Kojima Nobuo and Ōe Kenzaburō portrayed the ideological effects of these tropes through their works in the 1950s. Rather than simply dismissing these tropes, Kojima and Ōe engaged in an ideological critique by exploring the ways in which these tropes were practiced and sustained in specific social conditions. In particular, both authors rely on the portrayal of in-between figures who embody the tropes in order to demonstrate their specific effects in society. Kojima makes use of two Japanese American figures in his stories, while Ōe presents a Japanese interpreter and prostitute in his 1958 collection of short stories. In Kojima's stories, the nationality of the Japanese American individuals marks them as in-betweens; in contrast, Ōe's characters acquire in-between attributes through their careers. By portraying the interactions between such in-betweens (chūkansha, in Ōe's word) and other members of Japanese society, Kojima and Ōe attempt not only to reveal what is concealed by the tropes but also to trace conflicting desires within society. The in-betweens are centrally located in the conflicts between fascination with and revulsion for the other, and these conflicting desires manifest themselves through the bodies of the in-between characters.

After making his literary debut in 1948 with the short story "Kisha no naka" (On the train), Kojima Nobuo published a series of stories that focused on daily life during and immediately after the war. Japan's problematic relationship with the United States received Kojima's creative attention in several of these stories. For example, Kojima uses the nisei characters in "Enkei Daigaku Butai" (Yanjing University Corps) and "Hoshi" (Stars) to illuminate the power dynamics between the United States and Japan. Through figures existing in between the two countries, Kojima excavates the conflicts and tensions between the two countries that had largely been repressed in Japan during the immediate postwar years.

A contemporary of Kojima, Ōe Kenzaburō deploys a similar tactic by introducing a Japanese interpreter, prostitute, and homosexual male as in-betweens in his short stories. However, Ōe and Kojima differ in their readiness to name Japan's other. While Ōe's stories identify the United States and Europe as aggressive male figures in order to reveal the obsequious position of Japan, Kojima's "Enkei Daigaku Butai" is extremely hesitant to tackle the power dynamics between Japan and the United States. When Kojima deals with the presence of the United States through his depiction of the Japanese American figure in "Hoshi" two years later, he finally begins to articulate how deeply postwar Japanese society was defined in terms of its relations with the United States.[30]

Kojima's short stories need to be historicized within and against representations of Japan as hybrid. By consciously introducing the in-between
figures of Japanese Americans into his stories, Kojima participated in the
debate regarding Japan's hybrid identity. It could, moreover, be argued
that Kojima's writing was more historicist than either Katō's or Maruyama's in its exploration of historical conditions that led to eager acceptance
of the conceptualization of Japan as hybrid. Kojima allegorically represents these conditions in the form of an army unit at the moment of the
Japanese empire's collapse. In particular, languages and bodies become
the loci for the struggles of Kojima's characters to recast their identities
within the liminal space of the army unit. In "Enkei Daigaku Butai" from
1952 Kojima did not yet make forceful references to postwar Japanese
society, but he did lay a foundation for a more thorough pursuit of the
topic in 1954 in "Hoshi."

In "Enkei Daigaku Butai," Kojima focuses on the everyday lives of the
members of an army intelligence unit. The protagonist, Kojima—a name
written with the same characters as the author's name—narrates the
story.[31] In March 1944, Kojima is transferred from Shanxi province to an
intelligence unit in Beijing because he has a working knowledge of English. Kojima in fact volunteers for the unit in hope of being sent back to
Japan to do intelligence work; however, to his disappointment, he finds
that the unit is stationed at Yanjing University in Beijing. In the unit,
Kojima meets several strange characters, including a nisei soldier, Ahikawa, who is the illegitimate child of an American marine and a Japanese
woman (61, 67). Ahikawa resents his American heritage and is emotionally invested in Japan's victory. In contrast, Corporal Hanawa Zenjirō,
formerly a florist in Japan, is convinced that Japan will be defeated in the
near future.

Instead of making reference to the actual combat taking place throughout China, the plot focuses on the interactions of these three characters.
Even when battles in the Philippines are mentioned, they are conveyed
with no sense of immediacy. For example, Kojima remarks that "the Philippines are big islands and will take time to be defeated. The soldiers in
remote areas have become accustomed to the fact that the islands are in
the process of being defeated and have entered into the psychological state
of mind in which they thought nothing of it" (89). The unit appears to
be remote from actual battles taking place in Asia; the enemy, the United
States, appears only in the form of intercepted communications. Thus,
the characters in the story live in the amorphous, timeless space of the
war and the military. The narrator continues: "When I think about my
hometown, my heart aches. But what can I do? One gets bored with the
conversations [with one's families] that one ruminates, and forgets even

[familiar] faces. I even get totally bored with the fantasy that I will die" (89). Repressing all memories of the past and adapting oneself to the liminal space of the army seems to be the only way to survive.

However, this strategy of survival thoroughly alienates Kojima from that which was once so familiar to him, the Japanese language, while Ahikawa turns out to be the best suited to the unit's mission due to his exceptional language skills. Interestingly, the contrast between Kojima's and Ahikawa's relations to language prefigures the two opposing evaluations of Japan's hybrid culture forwarded by Maruyama and Katō in the 1950s. The story of Kojima's estrangement from his own identity, which unfolds metaphorically through his troubled relations with language in general and with his native tongue in particular, resonates with Maruyama's critique of celebrations of Japan's hybrid culture. For Maruyama, the foreign elements in Japan's intellectual milieu merely lead to a degenerative state of confusion. In contrast, the hybrid figure of Ahikawa and his suitability for the unit's mission embody Katō's positive evaluation of Japanese cultural conditions. The hybrid constitution of Japanese culture provides the basis for its vitality. Ahikawa's linguistic adeptness resonates, moreover, with the story's portrayal of his marked sexuality, clearly pointing to the generative possibility that Katō saw in Japan's hybrid culture. Perhaps for this reason, the text of "Enkei Daigaku Butai" itself is split in two and based on the contrast between the two characters' relations with the unnamed other, the United States.

The United States enters into the quotidian consciousness of the unit only through the voice of intercepted communication; its presence is at once immediate and distant. By contrast, China remains silent despite its inescapable presence in the lives of the unit members. For example, the scenes at the nearby brothel attest to the symbolic representation of China through the medium of Chinese female bodies. At the brothel Kojima uses a mixture of Japanese, English, and Chinese to converse with one of the Chinese prostitutes. However, this conversation remains "incoherent" (84). The woman embodies three languages since she has three names, one in each language: Toshiko, Julia, and a Chinese name that she writes on a wall in her room but never pronounces (84). The lack of sound for the Chinese name is symbolically salient: the name appears only as a trace among the other writings on the wall, a sign of the prostitute's past memories. The Chinese name is denied a synchronic presence and relegated to the past. Similarly, in both Katō Shūichi's postwar discussion of Japanese cultural hybridity and in Maruyama's negative evaluation of Japan's intellectual state, Asia—particularly China—disappears from the triad of Asia, Japan, and the West. Their discussions assume that China occupies an oppositional position with regard to the West, yet China remains a silent signifier and an ahistorical other to the West. Japanese hybridity is described solely in relation to the West in both Katō's and Maruyama's postwar articulations.

Thus, tropes of hybridity and in-betweenness assisted postwar society to conceal Japan's colonial experiences in wartime China. In Kojima's story, the silenced woman's Chinese name intimates that China was already absent in the minds of the unit members even before the end of the Asia Pacific War. The mission of the intelligence unit, to decipher American codes, is after all, wholly oriented toward the United States. The unit, with its strange dependence on the enemy country and slighting of China, prefigures postwar Japanese society.

In the prostitute's room, Kojima proceeds to efface China as the past by erasing all the writing on the walls. One morning he visits the prostitute while she is not in her room and decides to stay there anyway. After getting bored simply lying there, Kojima begins to scrub off the graffiti left by soldiers. The graffiti exist as a record of Japan's war against China in the prostitute's everyday life; numerous Japanese soldiers have left their marks on the walls.

Kojima does not know why he started the task, yet he feels compelled to finish washing the walls, since the clean spots are more conspicuous than before. After he completes the job, fatigue from the cleaning makes him fall asleep. He dreams that his parents, wife, and friends are washing his body before they place it in a coffin. When he wakes up from the dream, he realizes that what he did will annoy the woman since the graffiti constitutes "memorable letters" to her.[32] The image of the coffin suggests that washing the walls symbolically represents Kojima's departure from everyday life. Once he completes the process of both alienating himself from the past and its memories and losing contact with everyday life, the boundaries of his self disintegrate. Kojima begins to talk in another's voice: speaking like Hanawa, he identifies himself as Hanawa to a patrol officer. Kojima's irrational behavior illustrates Maruyama Masao's critique of the hybrid condition of the Japanese intellectual tradition a condition in which diverse elements simply remain fragmentary without a temporal axis. In the end, Kojima's dysfunctionality defies the generative possibility of hybridity: intimate contact with the Chinese prostitute in a trilingual environment only leads to the erasure of the past and the disintegration of his own identity.

By comparison, the Japanese American Ahikawa appears to be the only person in the unit who does not have a problematic relationship with language. Bilingual in English and Japanese and fluent in Chinese, Ahikawa is ideally suited for the unit's mission. In contrast, the Japanese soldiers have problems with English, while the Japanese of other nisei soldiers is rudimentary. Ahikawa's in-between quality—his Japanese and

American parentage and his fluency in Chinese—centrally locates him in an ironic fashion in the liminal space of the intelligence unit. This secure identity sanctions his act of conviction: Ahikawa publicly demonstrates his contempt for Hanawa, the defeatist in the unit, and even threatens to kill him in a theatrical, Kabuki-like fashion. Standing out against the noncommittal attitudes of his fellow unit members, Ahikawa ironically serves as the most outspoken "representative" of Japan. Ahikawa tries and succeeds in accentuating his Japanese identity in the marginal space of the intelligence unit, but his desire to be a loyal Japanese is perceived as excessive to this space, rendering him a somewhat comical figure. Within the unit which has already repressed the reality of fighting, Ahikawa's desire is an excess, for it reminds the unit members of the war that surrounds them.

Kojima figures Ahikawa's presence in the liminal space of the intelligence unit as an excess of sexual desire. Ahikawa serves as a constant reminder of the desires entangled in the conflict between the United States and Japan. His hybrid body, the product of such desires, represents contradictory desires of fascination with and revulsion toward the other. His hybridity manifests itself through his exceptional language ability and his undiminished sexual appetite. After Kojima finds Ahikawa defecating in a bush, they strike up a conversation in which the latter comments:

> Actually, I was having a hard time because I was also feeling the other urge there in the bush. Let's go have fun tomorrow [in the brothel]. Yeah, Ahikawa is prepared to die as a Japanese. I just resent my American father who gave birth to me. (79)

Ahikawa's sexual desire is so persistent that he cannot have full control over his body. He cannot defecate because he has a sexual urge. Ahikawa's sexual desire leads to a declaration of his readiness to die as a Japanese, yet, in the end, he admits to his American heritage. Ahikawa's hybridity becomes articulated and circulates in the form of sexual desire; his hybridity in turn marks sexual excess, which circulates in the unit whose mission is to decipher the enemy's language. In this sexually charged bilateral relation of the United States and Japan, China figures only as the medium through which these contradictory desires play themselves out. The sexual desires of the unit members and Ahikawa are thus mediated by the bodies of Chinese prostitutes. It is no accident that the lice infesting Ahikawa's crotch spread to other unit members via the Chinese prostitutes: the imagined community of the unit emerges through Chinese female bodies and the consequent infection with lice.

The author's critical insights into identity construction through language notwithstanding, Kojima's criticism of the military and postwar society in "Enkei Daigaku Butai" remains at the level of describing the fictional order of these spaces. The space depicted appears strikingly similar to the Japan that Katō and Maruyama outlined in their 1950s writings: a strange, static space without reference to the specific historical context that has produced it. Although the intelligence unit could exist only in relation to the exterior world, the conditions that created it—Japan's conflicts with China and the United States—simply disappear in the story. The presence of the other is figuratively acknowledged only through the sexual desires of the unit members for the Chinese prostitutes. Yet the protagonist of the story keeps erasing the memories and the community formed around the Chinese prostitutes, while the United States remains cryptically encoded. Kojima can only adapt to the liminal space of the unit by erasing the other in the external world.

Although the author's critique of this space is humorous and biting, it offers little insight into how desire for the other circulates in the unit and postwar Japanese society. Kojima waited two years until he intensified his pursuit of the shadow of the other through another Japanese American character in "Hoshi."

Invisible Japanese Americans

In "Hoshi" (Stars),[33] Kojima Nobuo introduces the figure of Private Jōji Sugihara into the imagined community of the Japanese army. Jōji is trapped in this space by a historical accident: the war breaks out while he is in Japan visiting his grandfather. His hybrid identity is established through such details as his education and his name. Jōji began junior high school in Japan but returned to the United States to attend college. His given name, Jōji, is itself a perfectly Japanese name that nevertheless translates well into the American *George*. His culturally hybrid identity determines his marginal existence in the army; this marginality in turn encourages him to embrace with intensity the fictive order of the army. This split between Jōji and George ultimately propels the narrative.

Although the story centers around Jōji's self-hatred and desire to find his own identity and community, it also deals closely with how other Japanese around him act out their own desires and anxieties through his identity. Jōji's hybrid identity in the story triggers the contradictory and sexually charged responses of Japanese characters toward Japan's other, the United States. Although Jōji is eager to forgo his marked in-betweenness, he is constantly reminded of what he "is," a nisei in the army. They even give him the nickname "America." Senior soldiers use Jōji to express their simultaneous revulsion toward and desire for the United States. They force him to "answer all sorts of questions about California and American women" and demand that he speak English and sing jazz

(119/116). When he refuses to comply with their demands, Jōji is rewarded with "Western-style cooking" (a beating from senior soldiers) or
subjected to "American sight-seeing" (the soldiers watching him "double
over in pain") (119–20/116). By beating Jōji, the unit members manage
to exorcise the very desire that their beating sessions bespeak, their own
desire for Americanness. In this way, Jōji's hybrid identity functions as a
suture holding the tension of the community in the army unit, a suture
that announces the existence of the wound itself. It simultaneously expresses and conceals the tension between desire for and revulsion toward
the United States.

Facing the contradictory process of repression and accentuation of his
social identity, Jōji attempts to gain a Japanese self by reifying the abstract
hierarchy of the army in the form of the stars on insignia. The stars become symbols assuring his place in the army. Jōji turns himself into an
ardent admirer of the stars, finding the community that he longs for
among them. The army to which Jōji is initiated exists as liminal space in
which the stars provide the only orientation. For example, when Kojima
describes the death of some Chinese soldiers, the only reference to the
actual war in the two stories, their bodies are reduced to the symbolic
signifier of their ranking, their stars. One of the soldiers receives a brief
description:

> One of the dead soldiers, dressed in a sky-blue padded uniform, lay face down
> at the side of the path. One of our men nudged the body over with his foot and
> stared at it. There, in the same location on his neck, the dead soldier wore a
> single white star against the black of his collar. The meagerness of that enemy
> star—though it wasn't an absolute meagerness—made me feel close to the dead
> man. Or was it just because he was now a corpse? (126/121)

Jōji Sugihara feels an affinity with the dead Chinese soldier through the
"meagerness of that enemy star," an abstract sign that embodies the military hierarchy. The army for which Jōji serves is an imagined community
through and through, separate from general history and society. Sociohis-
torical memories are obliterated in the military to be substituted by its
own sociality and temporality, which are symbolized by official rank. People are reduced to their stars, the signifiers of their rankings. The sheer
materiality of the soldier's corpse, devoid of historical and social reference, ironically provides the basis on which the stars can communicate
among themselves. Jōji's empathy toward the Chinese soldiers is explicitly
couched as that from one star to another.

Jōji also finds consolation by contemplating an existence more marginal than his own, that of Private Hikida. Hikida's inability to adapt to
army life makes him a perfect object of abuse in his unit. Thanks to Hikida, Jōji not only is relieved from daily mistreatment, but also creates

situations in which Hikida is abused. So long as he is with Hikida, Jōji feels safe, as if he were wearing "a cloak of invisibility" (121/118). Hikida becomes a mirror through which Jōji reflects and externalizes his marginality in the army; in the following description of Hikida's ugliness, Jōji admits to knowing how he himself must appear to others:

> His ugliness had little to do with his awkward posture, or the fact that his uniform was always in disarray because his spare time was all devoted to receiving upbraidings for his idleness. Rather I felt that the measly single star on his collar deserved a better setting than his tiny eyes and his long, pale, downcast face with its three moles. Indeed his looks were an insult to that star. Even one star was too exalted for him. He made me wish that someone had invented an even humbler insignia.
>
> I couldn't bear thinking about the way others viewed me. But vaguely I sensed they felt that I was a disgrace to my own star, too. By insulting one star I was insulting every other star. (120/117)

Jōji is deeply aware of and anxious about his low status in the unit and yearns for a more permanent way to differentiate himself from Hikida. He wishes there were a visual sign—"an even humbler insignia"—that would place Hikida on a lower place in the military hierarchy. The absence of such an insignia, however, only makes Jōji fixate on Hikida's appearance. Thus, Jōji takes Hikida's ugliness as the sign of Hikida's marginality: Hikida's more marginal status renders Jōji's hybrid identity invisible to the other members of the unit.

Contact with local Chinese people also provides Jōji with great comforts since they do not know that he is a nisei. After Jōji is promoted to private first class, he and Hikida (who remains buck private) are assigned to stand watch at the city gate (128/123). Although this assignment allows them to speak with the locals and thus quench their thirst for human contact, this "dream" assignment is short lived. After witnessing their lax security at the city gate, their senior soldier kicks Jōji to the ground, reminding him and the locals of the reality of the army. After this incident, Jōji grows to resent Hikida all the more for maintaining a sympathetic attitude toward the Chinese locals. Hikida simply does not care about being part of the army hierarchy. Without such emotional investment, Hikida cannot be thought of as the lowest supporter of the army hierarchy. When Jōji eventually beats Hikida atop the city wall, Hikida turns the tables by reminding Jōji of his marginal status: "Hikida, still huddled on the ground, muttered petulantly, 'You're not a Japanese after all. You aren't! You aren't!' "(132/126). Although Jōji wants to and does believe that the hierarchy of stars is the basis of the absolute order, Hikida reminds Jōji of his marginalized status outside the army.

Soon after the incident, Hikida is transferred to a unit in Southeast Asia, and Jōji loses his "indispensable" man, or star (128/123). Jōji has to face his own hybrid identity without the protection of "a cloak of invisibility." Jōji is assigned to be an orderly to one Captain Inoma, who takes up the task of creating a loyal Imperial Army soldier out of Jōji. One of the first orders that Inoma gives Jōji is to erase his past: "PFC Sugihara Jōji! You're going to have one hell of a time becoming a Japanese soldier. You will consider today the last time you have any past whatsoever" (136/128). Jōji is ordered to conduct the double act of marking and forgetting his own past by writing a personal history and "Journal of Self-Examination" (136/128) as the first part of his reeducation. Inoma simply tears up Jōji's personal histories, and Jōji has to contemplate his superior's act in his journal. Inoma demands that Jōji express his past in writing only to repress it. By learning to articulate and simultaneously repress his identity as a Japanese American, Jōji finds the way to be a loyal Imperial Army soldier.

Even more effective in inculcating army values in Jōji is the following assignment: "he came up with an unusual method of testing my loyalty. He had me prepare three separate collar insignia of captain's rank. While he slept at night, I was to rotate them on his uniform every now and then. By doing that, of course, I was unable to forget even in my sleep that he was a captain" (136/129). The captain's reeducation of Jōji is so successful that Jōji begins to see him as a star: "I let the notion grow in me that the captain was himself a star, and that stars had an innate grandeur about them" (136/129). Furthermore, Jōji begins to personify the three sets of Inoma's insignia as his brothers and sister; he finally finds his imagined community among the stars that he names Tom, Frank, and Kate. Note that he gives the stars his brothers' and sister's American names. Jōji thus finally finds a way to make the community of stars in the army his own, simultaneously reducing his family at home into a community of stars.

This equation between stars and individuals, including himself, completes his reeducation, yet Jōji discovers that bodies of individuals do not fit neatly into the equation. He is shocked to see Captain Inoma's naked body as he washes his back: the arbitrary relations between the signifier and the signified—Inoma's rank and his masculine body— throw Jōji. Jōji recalls his fatal discovery of Inoma's body:

> One day when I was attending the captain in his bath, he climbed out of the tub and plopped himself down in front of me. I felt as though a powerful electric shock had run through me. I couldn't shake off the peculiar sensation that Kate was still clinging to the nape of his neck. Why should I be so stunned to see the captain nude, without his uniform? Who in fact was this naked man before me?

He was muscular, to be sure, but was there such a great difference between me
and this man with the close-cropped hair when both of us were in the buff?
(137–38/129–30)

Although he manages to reregister the naked man in front of him as Captain Inoma, he has "a sluggish, uneasy feeling, as though a cog had slipped
out of place" (138/130). Inoma's naked body and his bodily existence in
everyday life disturbs the sense of order Jōji found by matching individuals with stars. As a consequence, Jōji begins to notice that "there was
something wrong with the way he gulped his tea, the way he refilled his
rice bowl, the way he snored in his sleep, and the way he spat out the
window each morning" (138/130). Jōji is shaken when he finds living
bodies of individuals beneath the abstract signs of stars.

Once he discovers the chasm between the signifier and the signified, he
grows even more fixated on the stars. Indeed, when he sees a chief of staff
in Beijing, he is mesmerized by the chief's stars and forgets to salute. Jōji
even starts taking a few steps toward the chief until he is stopped by a
"stentorian shout" (139/131). His disrespect toward the chief of staff en-
rages Inoma, who insists that Jōji commit suicide with a sword. The life
of Jōji, however, is saved by a comic discovery: both he and Inoma are
surprised to discover that Jōji's navel is shaped like a star. Not only does
Jōji find his ideal community among the stars, but has always already
been a star.

At this moment of total identification with the stars, Jōji's self seems to
disintegrate. After escaping Inoma's punishment for his irreverent behavior toward his superiors, Jōji wanders through the army compound in a
hallucinatory state. He even manages to escape from the army compound,
only to lose control over himself:

> In a frenzy I leaped a fence and came out on a road. I have no idea how long I
> walked, where my feet led me, what I did, or even if I was really in Peking. I
> had the feeling I had fallen off the planet altogether. I dropped to the ground
> and cried out: "Army Private Sugihara Jōji! Where am I? Get me out of here!!"
> (145/135)[34]

Jōji's process of reeducation is finally complete: he has internalized the
aura of the stars and cannot function outside of the army compound.

During the war, Jōji lives a fictional life in the army, a life that assumes
the eternal conflict between Japan and the United States. However, the
fictive hierarchy that Jōji grows to accept during the war suddenly disintegrates as the war comes to its conclusion. Following the defeat of Japan,
one fiction is immediately displaced with another that promotes the
mutual interests of the United States and Japan. During the war, the hybridity of Jōji's identity had to be repressed (yet marked as a trace of this

tension) in order to maintain the fictive hierarchy of the army. In contrast, the newly imagined community of postwar Japan was eager, like the Japanese army immediately after the war, to appropriate this hybrid identity (his affinity with the United States) in order to erase memories of the past conflict with the United States. Jōji is once again placed at the site of tension, this time as an interpreter, assigned to conceal the gaping wound inflicted by Japan's defeat. Although Jōji's prescribed role seems to change drastically once Japan is defeated, his function as the suture remains constant.

In Kojima's story, the aura of the stars tarnishes very quickly after Japan's defeat. Nevertheless, the Japanese army manages to maintain a semblance of the order within itself. At the end of the war, the two stars that Jōji carries are "imbued with my memories, my experiences" (146/136). He vaguely desires to "continue living the sort of life in which stars would play a part" (147/136). Having learned to live in the self-enclosed community of the stars, life outside has become difficult to imagine. Yet the behavior of his superior officers, particularly that of Inoma, begins to disturb Jōji's sense of hierarchy in the army. Inoma orders Jōji to remember English again, the language that the officer had been so insistent on erasing from Jōji's memories. Jōji is appointed to the task of translation, interpretation, and teaching volunteer officers. Inoma also forces Jōji to wear an officer's civilian clothes and use his given name when teaching English to his superiors, criticizing Jōji for introducing himself to the class as "Army Private Sugihara Jōji." Inoma insists: "All you need tell them is the name your parents gave you—Sugihara Jōji. In fact, just plain Jōji is good enough" (148/137). In sum, Jōji's psychological problems stem from the reversal of the process that he had to go through to adapt to the "normalcy" of the army. Jōji has been deprived of the rank he had grown into and once again thrown back on his origins; this time, however, the army is eager to appropriate his marginality.

For Jōji, the stars finally begin to recover an association with the world outside of the army, strange as it seems. Soon after the defeat, all of the members of the army are promoted one rank: such inflation of the rankings and the absurd motivation of his superiors who have made the decision instill a degree of cynicism in Jōji. His secure relation to the army hierarchy is further challenged by Inoma's humiliating request for a job at his father's farm in the United States. All this perhaps prepares Jōji to rediscover the stars outside of the army:

> The autumn sunlight that shone through the trees from the vast Peking sky made his [Inoma's] platinum stars [on his insignia] shimmer. The sight made me remember something I had forgotten for a long while—the stars and bells on a Christmas tree. I felt as though I could hear voices singing "Merry

Christmas!" somewhere. What a bizarre association to make, I thought. (150–51/139)

The associations are "bizarre" to him since they are completely out of the context of the army, the context in which he has buried himself. The United States returns to Jōji's mind as stars. It turns out that stars themselves are hybrid, imbued with Jōji's geohistorically specific experiences. Jōji looks at the stars as a Japanese soldier in Beijing and remembers Christmas in the United States.

On an LST for repatriation to Japan, Jōji's attitude toward the army hierarchy reverts back to ambivalence. It is clear that he is still emotionally invested in the hierarchy of the army, yet he is "incensed that even this man [the American staff sergeant] was caught up in the system of rank" (153/141). However, Jōji is quite unprepared for the incident that later takes place on the LST: right before the ship reaches the shore of Sasebo, American soldiers begin tearing off insignias from the collars of Japanese noncommissioned officers to collect as souvenirs. The hierarchy of stars in the Japanese army is displaced by the United States' military power. The scene that takes place on the LST that repatriates Jōji's unit and thousands of other soldiers back to Japan is highly symbolic. Jōji has the following exchange with one of the American soldiers:

> "Do the repatriates always have their stars taken away like this?"
> "This is our first voyage. I don't know what anybody else does."
> "Does Sergeant Brown allow you to confiscate stars?"
> "He wants them more than anybody."
> "What happens if this leads to trouble among our men?"
> "This!" He pretended to be firing a machine gun. (156/143)

The authority of Japanese stars is gone, and they are reduced to quaint souvenirs for American soldiers. What replaces the order and hierarchy of the Japanese stars is U.S. military superiority.[35]

The postwar Japanese society that Jōji anticipates is already shot through by the presence of the United States, and the community of stars Jōji once belonged to has been displaced by sheer American power. Similarly, on the American LST, the old stars lose their magic in the eyes of the Japanese soldiers: once the American soldiers retreat with their trophies, the Japanese in the hold begin ripping their own stars off from their uniforms. Jōji tries to stop them, to no avail: even his own stars are ripped off and trampled by another soldier. Later, Jōji finds Inoma on the deck wearing a pair of American army boots: an American officer has taken Inoma's boots and knapsack. Suddenly, Jōji makes a leap in his associations: he "recalled that his [Inoma's] feet were larger than average. . . . Inoma and the other soldiers were now looking for new stars"(158/

144). Inoma's large feet give a sexual overtone to his desire for the other; though they are momentarily deprived of their protection, they are immediately wrapped in a pair of American boots. Inoma's naked desire to wear new stars has already found a new object in the material presence of the United States.

When Jōji finally enters Sasebo Harbor, he is shocked to discover that "the hills were the color of the khaki uniform I wore" (158/144). The Japan to which he looked forward to returning is nothing more than an extension of the army and its vacuous space. Worse yet, there are no more stars. Historical and social memories of individuals were sacrificed in both the pre-1945 Japanese army and postwar Japanese society in order to maintain a fiction that these communities stood above history. The imagined communities of the army and postwar Japan share the same feature at the end of Kojima's fiction—the neutral color (chūkanshoku: literally, the in-between color) of khaki—into which all the stains and dirt of history have vanished. It turns out that the liminal space of the army of Jōji's experience is not an exception but rather the rule. Jōji realizes that he will have to repeat his former experiences all over again now that he has reached Japan. Jōji has to find a new set of stars within postwar society, which demands that its members repress past memories of the war. In order to fully embrace the stars of the American flag, postwar Japanese society needs to conceal past conflict with the United States.

In "Stars," Japanese society after the war turns out to be an extension of the liminal space of the army; the army's response to defeat prefigures the drastic change that Japanese society will experience. The difficult experiences of Japanese Americans during the war have gone unremarked since they are reminders of Japan's war against the United States. On the other hand, Japanese Americans remain inconspicuous within Japan despite the popular desire to cast Japan as a hybrid society. The perceived in-betweenness of Japanese Americans was appropriated by postwar Japanese society as a screen behind which to hide itself. After the surrender of Japan, Jōji's hybrid identity is resurrected in the army as a tool to conceal its principal role in the war and promote its newly found affinity with the United States.

It is important to emphasize in this conclusion the historicity of (non)-representations of Japanese Americans in Japanese society. Images of Japanese Americans have reflected the history of the two countries' contradictory relations: Japanese American identity became a locus where the tension of desire and revulsion was played out. Not surprisingly, strategies to represent Japanese Americans have drastically shifted, from repression of difference during the war to recasting Japan in the images of Japanese Americans in the 1950s. Kojima Nobuo's short stories illuminate this shift and the postwar representational strategy that appropriated Japanese American identity.

As a perfect illustration of this strategy at work, we can point to a criminal case of 1950. Many gruesome and media-worthy crimes occurred in immediate postwar Japan, but the armed robbery that took place on September 22, 1950, in Tokyo acquired notoriety not because of what the robber accomplished but because of what he said to the police—"Oh, mistake"—when he was apprehended. After the perpetrator managed to rob a car that was transporting cash, he hid with his girlfriend at her apartment. When the police arrived at the apartment two days later, the suspect pretended he was a nisei who did not understand Japanese, trying to hide his criminal behavior by casting himself as a Japanese American. His one line of English, "Oh, mistake," immediately became a popular phrase of the year.[36] Such appropriation of Japanese American identity, as Kojima demonstrated, similarly constituted postwar Japan's desperate attempt to conceal its own criminal past. This minor criminal drama caught the attention of the nation precisely because it tapped a deep anxiety lying beneath the repression of the past, an anxiety about getting caught in the midst of pretense. The Japanese media were quick to label this case as a crime representative of postwar youth, a caricature of the postwar desire to emulate everything American. Ultimately, the embarrassment and humiliation that this case stirred—feelings that Kojima's antiheroic characters similarly invoke—touched on the anxieties of many Japanese about facing (and also perhaps wanting to encounter) what was repressed in their postwar representations of Japan. Japanese Americans appeared only as traces of conflicting Japanese desires directed toward the other. Even when Japanese Americans were visible, they were discussed only through the surrogate figure of a Japanese impersonator.

Sudden Muteness

In 1953, another incident involving an in-between figure left an impression on Japanese society. After a short exchange, a quarrel developed between three GIs and a Japanese pimp on the Sukiya Bridge in downtown Tokyo. The GIs threw the pimp from the bridge into a moat, drowning him. Although this minor incident seems not to deserve mention when compared to the ruinous landscape of the years just after the war, it possesses great significance in Ōe Kenzaburō's collection of short stories, *Mirumae ni tobe* (Leap before you look) (1958).[37] The event is mentioned in two separate stories, and the reader is further reminded of the fact that the Japanese at the scene did nothing. They did not lynch the GIs, but instead simply watched while the poor man drowned. Ōe recalls this incident as the pinnacle of humiliation, a humiliation that Japan internalized in the immediate postwar period. A pimp embodied Japanese society's humiliation, and his death in a humiliating way did not elicit a strong reaction on the part of Japanese bystanders. Their inaction reveals that the very sensation of humiliation had been erased from the minds of many. In the collection, Ōe consciously portrays what he calls in-betweens—a Japanese interpreter, Japanese prostitutes who serve foreign clientele, and a Japanese gay man with a French partner—in order to explore the conflict "between the foreigners [Americans and Europeans] as the dominant and the Japanese in the obsequious position."[38] Ōe uses the in-betweens as the figures that embody the sexual desire beneath their relations. Even the body of the interpreter is described with sexually charged images.

Ōe's project is more nationalistic than Kojima's: Ōe urges his readers to imagine their own community by shedding their obsequiousness for a moment. Ōe's literary imagination resonates with Benedict Anderson's observation that a modern nation unites by mourning over its loss.[39] Postwar Japan lost its ability to mourn and unite since memories of the loss in the Asia Pacific War had been carefully masked. In order to reconstruct its own agency through mourning, Japan had to excavate such memories of loss and humiliation. Ōe yearns to reinscribe this loss on Japan's history and insists that this is a loss over which the Japanese can mourn.

When Ōe wrote *Mirumae ni tobe* during the second half of 1950s, anti-American feelings in Japan were on the rise. The tenacious movements against American bases that developed in Sunagawa, Tokyo Prefecture, and Uchinada, Ishikawa Prefecture, gained the sympathy of the Japanese left. An incident in which an American soldier intentionally shot a Japanese woman who was gathering bullet shells within an American base and the Japanese government's inability to effectively prosecute the soldier also outraged many in Japan.[40] These cases revolved around specific losses—land and the life of a woman—and the nation responded with rising nationalistic sentiment against the United States. In the following section, I turn to Ōe's story, "Totsuzen no oshi" (Sudden mute), in order to trace his attempts to recover the foundational loss of postwar Japan by relocating and retelling the story of the man who drowned in downtown Tokyo.

"Totsuzen no oshi" is set in a remote village in the mountains, a familiar scene for the readers of Ōe's early works. At the opening of the story, a group of five GIs and one Japanese interpreter arrives at the village on a mission that is never explained. The village seems to be an idyllic space devoid of historical references. Although fearful about the arrival of the victors, the villagers are fascinated by the Americans. Adult males and children curiously watch the arrival of the GIs from distance, while the women stay inside their houses. The soldiers maintain cordial attitudes toward the villagers, at least at the beginning of the story, and the villagers seem to reciprocate the soldiers' goodwill. After an initial exchange, one soldier expresses through the interpreter his appreciation for the villagers' welcome. The villagers are reluctant to return to their work and instead watch the soldiers with a sigh, a sign of admiration.

It is, in fact, the interpreter who disturbs the otherwise idyllic encounter between the American soldiers and the villagers. All of the communications between the soldiers and the villagers naturally take place through the interpreter, who maintains an arrogant attitude toward the villagers. In return, the villagers detest the interpreter. Although the specific source of the villagers' feelings is not identified by Ōe, the combination of the interpreter's arrogance toward the villagers and his obsequious attitude to the soldiers seems a likely cause. The language the interpreter uses to the villagers is rough and almost always spoken in an imperative form, while he refers to the soldiers as *konokata*, a honorific third-person pronoun. This discrepancy in his posture toward the villagers and the soldiers is clearly established at the beginning of the story.

The children of the village certainly share the adults' feelings toward the interpreter and the soldiers and express them more blatantly. Left with the soldiers after the adults leave the school grounds, the children observe the soldiers as the they begin their maintenance jobs. Especially after the interpreter climbs into the driver's seat of the jeep, the children can watch the soldiers with impunity: "The soldiers seemed quiet and polite, and they were tall and had broad shoulders. They looked splendid. The children gradually shrank the circle and came closer to the soldiers to watch them better" (109–10). The soldiers eventually go down to a creek to bathe, and the bodies of the soldiers in the water impress the children. The interpreter's body suffers by comparison:

> The children were soaked with sweat, yet they kept sitting quietly on the bank and watched the foreign soldiers. The interpreter came down there, too, and stripped his clothes off. His skin looked yellow-brown, and, furthermore, he had no body hair. This entire body appeared slippery and filthy. In contrast to the soldiers, he walked into the creek holding his groin firmly. The children laughed out loud with some contempt at the way the interpreter did it. The foreign soldiers did not seem to care about the interpreter, either. (110)

The interpreter receives no respect from either the American soldiers or the children: his body appears "slippery and filthy" because of its Japanese features, and the children laugh at him because of his Japanese mannerisms. The Japanese body underneath the American uniform embodies the obsequious desire to identify with the victor, yet its corporeal reality constantly reminds the reader of the impossibility of such a project.

A minor crisis develops when the interpreter emerges from the water and finds that his shoes are missing. Just as in Kojima's story, large feet exposed without shoes embody the interpreter's desire to embrace the new order. The interpreter's feet are "ugly" because they remind the villagers of their own desire for the other, that which they do not wish to admit to themselves. The figure of interpreter represents the career trajectory of officers like Inoma, who gratuitously upholds the American legitimacy at the end of the war. In "Stars," Captain Inoma manages to slip his feet in American boots after the war, and the boots are a sign of his obsequious attitude. Similarly, the interpreter in Ōe's story protects his "large and ugly" feet with a pair of American shoes (118). But the material manifestation of the interpreter's new American identity is gone. The villagers are quickly assembled at the school again so that the interpreter can demand the recovery of the shoes. A consequent search merely yields the shoelaces, which have been cut with a sharp knife. Moreover, the search only heightens the contrast between the villagers' contempt for the interpreter and their admiration of the American soldiers. When one of the soldiers also begins to search for the shoes on the bank of the creek bank, "the adults and children of the village all let out a hot sigh [in admiration of the GIs]. The villagers, all of them, feel relieved from the tension regarding the foreign soldiers" (114). However, this feeling does not last long: the interpreter's anger over the discovery of the shoelace revived "the awkward feelings mixed with fear among the village people" (114–15). The interpreter, the in-between figure of the story, brings back to the surface the anxiety that the villagers have managed to suppress, the anxiety they have toward the American soldiers.

Even after another round of futile searching, the interpreter insists that his shoes be recovered; demanding the villagers' cooperation, he only encounters their silence. In the course of discussions with the village head, the interpreter out of frustration hits the man in the face. The slap awakes the villagers' hostilities toward the Americans soldiers. The event triggers a chain reaction: the village head starts walking away from the interpreter; the interpreter tells him to stop and says something to the soldiers; a soldier holds a gun and shouts something; the village head becomes scared and starts running and then is shot to death by the soldier. The son of the village head witnesses the entire sequence of events from the soldiers' arrival to his own father's death. Holding his father's body, the boy cries; at that moment "the boy possessed his father by himself" (120). The boy's mourning over his father's death unites the village and restores the tension with the American soldiers. The villagers join the boy in mourning first by ceasing to speak and second by eradicating the interpreter, the person whose function is to speak.

On the evening following the incident, the son of the village head visits
the interpreter, who misunderstands the boy's presence as a gesture of
reconciliation. Believing that the boy is showing him where his shoes are,
the interpreter follows him to a quarry. The interpreter speaks incessantly
to the boy, who does not return a single word on the way. Once they
arrive at the quarry, however, even the interpreter's voice is silenced:

> They crossed a bridge covered with dirt, and descended on the stairs, which
> were slippery with the wetness of fog. From the darkness underneath the bridge,
> an arm appeared and covered the interpreter's mouth. Then, the bodies of sev-
> eral adults, covered with coarse hair, with muscles bulging like rocks, sur-
> rounded the interpreter, with their withered sexual organs exposed. The inter-
> preter was slowly pulled into the water as the several naked bodies clung onto
> him. Those who could not hold their breath any longer released the interpreter's
> body and returned to the surface of the water. After taking a breath, they then
> dived back into the water to embrace the interpreter's body. The adults took
> turns and repeated the operation, for a long time, then climbed onto the stone
> steps, leaving the interpreter's body in the depths of the water. (123)

Everything proceeds in complete silence. The villagers reject all possibility
of mediation with the Americans by eliminating the function of the interpreter as mediator. It is the very function of speaking that the villagers
intend to eradicate. By drowning the interpreter with their own hands,
the adults in the village refuse to communicate with the former enemies.
When the villagers literally "embrace" the body of the interpreter, the
sign of their obsequiousness, their emasculated bodies with their "with-
ered sexual organs" assert their male subjectivity, in the form of masculine
bodies that are "covered with coarse hair, with muscles bulging like
rocks." Through the sacrificial killing of the interpreter, the villagers
recognize and eradicate the part of themselves that is obsequious to the
Americans.

By mourning the loss of the old patriarchy embodied by the village
head, the villagers also reestablish a community among themselves, a
community that does not require verbal communications. The villagers'
moves are synchronized as if they constitute an organic whole. The Americans who shot the village head are not the subject of the villagers' punishment because Ōe's communitarian ideal does not demand the annihilation
of the other. The village community simply needs to recognize its organic
unity. The interpreter who ushers the other into the village becomes
the obstacle for the community's self-realization and hence must be
eliminated.

The next morning, the body of the interpreter, his white feet sticking
out of the water, is discovered by the American soldiers. The villagers

show no sign of concern: when the soldiers try to mobilize the villagers to carry the body, they act as if the soldiers do not even exist. Nobody, including the children, pays attention to the soldiers' departure:

> A girl was petting a dog's ear at the place where the road exited the village. The man who had the most clear blue eyes among the soldiers threw a wrapped sweet to her. But both girl and dog continued their play without any motion to retrieve it. (125)

The murder of the village head leads to the villagers' active refusal to respond to the soldiers' solicitations; this last scene is unlike any other in postwar Japan, where the sight of children flocking around GIs and begging for sweets was ubiquitous.

In this way, Ōe emphasizes the unsightliness of the sutures that bind Japan and the United States and what they concealed: the body of the in-between represents the obsequiousness that glosses over the tensions between Japan and the United States. Through its ending, the plot undoes the sutures and lets the chasm open. "Totsuzen no oshi" is about the history that never took place in postwar Japan. Ōe yearns to see the Japanese face the wound inflicted on the surface of history by defiantly refusing to be in an obsequious position; he finds that potential in a mythic, remote mountain village. However, in actuality, many eagerly welcomed the American occupation forces and desired to repress the traumatic experience of their loss. Although the narrative begins with the all-too-familiar scene of an encounter between American soldiers and Japanese villagers, the story takes a fantastic turn with the death of the village head. This elimination of traditional authority—the village's father figure—awakens a sense of community in the village. This loss restores a sense of conflict and makes mediation impossible between the two parties. Through mourning, the villagers reconstruct the communal identity of the village, and, in this process, the mediation and the compromise with the former enemy must be rejected.

Ōe renders visible the historical tension between Japan and the United States (and Western European nations). In so doing, he offers an allegory of the fundamental loss and mourning that unite a remote village. The in-between figure of the interpreter embodies the humiliating attitude displayed by the Japanese on the downtown Tokyo bridge where they watched a man drown. That attitude had to be drowned. By actively drowning the interpreter, the villagers enact their determination to face loss and restore their historical agency.

However, in the actual historical conditions of postwar Japan, the fundamental loss was concealed underneath the foundational narrative, which effectively deployed the trope of in-betweenness and hybridity. The ultimate authority figure in Japanese society—the emperor—did not die. Rather, he became the most visible in-between figure in the postwar period, a figure who mediated between Japan and the United States.

The Emperor's Sudden Muteness

The epilogue to Yoshida Yutaka's *Showa Tennō no shūsenshi* (The end of the war and Emperor Showa) contains a revealing anecdote involving the Japanese emperor. Emperor Hirohito and Empress Nagako were on their way to Europe when they stopped at Elmendorf Air Force Base in Anchorage on September 27, 1971. Richard Nixon welcomed them at the base and, in the ceremony held there, gave a speech emphasizing the friendship between the United States and Japan.[41] Nixon stressed that their meeting occurred in an in-between place, Alaska—equidistant from Tokyo and Washington. When it was the emperor's turn to reciprocate with a word of goodwill, he was unable to speak. Standing before five thousand Americans, no sound came out of his mouth, even though his mouth was moving in an attempt to speak. This lapse lasted only a few seconds, and the next day the newspapers reported his speech as if nothing unusual had happened.[42] However, this mishap was not a failure of the microphone. According to the recently published diary of Grand Chamberlain Irie Sukemasa, the emperor previously experienced these symptoms in June 1970. Another diary entry confirms their recurrence during the night of the welcoming ceremony.[43]

The emperor's aphasia in the celebration of Japanese-U.S. friendship illuminated the underlying chasm in postwar relations between the two countries. The emperor failed to perform his postwar role as a mediator twenty-five years after he announced the acceptance of the Potsdam Declaration on the radio in his high-pitched, frail voice.

Indeed, his voice was a target of zealous nationalists who attempted to keep Japan fighting. After Hirohito's so-called divine decision to accept the surrender terms specified in the Potsdam Declaration, he recorded the imperial rescript announcing the end of the conflict. The announcement was scheduled to take place on August 15, 1945. However, young army officers made one final attempt to interfere with the Japanese government's war-terminating process by seeking to destroy the disk on which the imperial rescript was recorded. While the officers' insurrection ended in failure and the recording was broadcast as scheduled on August 15, 1945,[44] we must take note of the symbolic significance of the act: since the imperial enunciation signified Japan's compromise, it was the emperor's voice that the officers tried to silence.

In 1971, it was the emperor's body that reenacted the loss and transgressed—albeit only for a moment—his assigned role in the foundational narrative. The emperor's sudden muteness attested to tension on the sutured surface of postwar United States–Japan relations. The sutures were maintained and reaffirmed, as Ōe portrays, through the act of enunciation, yet the sutures mark exactly that which they hide. Subjected to the gaze of Americans, the emperor's body revealed a fundamental disjuncture in postwar relations between the former enemies.

Although Yoshida claims the emperor's mishap was significant enough to form a lasting image of the emperor, his primary reaction was embarrassment. He had to turn off the television, because he felt too embarrassed to watch the emperor struggle. Yoshida speculates that many of his postwar generation (Yoshida was born in 1954) shared a similar experience in forming an image of the emperor. Yoshida's reaction suggests this moment of rupture arrived in postwar Japan too late and too briefly: it managed only to invoke an uneasy feeling of embarrassment among Japanese viewers, and the Japanese media had no problem in filling the gap with their own flood of enunciations celebrating the two countries' friendly relations.

4

Naming the Unnameable

Forgetting is to dis-remember
The sadness of the heart
That vows to forget
When it cannot

The person that one cannot forget
Is the person who is afar
People always urge one
To forget the person whom one cannot forget
  Kikuta Kazuo, Kimi no nawa

IN THE 1950s, the prominent intellectuals Maruyama Masao and Katō Shūichi identified Japan as an "in-between," liminal entity, thereby undercutting the effects of the nation's loss in the Asia Pacific War. This cultural configuration thus camouflaged the disjuncture created by defeat. The historically specific conditions of the postwar period were projected back onto Japan's past: Japan had always already been fragmentary and open to foreign cultural elements. Maruyama's and Katō's discourses, which commanded much attention in the 1950s, managed to preempt the trauma of loss through their particular reconstitution of Japan.

However, excavations of the rupture in the recent past were not necessarily absent in the 1950s, as demonstrated by such authors as Kojima Nobuo and Ōe Kenzaburō. By placing fictional "in-between" characters at scenes of rupture such as defeat by, and encounters with, Americans, Kojima and Ōe carefully explore that the trope of in-betweenness could be deployed to suture historical disjuncture. Such in-between characters literally embody the sutures. Simultaneously announcing and concealing the wound, the characters' bodies emerge as the sites where the reader is faced with contradictory desires: the desire to conceal and the desire to encounter memories of the past. Whereas Kojima magnifies each stitch in order to show the contradictory forces at work, Ōe impatiently undoes the sutures in an attempt to cut open what he believes is a festering wound inside.

The desire to encounter the past in an in-between location also found mass cultural expressions in the 1950s. In this chapter, I will discuss the

popular radio melodrama *Kimi no nawa*, the monster film *Godzilla*, and
the arena of professional wrestling as sites haunted by memories of the
past. When consuming these fictional representations in the popular
media, the audience "returned" to and found means to exorcise the monstrous past. Such encounters were not direct confrontations with past
memories since such a practice was prohibited by the foundational narrative. Nevertheless, mass culture afforded alternative forms for past memories. Although memories may have become visible in the cultural realm of
postwar Japanese society, they remained suppressed in political discourse.
Narratives of love and the grotesque bodies of a monster and professional
wrestlers became the preeminent media for historical expression within
the liminal space of postwar Japan.

Moreover, Japan's wartime memories were mediated through images
of the other as the United States. The foundational narrative of postwar
Japan managed to conceal past memories of animosity toward the United
States for its role as hostile other. To recognize the otherness of the United
States was to encounter the otherness of Japan's own past in the period
immediately after the war. The trope of in-betweenness, however, allowed
postwar Japan to leap over this historical disjuncture to identify with
American material culture. At the same time, by facing the inhibition of
the foundational narrative, mass culture oscillated in its expression of the
otherness of America: America was either absent or monsterized. Mediated by the images of the United States, historical memories perhaps existed as apparitions, in the liminal space of postwar Japan. Disappearing
when confronted with a desire to recover historical continuity, they resurfaced as monsters when they met with the desire to encounter memories
of loss and to name the unnameable.

These contradictory desires shaped Japanese mass culture in 1950s,
producing various strategies to represent past memories in such forums
as a radio drama, a series of films, and professional wrestling. The hero
and heroine of *Kimi no nawa*, Godzilla, and the wrestler Rikidōzan each
embodied tensions with memories of the past, becoming in the process
cultural icons of the 1950s. The cultural forms that I discuss in this chapter were also the subject of gender divisions: *Kimi no nawa* primarily
appealed to a female audience because of its heroine's brave struggle with
unyielding circumstances, whereas Godzilla and professional wrestling
tended to attract male spectators because of their graphic references to
war. In addition, the gender of the protagonists of these cultural expressions corresponded to the gender divide in their targeted spectators.
Nonetheless, despite differences in form and spectatorship, all three cultural productions provided opportunities to encounter that which had
been excluded in the trajectory of postwar history. Memories of the war
and images of the United States as an enemy country were made visible

and reappropriated into postwar society through these forums. My readings in this chapter focus on the project of excavating the past carried out in these three otherwise disparate cultural forms.

Markers of Loss

> Looking at the people passing by, Machiko [says]:
> "Various changes may occur to the people who
> cross this [Sukiya] bridge. . . Only the appearance
> of this bridge will always be the same."
>   *Kikuta Kazuo,* Kimi no nawa, *3:157*

Less than a month away from the conclusion of the occupation in April 1952, NHK (Nihon Hōsō Kyōkai, Japan Broadcasting System) began airing the radio drama *Kimi no nawa* (Your name is?). Ninety-eight episodes of the popular program were aired over two years. While the radio show was still in progress, it was also turned into a film, which was released in three parts in 1953 and 1954. The film was also an immediate hit and broke all box office records.[1] The popularity of the film was such that it even sparked a fashion trend: the way the heroine wore her scarf was called *Machiko-maki* and copied by many women (fig. 7). When the radio show finished in 1954, the drama was then published as a four-volume novel.[2]

Literary critic Isoda Kōichi reads the story of *Kimi no nawa* as postwar Japan's quest for its identity at the particular juncture of history when Japan was regaining its independence.[3] Although only a passing remark by Isoda, it accurately points to the link between a quest for the past and a desire to rectify the present within the narrative of *Kimi no nawa*. There are two contrasting motifs, however, concerning the heroine's relationship with past memories. The first part of the drama establishes the impossibility of encountering the past. In this part, the drama centers around the heroine's desire to recover the past, yet the process of recovery is hampered by her fear of encountering the very object for which she longs. Once the hero and heroine meet, the tone of the story radically changes. The meetings and separations of the hero and heroine in the second part ultimately lead to a recovery of the past—the happy ending.

A brief plot summary should suffice to show this shift from missed encounters to the process of healing. Atomiya Haruki and Uji'ie Machiko meet for the first time by the Sukiya Bridge in downtown Tokyo during the U.S. air raid of May 24, 1945. They save each other's lives and promise to meet again on the bridge exactly six months later. Although Haruki asks Machiko what her name is (*kimi no nawa*), they decide not to learn each

Figure 7. Uji'ie Machiko (Kishida Kyōko) and Atomiya Haruki (Sata Keiji) on the Sukiya Bridge. *Kimi no nawa*, 1953.

other's name until they meet again on the bridge. While Haruki returns to the spot every half year, Machiko is unable to do the same because she has had to leave Tokyo to be with her uncle's family in Sado. Machiko manages to trace Haruki from a rather fortuitous set of clues, and she becomes able to see him if she wants to. However, fear overcomes her. She decides to marry Hamaguchi Katsunori, a man who has been helping her in her hunt for Haruki. Machiko finally shows up on Sukiya Bridge a full year and a half after the initial encounter, the very eve of her wedding with Katsunori.

Machiko's marriage with Katsunori turns out to be a disaster. Sensing Haruki's shadow in Machiko's mind, Katsunori accuses Machiko of imagined infidelities. Katsunori's protective mother, who lives with them, further aggravates the problem. Machiko eventually decides to leave Katsunori to return to Sado, where she discovers that she is pregnant. Although Haruki visits her at Sado to be united with her, her pregnancy prevents their union. In the film version, Haruki encourages Machiko to return to Katsunori, whereas in the radio and book versions it is Machiko who has second thoughts about leaving Katsunori because of their child. However, in all versions Machiko miscarries the baby and then decides to leave Katsunori for good. Knowing that refusal is the only means left for him to avenge himself on Machiko and Haruki, Katsunori does not grant Machiko's request for divorce. In the end, however, the tension is resolved through the sincerity of Haruki and Machiko. The two remain in a strictly platonic relationship, and the purity of their lives dissolves all obstacles, including Katsunori's stubbornness. Finally overcoming Machiko's illness and the physical distance that separates them—Haruki is posted in Europe for his job—they are happily united.[4]

The subplots root the story more concretely in the confusion of immediate postwar Japanese society. The narrative of healing is played out in various minor stories of self-improvement. Impelled by circumstance, some of the supporting characters engage in illegal activities, such as prostitution or smuggling rationed food. Even Haruki's own sister is tricked into prostitution when she arrives in Tokyo to seek a job. Yet thanks to their sincere efforts to rise above the situation (Haruki rescues two prostitutes from destitution by finding jobs for them), many of these characters succeed in returning to quiet lives as ordinary citizens. Selfless assistance to fellow unfortunates is also crucial for "healing": the two prostitutes rescued by Haruki manage to reestablish their lives with the help of, and by helping, an elderly former army officer; later they also help out Haruki's sister. In their struggles, sincerity and silent endurance are proved to be the answer to the evils of society; abiding by the law enables the characters to gain legitimacy within society.

Yet *Kimi no nawa* provides more than just moral tales of overcoming obstacles with one's determination. Machiko's adventures are as much about her desire to escape her present misery as about her struggle to face the unnameable past. The story never really clarifies why Machiko decides to marry Katsunori rather than Haruki at the very moment when she finally locates Haruki's whereabouts. Although the author, Kikuta Kazuo, does offer an explanation later in the book, it comes rather too late and only as a retrospective gesture. According to the author, Machiko's prewar and wartime education disproportionately emphasized obligation to others and de-emphasized individual feelings of love. Faced with the kindness of Katsunori, Machiko's sense of obligation overpowers her feelings of love. Even so, she cannot forget Haruki (4:31). Hence, Machiko is caught between the old social mores and a new mode of behavior, and her tragedy is typical of this period of transition.

Perhaps it is possible to generalize and explain away Machiko's trauma as the product of social changes. In the author's own interpretation, *Kimi no nawa* is about Machiko's fight against an oppressive past of traditional mores. However, I would like to call the reader's attention to the radical aporia inside the story that resists an explanation that would reduce Machiko's struggle to a mere reflection of social conditions. The first half of the story in particular suggests that her love is hopelessly entangled with memories of loss. Her love is a process of recovery, recovery from the loss she suffered in the war. Machiko actually desires to return to the old social mores in order to reconstruct what she has lost: her family. Her love object—Haruki—reminds her of the impossibility of such reconstruction, since he is a marker of the very loss she tries to recover.

Memories of loss haunt Machiko throughout her quest for her true love. After leaving Sukiya Bridge, Machiko learns that her parents are missing. Only "after looking for them like a crazed person" does she find her parents' bodies (1:12). Haruki becomes a surrogate for the loss she suffers in the war: "If her parents were alive, she might have forgotten her promise with the young man. However, for Machiko, who has lost both her parents, the young man whose name she does not yet know, who is like a second parent, is the only person in the world about whom she reminisces" (1:12). The loss that she suffers is specific: she loses her parents and their house during the war. Nevertheless, the story does not dwell on her bereavement: only at one point of the book does she recall her parents (3:236). Perhaps her loss did not need to be constantly set before the audience, who had undergone similar experiences. Such loss was ingrained in the readers and Machiko. In Machiko's case, however, her loss is marked by Atomiya Haruki and the Sukiya Bridge. The same night that she finds her true love, she loses her parents. Although Haruki and the Sukiya Bridge are positive signifiers for her rescued future, a return to Haruki means a return to memories of her loss.

Machiko's fight is thus not so much against the past and traditional social mores, but against the loss of social mores and consequent confusion in postwar society. Were her parents alive, she would not be thinking about Haruki. She would be happily married with Katsunori, because the problems in their marriage derive largely from her orphan status: she is vulnerable in Katsunori's family since she has lost her own familial support (1:12). The loss of her parents in the war causes her misery and drives her out of the marriage, but she cannot fill this loss with Haruki, for he himself embodies the original loss. Images of Haruki appear as ghostly forms of the past and haunt her: "Hearing the story about Haruki exchanged between Katsunori and Kengo, Haruki's close friend, she believed it must have been a ghost of the man whom she left that night during the war" (1:187). The ghost in the form of Haruki returns to remind her of the loss she suffered in the war. Her decision to marry Katsunori is ultimately an attempt to recover the loss with an embodiment of social mores: Katsunori is a career bureaucrat who aspires to succeed within the bureaucratic system.[5]

The missed encounters with Haruki serve as buffers to protect Machiko from encounters with her loss. Although her marriage to Katsunori is supposed to end her struggle with her memories, even with a new family Machiko is unable to forget Haruki because memories of loss, embodied in Haruki, remain with her. Katsunori and his mother, guardians of traditional patriarchy, sense the past within Machiko's heart and try to exorcise this past. They accuse Machiko of secret meetings with Haruki and try to force her out of this imagined relationship. Before their marriage, Katsunori helps her with the process of naming the unnameable—finding the name of Atomiya Haruki—and it is he again who identifies the shadow of Haruki in their marriage. His and his mother's attempts backfire: their acts of suppression root her memories of Haruki more firmly in Machiko's mind. Unable to fit within the patriarchy represented by Katsunori and his mother, Machiko realizes that she has to leave in order to live with her memories of loss and return to Haruki, even if it can only lead to another unhappy marriage (4:130). When she decides to be with Haruki, Machiko is finally ready to face what she has lost in the war.

Now her own resistance, the obstacle to the couple's full reunion, becomes externalized in the narrative. Katsunori and his mother do everything in their capacity to prevent Machiko and Haruki from being happily united. The focus shifts from Machiko's internal struggle to a battle between the sincere protagonists and the evil forces in society. The struggle with past memories is displaced by a fight against the evil forces of the past, that is, the feudal family structure that refused to let Machiko go. Machiko again becomes trapped in an impossible situation, only this time one created by external forces. Katsunori's mother makes it impossible for Machiko to continue her married life with Katsunori. Meanwhile, Katsunori acts as the jealous head of the patriarchy and refuses to give a divorce to Machiko. The story moves away from Machiko's ambivalent relations with past memories and equates liberation from the past with victory over evil.

This victory, however, does not come from aggressive challenges but from the efforts to restore the original functions of such forces. This rather conservative approach of Kikuta is particularly interesting when placed against Japan's newly restored independence. The traditional elements in Japanese society represented in the form of patriarchy clearly inflicted damage on Japanese society in the past, yet Kikuta suggests that doing away with them is not the solution for postwar society. Patriarchy could be overcome only through recuperating its original functions.

Although Machiko and Haruki briefly contemplate running away in defiance of the legal entrapment devised by Katsunori, in the end Machiko seeks a pardon from the patriarchy. The lovers endure three years of complete separation in order to attain Machiko's divorce: a mediator suggests that Machiko be separated from Haruki while seeking her divorce in order to soothe Katsunori's feelings. Hence, the narrative of *Kimi no nawa* does not challenge conventional social mores. The target of blame is rather the absence of such mores in postwar society. The strategy that Machiko and Haruki ultimately choose actually contributes to the recovery of patriarchy because it insists on the couple's maintaining platonic relations until they can legally marry. When he discusses the conditions of the divorce, Haruki emphasizes how clean (*seiketsu*) their relations are (4:97). Machiko and Haruki's desperate plea falls on deaf ears, but they persevere in supporting patriarchy by restraining their bodily desires.

If we venture beyond the main story here, it becomes very clear that sexual desires and their seemingly unhampered flow in postwar society are to be condemned: female sexuality in particular is demonized as destructive to social mores. If we see the social problems of prostitution and interracial children as standing in for the larger issues of Japanese defeat and the presence of the United States, the story of *Kimi no nawa* reverses the causal relations between the defeat and subsequent social confusion. In this reversal, repression and normalization of the problem—female sexuality—become the means to recover the social order and erase the larger causes looming behind the social problems. In contrast to the eventual happy ending for Machiko and Haruki, relations in the drama initiated by lustful females end disastrously. Kengo, Haruki's close friend who is in love with Haruki's sister, reluctantly enters into marriage with another woman, Nami, after submitting to her sexual advances on a beach. "Kengo was tired of thinking about Yukie [Haruki's sister]. The body of Nami, who is there right in front of his eyes, emits a fresh fragrance, waiting to be picked like a fruit that had just ripened" (1:116). Their marriage does not last long: Nami destroys herself in her burning jealousy toward Yukie, Kengo's true love. After stabbing Kengo with a knife, Nami kills herself.

Yumi, the illiterate Ainu woman whom Haruki meets in Hokkaido, similarly encounters a disastrous end in her passionate pursuit of her love object. Haruki meets Yumi when he retreats to his friend's farm in Hokkaido to recover from his frustrated love. Yumi has an exotic appearance: "Her eyes are sunken like the eyes of a white person; she is an Ainu girl who looks like a wild Spanish or gypsy girl" (3:64). The sexual energy that Yumi emanates is equated with the otherness of her existence: She embodies a negative force that needs to be repressed. True to her passionate nature, Yumi immediately falls in love with Haruki and declares that she will marry him. Haruki vaguely replies that he will consider the possibility. However, Yumi realizes where Haruki's heart truly belongs when Machiko visits Haruki in Hokkaido. In the film version, Yumi kills herself by throwing her body into Lake Mashūko. The radio show and novel complicate the scenario by having Yumi fall into the lake by accident. Yumi's Ainu fiancé, who tries to rescue her, panics and dies, while Yumi survives the accident. She is condemned to reflect on the negative effects of her own desire.

In the narrative logic of the story, female bodies and sexuality need to be subjected to the process of normalization. Even prostitutes can have happy lives once they repent their acts and subject themselves to the normalization process. When Haruki contemplates marrying Yumi, he focuses on her education (3:123). In a letter to a friend in Tokyo, he writes, "Well, my interest, such as it is, is mostly in giving some polish to Yumi, a wild child. When it turns into real affection, I will think about marriage with her" (3:131). Wild female sexuality, a sign of otherness, is there to be tamed and normalized. On the other hand, wild male sexuality, that of the GIs, can be tamed only indirectly, through the process of healing. As one of the issues under erasure, male sexuality can be addressed only by normalizing its product. Toshiki, an interracial child born to a Japanese prostitute, thus receives instant encouragement to "be a good child" (4:310–11).[6]

In Kikuta's narrative of normalization and repression of female bodies and sexuality, the success of Machiko and Haruki's strategy depends on their willingness to submit Machiko's sexual desire to patriarchal will. They must convince the patriarch Katsunori that accepting loss will not lead to sexual promiscuity and thus to the destruction of social mores.[7] Their task is to tell the patriarchy that the task of normalization in postwar Japanese society is finally over: Machiko is ready to return to memories of loss without incurring dire consequences. The cost is almost complete denial of Machiko's bodily functions: she nearly dies from illness before she gains a pardon from Katsunori. Haruki returns from France in the hopes of seeing Machiko just once more before she dies.[8] However, Machiko survives the illness and awakes to Haruki, an ending perfectly suited to this melodramatic narrative.[9] The forces of normalization remain highlighted in the conclusion, which takes place in the sanitized space of a hospital, an institution dedicated to the normalization of body functions. It is the loss itself that is tamed and normalized. Under the regulatory forces of postwar society, memories of loss are finally rendered safe.

The other, the existence of which is intimated through wild sexuality, needs to be repressed from this safe place. Only its dangerous sexuality is identified and normalized in the domestic sphere of the story. Healing is thus a process through which to reestablish the nation by excluding the other within. Interestingly, the novel never mentions the name of the other—the United States—even when it discusses the issue of interracial children. When "otherness" is attached to a specific country in the story, that country is invariably a European one. The complete absence of the United States reveals the story's strategy of healing: it represses the United States and the damage inflicted by it, while normalizing what cannot be repressed. The story mentions the normalization of the interracial child, but never refers to GIs.

In order to complete this normalization of the domestics sphere, the story offers a final resolution by reworking the opera *Madame Butterfly*.[10] *Kimi no nawa* makes two specific references to Puccini's 1904 opera. On the first occasion, Toshiki and his mother, barely living above the poverty line, find themselves in the highly unlikely situation of going to see *Madame Butterfly* at the theater. The tragedy of Cho-Cho-San, who falls in love with an American naval officer and is betrayed by him, reminds the listeners and readers that the intrusion of a dangerously sexual other is nothing new to Japan (2:173–79). The second reference to the opera moves the story forward to reworking such detestable memories, the other's betrayal (4:272–73). Machiko and Haruki visit Nagasaki, the location of Puccini's opera, before Haruki leaves for France. Their guide compares their fate with that of *Madame Butterfly*. Haruki quickly retorts that he would never be unfaithful like Pinkerton in the opera. These references to *Madame Butterfly* are crucial in setting up the climax of the story: Haruki does indeed faithfully return to Machiko in the end. By exorcising the American from the tragedy, *Kimi no nawa* rewrites the opera as a domestic—familial and national—drama. It is a Japanese male who departs and makes an eventual return, thus foreclosing on possible disruption by the other.

Before I move on to the next section, I would like to make one final point. While Machiko believes that "only the appearance of this [Sukiya] bridge will be always the same" (3:157), real life did not bear out her faith. In 1957, three years after her happy reconciliation with the past, the Sukiya Bridge was demolished for an expansion of the subway system.[11] The economic development of postwar Tokyo necessitated modern traffic systems. In 1960, the Metropolitan Expressway Public Corporation completed construction of an expressway over the spot where Sukiya Bridge used to stand.[12]

Sukiya Bridge was a liminal space where the confusion of postwar society manifested itself in various forms. Kikuta Kazuo saw the bridge, standing in the midst of a field leveled by air raids, as symbolic of Japan.[13] Prostitutes, orphans, shoe polishers, and others loitered on the bridge seeking foreign customers. In 1948, there was even a flyer posted on a bridge post that read: "My life for sale."[14] That same summer, the female leader of a new religious sect that preached salvation through dancing performed on Sukiya Bridge with her followers.[15] The bridge was also explicitly made a symbol of injured nationhood: a religious altar dedicated to those executed in the Tokyo Trial was set up on the bridge in 1948 shortly after the execution. Five years later, GIs threw a Japanese pimp into the water from the bridge, an incident, as we may recall, that left a deep impression on Ōe. As Tokyo recovered from the devastating damage of the air raids, the Sukiya Bridge became an object that physically and perhaps symbolically hampered modernization. Sukiya Bridge made way for the elevated expressway's New Sukiya Bridge. Tokyoites lost a major marker of the loss they suffered during the war. Loss itself was being lost through the disappearance of signs of loss and destruction. Kikuta in 1953 comments with irony on the appearance of Japan: "Right after the war, the traces of destruction were miserably displayed both in the towns and countryside. The streets were filled instead with cheerful oaths, vows to never engage in war again. Now we have the reverse, and the towns and countryside are beautiful" (4:12). Nevertheless, even without the specific markers of destruction, the memories of loss remain and haunt the metropolis in a more amorphous form. For Machiko, loss had been placed at one degree of separation, mediated by the symbolic markers of the Sukiya Bridge and Haruki.[16] Those who have struggled to face memories of the past since Machiko's time must begin their quest by first searching for the markers of loss.

Monstrous Memories

> It was the [atmosphere of] the time period [of
> the postwar]: I even thought Godzilla was like
> the souls of the Japanese soldiers who died in the
> Pacific Ocean during the war.
>   *Ifukube Akira, music director for* Godzilla

In the 1950s, the post-Machiko phase of postwar Japan, monstrous bodies became replacements for tangible markers of loss. Memories of the war, even without specific markers, were still ubiquitous in postwar society. However, increasingly removed from the scene of destruction and devoid of particular references, the memories were transformed into amorphous destructive forces. Monstrous forms that defy human comprehension were burdened with the mission to represent memories of war loss. The film *Gojira* (Godzilla) is one such product of the specific historical conditions of mid-1950s Japan, from which markers of loss were steadily disappearing. Godzilla, in fact, returns to Sukiya Bridge in this 1954 film, ironically only a short time after the reunion of Machiko and Haruki. When Godzilla attacks downtown Tokyo, it lands on Shinagawa and passes through Ginza while heading toward the National Diet building. A newscaster announces that Godzilla is heading toward the Sukiya-bashi area, and next we see Godzilla crossing—and in the process destroy-ing—Sukiya Bridge.[17] Whether or not Godzilla returns to downtown Tokyo in search of the marker for the memories of loss, the monster reen-acts the scene of wartime destruction from which these memories origi-nally emerged.

The narrative of *Godzilla* operates within the discursive space of the foundational narrative and faithfully effaces the name of the United States, even though the United States looms behind the original destruc-tion. Memories of loss, inseparably tied with images of the United States, similarly remain unnamed, even as they fill the screen. The foundational narrative relegates memories of loss and images of the enemy to the abject, that which is constitutive of history but which cannot be named. The monstrosity of Godzilla is a mimetic embodiment of the abject: the devas-tating effects that the monster inflicts are real, yet they cannot be identi-fied. The monster's dark surface is inscribed by memories of the war, yet the inscriptions remain unreadable to the audience. The grotesque figure and repudiating cry of the monster defy human identification with or understanding of the monster.[18] The darkness that prevails in *Godzilla* enhances this unreadability.

In 1954, awakened from its eternal sleep by American nuclear testing at the Bikini Atoll, Godzilla attacks Tokyo. In real life, such nuclear testing and the *Lucky Dragon* incident were instrumental to the creation of the monster film. In March 1954, a Japanese tuna fishing boat, the *Daigo Fukuryūmaru* (*Lucky Dragon V*), was caught in nuclear fallout, and all twenty-three crew members suffered from radiation exposure. News of the *Lucky Dragon* broke a long silence on nuclear warfare in Japan, imposed on occupied Japan through strict U.S. censorship.[19] *Godzilla* hints at American involvement by making allusions to the *Lucky Dragon* incident in its opening scene.[20] Nevertheless, direct references to the United States are conspicuously absent: there is not even a hint of the U.S. responsibility in the subsequent destruction of Tokyo by the mon-ster.[21] The producer, Tanaka Tomoyuki, saw Godzilla as an allegory for the new destructive power that human beings face, disembodied from its specific geopolitical origin.[22] Frustrated by this omission of American responsibility in the film, one writer later insisted that Godzilla should have crossed the Pacific and attacked American cities, since the United States was responsible for nuclear testing and thus for the return of the monster.[23]

The United States is excised in other ways as well. The story proceeds as a purely domestic affair. Godzilla destroys Japan and is subsequently killed by Japanese without external assistance. An invention by a Japanese scientist—the Oxygen Destroyer—kills the monster and saves Japan from total destruction. Literary critic Kobayashi Toyoaki points out the film's conspicuous exclusion of U.S. forces from battle scenes against the monster.[24] In 1954, although Japan's National Police Reserve of 75,000 was reorganized into the Self-Defense Forces, numbering 150,000, a much larger contingent of 210,000 American military personnel was still stationed in Japan.[25] In 1954, the concerted attack that the film portrays would have been possible only with the help of American forces.[26] Nevertheless, the Japanese Bōeitai (Defense Forces) and Kaijō hoantai (Maritime Security Forces) are solely responsible for the attacks against Godzilla. If the monstrous body of Godzilla indeed embodied American nuclear threats, it is only logical that the Japanese forces alone should attack. The American forces by definition could not.

Thus, the United States returns as an enemy—albeit an unnamed one—through the figure of Godzilla, invoking memories of the war. After Godzilla passes through, Tokyo's cityscape resembles the ruinous scenery created by the American air raids, particularly those on Hiroshima and Nagasaki. In a hospital, a Geiger counter reveals that even children who escaped immediate physical injury have been exposed to radiation. During Godzilla's rampage in Tokyo, a woman squatting behind a building, incapable of moving farther, holds her child close and says: "We are soon going to Father's place"—that is, the grave. The father of the child probably died in the war, and Godzilla becomes the agent that reunites mother and child with the deceased figure. Even the attacks by Japanese fighter jets are of no use in destroying the monster, in much the same way that Japanese interceptors were almost useless against the hundreds of B-29s.[27] The staging of these scenes directly reflects the film creators' experiences in representing the war: the two men in charge of the film's creation—director Honda Ishirō and special-effects director Tsuburaya Eiji—had previously collaborated on the production of dramas with war themes in 1953 and 1954.[28] In particular, the destruction scenes owe much to Tsuburaya's experience in films acclaimed for their special effects such as *Hawaii, Malay oki kaisen* (The sea battles at Hawaii and off the Malay shore) (1942) and *Katō Hayabusa sentōtai* (The Katō falcon flying brigade) (1944). Honda later confided to a newspaper reporter that Godzilla's destruction of Tokyo was indeed produced in the image of the Tokyo air raid of March 1945.[29]

Not only memories of loss but also the loss itself—the souls of the war dead—return to Tokyo in the form of Godzilla. Ifukube Akira, the music director of the film, recalls that for his generation Godzilla was "like the souls of the Japanese soldiers, who died in the Pacific Ocean during the war."[30] Film critic Kawamoto Saburō argues that the darkness of the film stems from the fact that these returned souls of the dead soldiers are still under the spell of the emperor system. After destroying Ginza, the Diet building, and the television transmission tower in Kioichō, Godzilla is only a short distance from the Imperial Palace. In the end, Godzilla destroys only the prosperous downtown Tokyo that has been so quick to erase traces of the war, but leaves unscathed the residence of the emperor who had been instrumental in repressing war memories.[31] Kawamoto seizes on this moment to make the following points: "Those who died in the war are still under the spell of Japan's emperor system. Godzilla cannot destroy the Imperial Palace in the end. These who criticize Godzilla's inability as a sign of incomplete critical thinking in *Godzilla* do not know the 'dark' spellbinding force of the emperor system."[32]

The monster thus embodies both Japan's loss and the United States that inflicted that loss; the emperor becomes the unnamed historical condition that necessitated this dual embodiment of the monster. Since the United States refrained from destroying the Imperial Palace in its strategic bombing during the war, it makes sense that Godzilla as a proxy for the United States spares the Imperial Palace from ruin. As discussed previously, the emperor was needed by both the American and the Japanese governments for the resolution of the war: through his role in the foundational narrative of the postwar, the emperor helped forge Japan's alliance with its former enemy. The foundational narrative lumped together the two contradictory images of the loss that Japan suffered and the United States that inflicted that loss, and then relegated them to the status of the other. The fact that Godzilla—the monstrous embodiment of that which is excluded from history by the foundational narrative—does not destroy the Imperial Palace, the symbol of historical continuity, only attests to the firm hold of the foundational narrative in Japan in 1954. Ironically, through his absence in the film, the emperor proves his worth in the foundational narrative.

Godzilla eventually returns to the sea yet still needs to be subdued in order to prevent further destructive encounters with past memories. Godzilla is burdened with contradictory missions: to simultaneously re-present the traces of history and to be erased from the surface of the earth. The film reenacts the foundational narrative, the known formula that works, in order to arrive at the final resolution of the crisis: a secret weapon combined with the self-sacrifice of an individual. We must note, however, a major modification to the foundational narrative: the sacrifice made by Dr. Serizawa, the inventor of the Oxygen Destroyer, is final. After confirming the effectiveness of his weapon, Dr. Serizawa kills himself in order to prevent proliferation of the weapon. The use of a weapon powerful enough to destroy all life inside the Tokyo Bay counters the effects of the hydrogen bomb that awakens the monster. This final weapon, however, does not proliferate like nuclear warheads. The death of Dr. Serizawa and the disappearance of his body guarantee the finality of the Oxygen Destroyer's use and promise to close down the possibility of the monstrous return of the past.

Hence, the film's conclusion refuses the trajectory of the foundational narrative manufactured through the figure of the emperor.[33] The film brings the audience back to the scene of destruction, a space shared with the war dead. The audience is then provided with a final closure to memories of destruction by a Japanese character. Dr. Serizawa's invention and final intervention destroy the monster. However, through his act of bringing about a final resolution, Dr. Serizawa remains forever at the scene of destruction, joined by the souls of the dead at the bottom of the sea. Previously, the film has established that Dr. Serizawa had been injured in the war and has been determined to stay aloof from postwar society; his final act completes his reunion with the community of the war dead. The young scientist's self-sacrifice is an act that stubbornly refuses absorption into the historical narrative.

This particular Godzilla is laid to rest through his sacrifice, yet Godzilla keeps returning as long as postwar Japanese society exists and prospers under the aegis of the United States and keeps forgetting the war dead. Godzilla also returns to act out the deep-seated anxiety in Japanese society regarding nuclear weapons. The monster, which both embodies the war deceased and is empowered by the United States' nuclear weapons, serves as a grotesque caricature of postwar Japanese-U.S. relations.

The success of *Godzilla* established the genre of monster films in Japan and encouraged the production of sequels.[34] The first sequel, *Gojira no gyakushū* (Gigantis, the fire monster) came in 1955, but seven years then intervened before Tōhō began producing Godzilla films almost yearly.[35] Although the sequels all featured Godzilla, the later productions radically transformed the nature of the monster. The sequels did not inherit the original's critical perspective on the foundational narrative. Film critic Chon A. Noriega offers a reading of the changing roles of Godzilla in the shifting international political environments, particularly in relation to U.S. and Soviet policies toward nuclear weapons during the Cold War.[36] Godzilla becomes a "hero" who reflects the détente of the 1960s and returns in the 1980s against a backdrop of increasing Cold War tensions. Although Noriega presents an astute reading of Godzilla films in a historical context, Godzilla's semiotic meaning in relation to international politics was not the only thing that changed. Both the monster's body itself and its relations to Japan's war memories were drastically altered in the film's sequels.

The awkward movements of the monster enhance the irrational nature of its destructive acts (particularly in the original *Godzilla*). The technology that produced Godzilla improved over the years, but this improvement adversely affected the artistic effects of the production. The first Godzilla bodysuit created by the Tōhō special effects team was extremely heavy, weighing almost two hundred and twenty pounds and assembled with little regard to the body dimensions of the actual actors.[37] Hence, the sense of sheer materiality that the first Godzilla exuded was rather fortuitous: the actor simply could not move swiftly. The monster could barely lift its feet more than an inch, fell down frequently, and had to be helped up by other staff members.

The original film and the first sequel were black-and-white pictures. In the films, Godzilla attacks cities only during the night: impressive darkness prevails in both films. In contrast, the Godzilla of the 1960s appears in broad daylight and in color. The monster no longer destroys cities; it merely participates in fights against other monsters at a safe distance from urban areas. The monstrosity of Godzilla becomes completly tamed, and its swifter movement emulates human behavior. Its fights with other monsters are nothing but replications of professional wrestling matches that had become popular through the pioneer work of Rikidōzan, whom I will discuss in the following section.

In fact, in the first sequel, *Gojira no gyakushū*, the humanization of Godzilla is already in progress. Godzilla's fight against another monster, Anguirus, suggests the fact that the monstrosity of Godzilla alone can no longer sustain the narrative of the film. By borrowing performative representational strategies from professional wrestling, and by having it fight other monsters, the film attempts to rescue Godzilla's monstrosity from banality. This attempt, however, only encourages the taming of the monstrosity—the production of a narrative that anthropomorphizes Godzilla. The narrative structure based on a rivalry among monsters was reconfigured in the 1960s into the binary representation of monstrous bodies, the depiction of good versus evil.

Nevertheless, despite this shift in narrative strategy, *Gojira no gyakushū* continues in the vein of the original in its allusions to the war's destruction and in its resistance to a final resolution of the tension between Japan and the United States provided by the foundational narrative. In *Gojira no gyakushū*, the monster, attracted by light, lands at Osaka during nighttime; the same behavior pattern that the first Godzilla demonstrated in Tokyo. In order to prevent Godzilla's landing in Osaka, a strict restriction on lighting is placed on the city. Such restrictions echo regulations on lighting experienced by the audience a decade before, when it was feared that lights would invite American B-29s. After destruction, the city appears desolate and resembles scenes immediately after an air raid. Parallels with the war continue in Godzilla's return to another Asia Pacific War landmark. Although Godzilla is first detected on an island not too far from Osaka, it ends up, for no apparent reason, on an island north of Japan in the Sea of Okhotsk. Yet Godzilla appears to be aware that the island is its final destiny and the place of its death. Like the Japanese defense unit left on Attu in the Aleutian Islands in 1943, left to fight to the last soldier, Godzilla indeed dies surrounded by ice and snow.

Finally, an act of self-sacrifice is once again the mechanism that subdues Godzilla: a group of young veterans sacrifice their lives in an operation to contain the monster. Two commercial pilots, Kobayashi and Tsukioka, voluntarily participate in the Bōeitai's maneuvers to keep the monster on the island; they are regarded as honorary members because during the war they belonged to the same flying squadron as the Bōeitai's pilots. The Bōeitai's flying unit shows a remarkable continuity from the war: it appears to have remained intact even after the war! Kobayashi flies too close to Godzilla and crashes into the ice-covered mountainside, but his death proves to be an inspiration to the Bōeitai pilots. The avalanche that his crash causes turns out to be the solution to the problem. The entire flying unit devises and follows a highly demanding mission: flying through a narrow gorge and bombarding the ice walls in order to trap Godzilla in fallen ice. A number of F-86s inadvertently crash into ice walls and create an avalanche. Although it was not designed to be a suicide mission, the young pilots' sacrifices are crucial in fighting the monster. In the final scenes of the film, Tsukioka, who survives the mission, reports to Kobayashi that they managed to contain the monster.

The film is thus an answer to those who died in suicidal missions and in Japan's desperate war efforts overall. Although it invites the Japanese audience in 1955 back to the moment of the war's resolution, the film's conclusion departs from that of the original *Godzilla*: it accepts the trajectory into the postwar by rendering the sacrifices in the war comprehensible to the audience. In the original *Godzilla*, the monster embodies a stubborn rejection of this trajectory. However, in the sequel, monstrosity becomes confinable and history understandable through the acts of the young pilots. The strong continuity that the film portrays within the Bōeitai unit assures the audience that sacrifices made during the war are not wasted in postwar society; such sacrifices are indeed the basis of the nation's security. Japan by itself managed to contain the external threat through sacrifices made in the past (and by extension the present), thereby making possible the Japan of today. In the next chapter, I will further discuss this desire to link Japan's postwar prosperity with the wartime sacrifices against the backdrop of the historical conditions of 1960s Japan.

As Tōhō produced eight more Godzilla films during the 1960s, the distance between the sites of production and memories of the war widened, and the critical power of Godzilla was proportionately diminished. In *King Kong vs. Godzilla* (1962), Japan was rescued from the menace of Godzilla by King Kong, an icon of American popular culture. Thus, the film uncritically replicates the foundational narrative of the postwar period: the United States rescues Japan from a Japanese monster. Moreover, it is also a Japanese woman who becomes the object of King Kong's desire. There is even a scene in which King Kong stands on the National Diet building with the woman in his hand, graphically representing the meaning of the rescue: sexual submission to the United States. The banalization of Godzilla's monstrosity does not cease there. In the 1964 *Sandai kaijū: Chikyū saidai no kessen* (Ghidrah, the three-headed monster), a film produced in the year of the Tokyo Olympics, Godzilla was finally transformed into a defender of humanity by entering into an alliance with two other earthly monsters, Mothra and Rodan, against King Ghidrah, a monster who arrives from outer space. Mothra serves as a mediator between Godzilla and Rodan for the larger cause.

Although in the mid-1960s Tōhō began targeting children as the main audience for the Godzilla films, Honda Ishirō, who directed the first six, claimed that he did not consider children as his audience during the production of the original *Gojira*.[38] This shift in the targeted audience confirms the banalization of the monster in the series, the effects immediately discernible even in the quality of production.[39] Godzilla comes to faithfully reproduce human ways: it begins to act like a human and even becomes a "mother" in 1967. The son, Minilla, even speaks Japanese—the ultimate domestication of monstrosity. In 1960s Japan, a place overflowing with optimism inspired by economic growth, the monsters could not find a place other than as caricatures. The darkness that prevailed in the first two films of the mid-1950s had vanished from the screen and Japanese society.

Markers of loss were quickly disappearing in the 1950s in Japan's cities and countryside; Godzilla returned to reinscribe loss on the urban surfaces. However, the effect was not long-lasting. The monstrosity of Godzilla, the ultimate rejection of postwar Japan, was tamed and transformed into a guardian of postwar Japan's prosperity. In the next chapter, I will discuss the material conditions that erased the markers of loss. The 1964 Tokyo Olympics were instrumental in bringing these conditions into postwar Japanese society. However, before moving on to a discussion of the beautification and sanitization of Tokyo, it is still necessary to examine the monstrous body of Rikidōzan in order to explore another closely intertwined popular strategy for representing memories in the 1950s and early 1960s.

Performing the Nation

> The virtue of all-in wrestling is that it is the spectacle of excess.
>
> *Roland Barthes*, "The World of Wrestling"

> Pro wrestling, yes, one has to watch it with dead seriousness.[41]
>
> *Muramatsu Tomomi*, Watakushi puroresu no mikata desu (I am on the side of pro wrestling)

The professional wrestler Rikidōzan was always required to perform extraordinariness for spectators. In his collection of essays on professional wrestling in Japan, sports reporter Fukuda Kazuya offers an anecdote that exemplifies the "extraordinariness" fundamental to the existence of pro wrestlers.[40] When Rikidōzan ran into the American wrestler Dick the Bruiser in a New York bar, the American tore the cap of his beer bottle in four and blew the pieces toward Rikidōzan. Watching this, Rikidōzan began eating the shot glass out of which he was drinking. Respecting each other's extraordinariness, the two wrestlers drank together until dawn. The accuracy of the anecdote does not concern us here, since it is primarily included to show the performative aspect of pro wrestlers' lives.[41] Although much of Rikidōzan's legend has been debunked as phony from the very beginning of his career, in the 1950s and early 1960s millions of Japanese nonetheless cheered Rikidōzan's performances, admiring his extraordinariness. In his performances, many saw hope for their country as it emerged from foreign occupation. Rikidōzan has been called the second most famous person in postwar Japan, next only to the emperor.[42]

Rikidōzan established Western-style professional wrestling as a popular entertainment in Japan in the 1950s, and his articulation of nationalism through his bodily performance for the defeated nation was a critical component in his astonishing success. After training and fighting in the United States for thirteen months, Rikidōzan fought the first televised professional wrestling match in Japan on February 19, 1954. It did not take long for the uninitiated to convert themselves into avid fans of Rikidōzan. Rikidōzan and his tagmate, Kimura Masahiko, fought against the American Sharpe brothers (Ben and "Iron" Mike) in the main events of a three-day series (fig. 8). The Japanese tag team did not win the first

Figure 8. Rikidōzan (center) and Kimura in their match against the Sharpe brothers, Kokugikan, February 1954. Courtesy of Mainichi shinbunsha.

match. However, by the end of the series tens of thousands of Japanese were fervently cheering for Rikidōzan inside the Memorial Hall in Tokyo and in front of "street TVs" that Nihon Television set up in public spaces—so fervently indeed that one man in Tokyo died from a heart attack.[43]

The people who rushed to the Memorial Hall or gathered around the public television sets during the series were mesmerized by the dramatic role reversal that took place before their eyes: a Japanese man beat up two huge Americans. There was a sense of moral justice in his performance. During the match, the American wrestlers targeted Kimura, the weaker of the two Japanese, and resorted to dirty tricks. Rikidōzan, by contrast, showed that he adhered to principles of fairness, enduring hardship and rescuing Kimura. Finally he exploded in anger and beat his opponents down with "karate chops."[44] The endurance he exhibited, withstanding the dirty tricks of the American tag team—which included jumping into the ring without tagging, fighting only in their own corner, and saving their energy with quick tags—gave him the moral authority to resort to such final means in settling the conflict.

The Americans' tactics were benign in comparison to what soon became common practice in Japanese professional wrestling.[45] However, for an audience unaccustomed to the violence of wrestling performances they were enough to brand the Sharpe brothers as dirty. The trickery gradually escalated as many more American and often foreign wrestlers came to fight in Japan; this was all part of Rikidōzan's masterful plan in marketing wrestling. The matches gradually grew more violent, with bloodshed becoming routine at about the time that television began color broadcasting.[46]

From the time of his debut in Japan, Rikidōzan's wrestling reproduced the familiar tropes of the sincere self and the evil other, also staples of Japanese wartime propaganda. According to some propagandists, Japan represented the sincere intentions that would prevail in the end, despite the tenacious intervention of evil forces.[47] Although war is an undesirable means, Japan had to resort to war since its supply of raw materials had been severed by the ABCD (American, British, Chinese, and Dutch) encirclement and in order to liberate Asian colonies from European rule. It is not difficult to see a similar narrative in Rikidōzan's matches. Rikidōzan initially fought without karate chops in the matches because such moves are devastating and their legitimacy is rather questionable. (Many foreign wrestlers complained that karate chops are just as illegal as beating opponents with a fist.) After enduring the foreign wrestlers' dirty attacks and seeing his tagmate in trouble, Rikidōzan began beating his opponents mercilessly with a distinctively Japanese final "weapon."[48] In this sense, the drama that his performance produced in the ring was a faithful reproduction of wartime propaganda, the appeal of which did not disappear in the postwar period.

Rikidōzan defended the threshold of postwar history both from the demonic threats of the other and from memories of Japan's humiliation. Rikidōzan made the otherness of the United States and memories of Japan's defeat visible to the Japanese audience and then proceeded to exorcise these ghosts. The familiar trope of the opposition between the sincere self and the evil other was burdened with memories of Japan's recent past: a denial of otherness was also a rejection of Japan's recent history. In other words, Rikidōzan cast himself as a suture that prevented a rupture in historical continuity, a rupture caused by foreign bodies. The bloodshed he endured during the matches became a requirement for him to carry out the function of a suture. The skin of his forehead was torn by the attacks of the monstrous other; the blood signified Rikidōzan's heroic efforts to prevent a similar rupture in the nation's historical consciousness. Rikidōzan's bodily performance rehabilitated Japan's nationhood by casting Japan as a victor in the bloody fight against its adversary, the United States.

The recollections of the photographer Seto Masahito speak for many contemporary Japanese people's encounters with Rikidōzan on television, even though the circumstances under which he saw the wrestler were unique. Born in Thailand in 1953 to a Japanese father and a Thai mother, Seto moved to a village in Fukushima Prefecture with his father when he was eight. He saw Rikidōzan for the first time in the 1960s, when the wrestling matches had already escalated in their violence:

> ["Classy" Fred] Blassie, with his disheveled blond hair, did unthinkable things like biting; he was an animal and an enemy. Covered with his own blood, Rikidōzan staggered. I even thought he [Rikidōzan] might be bitten to death. Yet once Rikidōzan swung down the legendary weapon, his karate chop, exerting all his strength, even the golden-haired animal looked like a lamb. With each swing, power filled Rikidōzan's body, the product of his daily training. Just looking at the scene, I was encouraged.[49]

Behaving like animals, American wrestlers acted out Japan's worst fears of the American other. Fairness and rules had no place in the fights against them; Rikidōzan had to use his final weapon against the demonic other.

Seto's encounter with Rikidōzan coincided with the discovery of his Japanese identity:

> I felt I saw the "Japanese" in Rikidōzan as he charged the wrestlers who came from overseas and looked like monsters. That was the process . . . through which I became Japanese. Even without knowing where Rikidōzan came from, looking at his brave figure, I wanted to become Japanese.[50]

The boy from Thailand found the quintessential Japanese figure in Rikidōzan.

Millions of Japanese similarly found encouragement in Rikidōzan's fighting style in the 1950s and early 1960s, even without knowing where he was from[51]—Rikidōzan was, in fact, originally from Korea. He arrived in Japan in 1940 as a sumo hopeful and did not become a Japanese citizen until 1951.[52] Although he confided in his close friends, Rikidōzan publicly lived as a Japanese who was born in Japan, and the traces of his Korean ancestry were erased from his public persona. Even biographies written after his death claimed that Rikidōzan was born in Kyushu, and they included stories about his childhood there.[53] Ironically, Rikidōzan had to repress his own otherness in Japanese society, as he defended it from foreign invasion. His Korean identity was discursively transformed into that of a Japanese in the binary oppositions between Japan and the American other. Signs of Japan's colonial past were repressed in order to sustain the drama he created in the wrestling ring. When Rikidōzan was still alive, rumors that he was a Korean spread, as if that information were enough to question the legitimacy of professional wrestling.[54] In this drama, Japan could not be rescued by a former colonial subject: that job was reserved solely for a Japanese hero.

Nonetheless, the "Japanese" that Rikidōzan created for a Japanese audience mercilessly discarded prewar Japan. Rikidōzan marketed professional wrestling as a new and American fighting style that superseded its Japanese counterparts. Ten months after the fight against the Sharpe brothers, he fought and knocked out his former tagmate Kimura Masahiko only fifteen minutes and forty-nine seconds into their scheduled one-hour match. Kimura's image as a judo champion had been stigmatized in the match against the Sharpe brothers: he had been the weaker of the two, constantly rescued by Rikidōzan's karate chop. Afterward, Kimura suggested both that the match had been rigged and that Rikidōzan would be no competition if he fought seriously.[55] Kimura's provocation eventually led to the one-on-one match against Rikidōzan in December 1954.[56]

Kimura's challenge to Rikidōzan, however, stemmed from business considerations more than personal vendetta. The International Professional Wrestling League that Kimura helped to establish in April 1954 was not nearly as popular as Rikidōzan's Japan Professional Wrestling Association. The match between Kimura and Rikidōzan was a business deal in which Kimura's league would boost its popularity with the help of Rikidōzan. The match was the first of many to come and was supposed to end in a draw. At least, that was how Kimura understood the match.[57] However, Rikidōzan had a different plan—Kimura walked into the ring completely unprepared, and shortly after the match began he was knocked unconscious. Rikidōzan effectively finished his challenger's career as a professional wrestler and reinforced the hegemony of his wrestling organization.[58] The outcome of the match also announced that judo—Japan's national pride—was no match for professional wrestling.[59] With his karate chop, Rikidōzan easily knocked out the legendary judo champion (rumored the best in history) and vividly demonstrated to the audience that Rikidōzan's new fighting style was far more effective.[60]

As a hybrid of American sports and Japanese martial arts, the karate chop served as a sign of Japaneseness against the foreign wrestlers, while signaling its American quality. The Japaneseness that Rikidōzan defended was not the pure self of prewar Japan; rather, it was the image of a Japan already imbued with American icons. Rikidōzan embodied the hybrid identity of Japanese who would be capable of defeating both American and traditional Japanese competitors. To defend this hybrid identity, he not only had to beat American wrestlers but also had to denigrate traditional Japanese martial arts.

Therefore, although Rikidōzan carried associations with sumo wrestling, sumo served as a caricature in his promotion of professional wrestling. In 1955, the president of Japan Pro Wrestling Enterprises, Nitta Shinsaku, introduced the former *yokozuna* (the highest ranking) champion Azumafuji as a Western-style wrestler, hoping to curtail Rikidōzan's ever-growing popularity.[61] Rikidōzan had been acting too big for Nitta: the wrestler had grown dissatisfied with the financial compensation provided by the Nitta's company, despite the fact that he owed much to Nitta's personal support in launching professional wrestling as popular entertainment in Japan.[62] Nitta gambled that another powerful star would deflate Rikidōzan's ego. However, the former sumo champion only found himself constantly beat up by foreign wrestlers and rescued by Rikidōzan.[63] Indeed, one of the most memorable moments for Rikidōzan fans was a match between Azumafuji and the Mexican wrestler Jess Ortega in 1955. Azumafuji did not put up much resistance and was beaten unconscious. However, despite the fact that it was a singles match, Rikidōzan jumped into the ring and applied his karate chops to Ortega, who then fell out of the ring.[64] The scene was a bit too perfect, probably prearranged by Rikidōzan and Ortega, but the crowd simply loved it. Azumafuji, moreover, damaged his own image in another match when he attempted to stop a fight between Rikidōzan and Ortega. Azumafuji's tagmate, Rikidōzan had slammed Ortega's head twice into a corner steel pole; Ortega's head was covered with blood, and his wound later required some twenty stitches. Making a feeble attempt to stop the ringside fight, Azumafuji caught his thumb between Ortega's head and the steel pole and broke it.

The former sumo champion never matched Rikidōzan in the presentation of this new form of entertainment, and the authority of sumo plummeted along with the formidable reputation of Azumafuji.[65] Rikidōzan understood the showmanship of Western-style wrestling, the entertainment form that originated in Europe and grew popular in the United States. He promoted it as a new, American sport, while relentlessly demoting the Japanese martial arts that embodied premodernity in his ring. Rikidōzan himself instantiated the Americanness of professional wrestling for the spectators: through hard training, he transformed his body from one of a sumo wrestler to a more muscular form. Moreover, he drove around in a Cadillac on the narrow streets of Tokyo and enjoyed a motorboat in Zushi, when even the star professional baseball players could not afford these luxuries.[66]

Although Rikidōzan's performance was a nationalist project, it represented neither simple nostalgia nor a restoration of the pre-1945 Japan. The Japan that he represented was already Americanized, and the appeal of his wrestling stemmed from the spectacle of beating American wrestlers at their own game. His performance prefigured the story of Japan's corporate warriors during the period of high-growth economy: Japan excelled under the hegemonic rule of American capitalism and beat the United States at its own game. Rikidōzan's ever-growing business operations attested to a link between the nationalist performance within the wrestling arena and economic drive: by the time he died in 1963, Rikidōzan owned upscale apartment buildings, a sports complex, a supermarket, a restaurant, a boxing club, and Japan Pro Wrestling Enterprises. He was also involved in constructing a golf course and planning to build a yacht harbor.[67] His business success was the direct product of his nationalist performances, which urged spectators and himself to excel within the confines of American games.

However, Rikidōzan had to battle suspicions of rigging and to maintain the effectiveness of his own performance. Although most Japanese spectators believed that the fight with the Sharpe brothers had been genuine, many soon began to suspect that the matches were rigged. Furthermore, it did not take long for them to figure out the general pattern of Rikidōzan's matches. The enormous popularity of wrestling began slipping away, so Rikidōzan increased the level of violence in the ring. The tricks of the foreign wrestlers grew more vile, and bloodshed became more common.[68] Furthermore, Rikidōzan mystified the foreign wrestlers' finishing techniques and created narratives as to how he would challenge and defeat them in each series.[69] Through his bodily performances and narrative constructions, he struggled to legitimate professional wrestling matches.

Nevertheless, despite his efforts to enhance wrestling's appeal as genuine, its popularity kept declining until 1959, when he hit upon a new format. The key to revitalizing interest proved to be a tournament format that Rikidōzan introduced. In the summer of 1959, Jess Ortega, King Kong, and Mr. Atomic joined the Japanese wrestlers Rikidōzan, Toyonobori, and Endo Kōkichi for a World League series that was met with great enthusiasm.[70] Muramatsu Tomomi attributes the success of the series to its function in authenticating the matches: the process of elimination in the tournament lent authenticity to the final match between Rikidōzan and Ortega. The World League matches freed the narrative structure of professional wrestling from a binary opposition between Japan and the other. The bilateral rivalry between Japan and the United States was resolved through international competition. The format of an international tournament constructed the championship offered in Japan as an object that the "world" desired to attain, transcending the local rivalry between Japan and the United States. The internationalism exploited by the World League matches appealed to Japanese spectators because it offered a narrative progression away from the U.S. hegemony. Five years later, the nation fully accepted the ideological effects of international competition when it embraced the Tokyo Olympics as a national project.

Rikidōzan himself ardently supported the Olympics; as a special correspondent of *Supōtsu Nippon*, he arrived in Rome for the 1960 Olympics and gave pep talks to the Japanese athletes there. In 1963, he donated ten million yen, a portion of the profit from the 1963 World League matches to the Olympic cause. However, Rikidōzan did not live to see the success of the Tokyo Olympics. On the night of December 8, 1963 (exactly twenty-two years after Pearl Harbor: it was already December 8, 1941, in Japan when the attack took place), he got into a fight with a gang member and was stabbed in the lower stomach. Although he was immediately hospitalized and the wound did not appear serious, he died a week later, at the age of thirty-nine.[71] His sudden death became the subject of much speculation; one rumor claimed that his body had already been crumbling from years of taking large doses of stimulants for wrestling matches, alternating with sleeping pills.[72]

Rikidōzan needed excess violence to maintain his performance of nationhood beyond the question of authenticity and phoniness. Through his body, Rikidōzan enacted the violent past of the nation in popular memories, and he offered his body as the site where past memories could be overcome. The nation's violent past revisited his body with full force, and Rikidōzan had to counter with his own excess violence. In each match, he proved that he was powerful enough to endure the weight of the past and exorcise it with his karate chops. In other words, he performed with dead seriousness the spectacle of excess in order to produce a new narrative for the nation. By emphasizing the seriousness of his production—by abusing his body—he fulfilled his role as a producer of postwar Japan's mythology.[73] Through his often bloody bodily performance, Rikidōzan simultaneously sensationalized and banalized the violence into a myth. Rikidōzan enacted and signified the violent encounter with the (American) other in the ring through the myth that he choreographed. But when his material body could no longer sustain the production of myth, that function was absorbed by the larger, more legitimate international competition of the Tokyo Olympics.

Disappearing Markers of Loss

The three popular cultural forms that I have discussed in this chapter revolved around liminality, either creating liminal spaces or featuring liminal figures. At the threshold of postwar society, Machiko and Godzilla sought the signs of their past. On the other hand, Rikidōzan stood at the threshold defending the nation from its own violent past. However, these distinctive forms of liminality disappeared by the mid-1960s. The Sukiya Bridge had been demolished even before the 1960s. Godzilla became a good monster in 1964. Rikidōzan's life was cut short in 1963. There seems to have been no space left for them in 1960s Japan, so eager was the nation to erase the signs of liminality. In a high-growth economy, markers of the war and the occupation were fast disappearing.

Furthermore, this liminality was reduced to a banal sign of Japan's uniqueness in the form of *nihonjinron* discourse, as I discussed in the previous chapter. As Japan regained its political independence and international status through economic growth, *nihonjinron* gained ascendance as ideological support for postwar Japanese national pride. It discursively constructed Japan as a liminal, hybrid entity and found historical continuity within this liminality. According to this line of argument, the current historical disjuncture was nothing new in Japan: Japan had always already been imbued with disjuncture that was created by the other. Against this ideological characterization of Japanese history that naturalized the disjuncture, the representations of disjuncture in *Kimi no nawa*, *Godzilla*, and Rikidōzan simply became invisible to postwar critics.[74] Branded as mere corrupt copies of the European and American forms of cultural productions, their tremendous appeal to the contemporary audience received dismissive treatments in discussions of postwar culture.[75]

What motivates the readings in this chapter is my concern for the representations of the past in these popular cultural forms. Their appeal to contemporary society demonstrated that many of its members were still grappling with their own memories of past. Various strategies were devised in the 1950s to deal with the memory of loss; spectators revisited and transformed such memories with the help of such strategies. In the next chapter, I will examine the strategies of the 1960s to erase past memories once and for all. Against the radical transformation of the 1960s Tokyo cityscape, the 1964 Olympics became an arena that accommodated the contradictory desires to encounter and erase memories of loss. Before moving on to a discussion of the Olympics, however, one last monster in postwar Japanese society needs to be discussed—Prime Minister Kishi Nobusuke.

5

From the Anti–Security Treaty Movement to the Tokyo Olympics: Transforming the Body, the Metropolis, and Memory

STARTING IN THE 1950S, the high-growth economy rapidly transformed the everyday environment that surrounded the individual Japanese body. Both the cityscape and the private realm of the household were drastically changing. Many Japanese began living in the small, yet functional space of *danchi* (modern public apartments), which were objects of envy at the time.[1] *Danchi* space was also filled with household appliances, the use of which began to spread in the late 1950s and 1960s.[2] In the "dining kitchens" (eat-in kitchens) of *danchi*, women benefited from the convenience of rice cookers and refrigerators.[3] The so-called "three imperial regalia" of the 1950s (refrigerator, washing machine, and television) became affordable to most families by the mid-1960s. By February 1965, 62 percent of Japanese households owned a refrigerator, while washing machines and television sets were in 73 percent and 90 percent of households, respectively.[4] Those who used to look at *Blondie* with envy could now create their own version of this modern quotidian space.

Ueno Kōshi describes the transformation of the space that surrounded the body in terms of the disappearance of darkness in 1960s Tokyo: the interstices that used to exist in quotidian space were eradicated in the functional space of *danchi*, while artificial lights filled the darkness of the city.[5] Quoting statistics indicating the increasing institutionalization of birth and death, Ueno detects the dissipating ontological darkness behind the disappearance of physical darkness. In 1955, only 18 percent of births took place in hospitals, while 82 percent occurred in homes or elsewhere. However, by 1965 the proportion of hospital births grew to 84 percent. As for deaths, a similar trend occurred during this period, though the changes were less dramatic. The proportion of deaths taking place at medical facilities gradually grew from 9 percent in 1947 to 57 percent in 1980.[6] Thus, birth and death, the moments when Japanese bodies were introduced into and ushered out of the social realm, also came to be observed in the bright, sanitized space of modern medical institutions.

Japanese people worked harder and many longer hours to sustain the high economic growth of the 1960s and to make possible the radical transformation of their living environment. The peace and prosperity of postwar Japan produced a modern living space. In this emerging clean, bright space, traces of loss and the past seemed to be fast disappearing. Yet memories of the past and its loss were far from being fully dissipated in the modernized everyday life. In this chapter, I focus on the two events that swept Tokyo—the popular protest against the United States–Japan Security Treaty of 1960 and the spectacle of the Tokyo Olympics of 1964—to examine the tenaciousness of war memories during the early 1960s. For many, the anti–Security Treaty movement and the Olympics served as opportunities not only to remember their own experiences of the war but also to tame devastating memories before they engulfed postwar economic prosperity.

The Anti–Security Treaty Movement

In the last four decades, the anti–Security Treaty movement has commanded scholarly and journalistic attention as a political event. My discussion here relies on these preceding discussions, which have primarily focused on the movement's political ramifications. Although the protest against the Security Treaty was political, my concern is not confined to contemporary political issues. This section treats the movement as an arena in which postwar Japanese society was reminded of its problematic relations with nationalism and its own past. Moreover, I argue that bodies and bodily images once again became conduits with which to re-present memories of the past at this particular juncture of Japanese history.

In the first half of 1960, Japan was shaken by the popular political movement against renewal of the United States–Japan Security Treaty. As Japan regained its economic power in the postwar years, the Liberal Democratic Party (LDP), led by Prime Minister Kishi Nobusuke, sought to revise the original 1951 treaty in order to make it more equitable. Liberals and leftists opposed the new treaty on the grounds that it permanently subordinated Japan to U.S. strategic interests. During debates on the nature of the new security treaty, these groups expressed a desire to maintain a neutral stance with regard to U.S. hegemony in East Asia. Yet despite the efforts of opposition parties and labor organizations to mobilize opposition, the movement did not reach a mass level until Kishi's forceful maneuvering in the Diet to pass the new treaty sparked a sense of crisis across a broad social spectrum.

After Kishi's government forcefully pushed ratification of the renewed treaty in the Diet, the focal point of the movement shifted away from the international ramifications of the treaty to domestic democratic order in postwar Japan. In effect, strong reactions to Kishi's forceful tactics simplified the complex issue of democratic order within the United States–Japan

Security Treaty system. The issue of the treaty's renewal illuminated the contradictory state of Japan's democracy, which depended on the hegemony of the U.S. military in East Asia. In postwar Japan, democracy was inextricably linked to past memories of the war and a reemerging sense of nationalism. But, standing for the postwar democracy against the autocratic political authority, the organized Left and a large number of participants in the opposition movement narrowed their scope to attack that which Kishi represented: the return of the pre-1945 militarist legacy.

To discuss the diverse aspects of the anti–Security Treaty movement of 1960, it is first necessary to explain what Kishi aspired to achieve through the renewal of the treaty. Defined largely by the power dynamics of the two countries in the immediate postwar years and the strategic needs of the United States in East Asia, the 1951 Security Treaty granted large latitude to the U.S. military in Japan, while there was no specific U.S. responsibility to defend Japan against an attack by a third party. In revising the treaty, Kishi hoped to redefine the two countries as equal partners by articulating mutual military responsibilities and to reestablish Japan as the leader of Asian nations.[7] Although the U.S. government was not initially open to Kishi's proposal, two developments brought the United States to the negotiating table. First, the technological advancements of the Soviet Union, as demonstrated by its successful launching of *Sputnik*, directly challenged the strategic advantage of the United States, and, second, the United States needed to secure its Okinawan bases in the face of strong opposition within Okinawa.[8]

On January 19, 1960, at the White House, Prime Minister Kishi Nobusuke and President Dwight D. Eisenhower signed the revised Treaty of Mutual Cooperation and Security between Japan and the United States of America. The new treaty was not as lopsided as its predecessor. Article V emphasized the bilateral nature of the contract: "Each Party recognizes that an armed attack against either Party in the territories under the administration of Japan would be dangerous to its own peace and safety and declares that it would act to meet the common danger in accordance with its constitutional provisions and processes."[9] Specific items of the 1951 treaty that offended Japan were also eliminated, including Article I, which gave the United States the right to intervene in Japan's domestic disturbances, and Article II, which prohibited Japan from granting bases to other countries without prior U.S. consultation. Article X of the 1960 version specified that the term of the treaty would be ten years; moreover, either party could terminate the treaty with one-year notice of such an intention. Furthermore, Article II of the new treaty promoted close economic mutual assistance between the two countries.[10]

However, bilateral responsibilities did not mean absolute equality between the two countries. As indicated in Article VI, Japan was defined as a strategic outpost of the United States: "For the purpose of contributing to the security of Japan and the maintenance of international peace and security in the Far East, the United States of America is granted the use by its land, air and naval forces of facilities and areas in Japan."[11] Because its constitution specifically prohibited such activities, Japan could not render military assistance to the United States, and, as a result, the mutuality of Article V was undermined. Article VI compensated for Japan's lack of military maneuverability by granting various rights to the United States. The U.S. government did not expect Japan's direct military assistance, but it needed free access to bases in Japan.

Kishi and his supporters within the LDP wanted to break away from the legacy of the occupation.[12] Yet the new treaty did not change the fundamental nature of the two countries' relations: Japan gained concessions only through actively recognizing and internalizing U.S. strategic interests in East Asia. The new treaty fell short of what Kishi had envisaged as an expression of truly equal U.S.-Japanese relations: a military alliance with the United States. Kishi and other conservative leaders desired to achieve this goal by revising Japan's own postwar constitution, making it legal to dispatch Japanese forces overseas in case the United States needed such assistance. Although there was considerable support for constitutional revision in the early 1950s, support waned as Japan began to enjoy economic prosperity in the second half of the decade and the 1960s.[13] Japan's economic success under the Security Treaty diverted popular discourse and the attention of conservative political leaders away from nationalistic calls for constitutional revision.

Despite the fact that the new treaty did not resituate the two countries as equal partners, it nonetheless marked a new beginning for U.S.-Japanese relations. In order to celebrate the ratification of the treaty, Kishi requested that Eisenhower visit Japan; in exchange, the crown prince and princess were scheduled to visit the United States.[14] Upon Eisenhower's arrival, Emperor Hirohito was to welcome him at the Haneda Airport. Unlike the humiliating photographic image of MacArthur and Hirohito in 1945, the parade of Eisenhower and Hirohito in an open car was to have been an opportunity for Japan to boast of its new, more equal partnership with the United States to the world. Kishi planned to have the treaty ratified in the Diet by the time of Eisenhower's visit, which was scheduled for June 19. For this purpose, the treaty needed to pass the House of Representatives by May 19: once the treaty was approved by the House of Representatives, it would be automatically ratified in a month, even without the deliberation of the House of Councilors.

However, the Socialist and the Communist Parties in the Diet voiced strong opposition to the revised treaty; both parties feared that the militarists were once again to bring Japan into a war in Asia by entrenching

Japan in U.S. strategic planning for East Asia. It seemed that the Kishi administration was about to revive the pre-1945 legacies in postwar Japanese politics with the assistance of "U.S. imperialism." Thus, during an official visit to the People's Republic of China in March 1959, Asanuma Inejirō, the secretary general of the Socialist Party, declared that "U.S. imperialism is a common enemy for both the Chinese and Japanese peoples."[15] The Japan Communist Party similarly insisted in the late 1950s that Japan was subjugated to U.S. imperialism.[16]

The revised Security Treaty was scrutinized and criticized in the Diet sessions; the opposition tenaciously questioned in particular the definition of "the Far East" as the area of the possible U.S. action, as well as the practicality of the "prior consultation with the Government of Japan" by the United States in case of military action.[17] When the Socialist Party resorted to a delay tactic by staging a sit-in in the Diet building, Kishi was determined to steamroll over all opposition. On the night of May 19, he called in five hundred policemen to remove Socialist Party members who were blocking the House speaker's entrance into the assembly.[18] In the absence of the Socialist Party members and dissenters within the LDP (who chose not to be at the session), the revised Security Treaty was approved by the House of Representatives in a few minutes. In this way, Kishi managed to force his plan through the Diet. His tactic backfired, however.

Among the Left, the issue of the treaty's revision had provided the focal point to anti–Security Treaty sentiment; an organized opposition movement was already under way by this point. In March 1959, 134 organizations, including the Communist Party, the Socialist Party, the General Council of Trade Unions (Sōhyō), and student unions, created the National Council for Prevention of a Revision of the Security Treaty (Anpojōyaku Kaitei Soshi Kokumin Kaigi).[19] One year later, the number of organizations involved in the National Council increased tremendously, with 1,633 organizations participating in March 1960. Nonetheless, the issue of revision was too abstract for many, and mobilization by the opposition groups lacked the enthusiastic support of their members.[20] Ultimately, it was anger toward Kishi Nobusuke that motivated a wide range of citizens to join the opposition rallies on the streets of Tokyo. A wide variety of people, from high school students to nursing-home residents, took to the streets and expressed their frustration through massive rallies—the first public protest for many of them.[21] Tens of thousands of protesters day after day surrounded the Diet building, the prime minister's residence, and the American Embassy. As many as 5.6 million people throughout the nation participated in the June 4 general strike. Not only public transportation workers but also twenty thousand stores took part.

The forceful tactics employed for the passage of the revision in the Diet rendered the complicated issue of the treaty's revision into a simple binary: Kishi represented in an easy-to-recognize form the dark forces in Japanese politics that challenged the postwar democratic order. Kishi's career and action in this matter signaled the return of the dark forces, the residual elements of the pre-1945 Japan, which sought assistance from its former enemy, the United States. As a young bureaucrat, Kishi had been responsible for the industrial development of Manchuria; he later served as minister of commerce in the Tōjō administration. In the immediate postwar period, he was incarcerated as a Class A war criminal awaiting trial. However, reflecting a shift in the international political climate, the Tokyo Trial did not extend beyond the sentencing of the first twenty-eight defendants; Kishi was eventually released.[22] As the San Francisco peace treaty came into effect in 1952—Japan regained its independence and the GHQ's political purge of Kishi lost its effect—Kishi publicly rejoined the conservative sector in Japanese politics, easily climbing up the party hierarchy. In 1957, he became prime minister, triumphantly returning as the nation's leader despite his wartime activities.[23] His return could even be called "monstrous" in a society so eager to repress the legacies of the war.

Many called Kishi "*yōkai* of the Shōwa era" (*yōkai* are monstrous premodern creatures that survived in the liminal space of modern Japan, defying scientific explanations), for he embodied the return of wartime Japan.[24] This monster was at the heart of the political turmoil of 1960. This particular *yōkai* of the Shōwa era managed to return from the netherworld before 1945. Kishi brought back with him the monstrous qualities of the repressive pre-1945 Japanese political system. Kishi was a stand-in for the military regime, against which the Japanese should have collectively fought but did not before the defeat of Japan, as well as for the humiliation that this regime brought to Japan. The "*yōkai* of the Shōwa era" was truly monstrous, but not powerful enough to defeat the United States, the master of modern science. By affirming the subservient position of Japan to the United States in the new security treaty, Kishi served as a reminder of the earlier drama in which Japan had been defeated and tamed into a subordinate client state. The anti-revision movement, thus, became an opportunity to tackle the unresolved past in postwar Japan. Millions of Japanese took to the streets and supported general strikes to express their anger over Kishi's coercive tactics.

Even prior to the Security Treaty revision, Kishi had already demonstrated his autocratic inclinations. On October 4, 1958, the official talk on the revision issue began between Foreign Minster Fujiyama Ai'ichirō and Ambassador Douglas MacArthur II (nephew of General Douglas MacArthur).[25] Four days later, anticipating the political turmoil in the process of revising the Security Treaty, Kishi's government introduced the

Police Duties Performance Law Bill to the Diet. The Police Bill would have legitimized preventive measures by the police in their search, interrogation, and arrest; later, Kishi himself admitted that this bill was a preparatory step for forcefully realizing the revision of the Security Treaty.[26]

However, despite Kishi's strong tactics, the bill was defeated in the Diet. The Socialist Party immediately voiced its opposition to the bill, and sixty-six organizations formed a People's Council against Malrevision of the Police Duties Law (Keishokuhō Kaiaku Hantai Kokumin Kaigi) five days after the introduction of the bill. The opposition found support among ordinary citizens as well as the Japanese media. Although Kishi tried to pass the bill by extending the Diet session on November 4 (it was due to end on November 7), the Socialist Diet members countered this move by boycotting the session; the next day, six million workers participated in strikes in protest against the bill. Moreover, even powerful LDP members dissented from Kishi's program and began criticizing him openly. In the end, Kishi admitted his defeat: on November 22, he met the Socialist Party chairman Suzuki Mosaburō and agreed to shelve the bill. This opposition group's success in blocking the Police Bill led the organized opposition to protest against another one of Kishi's forceful moves, the ratification of the revised Security Treaty.

Maruyama Masao claimed that Kishi's authoritarian maneuver simplified the issue regarding the revision of the Security Treaty by turning it into a choice between democracy and authoritarian power.[27] Takeuchi Yoshimi's cry of "minshu ka dokusai ka" [democracy or dictatorship] captured this sentiment, which reduced international politics to domestic affairs as well as to a simple either/or choice.[28] The United States disappeared in the contrast made between democracy and dictatorship. By upholding democracy as the central issue, these intellectuals turned away from the historical conditions that brought democracy to postwar Japan. Democratic postwar Japanese society never existed as an abstract construct, but always as a historically specific condition under the hegemony of U.S. military power in East Asia. Furthermore, the wartime mobilization system was instrumental to the democratization of the postwar Japanese economy and society.[29] To reflect on the contradiction of the postwar political situation, the opposition movement participants needed to focus on the enigmatic relations between "democracy and dictatorship" in the political order realized under U.S. hegemony. However, by narrowly focusing on the either/or of "democracy or dictatorship," Maruyama and Takeuchi demanded that the participants in effect unconditionally embrace the legacy of the U.S. occupation, and many in the movement accepted Maruyama's and Takeuchi's call to reduce the issue to the fight between the democratic present and autocratic past.

Yet, despite the participants' emotional reactions to Kishi's coercive tactics and their effects in reducing the issue to a simple binary, the past still haunted the movement in various forms. In the minds of many participants, memories of the war and Japan's defeat collided with a rising sense of nationalism in postwar Japan. In his 1966 book *Protest in Tokyo*, George Packard identified this tension in the movement between a re-emerging sense of national pride and experiences of the war and defeat:

> It was not surprising that the war and the defeat were vital issues in the process of reconstructing national pride. The ready acceptance by the Japanese of the occupation and their swift embrace of democracy have led many foreign observers to conclude that the memories of the war already belonged to the dim past. Nothing could be further from the truth. The war and defeat were still the central facts in the lives of most adult Japanese, breeding feelings of guilt, inferiority, and insecurity. The psychological wounds on this proud and sensitive people would probably not heal until the present generation of college students took over, and the scars were apparent in 1960 to those who would look beneath the surface.[30]

Confirmation of Japan's subordinate position in the new treaty and Kishi's autocratic political maneuvering revived such memories of "guilt, inferiority, and insecurity" in the nation.[31]

Shimizu Ikutarō, an intellectual who was deeply committed to the anti-treaty movement, similarly identified in his recollections a nationalistic strain in the emotional responses of the participants. The opposition movement gained unprecedented support because it offered an outlet for the nationalism that had been "cooped up in a dark corner" of postwar Japan. Only fifteen years had passed since Japan's defeat; it was only to be expected that experiences and emotions from the recent past shaped the movement.

> Almost all of the participants [in the anti–Security Treaty movement] knew the war. They knew life before the war, knew life during the war, and knew life after the war. They not only knew it; they managed to survive it. During this period, always feeling uneasy, they experienced many things. With each experience, they were swayed by deep emotions. Looking back [on this period], everybody's past was filled with anxiety, fear, rage, hunger, and humiliation. Certainly, some elements of these emotions were concerned with oneself or one's family. Yet other aspects obviously revolved around our nation, Japan. There was nationalism. However, in the fifteen years of the postwar period, the private aspect of those experiences and emotions was given the right to be on a raised, bright stage, while the nationalistic elements had been cooped up in a dark corner.[32]

The anti–Security Treaty movement served as an opportunity for the protesters to express what they had long repressed under the foundational narrative: nationalistic feelings embedded in past experiences and emotions. The sense of nationalism returned to Japan as its government attempted to reconfirm the foundational narrative with few modifications.

Shimizu discusses the importance of Zengakuren's (the All-Japan Federation of Self-Governing Student Associations) physical confrontation with authority in awakening nationalistic feelings among its participants.

> As the anti–Security Treaty struggle escalated through Zengakuren's reckless (or selfless) behavior, the struggle pierced a deep, only semiconscious layer of the people's spirit. The struggle stimulated the experiences and emotions hiding in that layer, and gave them unexpected opportunities for expression. When shouting the slogan, "Against the Security Treaty," many people were probably releasing old experiences and emotions, which for a long time they could not have rendered in words.[33]

Shimizu Ikutarō argues that Zengakuren's tactic of physical confrontation with the authorities awoke disturbing memories of the past in Japan. These memories returned to the heart of Tokyo in the form of the bodies of the student demonstrators. One of the students who was injured in the confrontation with the police force on June 15 later expressed his wish that his wound would not heal for the rest of his life, leaving a permanent trace.[34] He wanted his political experiences inscribed as a physical scar on his skull. His body would become not only the means but also the site of his continuous political struggle; the body could not only convey political messages but also preserve the memories of conflicts. In the initial stage of the high-growth economy of the late 1950s, the anti–Security Treaty movement rediscovered the bodies in politics.

The radical Communist League (Kyōsanshugisha dōmei) assumed the leadership of Zengakuren and led a rally of about ten thousand participants into the compound of the Diet on November 27, 1959. Zengakuren's confrontations with the police were desperate attempts to pierce the postwar social order that masked its own historicity, to reach a layer of unresolved tensions. During a June 15, 1960, attempt to break through the gates to the Diet compound, a female student, Kanba Michiko, was crushed to death, and many others were injured (fig. 9). Her death was the culmination of the bodily expression in the anti–Security Treaty movement. On June 16, the seven major newspapers in Tokyo carried a joint statement denouncing Zengakuren's acts and strongly urging the rally participants to defend democracy against the use of such violence.[35] Although the bodies were undertheorized by Zengakuren leaders, their tactics were successful in awakening something disturbing to those deeply invested in the postwar political system. For that, Zengakuren was denounced by the media, which had hitherto been sympathetic to the movement and other opposition groups. Zengakuren's bodily tactics had to be contained within the prodemocracy movement that equated the use of violence with the legacies of Japan's militarist past, that which Kishi represented.

Even as three hundred thousand people surrounded the Diet and the prime minister's residence in protest, the revised United States–Japan Security Treaty was automatically ratified without deliberation in the House of Councilors. Nevertheless, because of security problems, the Japanese government was forced to cancel Eisenhower's visit at the height of the demonstrations. Although the Self-Defense Forces were on standby, thirty tanks were ready for police use against the demonstrators, and both governments were determined to overcome the opposition, Kanba Michiko's death ultimately diminished the American government's trust in the Japanese government's ability to maintain order during Eisenhower's visit.[36] Under pressure from Washington, Kishi announced the cancellation of the American president's visit to Japan. The safety of the president and the emperor was the immediate security concern, yet this decision was also made to protect the image of the imperial family from injury potentially caused by a security blunder.[37]

The two governments exchanged the instruments of ratification on June 23, and on the same day, recognizing his responsibility for the political turmoil, Kishi Nobusuke resigned his position. The monster was finally ousted. On July 19, after almost one month of negotiations within the LDP, Ikeda Hayato was named the next prime minister. In his efforts to restore order and regain the nation's support, Ikeda announced "tolerance and endurance" as his administration's slogan, and he directed the nation's attention toward economic growth. The move from politics to economy, embodied in the Ikeda administration's income-doubling policy, worked extremely well.[38] An aid to Ikeda confided in a later interview his almost instinctive response to the protesters surrounding the National Diet building. Recognizing the tremendous energy of the demonstrators, he was convinced that "if this energy can be turned toward Japan's economic development, Japan will surely become an economic superpower."[39] Just as he had wished, the nation plunged into the pursuit of economic development in the following decade. Opposition to the United States–Japan Security Treaty was stilled. Many who had participated in the antitreaty rallies went ahead and enjoyed economic prosperity under the aegis of the Security Treaty itself.[40] Yet, after failing to stop the ratification of the treaty, the opposition experienced a sense of defeat. Kishi's

Figure 9. Zengakuren students who sat down in front of the National Diet Building, June 15, 1960. Courtesy of Mainichi shinbunsha.

resignation provided a symbolic resolution to the contradiction between memories of the past and Japan's present condition under U.S. hegemony. This minor victory, along with the cancellation of Eisenhower's visit to Japan, offered the participants and witnesses of the movement against the Security Treaty an alibi for accepting material prosperity, patterned after the lifestyle of the former enemy. The outcome of the House of Representatives general election in November 1960 indicated general support for the LDP, the party that had forcibly passed and ratified the new United States–Japan Security Treaty.[41]

Before closing the discussion of the antitreaty movement in the late 1950s, I would like call the reader's attention to the importance of bodily metaphors in its characterizations. Hosaka Masayasu, who participated in the movement as a college student, slips between politics and hygiene, characterizing the antirevision movement as follows:

> The anti–Security Treaty struggle was essentially an anti-Kishi struggle. The anti-Kishi struggle could also be called a struggle to defend parliamentary politics. Furthermore, seen against the stream of Shōwa history, the struggle was motivated by hatred toward the bodily constitution [*taishitsu*], thought, and feel [*hada'ai*] that Kishi, a prewar bureaucrat who turned prime minister, represented. If I might venture a bold hypothesis, the struggle was a "people's court" that regarded Kishi as "one otherwise responsible for the Pacific War." It could also be called the Japanese people's war criminals trial that came fifteen years late.
>
> People were embittered by the filthiness [*fuketsusa*] of the situation in which Kishi was trying to appropriate U.S. power, flattering the very country against which he, as a member of the [Tōjō] administration, declared war.[42]

Although Hosaka's summary was published in 1986, his use of bodily metaphors in discussing Kishi is intriguing because it revises the general perceptions of the anti–Security Treaty struggle.[43] By discussing the bodily constitution (*taishitsu*) and feel (*hada'ai*) of Kishi and the filthiness (*fuketsusa*) of his act, Hosaka reduced the politics that Kishi represented to the level of bodily states, while depicting the opposition movement in hygienic terms. Denunciation of Kishi was for the protestors a means to settle with their own past; when he finally resigned, much of the disturbing memories of the past, along with filthiness of Kishi, were washed out of the postwar political scene.

In an interview in the 1990s, Miyazawa Ki'ichi, who was an assistant to Ikeda Hayato at the time of the Security Treaty crisis, similarly characterized the mood after the treaty renewal by using a bodily metaphor: "The anti–Security Treaty crisis was like an event in which laxative is sprayed all over the body. We were all wondering what should be done. 'Tolerance and endurance' were the only means we had to deal with it."[44]

Miyazawa's bodily metaphor is also appropriate to describe the government's policies following the months of turmoil in 1960. To extend his metaphor, memories of the past were excreted from the body of Japan. Japan was suffering from acute diarrhea in 1960: it is no surprise that the Ikeda administration spent the next few years in a state of *teishisei* (laying low) and that Japan seems to have been obsessed about cleansing itself in the same period. The memories of the past resurfaced to the popular consciousness only to be cleansed in the clean, bright space of modern Japan. The body that enabled the physical expression of political oppositions was ironically caught in the matrix of rational production in the early 1960s. In the preparation for the 1964 Olympics, politics quickly receded from the streets of Tokyo as the city drastically changed its appearance and increased its cleanliness.

The 1964 Tokyo Olympics

Japan entered into a phase of high growth in the late 1950s, and the 1964 Tokyo Olympics provided further impetus to economic growth. Huge investments were made in the infrastructure of the city, including the construction of a bullet train system between Tokyo and Osaka. In addition to signaling economic recovery, the Tokyo Olympics symbolized the full acceptance of Japan back into the international community and marked Japan's future path. Yet signs of the past, particularly memories of the Asia Pacific War, also burdened events. The original Tokyo Olympics, which were to have been held in 1940 but were canceled because of Japan's deepening conflict with China, haunted the 1964 Games.[45]

In May 1959, the International Olympic Committee voted to hold the 1964 summer games in Tokyo; over the next five and half years, "Olympic fever" gradually increased. Media reports ridiculed the frenzied nationalistic tone of the project by calling the Tokyo Olympics a *seisen* (sacred war).[46] Certain contractors in charge of construction projects for the 1964 Olympics even used the term *gyokusai* (which literally meant "shattered jewel" but was a metaphor for mass suicide in the Asia Pacific War) to describe the enormity of the project.[47]

Thus, even as they signaled a new beginning, the Olympics also conjured up memories of war and destruction. One person wrote to a newspaper three weeks before the opening of the games: "Looking at the splendid Olympic facilities, whose construction is now complete, the memories of the desolate autumn after the defeat of Japan come back to me and I am filled with deep emotion. Who could have imagined back then today's conditions?"[48] In this person's mind, the material wealth of 1964 was juxtaposed with Tokyo's destruction in 1945. The nineteen years separating the war and the Olympics were skipped to create a link between the destruction of Japan in 1945 and its reconstruction in 1964.[49]

The impressive opening ceremony of the Olympics reminded the writer Sugimoto Sonoko of an event that took place at the same location twenty-one years earlier. In 1943, deteriorating war conditions forced the imperial government to lift the moratorium on student conscription. With the exception of students in the sciences, all male college students who passed the physical examination had to go to the front. On October 21, 1943, college students from seventy-seven schools marched in the rain at Jingū Stadium (later transformed into Olympic Stadium) as part of the farewell rally organized by the government. In Sugimoto's mind, this image from twenty-one years ago was superimposed over the scene of the opening ceremony:

> Twenty years ago, also in October, I was at this same stadium. I was one of the female students. We stood there on the ground in the autumn rain to see the student soldiers off to the front. The scene inside the stadium has completely changed. Yet the size of the track is the same, and I learned that its location is the same as twenty years ago. I could not stop the memories of that day, memories of the march of the mobilized students from returning to me.
>
> Around the royal box where the emperor and crown prince sat [during the opening ceremony], Prime Minister Tōjō Hideki had addressed the students, encouraging them to destroy the American and British enemies.[50]

The marching of athletes from ninety-four different countries conjured up memories of the students' mobilization for Japan's desperate struggle. Although the event twenty-one years before lacked the colors of the Olympic ceremony—the field was filled with black and khaki—Sugimoto intuitively felt that "today's Olympics is connected to that day, and that day is connected to today. I am fearful of this connection."[51] In the midst of the nation's celebration, she remembered its history and was fearful of the possibility of history's repetition.

When the literary critic Etō Jun returned to Tokyo in 1963 from his stay in the United States, he perceived a war in progress: "Seeing the major construction going on day and night, I felt the Japanese were fighting a war."[52] For Etō, the invocation of the war was not a simple sentimental recollection of the past; the Japanese were indeed living through a war again: "Unless the majority of people tacitly recognized this [the construction frenzy in Tokyo] as a kind of war, the Japanese could never bear this thorough destruction of their living conditions. However, in actuality, people calmly endured it. Almost everybody must have instinctively known that this 'war' was worth the sacrifice."[53] Though the enemy figure may have been invisible, people endured the sacrifice in the war of the early 1960s. Etō simply intimates that people acted similarly during the last war.

Ichikawa Kon's documentary film *Tokyo Olympiad* (1965), which begins with a scene in which buildings are demolished, further underscores this connection. Seeing the film twenty-four years after the Olympics, the writer Hashimoto Osamu reached the same conclusion as Etō regarding the nature of the 1964 Olympics and aptly called it "a documentary film of a war."[54] Yet the "war" is easily subsumed under Japan's recovery in the film's opening scenes. After a brief shot of the sun filling the screen, the camera captures the scene of a wrecking ball demolishing multistoried concrete buildings. The film then moves to scenes of working crews cleaning up these demolition sites. Throughout the opening scenes, the voice-over methodically lists the modern Olympic games from their revival in 1896 to the Tokyo games, including the cancellations of the Olympics by the two world wars and the exclusion of Japan from the 1948 London games. The trajectory of the history of the Olympic games into the period after World War II intimates that the disrupted circle has been repaired in the revived postwar games.

Next, Olympic Stadium, then the Olympic arena, appear on the screen. Under the superimposed title of "XVIII Olympiad Tokyo," the stadium stands as a monumental structure with the solemnity and grandeur of a religious building. Equally solemn images of the Olympic arena in the morning fog follow. The contrast between the demolition scene sequence and the serenity of the newly constructed Olympic facilities complete the cycle of destruction and reconstruction. When the voice-over finally reaches the end of the list, the 1964 Tokyo Olympics, the scene dramatically cuts to a busy street in Ginza, filled with noise.[55] The opening sequence confirms the narrative of recovery that swiftly lifts Japan from its wartime destruction in 1945 to its prosperity in the 1960s.

The memories of destruction that haunted postwar Japan were admitted into the Olympic arena insofar as they anchored a narrative of recovery from August 1945. It was the success of Japan that these memories ultimately invoked, and sufferings before 1945 were transformed into necessary conditions for the 1960s recovery. The juxtaposition of 1945 and 1964 in the Tokyo Olympic games encouraged spectators to make a short circuit from the destruction of 1945 to the reconstruction of 1964, leaving out the historical process of the nineteen years between. The painful memories of defeat were paired with eventual reconstruction and thus rendered benign. It was not the destruction of war itself, but postwar Japan's struggle to deal with the destruction, that the success of the Olympics assisted in masking. In this sense, the Olympics served as a powerful antidote to the anti–Security Treaty movement of 1960, which offered its participants opportunities to revisit their war memories. It is symbolic that Washington Heights, the U.S. military housing area in downtown Tokyo, was converted into the Olympic village and compound for the Olympic arena and pool. This landmark of Japan's defeat and U.S. occupation was removed from the cityscape to make way for an international spectacle.

The 1964 Tokyo Olympics offered the spectacular drama of Japan's recovery from its destruction during the war; the nation staged this drama of recovery by transforming the metropolis and training Japanese athletes' bodies. The cleansed and modernized urban space of Tokyo became an appropriate site to accommodate the bodily performances of a proud nation.

The Production of the Clean, Bright Metropolis

Tokyo was virtually under constant construction during the first half of the 1960s, as the city prepared for the Olympics. Hashimoto Osamu points out that residents often noted that the scenery of Tokyo drastically changed around the time of the Tokyo Olympics, but it is not common to hear the same observation regarding the much larger-scale destruction during the war.[56] Hashimoto maintains that the war did not, in fact, change the fundamental cityscape of Tokyo, which reemerged as it had been in the postwar period. It was construction in preparation for the Tokyo Olympics that finally eradicated the underlying prewar elements in the city. We can, moreover, extend Hashimoto's characterization of the Olympics as the crucial turning point of Japan's postwar history. It is precisely the juxtaposition between the destruction of 1945 and the construction of 1964 that helped to conceal what Tokyo had inherited from the time before 1945.

The metropolitan and the national governments poured money into the construction of badly needed infrastructure in the capital. Expenses directly related to the Olympic games reached 29.5 billion yen (81.9 million dollars at the time), while indirect expenses amounted to 960 billion yen (2.7 billion dollars), more than thirty times the money spent on direct expenses. The sum total of one trillion yen was an enormous investment considering that the national budget for fiscal year 1958 was about 1.3 trillion yen (3.6 billion dollars).[57] The construction of the bullet train system (Tōkaidō Shinkansen) received the lion's share, almost 40 percent of indirect expenses, while the construction of subways and roads (including a highway) respectively received 19.8 percent and 18.3 percent of the indirect expenses. In 1959, the Metropolitan Expressway Public Corporation was established in order to construct an express toll road system for the Olympics. A section of Metropolitan Expressway No. 1 opened in 1962.

Pre-1945 technological aspirations returned through construction of the Tōkaidō Shinkansen, which began in 1959. As early as the 1930s, planning was already in progress for a standard-gauge rapid train system (*dangan ressha*) that would connect Tokyo and Shimonoseki along a nine-hour route.[58] However, both the dire need for steel during Japan's war against China and the general military buildup delayed major construction indefinitely. In 1937, the year in which Japan entered into full-scale war against China, the Japanese government promulgated strict regulations on the size of iron structures (*Tekkō kōsakubutsu chikuzō kyoka kisoku*). Structures that required more than fifty tons of steel were not permitted. Consequently, construction of a six-story station building at Osaka Station was completely halted.[59] The Olympic stadium for the 1940 Olympics was not exempted from these regulations. Although the city of Tokyo proposed to build the main stadium with its hundred thousand seats partially in wood, the structure never materialized.[60] A plan for a bullet train system was drafted in 1939, and, despite a shortage of resources, its construction did begin at certain points of the projected line. However, by 1943, even this project was completely abandoned (although land purchases for the new line continued).[61]

The bullet train system would have been the pinnacle of Japanese railway technology and a symbol of 1930s technological aspirations.[62] However, when the plans were revived in the late 1950s, many within both the Japan National Railways (JNR) corporation and political circles regarded a rapid train system as already obsolete. They believed that airplanes and highway would eventually replace the railway. Some even compared the plan with what they saw as the epitomes of monumental uselessness: the pyramids, the Great Wall, and the Japanese mammoth battleship *Yamato*.[63] Although JNR had decided in 1952 to expand its transportation capacity on the existing narrow-gauge network, the president of JNR, Sogō Shinji, promoted the construction of a standard-gauge rapid train system.[64] Sogō's career trajectory further testifies to the persistence of pre-1945 experiences in the postwar revival of the bullet train system. He joined the National Railway System in 1909 and later served as director of the South Manchurian Railways (SMR). The SMR operated on standard-gauge tracks and in 1934 inaugurated the express train *Ajia-gō* (Asia) connecting Dalian and Xinjing, covering the distance of 438 miles in eight hours and twenty minutes.[65] Although the desire for territorial expansion into Asia—embodied in the name *Ajia-gō*—was frustrated when Japan was defeated in the Asia Pacific War, the streamlined rapid trains, a symbol of prewar aspirations, returned to postwar Japan, just as did the Olympics themselves. The recovery-oriented economy of the immediate postwar period obfuscated the prewar desire for colonial expansion and speed: survival was the primary concern. Yet, in the mid-1960s the bullet train system made a return to Japan and to Tokyo. With greater velocities and a high number of casualties in its construction (203), the bullet trains continued the incomplete project of modernization.[66]

The acquisition of key pieces of land for the construction of the new line was already in progress during the war. The national railway system had already purchased 19 percent of the required land by the end of 1943;[67] acquisition was easy and cheap since few could protest the national project purportedly essential to the war effort. Incendiary bombing by the U.S. forces also helped speed the process: land cleared by the bombing lost much of its value.[68] The land already in the possession of JNR facilitated further acquisition of land in the postwar period and largely determined the route of the rapid train system.[69]

The technology employed in the high-speed operations also stemmed from prewar technological know-how. Through developing high-speed fighter planes, aeronautical engineers acquired crucial knowledge regarding high-speed navigation. Such knowledge did not go to waste: as many as one thousand researchers who had pursued military-related research were hired at the Railway Research Institute after the war.[70] This prewar accumulation of knowledge and the application of aeronautical technology were crucial in designing the rapid train system.[71]

However, transportation was not the only area that received official attention. The presentation of the capital to outsiders became almost an obsession of administrative officials. With financial assistance from the Tokyo Metropolitan government, in March 1961, the New Life Movement Association Foundation (Shin-Seikatsu Undō Kyōkai) was reorganized into the Tokyo Metropolitan New Life Movement Association (Tokyoto Shin-Seikatsu Undō Kyōkai), an auxiliary organization of the metropolitan government. The association actively supplemented the metropolitan government's "Beautification of the Capital Movement" by mobilizing local residents for its own beautification program over the next three years. The association was successful in soliciting the participation of residents in its efforts. As many as one million six hundred thousand people, for instance, helped clean the streets of Tokyo on January 10, 1964.[72]

As if to continue an incomplete project, the wartime interest in regulating Japanese bodies, discussed in chapter 2, returned to the nation. The Ministry of Health promoted a National Land Clean-up Movement (Kokudo Jōka Undō) and National Exercises for Health Movement (Kokumin Hoken Taisō Undō).[73] Minister of Health Kobayashi Takeharu denied the existence of hidden motives behind these movements:

> The minister intends to promote peaceful "health exercises nationwide," like exercise programs on the radio, until they grow to be a "total exercise movement of eighty million." They are different from the wartime "Nation-Building

Exercises" [*Kenkoku Taisō*] and "Navy Exercise" [*Kaigun Taisō*] that were forced on the people.[74]

Contrary to his intention, however, the minister's denial eloquently reveals the wartime sources of inspiration for the movements and the regulatory impulse underpinning the ministry's promotion of cleanliness.[75] The term "total" in the "total exercise movement of eighty million" recalls wartime "total mobilization," while the desire to "clean up" the national lands resonates with the regulatory impulse over the Japanese body.

The chastity of the Japanese—particularly female—body was of great concern, as it was during the time Japan waited for the arrival of American soldiers right after the defeat. In the midst of frenzied preparations for the Olympics, popular magazines expressed the fear of the corrupting influence of foreign (American and European) male sexual desire: naive Japanese women might end up as victims. Established in July 1959, the Women's Bureau in the Tokyo Metropolitan Welfare Office actively campaigned to protect Japanese women from foreign, particularly white, males. Although their overall directive was to try to prevent women from falling into prostitution, the bureau organized a special campaign for the Olympics. Nakano Tsuya, head of the Women's Bureau during this period, describes the bureau's efforts as follows:

> First of all, we produced an educational film. Then we published seventy-five thousand copies of a pamphlet targeting young as well as adult women. We also organized about 130 lectures for regional leaders [in Tokyo] and requested support from journalists. . . . Although we could not close down the Turkish baths [establishments that catered to sexual services], we did manage to convince their managers to voluntarily refrain from operating [during the Olympics]. Furthermore, we organized meetings for interested parties and went through the school principals' association to spread the messages to high school and junior college [female] students. We even went to schools to give lectures on several occasions.[76]

The message that the Women's Bureau conveyed to young women in Tokyo was simple: just say no to temptation. Nakano explains: "We were worried because we saw cases in which young ladies of good background accompanied [foreign men], suspecting nothing, to bars or even their hotel rooms. We warned them that they should not cheerfully follow foreign, especially white, men. They should say yes or no clearly, and they should not enter their rooms."[77] Such efforts to discursively suppress Japanese female sexual desire for foreign males were supplemented by magazine articles that emphasized importance of saying "no" clearly and avoiding troubles.[78]

Meanwhile, in March 1964, the Tokyo Metropolitan Hygiene Office announced plans to increase its supervision over the Turkish baths and to subject workers at the Olympic facilities and employees of hotels, bars, and cabarets in the Tokyo area to blood tests for venereal disease.[79] Although some who were targeted by this announcement voiced their protest,[80] the annual report of the Hygiene Office indicates that the plan was in fact carried out.[81]

Although the money spent on improving Tokyo's hygiene was far less than that spent on the creation of a transportation network, a considerable amount (4.7 percent of the total) was allocated for this purpose. However, the task of making Tokyo hygienic was monumental. In the early years after the war, the metropolitan government did not have resources with which to deal with growing urbanization and associated problems; the Tokyo Olympics provided the necessity and opportunity to tackle them. However, in the mid-1960s, the metropolitan and national governments had barely begun the task of eradicating the prewar problems of Tokyo. They only managed to mask prewar conditions by covering the streets and rivers with concrete structures. It was indeed the growing economic power of Japan that made this concealment possible; in the immediate postwar years, Japan simply did not have the resources to carry out massive construction. The real recovery of the city was deferred until the 1960s, and even when the recovery process began, the solution was rather temporary.

For instance, the prewar infrastructure, or the lack thereof, could not deal with the postwar increase in excrement. In 1960, only 21 percent of the Tokyo ward area had a sewer system; most household waste water was dumped, untreated, into local rivers.[82] Human excrement was manually collected from each household until the introduction of "vacuum cars" (trucks with a suction pumps) in 1957. Until 1953, Seibu Railways ran trains carrying night soil to the outskirts of Tokyo, where it was used as fertilizer.[83] The unused excess was dumped, untreated, outside of Tokyo Bay.[84] Though the Japanese media promoted Tokyo as an international city (*kokusai toshi*), those who knew its actual hygienic state jokingly called the town *kusai toshi* (smelly city) or *unkokusai toshi* (city smelling of poop).[85]

Tokyo managed to deal with the enormous challenge of concealing its dirt and excrement by focusing its resources on areas associated with the Olympic games. Although the overall sewer usage rate in Tokyo only rose to 26 percent by the time of the Olympics, areas within the Yamanote line, particularly around the Olympic facilities, improved greatly.[86] For instance, Shibuya Ward, where most of the Olympic facilities were located, showed a dramatic increase in sewer usage. Only 3 percent of the ward benefited from the sewer system in 1959; the ratio grew to 60 percent by the end of 1964.[87] In constructing a sewer system, the metropoli-

Figure 10. On a Sumida River ferry, 1963. Photograph by Tanuma Takeyoshi. Tanuma Takeyoshi, *Tokyo no sengo* (Tokyo: Chikuma shobō, 1993).

tan government chose the easy way out: it simply put a lid on the city's small rivers and creeks, converting them into a sewer system.[88] In the course of the rapid urbanization of the postwar period, such creeks and rivers had lost self-cleansing abilities and had died long before. Industrial waste water added to the pollution. Thus, when trains passed over the Sumida River, for instance, passengers shut the windows in order to protect themselves from the river's stench (fig. 10).[89] Along the river, brass products grew dingy within a day or two, and turned black within a few more.[90] What the constructions of the new infrastructure concealed was the persistence of prewar hygienic conditions.

Tokyo had to be symbolically cleaned as well: there were attempts to regulate the city by making its space more visible to police surveillance. The Tokyo Metropolitan Police Department implemented a series of crime prevention measures prior to the Olympics aptly called *kankyōjōka katsudō* (environment-cleaning activities).[91] The police regarded Tokyo's entertainment districts as hotbeds of crime and strictly applied new metropolitan ordinances restricting their business hours (they could not serve alcohol after midnight).[92] The normalization of juvenile behavior also became a major concern for the metropolitan police. Young people were escorted out of the entertainment districts to protect them from the temptations of darkness. The metropolitan police endeavored to sanitize the

Figure 11. Disabled veterans panhandling on a Ginza street, 1962. They were probably forced out of downtown Tokyo as the police applied traffic regulations more strictly. Photograph by Tanuma Takeyoshi. Tanuma Takeyoshi, *Tokyo no sengo* (Tokyo: Chikuma shobō, 1993).

environment and create a "bright and crime-free town" (*hanzai no nai akarui machi*). The term *akarui*, which translates as "bright," was meant quite literally: the coffeehouses that remained open all night and which were favorite hangouts for minors had to maintain a specified level of brightness.[93] In October 1963, the metropolitan police report proudly announced that the department purchased one hundred illuminometers (instruments to measure brightness) to distribute to its branch offices throughout Tokyo.[94] Clean and crime-free Tokyo would exist as a bright space where nothing could hide in its interstices.

The presentation of the town was also a primary concern for the police. The sanitization of Tokyo involved not only crime prevention measures but also regulations of bodily functions in public spaces.[95] Indeed, the metropolitan police were closely involved in the metropolitan government's beautification campaign from the planning stages. Legislation against misdemeanor and traffic laws provided the police the means with which to regulate activities on the streets. In 1963, the police focused on posters without permits, illegal dumping of trash, obstruction of traffic, and illegal construction. In the following year, the police added to its list the "crime of urinating in street."[96] After mentioning this addition in 1964, the metropolitan police report continued to pronounce its commitment to the cause: "The metropolitan police reinforced its guidance and control mainly through the street presence of patrolling policemen, and has endeavored to sweep up the malicious violators who would damage the capital's appearance."[97] One might wonder just how "malicious" the act of urination could possibly be (fig. 11).

The environment—both in the sense used by the Tokyo Metropolitan Police and in a more general application of the term—surrounding Japanese bodies was radically transformed in the early 1960s. The goal of the metropolitan police to produce a clean space within Tokyo may simply have been a general desire to complete its panoptic vision. This desire was part and parcel of Japan's attempt in the 1960s to construct a more modern, rational space in Tokyo, and such a space could be materialized only through completing unfinished projects of the prewar regime.

The Beautiful Body of the Atom Boy

> Mr. Sakai holds the Olympic fire. He was born
> at the moment the new fire of the twentieth
> century, the atomic fire, ended the fighting on the
> ground, and he lived through a peaceful nineteen
> years.
>> Radio comment, Tokyo Broadcasting
>> System, October 10, 1964

> I am a nuclear A-bomb. I search and destroy.
>> Nike television commercial campaign for the
>> 1996 Atlanta Olympics

Changing bodily images attest to the rapid transformation of Japan from the 1950s to the 1960s. In the 1950s, monstrous bodies reminded Japan of its past destruction. In 1964, the Olympics presented healthy, aesthetically pleasing bodies to metonymically represent the nation and its past. In 1954, Godzilla was awakened from its eternal sleep by American nuclear testing at Bikini Atoll and attacked Tokyo. The monster was the abject object of history—the pre-1945 memories haunting postwar Japan—that many Japanese could not reconcile. Its monstrosity signaled the loss that could not be comprehended or atoned for. Memory returned to the city of Tokyo as a monstrous body, mercilessly destroying what had been reconstructed since the war. The monster also embodied the fear of nuclear warfare in the minds of Japanese people, fear reawakened by American nuclear testing. The monster's destruction of downtown Tokyo invoked the memories of nuclear destruction in August 1945. However, even the awesome monstrosity of Godzilla was reduced to a benign cultural sign in the prosperity of 1960s Japan.

The destructive power of the atomic bomb was similarly tamed through the rejuvenating power of youth in the Tokyo Olympics. The body of the final torch carrier easily leaped over the preceding nineteen years of postwar history. For the honor, the Olympic Organizing Committee chose nineteen-year-old Sakai Yoshinori, who was born on August 6, 1945, the day of the atomic attack on the city of Hiroshima, only seventy kilometers away from ground zero.

The selection was perhaps largely media-driven; the *Asahi shinbun* was deeply invested in drawing a connection between the atomic bomb and the Olympic fire. The paper apparently scooped the selection committee's decision on August 10, 1964, a few days before the official announcement, and published the story of the *genbakkuko* (atom boy) with great fanfare.[98] However, the selection committee postponed its official announcement, originally scheduled on August 13, in order to refute any connection with the newspaper. The August 13 issue of the *Asahi* then reported the names of the ten finalists in the selection of the final torch carrier as if the decision had not yet been made. The nature of the relationship between the committee and the newspaper was not clear; some speculated that the official decision was leaked to the *Asahi*, while others believed the paper's reporting influenced the committee's final decision. To go against the reports would only hurt Sakai.[99] Through the appearance of a selection process, the committee perhaps tried to present its choice without overtly encoding it. Nevertheless, the result of the selection process was just as the *Asahi* anticipated: on August 18, the committee announced Sakai as the final runner.

In reporting the decision of the selection committee, the *Asahi* emphasized the aesthetic quality of Sakai's running body:

His nickname has been "antelope" [*kamoshika*] since junior high. His slender body is filled with youthful power. . . . his well-balanced body and slim [*surari to nobita*] legs are suited for a swift runner.[100]

Another journal replicated this description of Sakai's beautiful body:

Sakai is slender and tall—five feet nine inches and 140 pounds. His legs are as fit as an antelope's. He is a typical middle-distance runner. The beauty of his running is outstanding.[101]

When this aesthetically pleasing body was juxtaposed with the destruction of Hiroshima, the narrative that emerged was all too familiar: Japan had recovered from the destruction of the war. The juxtaposition between memories of loss and Sakai's beautiful body simply served to dramatize the marvel of this recovery.

Edward Seidensticker claims that the selection of the final carrier was politically motivated, sensing anti-American motives in the selection of Sakai Yoshinori. He calls this reference to the atomic bomb Japan's "self-pity."[102] However, pride rather than pity appears to be the more appropriate word for describing what the aesthetic body of Sakai represented for the Japanese media. A reporter for the *Asahi* described the general reaction at his paper as follows:

We thought the personal history of Mr. Sakai would be catchy. Hearing of the atom boy from Hiroshima, I envisioned a young man who had been born in that *pika-don* [the sound and light of the atomic blast] and grew up. I thought he would be perfect news. Afterward, I was actually a bit disappointed when I heard [that he had actually been born in] Miyoshi City, tens of kilometers away from ground zero.[103]

It was disappointing for this *Asahi* newspaperman that Sakai did not rise like a phoenix from the ashes of ground zero, defying all heat and radiation. Yet the association was powerful enough to let the reporter see Sakai as the symbol of Japan's complete recovery.

Nostalgia for Bodies in Pain

The victory of the Japanese women's volleyball team over the Soviet team also confirmed the narrative that directly linked wartime experiences to post-1964 Japan. Before the Olympics, the Japanese media began calling the Japanese women's volleyball team *Tōyō no majo* (The witches of the Orient) for their determination to win. The story of the embattled bodies of the players also bespoke the persistence of war memories in the postwar period. Only victory in the final game transformed the hardship of pre-1945 into fond memories. The drama centered around the transformation of war memories into a glorious victory by the "witches of the Orient."[104]

Daimatsu Hirobumi, the team's coach, authored two books that explained his coaching philosophy to a general audience. The books made it to the bestseller lists in 1963 and 1964 and sold a total of almost one million copies.[105] His writings and interviews from this period amply testify that Daimatsu's coaching philosophy was deeply embedded in his war experiences. Drafted by the army in late 1941, Daimatsu survived battles in China and Southeast Asia, and he participated in the ill-conceived Imphal Operation in Burma. For five months during the rainy season, he retreated with his troops, gnawing on raw bamboo shoots. During the retreat, his hemorrhoids became so aggravated that he could not walk. Although at one point he was ready to give up and be carried on a stretcher, he realized that once he stopped walking, he would only grow weaker and die. So, he kept walking through sheer willpower. Deep drowsiness threatened to overwhelm him, yet he kept walking, telling himself all the while: "Don't sleep. Don't sleep. You are gonna die once you sleep." Many others did die. He claims that only those with strong willpower survived. His life philosophy emerged out of his own survival: he could accomplish anything insofar as he willed it. He applied this philosophy to his volleyball coaching, repeatedly telling his "war experiences to his players and demanding from them days of hard training, as hard as severing their relations with their parents and siblings."[106] Daimatsu also insisted to the players: "Games are like fighting with real swords. Sports today are either kill or be killed. The metaphor of killing may not be proper, but second place means nothing. Unless you are number one . . . , [your efforts] are meaningless."[107] Having made it through the war, Daimatsu returned to postwar Japan to finish his war and to justify his surviving it.

That is, sheer survival was not enough to vindicate Daimatsu's life philosophy. After the war, he was sent to Ahlone Camp, a British POW camp in Rangoon, Burma, where he experienced utter humiliation. In an interview, he focuses on the British female figures in the camp:

> I will never forget my experiences cleaning Indian and British soldiers' feces with my bare hands. (He closes his eyes softly.) Even when my friend was shot and seriously wounded by an Indian soldier, the British female medical major left him on the dirt floor. He died in the end. (He bites his lower lip.)[108]

Daimatsu realized that there was something beyond his willpower, outside of his control. Willpower could not change the fact that he was a member of a defeated country. Encounters with feces and death—the ultimate abject objects of history—marked the incomprehensibility of this reality. Though not life threatening, another aspect of camp life was equally humiliating to him:

> POWs had to clean their female officers' rooms. Female officers ordered us to wash their underwear. Right in front of our eyes, they undressed and threw their underwear at us. If we did not wash them as they instructed, we were severely punished. They didn't even think of the Japanese as human beings.[109]

The fact that the officers were female added to the POWs' humiliation. The officers' nonchalant attitude in undressing in front of them completely deprived them of their masculine pride. Then, Daimatsu and his fellow POWs were forced to take the embodiment of their humiliation—the officers' dirty underwear—in their hands for cleaning.

Through his miserable experiences in the POW camp after the defeat of Japan, he learned the reality of war: "winning is everything." As a result of these experiences, volleyball became for Daimatsu not merely a sport but a means of Japan's historical redemption. Daimatsu aspired to make those who had not treated the Japanese as human beings recognize their error by demonstrating the determined spirit of the Japanese to win volleyball games. Given that images of women figure prominently in crucial junctures of his POW experiences, it was perhaps more than a coincidence that he strove to win by training female bodies whose gender specificity he denied. At an early stage of his coaching career, Daimatsu made a conscious decision to disregard the players' sex by demanding that his players overcome menstruation through training. After a series of losses, he realized that he could make a winning team only by subjecting them to the level of training that male players endure. Winning was the team's mandate, and menstruation would not excuse loss.

> I can tell when the players have their periods. Their sweat during practice is different from the others': they sweat greasy sweat. Yet, as they keep practicing a year or two even with their periods, they will have bodies that can endure the same practice even with cramps. They cease to have downtime. In short, whenever they face games, their period no longer hampers their performance.[110]

Daimatsu represented the players' femininity in the specific corporeal term of menstruation.[111] Disregarding femininity and overcoming menstruation were equated in his coaching philosophy with winning volleyball games. Furthermore, winning games was a sine qua non for Japan's historical redemption.[112] His encounter with dirty underwear epitomized his sense of humiliation in the POW camp. Therefore, his players' menstruation had to be repressed in order to redeem himself and Japan from the memory of humiliation.

Although two players were added from other teams for the Olympic games, the Nichibō (Dai Nihon Bōseki) Kaizuka company team, first organized in 1954, basically constituted the national volleyball team.[113] At the textile factory, the players were doing desk work full-time between eight and four, sometimes until six. Only after working hours did they begin their practice session. Their every waking hour was spent either in production or in volleyball practice; their resemblance to wartime Japanese youths under total mobilization is striking. The training regime guided by Daimatsu's coaching philosophy was Spartan. The players were expected to play under the worst imaginable conditions; for example, Daimatsu demanded that they adjust to the sleep deprivation they experienced with overseas games by sleeping less overall. Before winning the world championship in Moscow in 1962, the players were sleeping on average only about five hours. By the Olympics, their sleeping hours were cut even further, to three and half.[114] During the world championship in Moscow, some team members played when suffering from physical injuries. Of the six starters, one played with a broken finger, another with beriberi, while two others had colds.[115]

Daimatsu even refused to let another player quit the team when she complained of a chronic kidney condition. Instead, he gave her words of encouragement: "Once you give up, you are lost. Don't give up. As long as you think your illness is nothing, you can cure it. By playing volleyball with your heart and soul, you have to cure the illness from the kidney."[116] He similarly insisted to the other players: "Rather than being afraid of injuries, get used to injuries. Train your body in practice, train yourself so that you can tolerate injury."[117] Daimatsu certainly practiced what he preached when he injured his right eye during a practice session. Although the injury was serious (he eventually lost almost all sight in that eye), he refused to be hospitalized on the grounds that he needed to remain to supervise the practice. He stayed in the company clinic, which did not have an ophthalmologist. He kept going to practice sessions and visited an ophthalmologist nearby.[118]

Daimatsu also emphasized the ordinariness of the players: as individuals, he claimed, they were rather untalented. According to Daimatsu, the only condition that they satisfied were a certain height and some experience with volleyball.[119] However, these ordinary working-class bodies were transformed through hard training into a team of international stature. In the process, the image of the sport itself was transformed. Volleyball had been seen as an inexpensive, working-class sport, for it could be enjoyed with just a ball and a small amount of space (fig. 12). Okuno Takeo reminds his readers that volleyball belonged to the desolate scenery of the immediate postwar years. Daimatsu's coaching career began in such a workplace:

It was toward the end of 1947 that Daimatsu Hirobumi became a coach for the Nichibō factory's women's volleyball team. In 1947, Japan was still in the midst of the postwar dilapidation and dearth. Daimatsu had just repatriated in June of the same year after a long time as a POW. [When I think about volleyball], I envision girls suffering from malnutrition hard at playing volleyball—the only sport that they could afford—in a corner of a dark, filthy factory. Volleyball was a sport for the poor. It was a sport of factories, a sport for lunchtime and factory rooftops.[120]

Volleyball belonged to the immediate postwar years and to a society that was yet to experience material wealth. It was part of the daily life and work spaces of many workers. Furthermore, Daimatsu's coaching style suited the typical labor relations of the textile factories, with a male foreman supervising female workers on production lines.

The female workers and the union at Nichibō Kaizuka complained to the management about Daimatsu's training; he was called "Daimatsu devil" and "an enemy of women."[121] However, as the team began to win (they won all four major titles in Japan in 1958), criticism subsided and the atmosphere within the company became more supportive. The players' success ultimately brought glory to working-class life. The volleyball players became figures the workers in the factory could look up to. Daimatsu was excited to overhear one section chief lecture his workers: "Look at the practice of the volleyball team. They are not receiving any money from the company for their volleyball practice. Yet they are doing it for the company. I want you to work with half, or even one-third, of their dedication."[122] In wartime Japan, it was common to hear, "Think about the soldiers who are enduring hardship at the front." The championships transformed the volleyball team from a sign of exploitative practices within the company to a symbol of voluntary effort to a larger cause. Their victory vindicated Daimatsu's method, which was no more than a postwar equivalent of wartime total mobilization. In the textile factory of Nichibō Kaizuka, the volleyball players became substitutes for the wartime soldiers. Through the familiar trope of self-sacrifice for a larger cause, the players and the workers lived the wartime within the postwar. The bodies of the players, which were covered with joint bands and tape, were the remains of pre-1945 days.

By winning the 1962 world championship, Daimatsu and his team achieved their goal. They had sacrificed enough and were ready to quit. Within several weeks of the victory, more than five thousand letters poured in from throughout Japan; 60 percent of these letters urged the team to quit, while the rest told them to continue until they won a gold medal at the Tokyo Olympics.[123] Daimatsu's mind was torn, but what finally swayed him was the thought that he and his team could in-

Figure 12. Tsukiji, Tokyo, 1962. A riverbed was transformed into a highway and became a temporary exercise ground for office workers until the highway opened for cars. Photograph Tanuma Takeyoshi, *Tokyo no sengo* (Tokyo: Chikuma shobō, 1993)

spire national pride for the Japanese living overseas, for the second- and third-generation overseas immigrants.[124] The team had to keep playing volleyball not only as a national undertaking but also to reconfirm nationalistic ties with Japanese immigrants. Once the decision was made, Daimatsu subjected the fatigued bodies of the athletes to further rigorous training: "From a point-blank range, from all possible angles, I threw balls at the players with all my strength like a rapid-firing gun. Day in and day out, I never relaxed my hand and kept bombarding the bodies that fell on the floor and did not move."[125] Daimatsu and his players spent the next two years on the court, perfecting their battlefield defenses. Daimatsu's use of military metaphors to describe these practice sessions bespeaks his heightened sense of mission, a mission to defend the nation's pride. Daimatsu re-presented battle scenes in the practice court, shouting at bodies that had been shot, blasted, which had fallen on the floor only to stand and fight again.

Although the stories that Daimatsu kept telling the team were filled with his war memories, his memories had already been sanitized into fond recollections. He spoke from the safe location of the postwar era, the position of a survivor:

> The hard training that I received at the officers' preparatory school in Baoding of North China, and my experiences at the front in life-threatening situations— nothing but suffering and scarcity—now return to me, one after another, as pleasant memories. I relate these feelings to my players: "When you marry and have a child or two in the future, you will sometimes look back at your youth. When that happens, those who have many memories are the happy ones. Though it is hard now, you are making that happiness right now."[126]

Future victory transforms hardship into fond memories, but there is no future without victory. Daimatsu was a victor in the war in that he survived it, while many others did not.

It is ultimately his survival that vindicates his philosophy of life, not the reverse. His philosophy did not necessarily save his life; there were many who endured similar hardships yet did not return to tell their stories. Daimatsu's insistence on converting hardship into fond memory appropriates the voice of the dead. Only in their silence can he make his claims. He identifies with the war dead, admonishing his players: "What about you with this much practice? You are still alive and breathing."[127] Daimatsu in the voice of the deceased, or, more accurately, the deceased in the voice of Daimatsu, exhort the players to push themselves to their corporeal limits. His statement should perhaps be read backward: you are still alive on the court, so show your willpower, which made your survival possible. For Daimatsu, the practice court of Nichibō Kaizuka became a space where he constantly sought to prove his worth. He owed the deceased an explanation of why he, not they, survived the extreme hardships of the war.[128]

The war ended for Daimatsu and his players only with their victory over the Soviet team (even on the very day of the final game, October 23, the team had a four-hour practice session).[129] The Japanese team summarily defeated the Soviets in three sets. The victory over the Soviet team was particularly sweet since the Soviet Union had been one of the most detested countries in postwar Japan for its declaration of war in the final days of the Asia Pacific War and its detention of Japanese POWs in Siberia.[130] The nation eagerly embraced the drama of hardship and eventual success; the television ratings for the telecast of the game reached an unprecedented 85 percent.[131] In a poll conducted immediately after the Olympics, the majority of the sample groups (79 percent of 515 people in Tokyo and 76 percent of 743 people in Kanazawa) listed volleyball as the most memorable sport in the Olympics.[132]

By winning the gold medal, Daimatsu was able to show his and his team's worth to the war dead. Past memories returned to 1964 Tokyo through the scarred bodies of the players. However, in the modern clean space of Tokyo, the powerful drama played for a prime-time audience managed to transform players' hardships into fond memories and into the necessary conditions for postwar prosperity. In the nostalgic recollections of the 1960s, popular magazines invariably featured the Japanese women's volleyball team. Its victory was a key event in the trajectory of Japan's postwar history, and many have remembered it fondly.

Productive Bodies

The return of such painful memories to the volleyball court had already been captured in the language of rational production. The efforts that Daimatsu insisted on extracting from his players to expand their range of defense a fraction of millimeter every day nicely dovetailed with rationalization efforts at production sites.[133] Like the quality control circles introduced to Japanese factories in the early 1960s, Daimatsu and his team strove daily to improve their "technology." Extra hours after the regular workday were spent perfecting their technique. Even the team's achievement in 1964, as with any technology, was destined to be superseded. Yamada Shigeo, the coach of the 1976 Olympics gold medal team, estimated that the 1964 Olympics team could only compete at the high school level twelve years later.[134] Their level of play may not measure up to that of later players, but the 1964 team embodied a trajectory of progress through their practice and victories. The Japan of the 1960s eagerly consumed this drama of hardship and progress, which was replicated in many popular sports dramas.

Finally, the team's victory provided a sense of resolution to the memories of the past. The injured bodies of the female volleyball players became conduits through which memories of the past returned to postwar Japan. However, in the process of their return, these memories were transformed and sanitized into a motivating force for constant self-improvement in a daily training regime. The players' bodies may have been loci haunted by the memories of the war, yet they were soon caught in the regulatory forces of production in the bright and hygienic space. In this sense, the body of Sakai Yoshinori can be seen as a functional equivalent of the women's volleyball players: their bodies were icons of the past, yet they transformed memories into necessary conditions for the rational and national project of progress.

6

Re-presenting Trauma in Late-1960s Japan

Hegel remarks somewhere that all great world-
historical facts and personages occur, as it were,
twice. He has forgotten to add: the first time as
tragedy, the second time as farce.
  Karl Marx, The Eighteenth Brumaire of
  Louis Bonaparte

Repetition betrays the weakness of similarity at
the moment when it can no longer negate itself
in the other, when it can no longer recapture
itself in the other. Repetition, at one time pure
exteriority and a pure figure of the origin, has
been transformed into an internal weakness, a
deficiency of finitude, a sort of stuttering of the
negative: the neurosis of dialectics.
  Michel Foucault, "Theatrum Philosophicum"

IN THE BRIGHT, sanitized space of 1960s Japan, memories of the war lost
their reference points, at least according to the assessments of the writers
Nosaka Akiyuki and Mishima Yukio. Both Nosaka and Mishima, however, clung to the physicality of bodies as their last resort for a reconciliation with the past. In this chapter, I discuss these two writers' desire to
keep returning to the point of history, the defeat of Japan, which postwar
Japan was eager to leave behind. Both Nosaka and Mishima deploy the
literary theme of repetition as a means with which to re-present the
trauma of Japan's defeat. By reenacting the trauma through gestures of
repetition, they stubbornly refuse the contemporary signification of the
event. However, their refusal failed to counter contemporary social discourse, which contained war memories into a set of banal images. I will
first discuss Nosaka Akiyuki's two short stories from 1967, "Hotaru no
haka" (The grave of fireflies) and "Amerika hijiki" ("American *Hijiki*")
in the following section. I will then explore the historical significance of
Mishima's final tetralogy.

Before discussing these texts, it is necessary to outline the social conditions of 1960s Japan that surrounded the issue of war experiences. In the

eighteen years following 1955, the Japanese economy experienced tremendous expansion. The second half of the 1960s was, in particular, a period of unprecedented growth. After a brief slump in 1965 after the Tokyo Olympics, the GNP grew 2.2 times in a mere five years, at the astounding average annual rate of 11.6 percent.[1] The media called the economic boom of this period the *Izanagi keiki*: the highest level of growth since the time of Izanagi, the mythical creator of the nation. During this period, Japanese people worked longer hours than ever in pursuit of better living conditions, and the outcome was rendered in visible forms in their daily lives.[2] The "three imperial regalia" of consumption (refrigerator, washing machine, and black-and-white television) quickly saturated the market;[3] the three Cs (car, cooler [air conditioner], and color television) then replaced them as the new ultimate objects of desire.[4]

In 1968, Japan's GNP surpassed that of West Germany and became second only to that of the United States among capitalist regimes. The media made use of another historical metaphor to celebrate this year, which was also the centennial of the Meiji Restoration, by labeling the time the Shōwa Genroku.[5] Known for its prosperity and ostentatious cultural taste, the Genroku era (1688–1704) was invoked to capture a sense of exhilaration in the society. Government regulations on building heights were lifted in the mid-1960s, and the first skyscraper—the Kasumigaseki building—was constructed in Tokyo in 1968. Meanwhile, the television commercial for Morinaga chocolate promoted the concept of unrestrained development by repeating the jingle: "Big is good" [*ōkii koto wa ii koto da*]. Popular sports dramas on television and comic magazines invariably emphasized the virtue of the struggle for self-improvement. It seemed that audiences enthusiastically accepted these blatant messages.[6]

The euphoria that enwrapped Japanese society in the late 1960s culminated in EXPO 70, whose overarching theme was the "Development and Harmony of the Human Race." Over six months, as many as sixty-four million people attended the EXPO in Osaka. In the festive space of the EXPO, references to the Asia Pacific War were carefully erased, most notably in the exhibit on Japanese history in the Japan Pavilion, which leapt from the Meiji Period to the present without bothering to account for what lay between.[7] "Development" in EXPO 70 appeared to be a linear progression away from painful memories of the war. By the late 1960s, bright images of progress overshadowed the ghost of the war in Japanese society. The success of the Tokyo Olympics and the nation's ensuing economic growth promoted a linear image of history that reduced the war to nothing more than a necessary condition for Japan's present day prosperity. The hardship and starvation suffered by Japanese people during and immediately after the war became an integral part of the narrative that everyone knew had a happy ending.

As illustrated by the heroes and heroines of sports dramas, the hardship and starvation of the war were necessary for the success of today's Japan: nostalgia toward the past retrospectively rescued Japan's encounter with wartime loss as a meaningful experience. Many in Japan accepted this reconstitution of their war experiences. Some, however, expressed objections, but they were not necessarily able to articulate the grounds for their doubts. For instance, in an NHK TV discussion broadcast in August 1969, some college students stubbornly rejected the unspoken premise of the older participants, who had firsthand experiences of the war and believed their experiences should be shared by younger generations.[8] The participants who survived the war years emphasized the significance of their experiences in understanding contemporary Japanese society. In contrast, at least half of the college students in the studio objected to what they saw as an uncritical association between wartime and contemporary Japan. These students did not appear to have a clear theoretical position from which to articulate their objections, yet they reacted with a clear "no" to a nostalgic representation of war experience, denouncing the practice.

In the 1960s, Asia had not yet reentered Japan's popular consciousness. Although on an individual level there had been serious attempts to contemplate Japan's colonial aggression and its consequences, such attempts did not gain media attention until the 1970s.[9] The accounts of war experiences circulating within Japan were almost exclusively concerned with the suffering and starvation of the Japanese alone, often leaving out the violence that Japan inflicted on other Asian nations during the Asia Pacific War. Japan's colonial past had been excised from the popular consciousness. Through a selective recounting of war experiences, postwar Japanese society redrew its national boundaries; within these boundaries, Asian peoples and their wartime experiences remained invisible.

A 1968 special issue of *Kurashi no techō* (Notebook of daily life) provides a good example of this exclusive focus on the suffering of the Japanese people.[10] The magazine, which as its title would indicate, normally revolved around matters of daily life, dedicated an entire issue to stories by its readers about their war experiences. The "war" was here defined only as the Pacific War, particularly its last phase, rather than the full fifteen years of continuous military engagement on the part of Japan.[11] Moreover, Hanamori Seiji, the editor of the magazine, situates wartime Japan as the central battlefield of the war. Although the "total war" aspect of the Pacific War comes through clearly, the magazine omits discussion of the daily lives of other Asian peoples, as well as what Japan's war did to them. The narratives of shared suffering in the book presume and confirm a national space. Letter after letter describes the writer's experiences of suffering in detail, dwelling in particular on starvation. After going through the 1,736 letters sent in by readers, Hanamori confesses, "I have not read writing like this for some time, writing that moves my heart and sinks into my chest. As the selection process progressed, a kind of excitement ran through my body."[12] The editor never specifies exactly what it is about the letters that excites him; he assumes that, based on their common experience, readers will understand his excitement.

Moreover, even the students in the NHK studio who were critical of the nostalgic representation of war memories did not challenge the national space of remembrance. They objected to the privileged status of the war experiences within these boundaries. Their objections included statements such as the following: "The war experiences cannot be communicated in an 'aha!' form"; "It is not clear what you want to us to inherit"; "What is the use of accumulating records of war experiences? They are useless if they are nothing but bragging or complaints"; and "It has been said that wartime society was dark. But our contemporary society still seems dark and depressing."[13] Although the students in the NHK studio questioned the unspoken premise of the war generation that articulations of their experiences were inherently positive, in their attempt to verbalize their criticism their perspective was confined within national boundaries.[14]

War memories did not disappear from postwar Japan, but they saturated quotidian life as white noise devoid of its original impact.[15] In this environment, any articulation of war experience risked immediate banalization. For this reason, the students at the NHK studio responded with skepticism. However, the desire to return to the traumatic experiences of the Pacific War did not disappear with Japan's prosperity, since the narrative of progress posited its losses as the origin of postwar Japanese society. The familiarity of the narrative simply transformed the eyewitness accounts into clichés. A desire to return to the original loss was countered by the forward movement of the narrative: articulation of the war experience could take place only in the form of repetition, trapped between the contradictory needs to remember and to forget the traumatic experiences.

In this chapter, I focus on the struggle of two writers to deal with their desire to return to the original loss in postwar Japanese history while resisting the banalization of such a loss in the 1960s. The series of works produced by Nosaka Akiyuki and Mishima Yukio in the late 1960s attest both to their repetitious articulation of this loss and to their attempts to subvert this repetitious movement. Nosaka and Mishima felt compelled to return to this loss, finding their literary imagination trapped in repetition. As Marx claimed in *The Eighteenth Brumaire of Louis Bonaparte*, repetition takes the form of farce—the sign of human agency's subordination to material conditions. Nosaka's and Mishima's antiheroes are farcical because they managed to insist on their existence as self-caricatures in prosperous postwar society. Unable to make references to the original impact of the defeat, these writers' repetitious returns to the past merely signaled their nostalgia for the past within Japanese society in the midst of high growth. However, repetition was also their strategic choice: they consciously sought the radical possibility of recuperating loss precisely in a gesture of farcical repetition. By insisting on faithful—and perhaps excessive—repetition, the antiheroes of their writings could step aside, albeit temporarily, from the narrative of progress.

Nosaka's and Mishima's critiques could not be permanent since their articulations were made possible by the very conditions they wished to criticize. Their critiques of postwar society could only take the form of farce since they were articulated by annihilating the very ground on which they stood. A Foucauldian subversion of historical narrative through repetition can perhaps exist only as an ephemeral strategy. In the farcical gestures of Nosaka and Mishima, which oscillate between the contradictory desires of remembering and of forgetting, readers witness the enormity of the task of articulating war experience within the affluent, clean space of postwar society.

Neither Nosaka nor Mishima was involved in the war as a soldier; both writers viewed the war from the perspective of young men in the homeland. However, their experiences were much different in degree of severity. Their respective distance from the war—or the lack thereof—appears to have affected the ways in which they reconstructed their war memories some twenty years later. Nosaka constantly revisits the days immediately before and after Japan's defeat, when he was a starving teenage boy. In contrast, for Mishima, who had managed to dodge the draft, the war always remained abstract and distant in his literary work. The Pacific War returns as an immediate experience for Nosaka, an experience which he must struggle to overcome. Unlike Nosaka, Mishima felt a drive to make up for his missed encounter with the war by claiming spiritual immediacy to the war dead and the emperor.

Despite the differences in their manner of reconstructing the past, the war served as the single most important literary motif for both writers in the late 1960s. Both writers sought to swim against the tide of their society, which eagerly abandoned memories of the war in pursuit of material wealth. Unable to find any resolution to their relations with the past, they began speaking out against the tactics deployed by others to exorcise war memories from society. Nosaka and Mishima were also keenly aware of the effects that their objections had, deliberately turning themselves into sources of embarrassment to their society. Furthermore, both Nosaka and Mishima focused on the body as a crucial medium though which to reencounter the traumatic experiences of the war. Yet the body as a site of historical reconstruction had already been discursively transformed in postwar Japanese history. Scars on the cleansed surface of the "body" were rendered decipherable; they became the symbols of the past struggle that paved the way for Japan's postwar economic success. Nosaka's and Mishima's obsession with the body in the late 1960s stemmed from their desire to re-present the traumatic experiences of the war against received readings of the scars.

Nosaka Akiyuki and Farcical Returns of the Past

Born in 1930, Nosaka Akiyuki was too young to be recruited into the military. He was fourteen when his foster father died in an air raid in June 1945; in the same raid, his foster mother suffered massive burns and their house was burned down.[16] His father's death and the hospitalization of his mother transformed Nosaka's life. His father used to work as an executive for a company that imported and distributed petroleum. Thanks to his father's status within a company that had such strategic importance to Japan's wartime economy, Nosaka's family never suffered from shortages of essential food items during the war. His father managed to bring home abundant cooking oil to barter for other food items on the black market. However, the sudden disappearance of his protectors forced Nosaka and his adopted sister to live with their relatives—a widow and her children (his foster mother was hospitalized for her burns, and after her discharge, she sought the help of relatives in Osaka). For the first time, Nosaka and his sister were confronted with the food shortage. After a dispute over food with the widow, Nosaka and his sister moved out of her house, first into a bomb shelter and eventually to his friend's house in Fukui Prefecture. Lacking food and the support of close relatives, Nosaka had to take care of his sixteen-month-old sister, who eventually died of malnutrition. Nosaka never recovered from a sense of guilt at not having been able to protect his sister.

In the postwar years, after making a living through a series of odd jobs, Nosaka found work as a song and scenario writer for television. In 1963, he published his first novella, *Erogotoshi tachi* (Pornographers), which the writers Yoshiyuki Junnosuke and Mishima Yukio welcomed with enthusiasm. Nosaka's writing, which explored the critical potential of the banal sexuality within modern quotidian life, strongly appealed to both writers.[17] Although his interest in daily life remained strong throughout his later literary career, Nosaka soon began deriving the themes of his stories from his own experiences in the days immediately before and after the defeat of Japan. In 1967, Nosaka published the stories "American *Hijiki*" ("Amerika hijiki") and "Hotaru no haka," for which he received a Naoki Literary Prize in the following year.[18] Both stories are semiautobiographical, with Nosaka's own war experiences deeply reflected in their details. Yet, the two stories depict Nosaka's experiences in diametrically opposed ways, attesting to Nosaka's own conflicting desires to represent and to foreclose on past memories.

"American *Hijiki*" is an attempt to recapture the past by retracing the past to repeat scenes of humiliation. In the story, which is set in Tokyo, twenty-two years after the conclusion of the Asia Pacific War, the visit of his wife's American acquaintances triggers memories of the immediate postwar period for the protagonist, Toshio. Despite his determination to act with pride toward his American guests, Toshio ends up acting in a hopelessly obsequious manner, just as he and many other Japanese had acted toward Americans during the occupation. Furthermore, Toshio's memories are intertwined with his deeply sexualized images of the United States. His return to the past demands that he reenact his humiliation through bodily, sexual actions.

One day, his wife, Kyoko, announces to Toshio that the Higginses, a retired American couple who reside in Hawaii, will visit them in Tokyo. Kyoko became acquainted with the Higginses during a trip to Hawaii and hopes to reciprocate the hospitality she received from them at that time. As Kyoko begins practicing her English before bedtime, it becomes clear that the sudden intrusion of the United States into their household forces Toshio back into his memories of humiliating encounters with Americans and the English language. Before August 1945, Toshio's generation had little opportunity to learn English in secondary schools, since the wartime regime identified it as an enemy language and suppressed it from the media and society. At Toshio's school, English classes were replaced by military drills. Even when an English teacher showed up in his class on rainy days, the situation was not much better:

> "The only English you kids have to know is 'Yes or no?' When we took Singapore, General Yamashita said to the enemy general, Percival"—and here he pounded on the desk, his cheek distorted in a nervous spasm, his eyeballs bulging—" 'Yes or no!' What valor." (44/439)

Students were taught to hate the enemies and their language.

Once the war was over, however, the very same English teacher expatiated about how wonderful the United States was. Even then, the students did not learn much English from him. All Toshio can remember from those days are the phrases *thank you* and *excuse me*, which the teacher pronounced "San-Q" and "Ekusu-Q-zu-mee." By the end of the lesson, the teacher once again managed to reduce communication with Americans to the bare minimum, and in this case, a single sound: "All you have to do is smile and say 'Q' and America-san will understand" (43/438). In the end, Toshio learned his English in a more practical way. He picked it up from a souvenir photographer and used his new language skills as a small-time pimp introducing Japanese women to American GIs. These circumstances defined Toshio's relation to English: the act of speaking English reminds him of his own and his countrymen's humiliating behavior in the early postwar days.

The English language was not the only sign that announced the defeat of Japan to the teenage boy, Toshio. To Toshio, the impressive physique of American soldiers seemed explanation enough of why Japan lost the war:

> [T]he soldiers I was looking at now had arms like roof beams and hips like millstones, and underneath pants that glowed with a sheen our civilian uniforms never had, you could see their big, powerful buttocks. . . . What magnificent builds! No wonder Japan lost the War. (60/448–49)

The sight leaves a lasting impression. He admits he is fascinated by Caucasian males and their physical characteristics:

> Often in a beer hall I'll see a sailor at a nearby table, or some foreigner who seems shabby if you just look at his clothes, but his face is all civilization and I catch myself staring at his three-dimensional features. Compared to the Japanese all around him, he's a shining star. Look at those muscular arms, the massive chest. How can you not feel ashamed next to him? (54–55/445)

The homoerotic gaze that Toshio casts on Caucasian males some twenty years later resonates with the image of the victor that the teenage boy attributed to American soldiers. Male Caucasian bodies—the material evidence of "civilization"—seem to bring Toshio automatically back to the immediate postwar days.

Toshio was thoroughly impressed by the material wealth of the United States when he saw the bodies of GIs. Yet he maintained a distance from it. Memories of the war—the knowledge that such materiality was directly responsible for his father's death—stopped him short of completely accepting the allure of the United States. In contrast, others around him seemed oblivious to the inconsistency in their own behavior. When an American plane airlifted food rations for American POWs in Japan in August 1945 after the emperor's announcement, Toshio was witness to a complete change in the behavior of the adults around him. Two months before, they were fleeing from objects from the sky; now, they were swarming to them. His neighborhood association council expropriated the American food rations and distributed them to its members. When Toshio's mother offered this food before a picture of her late husband, Toshio contemplated the incongruity of the situation: "It was so strange—helping yourself to something that belonged to the 'American and English Devil-Brutes' who had killed your father and then offering it up before his spirit!" (69/454). The material presence of the food obliterated memory of the conflict: people scrambled in the city ruins seeking to satisfy their bodily needs, their present concern for the body displacing past animosity for the enemy.

Because his bodily needs were not satisfied, Toshio could not eradicate memories of the past so easily: his postwar condition of hunger was the direct result of his father's death in the war. Insofar as his hunger persisted, the past lived on in him. Although he and his family appreciated American food, there was far too little, and some of the items did not even give them any satisfaction. Among the expropriated food rations for the American POWs, they found some stringy black stuff. No one could tell Toshio what it was. However, one neighbor ventured that it looked like *hijiki*—a kind of dried seaweed—so Toshio boiled it. It quickly turned the water a rusty brown. After Toshio changed the water about four times, the American *hijiki* lost its bitterness, though it was tasteless and coarse. He learned later that it was actually black tea leaves, which he and his neighbors had never seen. But, by then, everybody in the neighborhood had consumed the entire supply of tea leaves. The coarse taste of American *hijiki* was not only humiliating—a reminder of their parochialism—but unsatisfactory as well. There was no nutrition in it. To top it off, after eating the leaves, he and his neighbors used chewing gum—another substanceless food—to cover the bad aftertaste. On another occasion, one day in 1946, Toshio and his family received "a substitute rice ration—a seven-day supply of chewing gum." He carried home nine boxes of chewing gum, each of which contained two hundred fifty sticks of gum: "It was a good, heavy load that had the feel of luxury" (53/445). That "feel of luxury" vanished as they attempted to have a chewing gum dinner, twenty-five sticks for each. In the end, Toshio exchanged the rest of the gum for corn meal on the black market. Chewing gum—an American food par excellence—impressed on Toshio's mind the superfluousness of American material wealth.

In his actual life, Nosaka needed to have food in his mouth in order to feel secure. He even learned to regurgitate the food he had in his stomach, and would regurgitate food for his sister.[19] The sensation of hunger was for Nosaka (and Toshio) a reminder of the past, of the event that killed his father and caused his family's demise. The need to eat all the time stemmed from a desire to avert the past all together. Nosaka managed to obtain food on the black market by resorting to petty theft. The fictional Toshio, in contrast, is unable to satisfy his bodily needs with black tea leaves and chewing gum. Because they lacked substance, the American foods failed to subdue Toshio's hunger, and therefore to conceal past memories.

Although a distance of twenty-two years does not necessarily diminish his memories of scrambling for food, the gap makes it harder for Toshio to talk about them. The younger generations do not share with his generation a nostalgic desire to revisit war experiences or the empty feeling at the bottom of these experiences. Even Kyoko, who also experienced the war as a child, detects and chastises the nostalgic elements in such war stories:

> You just have to forget these terrible things. Every summer they come out with new war stories, more memoirs—well, I just hate it. I mean, *I* remember my mother carrying me piggyback into the air-raid shelter, *I* ate those starchy wartime foods, but I hate the way they dig up the War and bring back memories of August 15 year after year after year. It's as though they're proud of having suffered so much. (62/450)[20]

Although about ten years younger than Toshio, Kyoko feels to the same degree a helpless feeling of loss. A mere child during the war and the postwar confusion, when she reached her teenage years in the late 1950s, Japanese society was already beginning to replicate American material culture. Indeed, she is more concerned with her guests' feelings than with Toshio's. Kyoko pleads with Toshio not to talk about the war: "It won't make him feel very good to hear that your father was killed" (62/450). The loss of his father, which will serve as a reminder of the past conflict, has to be suppressed.

Toshio's younger colleagues at work give him similar, though less emotional, responses to his war stories. With vague smiles on their faces, they reject his recollections. Their rejection is perhaps more complete since they even refuse to acknowledge the effects of his story: "At the company, whenever he would let slip a remark or two on the air raids or the black market, the younger men would smile faintly as if to say 'Here we go again' " (62/450). In order to overcome their indifference, Toshio feels compelled to exaggerate his story in each telling. In "American *Hijiki*," Japan of the late 1960s appears to have succeeded in trivializing the traces of loss in its society. Without the means to inscribe his loss on the vague smiles, Toshio desperately repeats and exaggerates his stories. But the exaggerations only lessen their credibility.

Waiting at the airport for the Higginses to arrive, Toshio resolves to act with dignity, to speak only Japanese to them. Making this resolution, he feels the "thrill of striking back at the enemy" (71/456). However, to Toshio's "Yaa, irasshai," Mr. Higgins responds "in faltering but correct Japanese, 'Konnichi wa, hajimemashite' " (72/456). It turns out that, during the war, Higgins studied at the University of Michigan Japanese language program and was stationed in Japan in 1946 as a member of the occupation forces. Faced with this unexpected turn of events, Toshio's defense crumbles, and he produces a few English words in response. From then on, the course of events seems set: Toshio is thrown back on the role of pimp, the role in which he originally learned English.

After dinner, Toshio sends Kyoko and Mrs. Higgins home early and takes Mr. Higgins to a nightclub. There, Higgins begins to show his true colors. He is just a dirty old American: while he cleans his teeth with a rubber string, he displays to the hostesses nude photos that he has taken. Toshio gets the idea to arrange the following evening's activity for Higgins and himself: prostitutes. Pimping seems to be the only way Toshio knows to communicate with this American male. Toshio's hostile feelings toward Higgins occasionally surface, yet he resigns himself to being a procurer of sexual services. By repeating such humiliating acts, Toshio's tragedy turns into farce. He wonders,

> Maybe he feels that same nostalgia, recalling the days when he was here with the Occupation. Considering his age, the time he spent in Japan might have been the fullest period of his life, something he had been missing and reverted to the minute he came back here. That might explain his almost in-sulting behavior, his serene willingness to let me go on buying him drinks. That's not hard to understand. But the question is, why should *I* go along with it? Why should I be so happy to play the pimp the way the grown-ups did back then? (83/463–64)

Toshio's and others' acts of survival after the war constituted a betrayal of the past: by acting in a servile manner toward the former enemy, they managed to repress memories of past conflict. However, memories of the past did not dissipate from Toshio's mind. Ironically, it is precisely his memories of the trauma caused by the former enemy that haunt and force him to be obsequious. The more powerful the trauma, the greater the deception has to be.

Toshio expects Higgins to be impressed by the new Japan. But Higgins seems unmoved by the scenery of post-Olympics Tokyo. Neither the downtown highway nor the neon illuminations of Ginza produce any effect on him. On the third day after the arrival the Americans, Toshio arranges for a live sex show to take place in a hotel room. The male performer, Yot-chan, possesses a huge penis, which his agent claims he gets a "complex just looking at" (85/465). As the show begins, Toshio comes to a sudden realization:

> The reason I'm doing all this service for Higgins is that somehow, one way or another, I want to bring him to his knees. I don't care if it's by drinking him unconscious or driving him crazy over a woman, I want to turn this grinning, maddeningly self-possessed son of a bitch on to something—anything—Japa-nese and make him knuckle under. That's what I'm after! (85/465)

Toshio's hostile memories toward the United States revive in his mind as he and Higgins watch the show progress. Now, Toshio has an opportunity to impress and bring Higgins to his knees with a physical demonstration of Japanese prowess. Toshio can finally pay him back in kind for the humiliation of defeat by the United States

However, Yot-chan's penis fails to attain its "heroic stature" in the show. Toshio reacts to Yot-chan's struggle with a nationalistic cry in his mind: "What the hell are you doing? You're numbah one, aren't you? Come on, show this American. That huge thing of yours is the pride of Japan. Knock him out with it! Scare the shit out of him!" (86/466). Toshio's and Japan's pride is at stake in the sex show: "It was a matter of pecker nationalism: his thing *had* to stand, or it would mean dishonor to the race. Toshio almost wanted to take the man's place, his own thing now taut and ready. Noticing this, he glanced at Higgins' crotch, but nothing was happening there" (86–87/466). Once again Toshio fails to generate any reaction—emotional or physical—from Higgins. Despite his frustration, Toshio can identify with the plight of Yot-chan. Toshio would take Yot-chan's place if he could. And Toshio knows perfectly well why Yot-chan cannot perform in front of Higgins. Yot-chan is in his thirties and most likely experienced humiliation like Toshio's just after the war. The presence of Higgins probably reminded him of this shame, and Yot-chan "recalled, as clearly as if it were yesterday, the hopeless feeling when there was no more fleet, no more Zero fighters, recalled the emptiness of the blinding, burning sky above the burnt-out ruins" (88/467). The defeat of Japan and the presence of the United States deprives Yot-chan's and Toshio's bodies of active agency: they can only behave in a cringing manner. As demonstrated in his short-lived resolution to speak to Higgins only in Japanese, Toshio maintains his national pride only as private thought. Toshio's penis is "taut and ready" for the time being, but it would surely become useless once it encountered Higgins's gaze. Pecker nationalism is an impossible dream for their emasculated bodies to sustain. The emptiness cannot be satisfied with the material wealth attained by postwar society.

Nosaka returns to the memory of American *hijiki* at the story's end. After the ill-fated sex show in the hotel room, Higgins again demonstrates his rude arrogance by canceling his dinner with Kyoko and Toshio, though he is well aware that Kyoko is preparing a sukiyaki dinner for him and his wife. Similarly, Mrs. Higgins leaves the house to stay with her friend in Yokohama. Toshio and Kyoko are left with large quantities of sukiyaki ingredients—Kyoko had even bought expensive Matsusaka beef for the occasion. Snubbed by the Higginses, in his domestic space, Toshio feels compelled to gorge himself, without a hint of enjoyment, on Matsusaka beef, the Japanese form of material wealth. He finds that the beef he is methodically consuming is just as tasteless and superfluous as the American *hijiki* he had eaten in the immediate postwar period. The American guests may have disappeared from sight, but the excess beef reminds him of their lingering presence in his home and inside him. The story ends as Toshio stuffs his full stomach with the meat, while thinking about the American inside him. The Higginses will eventually leave, but the American inside him "will drag me around by the nose and make me scream 'Gibume chewingamu, QQ' " (89/468). Toshio can never escape the American inside him who simultaneously kept him alive and humiliated him.

Toshio wishes to rewrite the past by acting differently in his second encounter with the United States. However, he ends up repeating his earlier obsequious acts in a society that had eagerly left memories of the past behind. Postwar Japan's economic success, driven by a desire for American material wealth, makes it more difficult for Toshio to adhere to the sense of loss and humiliation that he felt at the time of Japan's defeat. The markers of loss and even images of America as the enemy had disappeared from the circuit of desire: the Japaneseness of Matsusaka beef displaces the Americanness of American *hijiki* and chewing gum. Toshio resists by desperately clinging to the vanishing image of the enemy: reproducing the feelings of shame and consuming excess beef are acts of re-presenting the loss and humiliation of the immediate postwar period in the midst of the consumerism of late 1960s Japan.

Scornful Laughter of the Past

In contrast to "American *Hijiki*," in which the protagonist survives the humiliation of the defeat, "Hotaru no haka" begins with the protagonist's death before the arrival of the American occupation forces in Japan, and the narrative returns to this death at the end of the story. The narrative encloses the protagonist's death in nostalgia for the past; framed by death, the story rejects the time after the war. The protagonist and his sister live in a temporality that perpetually repeats itself, their quotidian life punctuated only by American air raids. They die pure deaths in the space called Japan before the days of humiliation in the immediate postwar period.

In a contradictory fashion, Nosaka simultaneously recalls and represses his war experiences by recounting them in a fictional form. In this story, unable to escape from the past himself, he feels compelled to re-present it in postwar Japanese society. At the same time, the story is also an attempt to contain his past experiences safely in a separate temporal location; the story becomes a literary device with which to escape the haunting memories of the past. In spite of the stories' contemporaneity, their foci are contrasting. In "American *Hijiki*," Nosaka attempts to reawaken contained memories of the war in postwar society through his self-caricature, while in "Hotaru no haka" he tries to contain the disturbing memories through their aestheticization.

In "Hotaru no haka," the protagonist Seita is a teenage boy, whose parents die in June 1945 during an air raid at Kobe. Left alone to take care of his four-year-old sister, Setsuko, Seita struggles to survive. However, Setsuko dies of malnutrition within days of the war's conclusion. Soon after cremating Setsuko's body, Seita also dies of malnutrition. Seita tries hard to protect his sister, yet in the end succumbs to the force of circumstances. This focus on the two children and the timing of their deaths are crucial in the story's aestheticization of suffering. The children's suffering represents their ultimate victimhood in the war, as they fell victim to forces beyond their control and comprehension. Furthermore, as these children never encounter the humiliation that Nosaka himself experienced in the postwar period, envy for the material wealth of the victor would not corrupt the boy and his sister in the story. Seita and his sister die pure deaths before any chance of an encounter with Americans.

Seita and Setsuko are powerless in wartime Japan. Without the help of parents, they are forced to face a society in which each member is merely concerned with his or her own survival. Even the relationship with their remote relatives (a widow and her children) who offer them shelter turns sour when Seita and Setsuko cannot offer food for the family. Once the food Seita and Setsuko bring with them is gone, the widow constantly taunts them with their dependency and eventually drives them out of her house. Seita and Setsuko move to a bomb shelter dug into the bottom of a hill. Because they do not belong to a neighborhood association, they cannot possibly receive food rations. Even though they use the money in their father's savings account and resort to petty thefts, the children's health steadily declines.

As much as they are abandoned by it, Seita and his sister reject wartime Japanese society. It is Seita's own decision to leave the widow's house and live on their own. Seita decides to remove themselves from a war crazed society. Although their choice is not an active resistance to the war effort, Seita's and Setsuko's nondependency grants them immunity from the war guilt. They refuse to participate in the madness and they have to pay the price for this with their own deaths. Even Seita's acts of stealing become signs of passive resistance against a society that pursues war goals at the expense of the "innocent." The tragic end of Seita and his sister thus separates them from the selfish behavior of others during the war.

Nosaka uses the image of fireflies to convey the notion of the past. In the 1960s, fireflies were fast disappearing from the Japanese landscape because of industrial pollution and the use of chemical insecticides. One night outside the shelter, Seita points at the flickering lights of a Japanese fighter plane flying westward. Seita tells Setsuko: "That's a special attack corps [kamikaze] plane." She responds: "It looks like a firefly" (30). Seita later captures a hundred some fireflies and releases them inside a mosquito net. In the dim glow, he slips into childhood memories of a naval review in October 1935. Seita is brought back to the present by thinking of his father, who is serving as an officer in the navy; he wonders about the war his father is fighting. The next morning, half of the fireflies are lying on the ground, dead. Seita's sister digs a grave for the fireflies, and then tells Seita that she has learned of their mother's death, the death he was hiding from her. The kamikaze plane, Seita, Setsuko, their mother, father, and fireflies exist only to perish under forces beyond their control, gone in no time. The war is transformed into an ephemeral dream in the quotidian life of Seita and his sister, a dream that must end when the morning arrives.

Setsuko dies on August 22, 1945. Her emaciated body was covered with lice and ringworm. Seita cremates her body by himself. He, too, is already suffering chronic diarrhea, a sign of malnutrition. Exactly a month later, Seita dies of malnutrition in the Sannomiya Station, and as he lies on the floor of the station, his body is covered in his own feces. The miserable deaths of Seita and Setsuko are the symptoms of the irrational war. Seita and his sister harm nobody; they simply suffer to maintain their innocence within this war-crazed society.

In folk belief, it was widely believed that the deceased returned to this world in the form of fireflies. However, even these ephemeral markers of the past disappeared from people's daily lives in 1960s Japan. Nosaka buries his memories of the war in the grave along with the dead fireflies, markers of the dead and loss. Nonetheless, memories of loss did not disappear as did the fireflies, which were physical reminders of the loss. Memories stayed with Nosaka in the form of a guilty conscience for surviving the war; these memories resurface through his body. Nosaka finds himself compelled to keep revisiting the memories that he fictionalized and cleansed in "Hotaru no Haka."

Nosaka later openly admitted that he had aestheticized his own experiences in "Hotaru no haka." For example, in this short story, Seita's sister, Setsuko, is supposed to be four years old, while Nosaka's own sister died at the age of sixteen months. Moreover, Nosaka was not nearly as considerate as Seita is to his sister. In Nosaka's own words, he "can say with pride he loved Keiko [his sister], but, facing his own appetite, everything—love or kindness—lost its color."[21] In "Hotaru no haka," seeing his sister suffer from malnutrition, Seita ponders whether he can feed his blood or one of his fingers to her.[22] In actuality, his sister's soft thighs before she lost so much weight whetted Nosaka's appetite.[23] Nosaka tried hard to feed his sister, but he could not overcome his own hunger, eating her portion of their food with very little guilt at the time.[24] His sister soon began to cry all the time, day and night, because of her deteriorating health, whereupon he began hitting her with his fist to stop her crying. Nosaka believed at the time that his sister ceased crying because she was afraid of the pain. He learned only much later that it was likely that she stopped crying not because she feared the pain, but because she had suffered from a concussion.[25] The memory of his sister is linked to a sense of guilt in Nosaka's mind, the guilt of not being able to protect her.[26]

The biggest difference between his actual experiences and his fictionalized account is the fact that Nosaka survived the war to tell the story of his experiences. He feels tremendous guilt for surviving the war, and this guilt has driven him to revisit the past constantly. In his semiautobiographical stories that he began to write in the mid-1960s and that invariably took themes from his wartime and immediate postwar experiences, Nosaka traces and sublimates the memory of bodily suffering. His creative impulse was deeply embedded in a desire to reexperience the devastation of the war. In the course of normal, everyday activities such as watching television, sitting at a stadium, or strolling on a bustling street at night, he found himself slipping back to vivid images of the days leading up to and after the defeat of Japan.[27] He sought spaces where he could be left alone to be enveloped by his "delusions." These memories led Nosaka to create fiction; and as soon as he wrote these delusions down, they disappeared. Writing for Nosaka was a form of exorcism. Nevertheless, this double movement of conjuring up and exorcising memory only created a new sense of guilt in Nosaka, who was aware that what he wrote was no more than "self-justification."

After experiencing the air raid of June 1945, Nosaka was plagued by a sense of alienation from his own speech, which seemed to emanate from another.[28] The seemingly innate world of language became a fictive world to him after his tragic encounter with loss. For Nosaka, the production of narratives constituted a struggle to remedy this damaged relation to language and the exterior world. Yet, his attempts inevitably failed since the loss always exceeded language; it was loss that tore his language from the external world in the first place. Nosaka was caught in a perpetual motion as he attempted to represent the unrepresentable, driven by returning guilt. He could never fully re-present past experience, and he suffered at the same time from a recurring sense of guilt for his trying to escape from these traumatic experiences. Fictional writing failed to remedy Nosaka's plight, although he had no choice but to continue writing fiction to maintain a relation both with the exterior world and with memories of the past, even as he confessed the fictionality of his work. The strange combination of fictional accounts of his own life and essays that confess the fictiveness of his fictions appears to have been a desperate strategy to break away from the cycle of guilt. By self-critiquing the "lies" in his writing, he attempted to distance himself from his feelings of guilt.

Nosaka developed a dependency on fiction writing, as it were, much in the same way that he became dependent on alcohol. Much like an alcoholic, in his sober moments, Nosaka expresses his regrets for his dependency on fiction. His struggles with past memories took a toll on his body: he was admitted to the hospital six times for liver problems stemming from his alcoholism. He drank to numb the pain of his recurring memories. In the conclusion to his 1992 autobiography, *Waga shikkoku no hi* (A monument to my fetters), Nosaka declares that he will stop trying to "atone" for the past:

> "Fatty liver" refers to a liver condition caused by excess alcoholic consumption. This tends to happen in cases of [alcoholic] dependency, reflecting neither a weak will nor the lack of control. It is supposed to be an illness of the psyche. The past is scornfully laughing at me. Even since the publication of "Hotaru no haka," I tried to resist this scornful laugh by producing writings that repeated the same theme in the so-called "*watakushi shōsetsu*" [I-novel] style. My past [writing] has been just a superficial, deceptive act of atonement toward the past. There is no way of atoning for the past. I will never again write *watakushi shōsetsu*. I am not sure of the direction of my drifting. But, I have stopped my atonement. That is at least probably a more honest attitude.[29]

This statement announces that Nosaka's struggles to reconcile with the past ended in a personal defeat: his memories of war and loss defied his narrative strategy of encoding. His literary journey that began in the 1960s reached a point in the 1990s where he had to accept the "scornful laugh" of the past.

The postwar period for Nosaka had been marked by a series of attempted escapes from the burden of the past. He barely survived the air raids during the war, then after the war fled from his guilty conscience regarding this survival. In the 1960s, he managed to bury his past and his guilt in the circular narrative of "Hotaru no haka." The death of his sister was transformed into a beautiful death, while Nosaka's own guilty conscience was foreclosed by Seita's death. Yet Nosaka was trapped by his story's very success. Nosaka claims that he has not been able to reread the story; he cannot bear either the emotional pain that the story conjures up or the deception that the story offers.[30]

Although "American *Hijiki*" and "Hotaru no haka" present contrasting strategies in representing the past, they communicate the similar effects of past memories. The markers of loss may be erased, but memories will not easily disappear. Furthermore, without markers, memories return as unfixed, ubiquitous anxiety in the form of repetition. In "American *Hijiki*," the past insinuates its presence through the repetition of bodily gestures and humiliation, resisting the erasure of traces of the war among the economic prosperity of late 1960s Tokyo. On the other hand, the narrative of "Hotaru no haka" participates in this erasure of markers by attempting to cleanse war memories through their aestheticization.[31] Only later did Nosaka discover that the memories persisted. They haunted and compelled him to repeat his escape from the past.

The Farcical Death of Mishima Yukio

> There was no other sound. The garden was
> empty. He had come, thought Honda, to a place
> that had no memories, nothing.
> *Mishima Yukio*, The Sea of Fertility

In contrast to Nosaka's acknowledgment of his defeat by the past, Mishima Yukio kept up his fight until the last moment. He was perhaps more afraid of living farcical repetitions of the past than of admitting his defeat by it. To prevent farcical returns of the past, on November 25, 1970, Mishima destroyed his own body, the privileged medium through which the past returns. In the years leading up to his dramatic suicide, Mishima authored a story of repetition, the tetralogy *The Sea of Fertility* (*Hōjō no umi*), which cast light on his struggle with memories of the past.[32] *The Sea of Fertility* provides a key to reading Mishima's death as a desperate attempt to re-present war memories in their original intensity in the context of Japanese society of the late 1960s. Mishima saw radical possibilities in the repetition of history; he attempted to repeat the past, not as a farce, but as a tragedy through his own death. Yet his suicide managed only to announce the impossibility of achieving such a pure death devoid of historical meaning. Facing the difficulty of articulating war memories in late 1960s Japanese society, Nosaka Akiyuki oscillated between a farcical repetition and an uncorrupted death in his literary representation of the past. Mishima, by contrast, sought to "unsuture" the ideological closure of Japanese society by cutting his own body open. His death, however, met with sarcastic responses in a society where memories of loss were becoming banal: Mishima merely managed to die a farcical death.

In *The Sea of Fertility*, the past keeps returning to the present through repetition: Mishima chose the transmigration of the soul through four phases of modern Japanese history as the central theme of the tetralogy. The soul of Matsugae Kiyoaki, a teenage protagonist from an aristocratic family, keeps returning to the present time of his friend Honda Shigekuni.

The first volume, *Spring Snow* (*Haru no yuki*) begins in 1912, when Kiyoaki and Honda are both eighteen years old. Kiyoaki's illicit love affair with Ayakura Satoko, the fiancée of the son of an imperial prince, ends in tragedy. Satoko becomes pregnant with Kiyoaki's child; then, although she manages to abort the child, she decides to renounce the world by joining Gesshūji, a Buddhist nunnery, in Kyoto. Devastated by Satoko's decision, Kiyoaki falls ill. Without seeing her again, he dies in despair at the age of twenty, leaving a cryptic message to his friend Honda: "Just now I had a dream. I'll see you again. I know it. Beneath the falls" (18:394/389).

In the second volume of the tetralogy, *Runaway Horses* (*Honba*), Kiyoaki is reborn as a young Japanese terrorist, Iinuma Isao, whose only wish is to die to prove his uncompromising devotion to the emperor and the nation. Isao plots with a group of young men who share his indignation with the corrupt government of the 1930s to assassinate political and financial leaders. However, Isao's own father, concerned with his son's life, leaks the plot to the police. Isao is arrested and indicted for the plot, but Honda, an established judge by this time, gives up his job in order to defend Isao in court. Honda's defense is successful: although Isao is found guilty, the court suspends the sentence. In the end, however, Isao manages to kill a finance minister, taking his own life afterward.

The first two volumes suggest that Mishima intended to portray a dialectical process and its final synthesis through the tension between the protagonists' destructive, self-consuming passions and Honda's rational mind. Throughout the tetralogy, Honda serves as a witness to Matsugae Kiyoaki's reincarnations in different human forms. Honda, as the rational observer, embodies mundane, this-worldly concerns, in contrast to the blinding passions of Kiyoaki and Isao that compel them to action and eventual death. The contrast between the mentalities of Honda and Kiyoaki/Isao provides a schematic binarism throughout the tetralogy, which ultimately becomes a binary opposition between history and individual experiences. To be part of history, individual experiences must be shared by others. However, the uniqueness of Kiyoaki's and Isao's existence refuses such historical signification. Their untamable passions present excess to history, threatening its very foundation. Nonetheless, Honda's rational gaze renders their passion recognizable to history.

According to his posthumously published notes, Mishima originally envisaged a symmetrical and circular structure for the tetralogy:

> Honda is already in his old age. Some figures appear around him. Although they seem to be [reincarnations of] the protagonist of volumes 1, 2, and 3, they have completed their missions and are all fakes. [Honda] searches for the

protagonist throughout the four volumes, but he fails in his search. At last, when he is about to die at the age of seventy-eight, a boy eighteen years old appears suddenly and shines with eternal youth as if an angel.[33]

When Honda finally encounters this boy, "he is pleased and grasps this opportunity for self-enlightenment."[34] In Mishima's original plan, the return of unique individual passion in history leads to an unmistakable, genuine reconciliation between the past and present: the past will repeat itself, not as a farce, but as a final resolution between individual experience and history.

Mishima is successful in portraying this tension in the first two volumes. However, when he moves to the postwar portion of the tetralogy, individual passion loses its intensity and the narrative seems incapable of generating a sense of tension between individuals and history. The soul of Kiyoaki returns to Honda in the form of a Thai princess, Ying Chan, in the third volume, *The Temple of Dawn* (*Akatsuki no tera*), and as a teenage orphan, Yasunaga Tōru, in the final volume, *The Decay of the Angel* (*Tennin gosui*). Both characters lack passion of their own and are mere shadows of the earlier characters Kiyoaki and Isao. Meanwhile, Honda manages in the confusion of the postwar years to acquire a large fortune through his practice as a lawyer, while his cool demeanor is reduced to mere snobbery. Even his role as an observer degenerates. For example, he turns himself into a voyeur in his search for physical evidence of reincarnation—a cluster of three moles on the left side of her body—on Ying Chan's body. He invites Ying Chan to his villa, then observes her in her bedroom through a peephole.

In the final volume, Tōru appears as a double of Honda Shigekuni rather than the genuine angel of Mishima's note. Honda immediately recognizes his mirror image in Tōru's eyes when he meets the boy for the first time:

> Their eyes met. Honda knew that the cogs of the same machine were moving both of them, in the same delicate motions at precisely the same speed. Honda's duplicate down to the finest detail, even down to an utter want of purpose, was there as if bared to a cloudless void. Identical to his own in hardness and transparency despite the difference in their years, the delicate mechanism within this boy corresponded precisely to a mechanism within Honda, in terror lest someone destroy it, the terror hidden in its deepest recesses. In that instant Honda saw a workerless factory polished to a perfection of utter bleakness, Honda's mature self-awareness in juvenile form. (19:434/62–63)

When the soul of Kiyoaki and Isao returns to postwar Japan as Tōru, it is transformed into a "machine" devoid of emotional excess. Honda immediately discovers his double in Tōru, who works as a signalman for ships coming into Shimizu Harbor. Tōru's primary function is to gaze at the ships; he is a seer par excellence.

Tensions between the observer and the observed, between Honda's rationality and Kiyoaki's passion, and between history and individual memories are dissipated in the mirroring of Honda and Tōru. Individual passion, that which defies the linearity of history and motivates the circular movement of reincarnation, is now saturated with the homogeneous progress of time. Kiyoaki's and Isao's passion is transformed into a mere consciousness of self within the everyday life of Tōru, and there is no more possibility for the dialectical process of history that Mishima had envisioned for the final volume.[35] In Mishima's vision, postwar Japanese society tolerated passion only insofar as it worked like a clock and conformed with the linear progress of history. Mishima was probably commenting on his sense of staring at a place where memories of passion could no longer be articulated.

Images of decaying angels constitute the central motif of the anticlimactic final volume; decaying bodies of angels are juxtaposed with Honda's aging body and the miserable physical condition into which Tōru falls. On the fateful trip to the pine grove of Mio during which he discovers Tōru, Honda discusses with his close friend Keiko Buddhist images of the declining phase of angels. Honda explains to her the five signs of a dying angel: "the once-immaculate robes are soiled, the flowers in the flowery crown fade and fall, sweat pours from the armpits, a fetid stench envelops the body, [and] the angel is no longer happy in its proper place" (19:422/ 53). Amid the peace of postwar Japan, Honda encounters the decaying angel Tōru. History has lost its antithesis, and the possibility of dialectical drama has degenerated to mere memory. In the uniformly progressing time of postwar Japan, pure passion manifests itself only in its disappearance, trapped in Tōru's decaying body. In the end, Tōru finds himself deeply entrenched in the contemporary society and history that he believed he had transcended. Contrary to the angel of history that Walter Benjamin portrays as blown along by the storm of progress, forced to gaze on what progress had destroyed and left behind, Mishima's angel is hurled into the dirt, unable to fly with his wings beyond the perimeters of history.[36] The storm of progress in postwar Japanese society left even the angel among the debris of history.

To read *The Sea of Fertility* as a historical text, it is necessary to excavate what it leaves unarticulated: Mishima's own war memories. There are structural, more visible signs that connect the text to the war. First of all, the period that the story covers is equally divided by the Pacific War. The story begins in 1912, exactly twenty-nine years from the beginning of the Pacific War in 1941, and ends in 1974, which is also twenty-nine years after the conclusion of the war in 1945. Secondly, Mishima was twenty years old when he experienced the devastating defeat of Japan. The age twenty has central significance in the narrative as the ultimate proof of Kiyoaki's returning passion. Kiyoaki, Isao, and Ying Chan all die at the age of twenty. The reincarnations and predestined deaths of the protagonists at this age reveal Mishima's desire to return to this moment of devastation. It was also twenty years after the conclusion of the war, in 1965, that Mishima began writing *The Sea of Fertility.*[37] Mishima's own forty years of life at that point were equally divided into two twenty-year periods by Japan's defeat in 1945.

Given his careful calculation of the narrative plots in his other works, it is highly unlikely that Mishima did not consciously construct the symmetry of the narrative in this tetralogy. Nonetheless, there is remarkably little description of the actual conditions of the war in it. Honda spends most of his time during the Pacific War studying various religious doctrines on reincarnation. The section in the third volume that corresponds to the four years of the Pacific War is primarily filled with summary excerpts of religious doctrine. It is only the beginning and the end of the war that receive brief attention. The only description of the visible effects of the war is that of Tokyo after the incendiary bombing in May 1945, but even this occupies only a few pages (19:143–45/130–33). Although the war figures as a central location in the structure of the narrative, descriptions of the actual war are conspicuously missing. Paradoxically, the war insinuates its presence through its absence within *The Sea of Fertility.* Its absence in turn reveals Mishima's relation to his own war experiences, or lack thereof.

The idiosyncrasies of Mishima's "war experience" appear in relief if we contrast them to the ways in which certain members of older generations experienced the war. Isoda Kōichi argues that, for the generations of intellectuals who were older than Mishima and who gained their critical perspective from Marxism, the so-called divine war was an embodiment of sheer evil.[38] Isoda uses the writing of Haniya Yutaka, who was born in 1910, to explore this distrust. Isoda claims that Haniya's generation managed to gain a critical purchase by positing an exterior to the war. Haniya compares his war experiences to life within a "huge concentration camp." The metaphor of a concentration camp enabled Haniya to envision an exterior to the "total" system of the war. The possibility of an exterior afforded Haniya and his generation a distance from the war. Maruyama Masao (1914–96), an intellectual of Haniya's generation, remained emotionally uninvested in the war and felt absolutely no shock when he learned of Japan's defeat. His first response, which he shared with his colleagues at the Army Maritime Transportation Headquarters in Ujina, Hiroshima, was, "It is hard to look sad."[39] We might think of this exterior

to Haniya and Maruyama's generation as "history." Haniya and Maruyama found redemption in the progress of time. The ordinariness and
predictability of history outside of a concentration camp provided a
means to measure the suspended time within "the camp." Identification
with the future and progress provided a basis for critical thinking.

In contrast, there was no exterior for Mishima's generation. As Etō Jun
and Isoda astutely observed, the war was a "grace" to Mishima and many
others whose teenage years fell during the Pacific War.[40] They lived the
totality of the war as an all-encompassing experience: there was no chasm
between their interior world and the exterior of history. Temporal progress came to a halt, and history consisted purely of the passion of individuals without causal effect. The acts of individuals escaped historical signification and thus remained pure acts. The inevitable individual deaths are
embraced in the suspended, exhilarating time of the war. Therefore, the
war's end meant to Mishima the destruction of this liminal space that
enveloped youthful existence with seemingly eternal excitement. Moreover, beyond the destruction and omens of death, a mundane, quotidian
temporality awaited them in postwar Japan.

In Mishima's *Temple of the Golden Pavilion* (*Kinkakuji*), published in
1956, Isoda detects the sense of devastation that Mishima experienced
when he realized he would henceforth have to live an "eternal future"
within history. During the war, Mizoguchi, the protagonist of the story,
embraces the idea that soon he and the Golden Pavilion will unite in their
destruction:

> I was almost intoxicated with the thought that the fire which would destroy
> me would probably also destroy the Golden Temple. Existing as we did under
> the same curse, under the same ill-omened fiery destiny, the temple and I had
> come to inhabit worlds of the same dimension. Just like my own frail, ugly
> body, the temple's body, hard though it was, consisted of combustible carbon.
> (10:53/46)[41]

The Golden Pavilion and the protagonist could share a common destiny
only in their final moment of combustion. The Golden Pavilion not only
is an embodiment of beauty, but also stands as a metonym for an "eternity" that transcends the protagonist's unimpressive individual being. It
stands for "transcending or at least pretending to transcend such things
as the shock of the nation's defeat or national grief" (10:71/63).[42] The
physical being of the Golden Pavilion signifies the return of "eternity" to
the defeated nation. The eternal flow of history judges individuals and
renders them infinitesimally small.

The destruction of this symbol of "eternity" and his own body would
achieve Mizoguchi's total identification with "eternity." However, that
final moment he dreams of never comes. The Golden Pavilion and Kyoto

are saved from American incendiary bombing, and the war itself comes to an end on August 15, 1945. The protagonist despairs over the shattering of his sweet dream:

> "The *bond* between the Golden Temple and myself has been cut," I thought. "Now my vision that the Golden Temple and I were living in the same world has broken down. Now I shall return to my previous condition, but it will be even more hopeless than before. A condition in which I exist on one side and beauty on the other. A condition that will never improve so long as this world endures."
>
> The country's defeat was for me just such an experience of despair. Even now I can see before me the flame-like summer light of that day of defeat, August 15. People said that all values had collapsed; but within myself, on the contrary, eternity awoke, was resuscitated, and asserted its rights. (10:72/64)

The protagonist is now condemned to live eternity in the form of quotidian life. For Mizoguchi, the drama of the war ought to have culminated in his own death and the end of history. Instead, Mizoguchi survives the war and finds himself confronted with the beauty and eternity of the Golden Pavilion, which mocks his wretched existence. The end of the war brings eternal torture to Mizoguchi: he is condemned to live the uneventfulness of the future. The trauma for Mizoguchi is not the loss that he suffers during the war but the missed encounter with the loss at war's end.

Mishima attempts to re-present the war loss in the text of *The Sea of Fertility*. However, what he manages to excavate from the period can be characterized as a nonevent: nothing happens in Honda's life. The city of Tokyo goes up in flames, yet it does not affect Honda's being as an observer of history. Even the tragic deaths of the other characters, the most compelling elements in Mishima's mind, serve only as a literary device that propels the narrative of the story: Honda, for instance, never personally witnesses their deaths.

In life Mishima shied away from a heroic death during the final years of the war, preferring to wait for the collapse of the external world. In February 1945, at the age of nineteen, Mishima was drafted into the army, but evaded service due to a fever he had at the time of his physical examination. According to his semiautobiographical account in *Confession of a Mask* (1949) (*Kamen no kokuhaku*), the doctor who examined Mishima mistook his fever for a sign of incipient tuberculosis. Mishima himself did not correct the doctor's error (3:261/136)[43] and even raised his hand when the doctor asked the examinees who had tubercular episodes.[44] Although Mishima had fantasized about a beautiful death as a young literary genius at the early age of twenty, he did not hesitate to flee from the reality of death, and even its shadow. Mishima recalls the scene in *Confession of a*

Mask: "Once I had put the barracks gate behind me, I broke into a run down the bleak and wintry slope that descended to the village. Just as at the airplane factory, my legs carried me running towards something that in any case was not Death—whatever it was, it was not Death" (3:261/ 136).[45] Prior to the arrival of his draft notice, the protagonist, Mishima's alter ego, was mobilized as a student worker at an airplane factory, where he witnessed the workers rushing to a shelter each time an air raid siren sounded. In the same cool manner that he observes the "silent, impatient, blind mob" (3:260/134) rush toward the shelter, the protagonist declares that what he is running toward is "not Death."

To be more specific, the protagonist, or Mishima, ran away from the death in the everyday life of the military.[46] A heroic death is unattainable in the modern organization of military: there are only statistical deaths. He leaves the final resolution to history. After hearing the news of Hiroshima's destruction, he waits in anticipation:

> It was our last chance. People were saying that Tokyo would be next. Wearing white shirt and shorts, I walked about the streets. The people had reached the limits of desperation and were now going about their affairs with cheerful faces. From one moment to the next nothing happened. Everywhere there was an air of cheerful excitement. It was just as though one was continuing to blow up an already bulging toy balloon, wondering: "Will it burst now? will it burst now?" And yet from moment to moment nothing happened. (3:323/217)

This is his last chance to attain resolution: he and the exterior—history— will disappear in unity. The protagonist even declares that he did not care whether Japan won or lost the war: he just wanted to "start a new life" [umarekawaritakatta] (3:321–22/216–17). However, he learns a few days later that what he was waiting for would never arrive. He must then face the prospect of the future in the agony of "everyday life."

> I took the copy [of the August 10, 1945, note of the Japanese government accepting provisions of the Potsdam Declaration] into my hands, but even before I had time to read it I had already grasped the reality of the news. It was not the reality of defeat. Instead, for me—for me alone—it meant that fearful days were beginning. It meant that, whether I would or not, and despite everything that had deceived me into believing such a day would never come, the very next day I must begin that "everyday life" of a member of human society. How the mere words made me tremble! (3:322–23/218)

It is not the defeat of Japan but the prospect of the future in the form of daily life that devastates the protagonist. He is destined to live a nonevent in the homogeneous time of history.

Mishima's postwar period thus began with this sense of despair. He cursed the perpetuity of history within his postwar fiction, but his project to bring an aesthetic closure to his war experiences existed only as an impossibility in postwar Japan. As long as he continued to live the everyday life of postwar Japan, it was impossible to resurrect the dramatic quality of the war years. To achieve a reconciliation with the past he left behind, the homogeneous time of the postwar period had to be rejected by passion. Accordingly, Mishima's dramatic death was an attempt to return to August 1945 and retroactively refuse the historicity of the postwar period.

Before taking things into his own hands, however, Mishima maintained a distance from quotidian affairs in the postwar period. With markers of devastation still littering the scene just after the war, the transition from war to daily life was not a unilinear process, nor did it happen overnight. "[T]hat everyday life which I feared showed not the slightest sign of beginning," the protagonist of *Confession of a Mask* discovers to his surprise. "Instead, it felt as though the country were engaged in a sort of civil war, and people seemed to be giving even less thought to 'tomorrow' than they had during the real war" (3:324/219). In the confusion immediately after the war and in the process of slow recovery, Mishima could defer his encounter with an eternity of everyday life, cursing all the while the coming of the inevitable. So long as the postwar narrative of destruction and recovery did not take a firm hold over society, he could maintain a critical distance. Action that defies everyday life is still conceivable in the first days after the war; for example, in the text of *The Temple of the Golden Pavilion*, Mizoguchi finally achieves his goal by personally destroying the Golden Pavilion. Nevertheless, the homogeneous time of everyday life that Mishima so feared caught up with him in the 1960s. Loss was being lost in quotidian life, while the trajectory from destruction to material wealth became part and parcel of the postwar Japanese paradigm. Mishima reached a point where he could no longer articulate his despair: his desperate cries against postwar Japanese society were lost in the white noise of everyday life.[47]

Nosaka's strategy of invoking loss in postwar Japanese society was not an option for Mishima, since for him an encounter with loss had been indefinitely postponed. We must turn Mishima's own explanation of his despair upside down to comprehend its ideological nature. His despair in August 1945 was also a strategy for not feeling the loss he actually suffered. It is in the moment of the final resolution that he would manage to assemble the fragments of his experiences. Until then, they would remain fragmentary and indecipherable; and, as long as they remained in this condition, Mishima would never have to experience the impact of his loss. Despair over the missed opportunity, then, is merely a literary device to externalize his unwillingness to confront the loss of the war years. Mishima hastily invented an "exterior" on the day when he learned of

Japan's defeat, shying away from the task of confronting his war experiences. Instead of direct engagement, he placed the blame on the "exterior." He could then argue that he wanted to, but could not, embrace his loss because the war ended in an unexpected way. Mishima's postwar efforts to confront war experiences were sublimated into resentment toward the exterior—postwar Japan—that he eventually came to equate with the emperor.

The emperor, who stood on the side of history by participating in the production of the foundational narrative of postwar U.S.-Japanese relations, embodied the everyday life of the postwar period for Mishima. By laying the ideological ground on which postwar prosperity could be attributed to the emperor's human and humane decision, the emperor concealed the drama played in his name. Although Mishima came in the 1960s to revere the abstract being of the emperor as the ultimate synthesizer of individual acts of passion and history (33:397), Mishima maintained a deep resentment toward the historical figure of Emperor Hirohito.[48] Only the emperor could have brought about the final resolution of which Mishima had dreamed in the final days of the war, the resolution to its drama and the conflict between passion and history. However, the emperor chose to act as a constitutional monarch—a human being—for the sake of order and history, relegating Japan's entire experience during the war to barbarity and backwardness.

Mishima introduced his conceptual distinction between the emperor as cultural ideal and the emperor as political figure in "Bunka bōeiron," not to advocate the reconciliation of the two, but to emphasize the impossibility of such a task. The chasm between the two was not an obstacle but a buffer that separated Mishima from his war memories. Mishima's postwar resentment toward the emperor could be called Nietzschean in its demand for an exterior world:

> The slave revolt in morality begins when *ressentiment* itself becomes creative and gives birth to values: the *ressentiment* of natures that are denied the true reaction, that of deeds, and compensate themselves with an imaginary revenge. While every noble morality develops from a triumphant affirmation of itself, slave morality from the outset says No to what is "outside," what is "different," what is "not self"; and *this* No is its creative deed. This inversion of the value-positing eye—this *need* to direct one's view outward instead of back to oneself—is of the essence of *ressentiment*: in order to exist, slave morality always first needs a hostile external world; it needs, physiologically speaking, external stimuli in order to act at all—its action is fundamentally reaction.[49]

The external world—the world of the master—must exist for the slave to express his values in the form of resentment. Like the Nietzschean slave, Mishima needed an exterior to articulate despair in the form of resentment. Who better than the emperor himself to serve as the "master," as the existence worthy of his resentment? In this way, Mishima was able to direct his "view outward instead of back" to himself. The emperor's human body "physiologically" represented the external world.

Furthermore, Nietzschean resentment is a sign of the eternal return of the past to the present (re[curring]-*sentiment*). In 1960s, Mishima struggled to represent the past that returned the postwar in the form of resentment. However, the past that returned was not his own but that of others. So long as Mishima enunciated his resentment in order to avoid a confrontation with his own war experiences, he could not rely on these very experiences to serve as the basis for his resentment. For this reason, he had to turn to the experiences of others.

Mishima's work of 1966, "Eirei no koe" (The voices of fallen heroes), enunciates his resentment toward the emperor who opted to act as a human at certain critical junctures. The souls of the soldiers who participated in the February 26 incident (a coup d'état attempt led by young army officers) in 1936, together with the soldiers who died as kamikaze pilots, return to a shrine where a *kamugakari* (séance) is in progress. The first voices that speak through the medium claim that they belong to "the souls of those who were betrayed" (17:525), the souls of the young officers of the February 26 incident. They accuse the emperor of betraying them when they most needed his divine intervention. In spite of this, the emperor chose to identify himself with the very political order that the young officers tried to bring down.

Next, the voices of the kamikaze pilots claim that they, too, were betrayed by the emperor when he declared in the postwar that he was a mere human being. Only by remaining a god could Hirohito have given meaning to the sacrifices these souls made. The voices chant:

When Your Majesty declared Your humanity
The souls that died for the god are deprived of their names
Without a shrine to be housed
Still bleeding from the hollow chests
There is no serenity, even in the divine sphere
. . . .
It is acceptable to endure the humiliation
It is acceptable to accept irrefutable demands gracefully
However, only one thing, only one thing
Even with whatever coercion
Even under whatever oppression
Even with the threat of death
Your Majesty should not declare You are human

(17:562–63)

At the end of the chant, the resentful voices of the deceased repeat the question, "Why has the emperor become a human?" In this fashion, Mishima expressed his resentment toward the emperor and postwar Japan through the voices of the young officers and kamikaze pilots.

In order to invoke resentment toward the emperor's human acts, Mishima needed to identify with the voices of others, the voices of slaves. Because Mishima directed his resentment toward the exterior to avoid encountering his own memories and speaking in his own voice, the voices come from the young officers and kamikaze pilots who reject historical signification. The twenty-odd years that had passed and the material wealth of postwar Japan, however, managed to render banal the disturbing quality of their voices. In Mishima's fiction, the dead speak only in unison, their individuality resolved into the categorical identity of *eirei* (the fallen heroes). The deeds of young officers and kamikaze pilots had already been converted into signs of the safely contained past. Their voices were barely audible against the white noise of banalized war memories that filled society.

Before discussing Mishima's dramatic death, it is necessary to return to the anticlimactic closing scenes of *The Sea of Fertility* and their betrayal of Mishima's original intention to attain an aesthetic synthesis between individual passion and historical time. Throughout the tetralogy, the youthful deaths of the protagonists serve as ultimate proof of their reincarnation. However, only the first three die at the age of twenty. Honda, himself seventy-six, adopts Tōru, with the intention of controlling the radical possibilities that Tōru's existence poses to history by placing him under his strict tutelage in the mundane world. If he was able to witness the death of Tōru as an utterly worldly minded man, devoid of the intense passion of Kiyoaki and Isao, Honda could then prove his ultimate superiority as an observer of the historical process. History would finally prevail over their passion. If it were shown that Kiyoaki's and Isao's passions had no impact on history, Honda's own inaction would be vindicated. For this reason, Tōru has to die as an ordinary youth.

This plan is almost derailed when, after learning the secret of the reincarnations and Honda's ulterior motive from Keiko, Tōru attempts to commit suicide by consuming methyl alcohol. Mishima's subtly constructed narrative offers little at this point to explain Tōru's attempted suicide other than his almost maniacal belief that he is the chosen one. However, even his act of desperation is merely a reflection of his transparent consciousness: it is an act of self-love, lacking external purpose in the end. Tōru manages only to blind himself and subsequently lives a reclusive life with his mentally ill wife. By losing his sight, he can no longer maintain his superior sense of ego as a rational observer. His consciousness cannot transcend the historical conditions of his time. Condemned to live in everyday life as a this-worldly being, Tōru lives beyond the age of twenty as a nonthreat to history.

Honda wonders if there is another youth who must have died at the age of twenty of whom he is unaware. Yet, by this time he has lost the desire to locate this unseen youth. Although it is clear that Honda failed in his experiment, his perception of his role as an observer of the historical process remains unchanged. Finding comfort in the Buddhist doctrine of the eternity, he muses:

> If to die meant to return to the four elements, to dissolve into the corporate entity, then there was no law holding that the place of birth and rebirth need be no other than here. It was an accident, an utterly senseless accident, that Kiyoaki and Isao and Ying Chan had all appeared beside Honda. If an element in Honda was of exactly the same quality as an element at the end of the universe, there was no exchange procedure, once individuality had been lost, whereby they could purposely come together through space and time. The particle here and the particle there have precisely the same significance. There was nothing to keep the Honda of the next world from being at the farther side of the universe. (18:619/211–12)

Thus, the declining body of Honda is not a source of despair in this eternal temporal sphere. By identifying with the invisible mechanism of history, Honda looks forward to encountering future reincarnations of Kiyoaki.

When Honda realizes that he has cancer and his death is fast approaching, he attempts to bring closure to his life by revisiting a trace of Kiyoaki's passion in Kyoto. Straining his ailing body, Honda manages to visit the abbess of Gesshūji, the woman Kiyoaki loved and for whom he died sixty years earlier. Arriving at the mountain gate of Gesshūji, Honda feels that he "had lived these sixty years only to come again" (18:638/ 228). He needs the abbess as a witness and accomplice to his lifelong project of containing and encoding Kiyoaki's passion. Reminding the abbess of the plight of Kiyoaki sixty years earlier would transform his ever-returning passion into a pleasant memory. Memories, however, have their final revenge on Honda. When Honda prompts the abbess to recall Matsugae Kiyoaki, she insists that there was never such a person in her life. The abbess is firm on this point:

> No, Mr. Honda, I have forgotten none of the blessings that were mine in the other world. But I fear I have never heard the name Matsugae Kiyoaki. Don't you suppose, Mr. Honda, that there never was such a person? You seem convinced that there was; but don't you suppose that there was no such person from the beginning, anywhere? (18:645/234–35)

Shaken by the abbess's flat denial, Honda tries to refute her assertion with material evidence. But the seed of doubt quickly takes root in his mind, and he is compelled to retort: "If there was no Kiyoaki, then there was no Isao. There was no Ying Chan, and who knows, perhaps there has been no I" (18:646/235).

To his desperate rebuttal, the abbess replies: "That too is as it is in each heart" (18:646/235). Honda's project to find a resolution to the tension created by Kiyoaki's passion within the eternity of history is miserably crushed at the very moment he completes it. If there is no passion, the antithesis to history, then history itself does not exist. Devastated by his conversation with the abbess, Honda contemplates the emptiness of the garden of Gesshūji. Standing in this "bright, quiet garden, without striking features," he reflects: "There was no other sound [than the shrilling of cicadas]. The garden was empty. He had come, thought Honda, to a place that had no memories, nothing" (18:647/236). Honda ends his sixty-year journey overwhelmed by a sense of impossibility. There is no antithesis to history, let alone a synthesis between individual passion and history. The final resolution he had envisioned can be attained only as an erasure of history.

Peaceful, Peaceful Japan

Like Honda, Mishima found the late 1960s a time when memories, even of passion, were fast disappearing. Yet Mishima kept waiting for a final resolution. In the late 1960s, Mishima thought he saw one last chance in the social turmoil created by radical youths. American involvement in Vietnam spurred controversy among leftists over Japan's role in the war and, by extension, the United States–Japan Security Treaty that incorporated Japan in the U.S. strategic plan for East Asia. The reversion of Okinawa and the treaty, which could be terminated in 1970, became the focal points for leftist political protests. Rejecting the authority of the Japan Communist Party, radical sects and the Zenkyōtō (All-Japan Student Joint Struggle Councils) constituted the core of the New Left movement on university campuses. This movement took the initiative by adopting more confrontational tactics in its political rallies. Mishima saw the "international anti-war day" scheduled on October 21, 1969, as a possible turning point in postwar Japanese history, believing that the revolutionary situation created by the leftists would necessitate deployment of the Self-Defense Forces for the defense of the national polity. In the "manifesto" he prepared before his death, Mishima claims that he was ready to sacrifice his life with the members of his own paramilitary group, the Tatenokai

(Shield Society), in order to "rectify the nation's warped foundation" (34:528).[50] This was an opportunity, Mishima hoped, for postwar Japan to reconcile itself with its legacies from before 1945 by recognizing the Self-Defense Forces as a national military. Postwar Japan could reembrace its pre-1945 incarnation by reclaiming what had been renounced—war memories—for the sake of maintaining its quotidian order. Moreover, this reconciliation would be a violent process; by participating in the violence, Mishima could also reconcile himself with his own past left behind in August 1945.

However, his hope for a final resolution was frustrated again. The riot police, thirty-two thousand strong, had little problem keeping the rallies of October 21 under control; there was absolutely no need to mobilize the Self-Defense Forces. Mishima was bitterly disappointed and decided to take matters in his own hands. In his final bodily performance, Mishima single-handedly attempted to destroy the postwar paradigm that originated in the foundational narrative of postwar U.S.-Japanese relations, the everyday life that Mizoguchi so detested in *The Temple of the Golden Pavilion*.

On November 25, 1970, Mishima and four members of the Shield Society took Commandant Masuda hostage at the Ichigaya headquarters of the Self-Defense Forces.[51] They demanded that Mishima be given the opportunity to speak to the members of the entire Eastern Division of soldiers. The officer in charge complied, and Mishima began to give a speech based on his "manifesto" to about eight hundred men from the Eastern Division. Mishima urged the members of the Self-Defense Forces who were gathered there to revolt against the present restrictions in order to establish themselves as the national military. Mishima argued that the Self-Defense Forces had come to embody the postwar Japanese contradiction as defenders of the very constitutional system that prohibited the existence of national military forces (34:529). Only the Self-Defense Forces possessed the potential to challenge the deception that had corrupted the Japanese spirit. Mishima presented his case as a crisis of Japanese nationalism and vehemently urged the members of the force to break out of the U.S. hegemony (34:530).

However, his final desperate plea was jeered by his audience and drowned out by the noise of a helicopter hovering over the headquarters. Mishima's attempt to articulate the contradictions of postwar Japanese society (which Masao Miyoshi aptly calls "body speech") was reduced to pantomime (fig. 13).[52] After seven minutes of speech, Mishima abruptly shouted "Tennō heika banzai" [Long live the emperor] and retired. He then committed the ritual suicide; a Tatenokai member, Morita Masa-

Figure 13. Mishima gives his final speech at the Ichigaya headquarters of the Self-Defense Forces, November 25, 1970. Courtesy of Mainichi shinbunsha.

katsu, completed the rite by cutting off Mishima's head with a sword. Morita died in the same way with the help of another Tatenokai member.

With his bodily pain, Mishima tried to authenticate the voice through which he spoke his resentment. Mishima re-presented the past in order to challenge the complacency of the present. By dying, Mishima made sure that the past would return through his body, as a onetime event, its impact on history intact. However, Mishima's action merely proved the impossibility of his longed-for resolution. Although his death drew considerable attention—it generated revenue for both the news media and scholars—it made no dent in the everyday life of postwar Japan. Mishima asked the journalist Tokuoka Takao to witness the event on November 25. After hearing, outside the building, of Mishima's death inside, Tokuoka left shocked and fatigued. When he arrived at the slope leading to the main gate, he witnessed an incredible scene:

I saw several staff members playing volleyball a short distance away . . . around the area where the war records library used to be, on the right hand side of the street. It might have been a lunch break. There were four or five women and one or two men. This was the wonderful scenery of peaceful, peaceful Japan—it could not have been more peaceful. I felt nauseated.[53]

Mishima's death did not inspire any action among the members of the Self-Defense Forces, nor did it cause turmoil in society at large. His death was absolutely ineffectual. Tokuoka felt nauseated when he saw that peaceful, everyday life turned a deaf ear to Mishima's desperate cry.[54]

In the same month as Mishima's death, Toshiba EMI released a recording of a song that clearly marked this peaceful everyday life in postwar Japan. The song was entitled "Sensō o shiranai kodomotachi" (Children who don't know the war).[55] It has been remembered as a song that captured the optimism of late 1960s Japan.[56] A cheerful melody accompanies lyrics that celebrate the arrival of a new generation without experiences of the war:

After the war was over, we were born
Without knowing the war, we grew up
Grown up to be adults, we begin walking
Singing songs of peace
We want you to remember our names
It is children who don't know the war

If it is not allowed because I am too young
If it is not allowed because my hair is too long
The only thing left for me
Is to sing holding back my tears
We want you to remember our names
It is children who don't know the war

Fond of blue skies, fond of flower petals
Always smiling, wonderful person
Whoever it is, let's walk on together
Along the path the beautiful setting sun shines on
We want you to remember our names
It is children who don't know the war[57]
            (Used by permission of JASRAC
            License no. 9905441–901 © 1970 by MBS Planning Corporation)

The song announced a closure to the postwar struggle with war memories. The postwar youths who grew up "without knowing the war" claimed their rightful place in society. They had no experience of the war. They knew, however, how to enjoy peace. War memories were reduced to a perfunctory signifier, which haunted the postwar period only through their disappearance. Under the *akarusa* (brightness) of the "setting sun," the generation that did not "know the war" affirmed its own progress.

Mishima was well aware that passion had already been rendered benign, tamed in everyday life, just as Yasunaga Tōru was condemned to live as an ordinary being. Passion may return to the present, but only as farce, only to confirm what is in place in postwar Japanese society. Mishima tried to escape from the complacence of everyday life by re-presenting deeds of passion in postwar society. Yet, in his attempt to re-present the past in its original intensity, he merely managed to present the original event—his death—without its intensity. Mishima ironically demonstrated the extent to which the paradigm of postwar society has taken root. As Tokuoka saw on November 25, 1970, in its futility, Mishima's violent death underscored the entrenchment of peaceful everyday life.

The postwar struggle to contain the past began with the production of the foundational narrative and came to closure in the late 1960s. Even the sutures that foreclosed painful war memories were fast disappearing from Japanese society. Nosaka Akiyuki and Mishima Yukio reinvoked the past through re-marking wounds and sutures on Japanese bodies. Through the gesture of repetition, Nosaka and Mishima attempted to articulate their own war memories. However, their desperate critiques were ineffectual: their writings and acts failed to spark discussions of the war's legacies in Japan. It was only when the international political conditions of the Cold War (the condition that enabled Japanese society to forget its past) began crumbling in the following decades, that Japanese society seriously turned its attention to its own war and colonial memories. In the late 1960s, Nosaka and Mishima appeared more like the "setting sun" that shed its last ray on the path that the new generation was about to take.

Conclusion _____

JAPAN'S STRUGGLE to redefine itself by revamping the memories of its war loss culminated in a peaceful, prosperous everyday life in the late 1960s. The shattered image of the nation was reassembled, sutured, and rehabilitated during the quarter century following defeat. After struggling with its conflicting desire both to re-member and to forget its loss, postwar Japan managed to restore nationhood through a teleology of progress and the country's newly acquired material wealth. This recuperation of nationhood was an integral part of re-membering the past. Bodily images in popular culture that metonymically expressed Japan's nationhood were also transformed in the first twenty-five years of the postwar period. The malnourished and lice-infested bodies present immediately after Japan's defeat were physically and discursively recast as clean and productive by the late 1960s; bodies were detached from the memories of Japan's loss and cleansed of the nation's dirt, its memories of war.

Japan's efforts to distance itself from the legacies of the Asia Pacific War were aided by American Cold War politics. As I argued in chapter 1, the United States needed Japan as an ally in the Cold War, and Japan actively supported the U.S. hegemony in East Asia. The foundational narrative of postwar relations not only consolidated the two countries as allies but also turned the attention of Japanese society away from the country's colonial past. Japan was protected from its own past, so to speak, in this Cold War political paradigm.

As an example, the U.S. military was willing to conceal one of the most atrocious war crimes committed by the Japanese army. At various locations in Manchuguo, from 1936 until Japan's defeat, Unit 731, the biological warfare unit, killed more than three thousand human subjects (mostly Chinese) in experimenting on how to spread deadly pathogens (anthrax, cholera, plague, tetanus, typhoid, yellow fever, and many others) most effectively.[1] Immediately after the war, the U.S. military made a deal with the researchers who participated in the development of the bacteriological weapons: they gained immunity from prosecution for the crimes they committed in exchange for information about these weapons. The U.S. military leaders tried to secure this information lest the Soviet Union acquire it and undermine the U.S. national security. The conflict between the two superpowers overshadowed the local memories of Unit 731's atrocities: Japan's war experiences were transformed into useful information for the U.S. effort to fight the Cold War.

The United States also needed an economically strong Japan for its Cold War policy in East Asia. Not wanting to hamper the recovery of the Japanese economy, the United States insisted that Japan pay no reparations for its acts of aggression. Only four Asian countries—Indonesia, the Philippines, Vietnam, and Burma—maintained their claims to reparations from Japan in the San Francisco peace treaty. The terms of Japan's reparation payments were left to bilateral negotiations between the individual countries and Japan. Through prolonged negotiations, the Japanese government managed to gain key concessions from each of these countries: as a result, Japan ended up paying a smaller amount of money over a longer period of time. The payment of reparations, therefore, did not pose a great burden on Japanese society, whose economy was already moving into a high-growth phase.[2] In the end, Japan compensated twenty-eight countries, including a separately negotiated economic aid package with Korea.[3] Japan's total monetary payment amounted to 657 billion yen, or about five thousand yen (about twenty dollars at the 1980 yen-dollar exchange rate) per capita. Government officials saw the reparations and economic aid to other Asian countries, not necessarily as an acceptance of Japan's guilt, but as a foothold on economic advances into the region.[4]

Japan also heavily relied on the United States for its defense structure and did not make a heavy military commitment. The relatively low profile of Japan's Self-Defense Forces helped to evade the issues of military legacies in postwar society and keep the cost of defense low. Under the Cold War paradigm, Japan economically flourished while moving away from its wartime memories. This political paradigm, which strongly encouraged Japan's recovery after the war, culminated in the late 1960s and early 1970s with the U.S. involvement in the Vietnam War. Boosted by U.S. war procurements, the Japanese economy's astounding growth transformed the way Japanese bodies were discursively constructed. During the Vietnam War, the process of cleansing and dehistoricizing Japanese bodies, which began after the Asia Pacific War, reached its height. Just as bodies were cleansed of the traces of the past, Japan's nationhood was reconstructed through ahistorical, transparent images. *Nihonjinron* discourse, which portrayed a Japan that transcended its historical conditions, began to flourish.

However, just as the process of forgetting was completed within Japan, the external conditions that supported this process began to show signs of stress. In particular, the oil crisis of 1973 deeply shocked Japan: it threatened the bipolar structure of international politics on which Japan built its prosperous society. In the midst of the 1973 Arab-Israeli war, Middle Eastern countries demonstrated that they had an effective means—petroleum—to make their voices heard. A panic ensued in Japan, and the cleanliness of Japanese bodies was carefully guarded.

In October and November 1973, toilet paper became the hottest commodity in Japan. Sparked by the oil crisis and fear of a shortage of paper products, residents of *danchi* began lining up at stores and stocking up on toilet paper, facial tissue, disposable diapers, and sanitary napkins. A Shizuoka City resident managed to purchase a thousand rolls of toilet paper, enough to last five years if his family used four rolls a week.[5] The panic reportedly originated in early November in a northeastern part of Osaka, an area with a number of newly developed *danchi* complexes, and spread to the west and then to the eastern part of Japan.[6] The residents of these complexes knew that they needed imported oil to support their modern lifestyle and the cleanliness of *danchi*. The items hoarded expanded to include heating oil, detergent, matches, sugar, and even salt.[7] This surge in demand for such basic consumer items raised prices dramatically; in some areas, the price of a roll of toilet paper tripled within a few weeks.[8] The demand was such that petty theft of toilet paper rolls became rampant in Osaka's public buildings.

By the 1970s, Japanese society was already aware of the changing international political climate through its relation with the United States. So-called Nixon shocks—the establishment of diplomatic relations with the People's Republic of China and the implementation of dollar protection measures in 1971—alarmed the Japanese leadership since they signaled shifts in the political environment surrounding Japan. Yet, the 1973 war in the Middle East shook Japan's sense of security most severely because it threatened the basis of Japan's high growth economy—the stable supply of inexpensive oil. Tanaka Kakuei, who was inaugurated as prime minister in July 1972, optimistically proposed his plan to rebuild Japan's entire industrial structure on the assumption that a cheap supply of oil would continue into the indefinite future. In *Building a New Japan*, Tanaka claimed without a hint of concern that "Japan brings 92 percent of its total [petroleum] imports from the Middle East sources," and added that, "thanks to the use of giant tankers, it is just as if Japan had the world's largest oil field within its own borders."[9] This reliance on the Middle East for Japan's vital resource was actually, according to Tanaka, advantageous to Japan's economy.

The Arab-Israeli conflict, however, revealed Tanaka's optimism to be hollow. On October 6, 1973, Egypt and Syria launched surprise attacks on Israel. Although a cease-fire was declared sixteen days later, oil-producing countries that participated in the conflict began using oil as a strategic commodity in rallying international support for their cause. On October 17, six countries in the Persian Gulf raised the price of oil by 21 percent, and the Organization of Arab Petroleum Exporting Countries announced that it would reduce its exports to pro-Israel countries by 5 percent.

The fear of an oil shortage immediately undermined the image of a prosperous Japanese society, and many Japanese responded to this crisis by stocking up on what they believed to be the essential items of their daily life. There had already been signs of a paper shortage earlier in 1973. Social awareness of industrial pollution cases in the early 1970s slowed down the growth of paper production, while the demand for newspaper stock increased during the same period. Furthermore, the prospect of a shortage made paper an object for speculation, and dealers kept large quantities in reserve.[10] The Middle East crisis, however, proved an even greater threat since, had the supplies of petroleum from the Middle East been cut off, the entire distribution system in Japan would have been disrupted, and everyday items could have been in dire demand. Importantly, Japanese consumers first focused on hygienic items, including toilet paper, sanitary napkins, disposable diapers, and detergent. The modern style of living necessitated such items of convenience; yet the buying frenzy of toilet paper rolls in 1973 resulted from more than just material necessity.[11] It was also an attempt to stave off past memories of the war.

When the basis of Japan's economy—the source of postwar national identity—was threatened, many focused on their own and their family's cleanliness. Newly attained affluence, as I argued in chapters 5 and 6, enabled Japanese society to cleanse bodies of the memories of war in the postwar years. Nevertheless, with the imminent shortage of hygienic products, memories of the past returned to daily life. Those who stocked up on toilet paper and other paper products tried to defend their lives against this infiltration of the past by keeping their bodies clean. Indeed, references were made to wartime and immediate postwar experiences in the media: items such as sugar, salt, and matches had been under strict ration in these years.[12] In purchasing paper products and other items in short supply, people acted out their deep-seated anxiety that their society was not, after all, shielded from the past. Japanese bodies had to be kept clean and ahistorical lest they remind postwar society of wartime memories.

Government leaders feared that the Middle East crisis could undermine the entire industrial structure of Japan. Diplomatically ill-prepared to deal with the crisis, the government managed to secure oil from Arab nations by adopting a pro-Arab stance. In December 1973, Tokyo sent Vice Prime Minister Miki Takeo as a special envoy to eight Arab nations. With Japan's economic aid package to the region, OAPEC recognized Japan as a friendly nation and ensured the future supply of petroleum, albeit at a higher price.[13] With this diplomatic success, the Japanese economy swiftly adapted to the new international order, though it experienced a negative net growth of GNP in 1974.

Because the crisis was thus averted, postwar Japanese society maintained and even augmented its prosperity, which in turn further enabled the dissociation of Japanese bodies from the nation's war memories. Although the desire to remember the war loss did not disappear, from the late 1960s onward, Japanese bodies ceased to be the focal point of efforts to articulate memories of the Asia Pacific War. The focus clearly shifted after the late 1960s: in place of Japanese bodies, Asian bodies came to present the loci of struggles to signify the war loss. After the early 1970s when the Cold War paradigm began to show signs of stress, various issues related to the Asia Pacific War commanded the attention of the Japanese media and public.

The Vietnam War, the ultimate expression of the Cold War's bipolar tension, ironically reminded many Japanese of the existence of the third term outside the capitalist-Communist conflict. The images of Vietnamese peasants enduring American bombings invoked Japan's own memories of bombing near the end of the Asia Pacific War. The recognition of suffering Asian bodies reverberated with the postwar sentiment that posited the Japanese as war victims in the conflict against the United States. Nonetheless, the awareness of Japan's close ties to U.S. interests pointed to Japan's role as an accomplice to the U.S. involvement in its Asian war. The reversion of Okinawa to Japan in 1972 merely illuminated Japan's complicity in the war, for it failed to liberate Okinawa from its prescribed role as a Pacific outpost of the U.S. military.

As Japan developed closer ties with China and other Asian countries, memories of aggression within these regions were admitted into Japan's popular consciousness as well. The establishment of diplomatic relations between the United States and the People's Republic of China revealed a chasm in the bipolar structure of Cold War politics. (Following the United States, Japan reestablished its diplomatic relations with China in 1972.) In 1971, serialized reports by Honda Katsuichi on the violence and atrocities committed by the Japanese military in China created wide reverberations in Japan. Honda offered the first extensive coverage on how memories of the war had been articulated in China and generated a heated debate on the Nanjing Massacre of 1937; the debate, which still continues, centered around whether the massacre took place and, if so, how many Chinese were killed.[14] In the 1980s, Unit 731's human experimentation on Russian and Chinese subjects was widely publicized through Morimura Sei'ichi's best-selling book *Akuma no hōshoku* (Devil's feast).[15] In the mid-1980s, the screening process for Japanese history textbooks became a subject of international discussion. Neighboring Asian countries' severe criticism against the Ministry of Education's efforts to euphemize the history of Japan's aggression in Asia triggered disputes over the official representations of Japan's past. Prime Minister Nakasone Yasuhiro's first visit to the Yasukuni Shrine and the Liberal Democratic Party's initiative under his leadership to increase Japan's military preparedness in the 1980s led the Chinese and Korean governments to question Japan's official version of the history of the Asia Pacific War.

When the Cold War system, which eagerly overlooked Japan's past, collapsed in the late 1980s, Japan's colonial past continued to resurface through suffering Asian bodies. In Japan, the death of the emperor in 1989 aptly announced an end of the postwar paradigm. With the disappearance of Hirohito's body—the key element in the foundational narrative—war memories returned to the Japanese media, both as nostalgia and as critical reflection. The death of the monarch also announced that not much time was left for the survivors of the war to speak of their own experiences. Realizing that their bodies would soon perish, some came forward to tell stories that they had long silenced. The issue of "comfort women" entered the popular consciousness of Japan during this period thanks to the compelling accounts given by those who were coerced into sexual servitude for the Japanese military, and a fierce controversy ensued over the Japanese government's involvement in maintaining the "comfort women" system. As Suzuki Yūko claims, the voices of these women reached Japan only after a long preparatory period of tracing their history within 1980s Korea.[16] Correspondingly, the growing interest in minorities' issues in Japan created an audience receptive to their voices. However, the retrospective mood of the 1990s did not find Japanese bodies critical for its remembrance of the wartime past. Japanese bodies were long rehabilitated from wartime memories and offered little clues to remember the past. Instead Japanese society sought out Asian bodies, which remained outside the postwar paradigm. The suffering bodies of Asian people came to constitute the ground for remembering the traumatic experiences during the Asia Pacific War.

The images of suffering Asian bodies haunt post–Cold War Japan, demanding to be part of its war narratives. The challenge that Asian people's experiences poses can be met only through rigorous self-reflection on how long Japan managed to repress this challenge and how it sanitized the images of suffering Japanese bodies in popular consciousness. Critical discussions of Japan's aggression in Asia necessitate the production of a new collective identity that is capable of working through the nation's memories of violence. In order to imagine such an identity, one needs to understand how new images of Japan's nationhood were forged and maintained after the war, at the expense of memories of loss.

The collapse of the Cold War paradigm has helped Japan to grow more aware of its aggression in Asia. However, it has also liberated a powerful sentiment that seeks once again to confine memories of the war to Japan's relations with the United States. A reporter for *Asahi shinbun* writes about a poster that he saw in the summer of 1998 that stated, "The U.S. should repent to Jesus Christ. Hiroshima, Nagasaki, Nuclear Holocaust."[17] While the anti-American nationalism of this poster expresses what is concealed under the foundational narrative, it renders exactly the same ideological effects as the foundational narrative: it defines Japan as a victim of the war, erasing the war memories of its former colonial subjects. Fifty years after the conclusion of the Asia Pacific War, Japanese society appears to have come to accept political nationalism and anti-American sentiment. Yet such sentiment replicates the effects of the foundational narrative by negatively responding to it. Under the rubric of "healthy" nationalism, conservatives are attempting in the 1990s to silence memories of war loss among other Asian peoples. The process of discursively recuperating Japanese bodies is replicated in this conservative discourse: the "healthy" national body of Japan drives out the battered bodies of Asian females.

Kobayashi Yoshinori's 1998 *manga* (comic) *Sensōron*, is one such example of the problematic return of nationalism to postwar society. Capturing the popular desire to rehabilitate Japan's nationhood, *Sensōron* remained on best-seller lists for several weeks in 1998.[18] Deep-seated anxiety about shifting social paradigms motivates Kobayashi in his ideological battle against attempts to problematize narratives of Japan's heroic war. For him, Japan's nationhood must be free from any aggressive intent in order to be worth its members' sacrifices in the 1990s. *Sensōron* therefore categorically denies Japan's colonial aggression toward Asian peoples on the ground of insufficient evidence. Kobayashi dismisses accusations of Japan's aggression, arguing that it was necessary in a war against European imperialism: he urges that "we should be proud we had grandfathers who fought against racist Caucasians" in a full-page frame, which portrays youthful Japanese soldiers advancing in an oilfield.[19] Kobayashi's total identification with the scene is clear: the central figure who issues commands to the soldiers has the same facial features as Kobayashi's in the book.

With the reinscription of a heroic narrative of self-sacrifice about the war, Kobayashi seeks to overcome the crisis that he sees in 1990s Japanese society. Under the appearance of peacefulness, Kobayashi argues that social mores have been decaying. He lists symptomatic signs of this process after the burst of the so-called bubble economy: disintegrating families, the rising divorce rate, prostitution by housewives and high school girls, violence among junior high students. Sensing a large paradigmatic change in 1990s Japan, Kobayashi expresses his yearning for the status quo through his anxiety-ridden *manga*. In his mind, Japan's defeat in 1945 and its subsequent loss of nationalism are the underlying causes of all its contemporary social problems.

Kobayashi claims that Japan's nationhood, as the political entity that demanded its members sacrifice, has been thoroughly denigrated in the postwar understanding of history. Without the sense of civic responsibility (kōkyōshin) that only the state can support, postwar Japanese democracy, which promotes individualism, disintegrates into egotism. Therefore, Japan's nationhood and nationalism must be restored, for they are the moral backbone of society. For this purpose, Kobayashi denies all Japanese aggression toward Asian peoples and highlights the inhumanity of U.S. attacks on "innocent" civilian Japanese. Aggression belongs to the demonized other (Kobayashi casts the Soviet Union, the United States, Britain, China, and North Korea in this category); and it is against this vision of the other that Kobayashi produces images of Japan's nationhood.

Although Kobayashi seeks to critique the postwar social paradigm, his narrative ironically demonstrates how deeply it has taken root in popular consciousness. Contrary to Kobayashi's portrayal, what has been finally coming to an end in 1990s Japan is not an abstract moral system, but the historically specific condition of the postwar paradigm. Kobayashi may rediscover nationhood underneath social order, but what he easily overlooks is that postwar nationhood was produced in response to Japan's lost war. The self-sacrifice that Kobayashi demands from Japanese citizens has been a staple element in narratives that concealed the historical disjunction of the defeat. Facing the end of the postwar paradigm, Kobayashi nostalgically celebrates the certainty that the foundational narrative once commanded.

The brand of nationalism that Kobayashi forwards as the answer to Japan's current problems is vastly different from the aestheticized nationalism that Mishima articulated in the 1960s. The object of Mishima's criticism was the postwar paradigm: he desperately attempted to undermine political reality by counterpoising an aesthetic concept of politics (i.e., the emperor).[20] For him, death in war belonged to the realm of aesthetics, which postwar politics failed to encompass. On the other hand, Kobayashi tries to hold the crumbling postwar paradigm together by emphasizing the utility of the war's deaths. The sacrifices made by the war dead are valuable precisely because they laid the foundation for postwar society. In claiming the continuity between pre- and post-1945 Japan, Kobayashi conceals the historical trauma of 1945.

It is easy enough to dismiss Kobayashi's anti-American nationalism as ideological and historically uninformed. However, such a dismissal neither accounts for the appeal of this ideology nor understands resentment against the United States as a powerful paradigm through which to contemplate the past.[21] Only by working through the ideological effect of anti-American nationalism and its denial of the trauma can one imagine a new national identity that can embrace memories of Japan's colonial aggression.

The series of essays that the literary critic Katō Norihiro produced in the second half of the 1990s constitutes a belated attempt to work through the trauma of the defeat. The essays were reprinted with major revisions in his *Haisengo ron* (Thesis on the postdefeat).[22] Katō strives to comprehend and overcome the historical conditions that produced the xenophobic nationalism in postwar Japan. Katō insists that the people of a defeated country must live through the defeat after the war; however, Japanese people avoided facing the defeat by deceiving themselves that what the defeat brought was actually what they had wished for.

Katō locates a "twist" (*nejire*) in the contradictory condition that the postwar "peace" constitution was forced onto Japan by the United States with threats of superior (nuclear) military power. Caught in this double bind, the nation's history could not be drawn as a straight line any longer: it was forever "twisted" at its defeat. According to Katō, postwar Japan eagerly looked away from the "twist" by claiming that what the new constitution and ultimately the defeat brought to Japan—peace—was what its people spontaneously and independently desired. This aversion of the trauma caused Japan to experience a schizophrenic condition, a split into a pure inner self and an obsequious outer self. The inner self managed to shelter itself from the external political reality and to preserve an ideal image of Japan, whereas the outer self recast external demands as its own wishes.

In describing the pathology of postwar society, Katō Norihiro relies on the psychological profiles of Japan's nationhood forwarded by Kishida Shū. Kishida posits a nation as a viable unit of psychoanalysis and diagnoses modern Japan with a schizophrenic condition that originated in the mid–nineteenth century after its shock encounter with the West.[23] Although Katō limits his discussion to the postwar period, he fully accepts Kishida's diagnosis and prescribes a treatment analogous to individual therapy. Postwar Japanese society must face the deception at its origin: only by accepting the trauma of the defeat for what it is can Japan wholeheartedly address the issues of its war responsibilities.

Katō claims that even the war dead have been divided into two groups: the three million Japanese dead and the twenty million of other Asian countries. The inner self of postwar Japan has identified with its own war dead, while the outer self, which has dominated social discourse, has elevated victims of the war elsewhere in Asia. Katō argues that it is imperative to overcome this split in order to construct a collective subjectivity that is able to mourn the losses of both Japanese and Asians. Katō locates the reintegration of the Japanese psyche in its ability to mourn the three million Japanese war dead: only by embracing what the inner self zealously defends will Japan gain the ability to mourn the twenty million.

Elsewhere Katō Norihiro expresses his uneasiness toward the ways in which the images of suffering Asian bodies galvanized the debate in the 1990s over responsibilities for the war.[24] Katō senses the lack of desire within Japan to contemplate the legacies of the past in an everyday context. He locates a void within Japan, a void that prevents its citizens from truly feeling the sufferings of Asian peoples. Katō proposes to fill this void with an ethical and collective subject that would be capable of accepting the legacies of Japan's colonialism as "our" (*watashitachi no*) history. Postwar Japan should not exclusively depend on the exterior for its critical reflections: they must come from within.

The nationalistic undertone of Katō Norihiro's claims were immediately criticized. By accepting Kishida Shu's premise of collective psychoanalysis, he reinforces the national boundaries of the subject of his inquiry. The collective "we" (*watashitachi*) that includes the war dead constitutes the subject of mourning for Katō. Many critics express doubts about Katō's privileging of Japanese collective subjectivity.[25] Katō is well aware that he risks essentialism; yet he insists on taking this risk in order to construct a new nationhood that could embrace the trauma of defeat. His premise is that Japan can not innocently celebrate the production of borderless societies in late-twentieth-century capitalism. As the citizens of the aggressor country, Japan—"we" in Katō's discussion—has old business to settle. Only through embracing the historical "twist" at the beginning of postwar history can the Japanese people redefine their nationhood as something more open.

Categorically faulting Katō for the nationalistic undertones of his argument is not a productive strategy in reading his texts, primarily because such undertones stem from the thorny issue of Japan's war responsibility that he critically addresses. Responsibility remains a "national" question; in order for the postwar generation that did not even exist during the Asia Pacific War to claim moral responsibility, Katō has to posit a collective agency, one that is continuous from the prewar period. By ethically accepting the responsibility of the earlier generation as a Japanese citizen, one paradoxically becomes trapped in the constraints of nationhood.

While it is possible to mourn as an individual apart from one's nation, an individual act does not diminish the need to address the historical specificity of a nation's actions: millions of Asians were killed by *Japanese* aggression. The past act of a nation-state cannot be resolved at the level of individuals. The legacies of the Asia Pacific War demand that the citizens of Japan address the issues of responsibility as a nation.[26] There was no revolution in the postwar years that might have relieved the postwar government from its war responsibilities. Just as the prewar and postwar generations possess an ethical obligation to face these responsibilities, so too do Japanese citizens by the sheer fact that they live under the regime that has not settled its war legacies.

Katō Norihiro's writing is a response from the postwar generation (Katō was born in 1948) to the question of Japan's responsibility. As a member of the postwar generation, Katō seeks an ethical position from which to confront Japan's past aggression and simultaneously to resist the totality of nationhood this very position imposes on him. The final resolution between the inner and outer selves would be a paradoxical moment. Only when postwar Japan can accept the fact that three million Japanese died meaningless deaths can it reestablish its own national identity. Yet the acute awareness of loss, Katō hopes, will inevitably undermine the rigid definitions of Japan's nationhood.

I support Katō's position to the extent that it claims postwar Japan's need to contemplate the trauma of war and loss collectively. However, I find the lack of historical specificity in his theorization deeply troubling. Katō discusses postwar Japan as if it lived through a uniform time of deception after the defeat; in Katō's *Haisengo ron*, 1945 Japan unproblematically returns to late 1990s Japan. Little seems to have changed in the past half-century. In Katō's thinking, Japan and its people still live through exactly the same trauma or absence. Katō's explanation intimates that a psychological defense prevented the trauma from dissipating: the trauma has been repressed in postwar Japan, and hence it maintains its original shape and impact.

By historicizing the ways in which postwar Japan dealt with traumatic memories of the Asia Pacific War, this book has argued against Katō's claim. There has been no secure reservoir of trauma. The trauma of defeat and loss has been articulated many times over in the social and cultural space of postwar Japan, and its original impact has lessened in each articulation despite attempts to retain it. The scarred Japanese body was a central image in efforts to remember the pain of the past; yet, as postwar Japan removed the discursive markers of war and loss from its surface, so too did it erase the traces of the past from its bodies. It is highly indicative that Katō uses the term "dirt" (*yogore*) to describe the historical disjunction of 1945: he may believe that Japan's dirt still remains visible and accessible for those who live in the late 1990s. However, as this volume demonstrates, the cultural practices that accompanied postwar Japan's unprecedented material wealth cleansed the dirt from everyday life.

A simple ethical call is insufficient to change the historical conditions that produced a chasm in Japan. The chasm that Katō perceives in postwar society is not an empty space waiting to be filled with ethical commitment; it is already filled with layers of discursive practices that have transformed the meaning of defeat. Without critical reflections on the process through which the image of trauma has been transformed, the ethical subject that Katō demands would immediately be disoriented in Japan's discursive space. To gain a critical purchase on this space, one must be attentive to the historical processes that produced it after the war.[27] It is impossible to reach the original trauma by short-circuiting postwar history: one can merely hope to capture its resonance within postwar discourses.

As a strategy to re-member Japan's past, this book offers critical examinations of how Japan has forgotten its wartime legacies. The process of forgetting was far from unilinear: it was attained only within the contradictory desires to express and to repress the past. Through excavating the tension between forgetting and re-membering, this study foregrounds the historical conditions that produced memories of war in postwar Japan. The examination of postwar history is a sine qua non for treating these memories as a historical product. To construct a collective subject that can transgress traditional national boundaries, it is imperative to realize how postwar Japanese subjectivity has been produced and maintained through nationalized historical narratives. The chapters of this book illustrate the central significance of war experiences to the production and maintenance of a collective Japanese identity after the war.

Suffering Asian bodies have been central to Japan's renewed efforts to confront its wartime legacies; yet they do not offer an automatic answer to the challenge of excavating war memories. To contemplate Japan's past through the disturbing images of other Asian bodies, one must simultaneously examine how postwar Japan managed to cleanse the "dirt" from the surface of Japanese bodies and dissociate itself from its war memories. In the social and cultural space where bodily pain is absent, others' pain becomes at best abstract, and at worst unimaginable. Historical studies may not make the pain of others more comprehensible; but they do teach us how to resist certain narrative practices that reduce such pain to easy categorical knowledge.

Notes

Introduction

1. Ōgai Haruko, ed., *Ōgai Yatarō isakushū* (private publication, 1994). Unless otherwise indicated, all translations are my own.

2. I use the term *Asia Pacific War* throughout this book to emphasize that Asia as well as the Pacific were important regions for Japan's military actions, which began with the Manchurian Incident in 1931 and concluded with Japan's surrender to the Allies in 1945. For a concise overview of the political implications of various designations of the Asia Pacific War and a rationale for using the term, see Kisaka Jun'ichirō, "Ajia Taiheiyō sensō no koshō to seikaku," *Ryūkoku hōgaku 25*, no. 4 (1993): 386–434.

3. Dominick LaCapra's *History and Memory after Auschwitz* (Ithaca: Cornell University Press, 1998) provides critical readings of the key issues and texts within recent European and U.S. discussions of the wartime past. The essays in the *American Historical Review* 102, no. 5 (1997) forum on history and memory include extensive bibliographical information on the topic; see Susan A. Crane, "Writing the Individual Back into Collective Memory," 1372–85; Alon Confina, "Collective Memory and Cultural History: Problem of Method," 1386–1403; and Daniel James, "Meatpackers, Peronists, and Collective Memory: A View from the South," 1404–12. For a critical overview of the so-called Historians' Debate in the 1980s Federal Republic of Germany, see Charles S. Maier, *The Unmasterable Past: History, Holocaust, and German Identity* (Cambridge: Harvard University Press, 1998). Henry Rousso's *The Vichy Syndrome: History and Memory in France since 1944* (Cambridge: Harvard University Press, 1991) exemplifies France's efforts in the 1980s to reexamine its wartime memories. The United States' case is different from other countries mentioned here because it was victorious in World War II: the Good War posed no ontological threat to the American popular consciousness. However, as Maria Sturken points out in *Tangled Memories: The Vietnam War, the AIDS Epidemic, and the Politics of Remembering* (Berkeley and Los Angeles: University of California Press, 1997), U.S. consciousness was challenged by the Vietnam War and more recently AIDS.

4. Kuboshima Sei'ichirō, *"Mugonkan" e no tabi: Senbotsu gagakusei junreiki* (Tokyo: Ozawa shoten, 1997). Another volume by Kuboshima reproduces sixty-three of the works at Mugonkan: *Mugonkan: Senbotsu gagakusei "inori no e"* (Tokyo: Kōdansha, 1997). The information pertaining to Kuboshima and Mugonkan derives from these two volumes and my interview with him at Ueda, Nagano, on May 17, 1998.

5. Nomiyama Gyōji, Sō Sakon, and Yasuda Takeshi, *Inori no gashū* (Tokyo: Nihon hōsōkyōkai shuppan, 1977).

6. Kuboshima, *"Mugonkan" e no tabi*, 110. Nomiyama's account is somewhat different from the version Kuboshima renders. Nomiyama expresses the sense of

guilt that he felt for surviving the war when facing his deceased classmates' parents. See Nomiyama, Sō, and Yasuda, *Inori no gashū*, 70.

7. Nomiyama confirms Kuboshima's observation in his own writing. Almost a half-century later, Nomiyama was no longer able to find the dead among the bereaved families. Nomiyama Gyōji, *Shomei no nai fūkei* (Tokyo: Heibonsha, 1997), 199.

Chapter 1

1. This attempt began in 1993 and effectively died two years later, facing stiff opposition from the Air Force Association and the American Legion. For comprehensive accounts of the controversy, see Martin Harwit, *An Exhibit Denied: Lobbying the History of "Enola Gay"* (New York: Springer-Verlag, 1996); Barton J. Bernstein, "The Struggle over History: Defining the Hiroshima Narrative," in *Judgment at the Smithsonian*, ed. Philip Nobile (New York: Marlow, 1995), 127–256; and Saitō Michio, *Genbaku shinwa no 50 nen* (Tokyo: Chūōkōronsha, 1995); Lisa Yoneyama, "Critical Warps: Facticity, Transformative Knowledge, and Postnationalist Criticism in the Smithsonian Controversy," *Positions* 5, no. 3 (1997): 779–809.

2. John Dower scrupulously documents the two countries' propaganda efforts in producing images of the enemy during World War II. See *War without Mercy: Race and Power in the Pacific War* (New York: Pantheon, 1986).

3. I invoke the concept of melodrama here to emphasize the hyperbolic and aestheticized qualities of the political drama. The emotional investment that the drama encouraged was the key factor in its maintenance. For a critical discussion of the melodramatic genre, see Peter Brooks, *The Melodramatic Imagination: Balzac, Henry James, Melodrama, and the Mode of Excess* (New Haven: Yale University Press, 1976).

4. For instance, on April 15, 1996, the ABC television network program *Nightline* reported decreasing anti-Japanese feelings among Americans. Although one should approach this change with caution, the report is certainly encouraging. On the other hand, in the late 1980s, the Japanese media began paying more attention to the issue of Japan's responsibility for the war, specifically, its role as the aggressor against Asia. For instance, as Nakamura Masanori argues, the issue of "comfort women"—as many as a hundred thousand women, many from occupied areas, were forced into sexual slavery for Japanese soldiers—is a drastic example of the "unfinished history" that defies the sense of closure placed on postwar Japanese history. Nakamura Masanori, "Sengo kaikaku to gendai," in *Senryō to sengo kaikaku*, Kindai Nihon no kiseki, vol. 6, ed. Nakamura Masanori (Tokyo: Yoshikawa kōbunkan, 1994), 19–20.

5. Japan's House of Representatives (lower house) passed the Resolution to Renew the Determination for Peace on the Basis of Lessons Learned from History on June 9, 1995, in its regular meeting. However, the resolution managed to indicate Japan's responsibility only in vague language because of the fierce opposition within and outside of the lower house. For the official translation of the resolution and the political struggle over its content, see Fukatsu Masumi, "The Eclipse of Shōwa Taboos and the Apology Resolution," *Japan Quarterly*, October 1995,

419–25; John W. Dower, "Japan Addresses," *Journal of the International Institute*, fall 1995, 8–11.

6. Yoshida Yutaka detects anti-American feeling beneath the recent characterization of Japan's war efforts by the conservative forces in the government. For instance, Ishihara Shintarō of the Liberal Democratic Party recognizes Japan's responsibility toward other Asian countries; however, he claims that the Pacific War was also a struggle against imperialist powers and that Japan does not have unilateral responsibility for its conflicts with them. Ishihara's claim is directed largely against the United States. Yoshida Yutaka, *Nihonjin no sensōkan* (Tokyo: Iwanami shoten, 1995), 15–21.

7. Although the overall trend in recent surveys shows a decline in support among the American people for the decision to use the atomic bomb, a November 1994 joint survey by a Japanese broadcasting company, CBS, and the *New York Times* showed that 55 percent approved and 38 percent disapproved. In the same survey, 12 percent of the Japanese respondents expressed no moral objections to the bombing, while 80 percent of them disapproved on moral grounds. For a breakdown of the survey, see Saitō, *Genbaku shinwa*, 106–9. For the overall trend in the American opinion polls, see Gar Alperovitz, *The Decision to Use the Atomic Bomb: And the Architecture of an American Myth* (New York: Knopf, 1995), 672–73 n. 15.

8. I present a composite picture of the events assembled from various popular historical accounts, including the following: John Toland, *The Rising Sun: The Decline and Fall of the Japanese Empire, 1936–1945* (New York: Random House, 1970); William Craig, *The Fall of Japan* (New York: Dial Press, 1967); Pacific War Research Society, *Japan's Longest Day* (Tokyo: Kodansha International, 1968); Shinobu Seizaburō, *Seidan no rekishigaku* (Tokyo: Keisō shobō, 1992); and Nakamura Takafusa, *Shōwashi*, 2 vols. (Tokyo: Tōyōkeizaishinpō-sha, 1993).

9. Pacific War Research Society, *Japan's Longest Day*, 33.

10. Hosokawa Morisada, *Hosokawa nikki*, 2 vols. (Tokyo: Chūōkōronsha, 1989), cited in Irokawa Daikichi, *The Age of Hirohito*, trans. Mikiso Hane and John K. Urda (New York: Free Press, 1995), 93.

11. "Ryakugō 0649," in *Nihon no sentaku: Dainiji Sekaitaisen shūsenshi roku*, ed. Ministry of Foreign Affairs (Tokyo: Ministry of Foreign Affairs, 1990), 817–18.

12. Hidenari Terasaki and Mariko Terasaki Miller, eds., *Shōwa tennō dokuhakuroku: Terasaki Hidenari goyōgakari nikki* (Tokyo: Bungeishunjū, 1991), 129. For a discussion of the emperor's active involvement in the Asia Pacific War, see Herbert P. Bix, "The Showa Emperor's 'Monologue' and the Problem of War Responsibility," *Journal of Japanese Studies* 18, no. 2 (1992): 295–363.

13. Harry S. Truman, *Memoirs of Harry S. Truman: Year of Decisions* (New York: Doubleday, 1955), 428.

14. For a discussion on the subject within the early Truman administration, see Alperovitz, *Decision*, 33–79, 292–317.

15. Uday Mohan and Sanho Tree document the media discussion of the question of unconditional surrender in the spring and summer of 1945 in "Hiroshima, the American Media, and the Construction of Conventional Wisdom," *Journal of American–East Asia Relations* 4, no. 2 (1995): 141–60.

16. For instance, when the reply came, Secretary of War Henry Stimson was about to leave Washington for a vacation. See Barton J. Bernstein, "Understanding the Atomic Bomb and the Japanese Surrender," *Diplomatic History* 19, no. 2 (1995): 257.

17. Truman, *Memoirs*, 429.

18. *Newsweek* carried an article titled "The Face of the Defeat: An Emperor Remains" right after the defeat of Japan. While the article emphasized that the Allied response made "the emperor responsible to an Allied supreme commander," it clearly recognized the nature of the condition attached to Japan's "unconditional surrender" (*Newsweek*, August 20, 1945, 28–30). An article in the first issue of *Time* after the defeat of Japan describes the process of the negotiation between the Japanese leadership and the Allied countries. "U.S. at War," *Time*, August 20, 1945, 21.

19. Michael Sherry, "Guilty Knowledge," *New York Times Book Review*, July 30, 1995, 13.

20. Interestingly, both Hirohito's death and the fall of the Berlin Wall, the event that symbolized the end of the Cold War paradigm, happened in 1989.

21. As early as 1943, some government officials close to the throne started discussing and agreed on a plan to use the emperor's "divine decision" for finishing the war. For those who agreed on the plan in August 1945, the declaration of war by the Soviet Union and the explosion of the atomic bombs were "a help from heaven." See Yoshida Yutaka, *Shōwa tennō no shūsenshi* (Tokyo: Iwanami Shoten, 1992), 26–27.

22. Fujiwara Akira and Awaya Kentarō infer that the emperor was already committed to the resolution of the conflict in mid-June 1945; hence, the "divine decision" was not a sudden conversion. See *Tetteikenshō: Shōwa tennō "Dokuhakuroku"* (Tokyo: Ōtsuki shoten, 1991), 98.

23. Many Japanese did not understand the rescript because it was written in abstruse Japanese and because the broadcast was constantly interrupted by poor reception. Those who understood the gravity of the announcement did so by piecing together the phrases they heard. The Japanese government followed the rescript with other radio commentaries that emphasized a single point: the conflict was brought to conclusion by a "divine decision." The scene of people gathered around radio receivers to listen to the announcement marks the beginning of the postwar period for many Japanese. The scene appeared in many Japanese television dramas accompanied by the actual recording of the broadcast. However, Hirohito's voice was not replayed directly from the original recording plates produced in 1945. The original plates stayed in the Imperial Household Agency until 1975. When they were permanently lent to the Nihon Hōsō Kyōkai Broadcasting Museum in 1975, they were in no shape to be played. The recording that many Japanese heard in the postwar period was actually from a copy made from the original at the Civil Information and Education Section of MacArthur's General Headquarters. Ironically, Hirohito's voice, which many have regarded as the defining element of postwar Japanese history, was preserved by the American occupation forces. See Takeyama Akiko, *Gyokuon hōsō* (Tokyo: Banseisha, 1989), 75–79.

24. Actually, a somewhat toned-down version of the Potsdam Declaration was read as a part of the commentaries following the rescript. For the details of the program broadcast before and after the rescript's announcement, see Takeyama, *Gyokuon hōsō*, 92–147.

25. Washida Koyata, *Tennō ron* (Tokyo: San'ichi shobo, 1989), 43–46.

26. The emperor urged his subjects to do their duty in the war against the United States and Great Britain. The imperial rescript, for instance, begins:

> We by grace of heaven, Emperor of Japan, seated on the Throne of a line unbroken for ages eternal, enjoin upon ye, Our loyal and brave subjects.
>
> We hereby declare war on the United States of America and the British Empire. The men and officers of Our Army and Navy shall do their utmost in prosecuting the war, Our public servants of various departments shall perform faithfully and diligently their appointed tasks, and all other subjects of Ours shall pursue their respective duties; the entire nation with a united will shall mobilize their total strength so that nothing will miscarry in the attainment of Our war aims. (*Japan Times*, December 8, 1941, 1)

The rescript clearly identifies the emperor as the agent who declared the war and who urged his subjects to support Japan's war efforts.

27. Arai Shin'ichi, *Sensō sekininron* (Tokyo: Iwanami shoten, 1995), 161.

28. For instance, the image of the peace-loving sovereign was often used in letters sent by Japanese citizens to General Douglas MacArthur. A total of 164 letters, dated from November 1945 to January 1946, were sent. The majority of these defended the emperor; only nine were critical. See Sodei Rinjirō, *Haikei Makkāsā Gensuisama* (Tokyo: Chūōkōronsha, 1991), 82–143.

29. According to a survey published in 1947 by the United States Strategic Bombing Survey, 47 percent of the people who were surveyed in Hiroshima and Nagasaki after the atomic bombings felt "Fear—terror," 26 percent felt "Admiration," and 17 percent felt "Anger." Furthermore, the survey claimed that "the morale of the Hiroshima and Nagasaki area's populations after the bomb was dropped did not fall below that of the rest of urban and rural Japan." Table 1 demonstrates the relatively high morale among the residents of Hiroshima and Nagasaki after the atomic bombing.

TABLE 1
Japanese Confidence in Victory after Bombing of Hiroshima and Nagasaki

	Hiroshima and Nagasaki Area (%)	Rest of Japan (%)
Never had doubts of victory	19	11
Were never certain that Japan could not win	27	26
Were never personally unwilling to continue the war	39	28

Source: United States Strategic Bombing Survey, Morale Division, *The Effect of Strategic Bombing on Japanese Morale* (Washington, D.C.: United States Government Printing Office, 1947), 94–95.

Table 2 demonstrates that the morale in Hiroshima and Nagasaki after the nuclear attacks was comparable to the morale observed in cities that suffered from "medium" to little or no bombing during the war. As far as these figures indicate, the atomic bomb did have some effects on Japanese morale but fell far short of rendering a miraculous conversion of the Japanese.

TABLE 2

Japanese Morale, by Severity of Experienced Bombing

	Relatively Low Morale (%)	Relatively High Morale (%)
Heavily bombed cities, exclusive of Tokyo	56	44
Medium bombed cities, high percent of destruction	51	49
Medium bombed cities, low percent of destruction	46	54
Lightly bombed and unbombed cities	47	53
Hiroshima and Nagasaki	45	55

Source: United States Strategic Bombing Survey, Morale Division, The Effect of Strategic Bombing on Japanese Morale (Washington, D.C.: United States Government Printing Office, 1947), 94–95.

The Strategic Bombing Survey concluded from its investigations that "certainly prior to 31 December 1945, and in all probability prior to 1 November 1945, Japan would have surrendered even if the atomic bombs had not been dropped, even if Russia had not entered the war, and even if no invasion had been planned or contemplated." U.S. Strategic Bombing Survey, Japan's Struggle to End the War (Washington, D.C.: United States Government Printing Office, 1946), 13. Although bias in the U.S. Bombing Survey's investigations is possible, they provide a valuable perspective on the psychological responses to the atomic bomb as compared to conventional bombing.

30. Hachiya Michihiko, Hiroshima Diary (Chapel Hill: University of North Carolina Press, 1955), 82, cited in Ubuki Satoru, "Hibakutaiken to heiwaundō," in Sengo minshushugi, Sengo Nihon—Senryō to sengo kaikaku, vol. 4, ed. Nakamura Masanori et al. (Tokyo: Iwnami shoten, 1995), 100.

31. Hachiya, Hiroshima Diary, 100.

32. Tanimoto Kiyoshi, Hiroshima no jūjikao idaite (Tokyo: Kōdansha, 1950), cited in Ubuki, "Hibakutaiken to heiwaundō," 101.

33. Toyoshita Narahiko infers that Minister of Foreign Affairs Yoshida Shigeru's meetings with MacArthur on September 20 and with Hirohito the next day were part of the preparation. See "Tennō wa nanio kattataka," Sekai, February 1990, 251.

34. Douglas MacArthur, Reminiscences (New York: McGraw-Hill, 1964), 288.

35. Henry L. Stimson, "The Decision to Use the Atomic Bomb," Harper's, February 1947, 102.

36. MacArthur, *Reminiscences*, 288.

37. After a careful study of other contemporary sources, Matsuo Takayoshi offers the following as the emperor's original statement: "As for the beginning of the war, I had no intention to resort to an attack on Pearl Harbor prior to the declaration of the war. It is regrettable that, despite my best efforts, we could not help but start the war in the end. Its responsibility resides in me as Japan's sovereign." See Matsuo Takayoshi, "The First Meeting of Showa Tennō with General MacArthur: A Documentation," *Kyoto Daigaku Bungakubu kenkyū kiyō* 29 (March 1990): 87–88, cited in Irokawa Daikichi, *Shōwashi to tennō* (Tokyo: Iwanami shoten, 1991), 205–6. Irokawa's discussion of the first Hirohito-MacArthur meeting is left out of the abridged English translation of the book.

38. Matsumura Kenzō, *Sandai kaikoroku* (Tokyo: Tōyō keizai shinpōsha, 1964), 267.

39. MacArthur, *Reminiscences*, 288.

40. When a Japanese translation of his *Reminiscences* was serialized in 1964, the *Bungeishunjū* editorial office scrutinized MacArthur's account and pointed out a number of "exaggerations," "misunderstandings," and "contrary" facts. See Toyoshita, "Tennō wa nanio kattataka," 233.

41. Toyoshita Narahiko, " 'Kūhaku' no sengoshi," *Sekai*, March 1990, 105–11.

42. Douglas Lummis, "Genshitekina nikkō no nakadeno hinatabokko," *Shisō no kagaku*, June 1981, 18.

43. Matsuo, "First Meeting," 62.

44. Nosaka Akiyuki, "American *Hijiki*," in *Contemporary Japanese Literature*, ed. Howard Hibbett (New York: Knopf, 1977), 447.

45. Nosaka, "American *Hijiki*," 455.

46. This equation of physical and sexual prowess can be seen in Irokawa Daikichi's description of American soldiers as well. Irokawa includes his diary entry from May 1946 in his biographical note on the immediate postwar period. He uses the third-person pronoun to describe himself:

> Then another soldier came in front of the bench [at the train station] with a Japanese girl, practically carrying her. The tall American soldier, almost twice as tall as the woman, bent over and was absorbed in licking her all over her face. It was nothing as casual as kissing. The woman seemed to whisper something once in a while as she leaned on him, but her whisper was inaudible. Then the train that they had waited almost thirty minutes for came in. Even in the train car, the soldier, unconcerned about the people around, kept toying with her persistently. Thinking that the Japanese are taught about a completely strange way of love in this fashion, he was troubled by a vague longing [*mōnen*] which he was unable to identify as negative or positive. (Irokawa Daikichi, *Jibunshi* [Tokyo: Kōdansha, 1992], 137–38.)

Although Irokawa distances himself from the scene by describing himself in the third person, he readily admits that he is already part of the scene. The "vague longing" best describes his ambiguous feelings about the American presence and its corporeal display.

47. Ide Magoroku, *Sengoshi, jō* (Tokyo: Iwanami shoten, 1991), 20. Nosaka also mentions American soldiers' buttocks: "The soldiers I was looking at now had arms like beams and hips like millstones and, underneath pants that glowed with a sheen our civilian uniforms never had, you could see their big powerful buttocks" ("American *Hijiki*," 448–49).

48. Ide, *Sengoshi—jō*, 20–21.

49. Ueno Kōshi, *Sengo saikō* (Tokyo: Asahi Shinbunsha, 1995), 34.

50. Lummis, "Genshitekina nikkō," 16.

51. Takayanagi Kenzō, Ōtomo Ichirō, and Tanaka Hideo, eds., *Nihonkoku Kenpō seitei no katei* (Tokyo: Yūhikaku, 1972), 320, 322.

52. Takayanagi, Ōtomo, and Tanaka, *Nihonkoku Kenpō*, 322.

53. Takayanagi, Ōtomo, and Tanaka, *Nihonkoku Kenpō*, 324.

54. Mark Gayn, *Japan Diary* (Tokyo: Charles E. Tuttle, 1981), 129.

55. Kaneko Mitsuharu, *Zetsubō no Shōwashi* (Tokyo: Kōdansha, 1996), 181.

56. Yoshimi Yoshiaki, *Jūgun ianfu* (Tokyo: Iwanami shoten, 1995), 194–99.

57. The process of feminization did not take place overnight; it was already beginning during the war. Toward the end of the conflict, in popular writings warning of espionage, Japanese women were regarded as prime suspects because of their partiality for European and American men. See Aramata Hiroshi, *Kessenka no yūtopia* (Tokyo: Bungeishunjū, 1996), 187–88.

58. Satō Tadao, *Nihon eiga 300* (Tokyo: Asahi shinbunsha, 1995), 118.

59. Satō Tadao reports that in conversations he had with Chinese people at the 1992 Hong Kong Film Festival, this is the scene they most hated in the movie. See Satō, *Nihon eiga 300*, 119. There is also a general reference on this point in Satō Tadao, *Nihon eigashi*, vol. 4 (Tokyo: Iwanami shoten, 1995), 107. Gregory J. Kasza discusses the film's three different endings, which were shown in different regions—Japan, Southeast Asia, and China. The Chinese version emphasizes the happy ending for the couple, who personify "the two pillars of the Great East Asian Co-Prosperity Sphere." Gregory J. Kasza, *The State and the Mass Media in Japan, 1918–1945* (Berkeley and Los Angeles: University of California Press, 1988), 250.

60. Her passing was so perfect that she was later tried in a postwar Chinese court for treason but found not guilty because she was able to prove that she was Japanese (Satō, *Nihon Eigashi*, 4:107). Yamaguchi Yoshiko (Ri Kō-ran) published autobiographical accounts of her life in 1987. Yamaguchi Yoshiko and Fujiwara Sakuya, *Ri Kō-ran: Watakushi no hansei* (Tokyo: Shinchōsha, 1987). Her life was made into a musical by the Japanese theater group Shiki in 1991 (*Nihon Eigashi*, 4:348). Intriguing readings of the construction of gender and nationality in Ri Kō-ran's life and career appear in Miriam Silverberg, "Remembering Pearl Harbor, Forgetting Charlie Chaplin, and the Case of the Disappearing Western Woman: A Picture Story," *Positions* 1, no. 1 (1993): 28–42.

61. For Ri's pursuit of an international identity, see Iida Momo, *Sengoshi no hakken*, vol. 2 (Tokyo: Sanpō, 1975), 114–35. Gena Marchetti provides a critical reading of the film *Japanese War Bride* in her book *Romance and the "Yellow Peril."* The presence of the Japanese heroine, Marchetti argues, may promote the concept of racial unity in the film; yet the film ends up confirming the "traditional,

American, bourgeois, patriarchal home." Gena Marchetti, *Romance of the "Yellow Peril"* (Berkeley and Los Angeles: University of California, 1993), 175.

62. Murakami Yumiko, *Yellow Face* (Tokyo: Asahi shinbunsha, 1993), 162–65.

63. Awaya Kentarō, "Report 4," in Fujiwara et al., *Tetteikenshō*, 140–41.

64. See Yoshida, *Shōwa tennō no shūsenshi*, 239; Awaya Kentarō, "Tokyo saiban ni miru sengo shori," in Awaya Kentarō et al., *Sensō sekinin—sengo sekinin* (Tokyo: Asahi shinbunsha, 1994), 92–93; Uchida Masatoshi, *"Sengo hoshō" o kangaeru* (Tokyo: Kōdansha, 1994), 160–67; and Ikeda Kiyohiko, "Ōbei to Nihon no shokuminchi taiken no uketomekata no chigai wa naze shōjitanoka," in *Bokura no "shinryaku" sensō*, ed. Miyazaki Tetsuya (Tokyo: Senyōsha, 1995), 216–17.

65. Shindō Eiichi, "Bunkatsu sareta ryōdo," *Sekai*, April 1979, 47–48, cited in Nakamura Masanori, *The Japanese Monarchy* (Armonk, N.Y.: M. E. Sharpe, 1992), 120.

66. "Japan's Unpretentious Emperor: Hirohito," *New York Times*, September 30, 1975, 2.

67. Editorial, *Washington Post*, October 5, 1975, A6.

68. "Hirohito Meets John Wayne," *Atlanta Constitution*, October 9, 1975, 4-D.

69. For a succinct analysis of the film in relation to other Hollywood films that feature "geisha girls," see Murakami, *Yellow Face*, 168–85, esp. 181–84.

70. "Alpine Rest for Emperor after Sour Holland Visit," *Times* (London), October 11, 1971, 5.

71. "Ryōheika Ōshū no 16 nichikan," *Asahi shinbun*, October 12, 1971, evening edition, 8.

72. James R. Van de Velde, "Enola Gay Saved Lives, Period," *Washington Post*, February 10, 1995, A-23.

73. Although the Japanese government strenuously protested the U.S. government's use of the atomic bomb right after the attack on Hiroshima, the government found itself in the postwar period in complete agreement with the U.S. explanation for its use of the bomb. In a 1957 lawsuit, where victims of the atomic bomb challenged the legality of the atomic attack and demanded reparations from the Japanese government, the government requested that the court dismiss the case on the grounds that use of the bomb was legitimate under international law. The claim that the government presented to the Tokyo Higher Court reads as follows: "The use of the atomic bombs expedited Japan's surrender, and consequently prevented the killing and wounding of people of either country in belligerency, to which the continuation of the war would have led. Observing such conditions objectively, nobody can answer the question whether the dropping of the bomb on Hiroshima and Nagasaki was a violation of the international law." *Hanrei jihō*, no. 355, the section on the Tokyo Higher Court, December 7, 1963, judgment and factual background and appendix chart 3, quoted in Ienaga Saburō, *Sensō sekinin* (Tokyo: Iwanami shoten, 1985), 376.

74. Of course, this reading did not preclude struggles over the signification of the bomb. For instance, such efforts in postwar literary practice are carefully documented in John Whittier Treat, *Writing Ground Zero* (Chicago: University

of Chicago Press, 1995). Lisa Yoneyama discusses the discursive struggles to signify the bomb and *hibakusha*'s experiences in postwar Hiroshima. See Lisa Yoneyama, *Hiroshima Traces: Time, Space, and Dialectics of Memory* (Berkeley and Los Angeles: University of California Press, 1999).

75. George Orwell, *1984* (San Diego: Harcourt Brace Jovanovich, 1949), 36.

76. Senate Resolution 257, Congressional Record, vol. 140, no. 134, September 22, 1994: S 13315–16.

77. James Fallows, "Containing Japan," *Atlantic*, May 1989, 41.

78. Michael Crichton, *Rising Sun* (New York: Ballantine Books, 1993), 388.

79. Crichton, *Rising Sun*, 258.

Chapter 2

1. For the details of Hirohito's postwar imperial excursions, see Sakamoto Kōjirō, *Shōchō tennōsei eno pafōmansu* (Tokyo: Yamakawa shuppansha, 1989).

2. Shiba Ryōtarō and Handō Kazutoshi, "Shiba Ryōtarō sengo 50 nen o kataru," in *Iwanami shoten to Bungeishunjū*, ed. Mainichi shinbunsha (Tokyo: Mainichi shinbunsha, 1996), 14.

3. Kakei Katsuhiko, *Yamato bataraki* (Tokyo, 1929). The timing of Kakei's publication strongly suggests that the inauguration of a radio calisthenics program (*rajio taisō*) on NHK (Nihon Hōsō Kyōkai: Japan Broadcasting System) in 1928 inspired Kakei's ideological efforts. Kakei correctly observed the ideological potential of radio calisthenics. In 1939, NHK began broadcasting a program featuring "Dai-Nihon kokumin taisō," calisthenics exercises that the Ministry of Health had devised, along with two other preexisting exercises. Rajio taisō 50 shūnenkinenshi henshū iinkai, *Atarashii asa ga kita—rajio taisō 50 nen no ayumi* (Tokyo: Kan'ihokensha kanyūshakyōkai, 1979), 41–42, 92–93.

4. Ishibashi Takehiko and Satō Tomohisa, *Nihon no taisō—hyakunen no ayumi to jitsugi* (Tokyo: Fumaidō, 1966), 690–91.

5. Ishibashi and Satō, *Nihon no taisō*, 785.

6. According to Takahashi Hidemine, immediately after the war the NHK tried to convince the officers of CIE that their newly Americanized version of radio calisthenics was an instrument for Japan's democratization. See his *Subarashiki rajio taisō* (Tokyo: Shōgakkan, 1998), 170–85.

7. Tanaka Satoshi, *Eisei tenrankai no yokubō* (Tokyo: Seikyūsha, 1994), 195.

8. Sawano Masaki, *Raisha no sei: bunmei kaika no jōken to shite no* (Tokyo: Seikyūsha, 1994), 142.

9. The examinees were tested for their abilities in running, doing the long jump, throwing hand grenades, carrying weights, doing chin-ups, swimming, and marching. Kanō Masanao, "3 tairyoku no jidai," in *Momotarō sagashi—kenkōkan no kindai*, Rekishi o yominaosu, vol. 23 (Tokyo: Asahi shinbunsha, 1995), 31.

10. Sawano, *Raisha no sei*, 143.

11. Documents of the Ministry of Health report the actual number of operations as 538. Kōseishō mondai kenkyūkai, *Kōseishō 50 nenshi: Kijutsuhen, shiryōhen* (Tokyo: Kōseishō, 1988), quoted in Kanō, *Momotarō sagashi*, 37.

12. Yoshiko Miyake, "Doubling Expectations: Motherhood and Women's Factory Work under State Management in Japan in the 1930s and 1940s," in *Recreating Japanese Women, 1600–1946*, ed. Gail Lee Bernstein (Berkeley and Los Angeles: University of California Press, 1991), 278.

13. The Home Ministry pared the ten-year plan down to a five-year plan just as the Japan Association for Leprosy Studies recommended, with financial assistance coming from the Mitsui Gratitude Foundation (Mitsu Hōonkai). Fujino Yutaka, *Nihon fashizumu to iryō* (Tokyo: Iwanami shoten, 1993), 136.

14. Fujino, *Nihon fashizumu to iryō*, 84.

15. Fujino, *Nihon fashizumu to iryō*, 104.

16. The mechanism of exclusion was replicated inside the facilities. The financial needs of the facilities converted the patients into working bodies: their labor was needed to sustain the operation of the facilities. Unproductive bodies were segregated into "special rooms"—a euphemism for confinement cells. Sawano, *Raisha no sei*, 148–61.

17. In July 1941, five public facilities were transferred from municipal management to the state, and the total number of national facilities became eleven. The death rates at the two facilities in Okinawa were extremely high—38 percent and 78 percent—because of the land battle fought there. Fujino, *Nihon fashizumu to iryō*, 206, 275–77.

18. Tatetsu Masasumi, "Sensōchū no Matsuzawa byōin nyūinkanja shibōritsu," *Seishin shinkeigaku zasshi*, vol. 60 (1958), reprinted in *Koenaki gyakusatsu*, ed. Tsukazaki Naoki (Tokyo: BOC shuppanbu, 1983), 225; and Okada Yasuo, *Shisetsu Matsuzawa byōinshi* (Tokyo: Miyazaki gakujutsu shuppansha, 1981), quoted in Kanō, *Momotarō sagashi*, 39. At the Matsuzawa Hospital, 62 percent of the deaths in 1945 directly stemmed from malnutrition. Tatetsu, "Sensōchū no Matsuzawa byōin nyūinkanja shibōritsu," 225.

19. Tsukazaki, *Koenaki gyakusatsu*, 23, quoted in Kanō, *Momotarō sagashi*, 39.

20. Fukushima Kikujirō, *Sensō ga hajimaru* (Tokyo: Shakaihyōron-sha, 1987), 253.

21. Fukushima, *Sensō ga hajimaru*, 253.

22. For instance, in February 1945, the Kyoto Prefecture's Economic Security Section issued the guidelines mandating that a bathhouse be paired with another and alternate business cycles: two days open and two days closed. Hours were limited to four to five per business day. Shimizu Isao, *Manga ni miru 1945 nen* (Tokyo: Yoshikawa kōbunkan, 1995), 40.

23. Nihon kyōiku terebi shakai kyōikubu, ed., *8 gatsu 15 nichi to watashi*, quoted in Shimokawa Kōshi, *Dansei no mita Shōwa seisōshi* (Tokyo: Daisan shokan, 1992), 13.

24. Hayashi Shigeru et al., eds., *Nihon shūsenshi: maboroshi no wahei kōsaku*, vol 2 (Tokyo: Yomiuri shinbunsha, 1962), 85.

25. Tezuka Osamu, "Manga baka no ben," *Bungeishunjū*, August 1975, 86. Also see his *Bokuno manga jinsei* (Tokyo: Iwanami shoten, 1997), 62–65.

26. Restrictions on nighttime lighting were officially lifted on August 20. Iwanami shoten henshūbu, ed., *Kindai Nihon sōgō nenpyō*, 3d ed. (Tokyo: Iwanami shoten, 1991), 344. The return of light to the cities in nocturnal hours impressed

many and has been included in numerous literary scenes. For instance, see Nosaka Akiyuki, *Senso dowashu* (Tokyo: Chūōkōron sha, 1980), 96; Senō Kappa, *Shōnen H* vol. 2 (Tokyo: Kōdansha, 1997), 229. In addition, several contributors to *8 gatsu 15 nichi no kodomotachi*, a collection of childhood memories from the end of the war, describe lighting during the night as the most noticeable and exciting change right after the war. See Anohi o kirokusurukai, *8 gatsu 15 nichi no kodomotachi* (Tokyo: Shōbunsha, 1987), 50, 63–64, 72, 82, 104, 136.

27. Statistics Bureau, Office of the Prime Minister, *Japan Statistical Yearbook, 1950* (Tokyo: Nihon Statistical Association and Mainichi shinbunsha, 1951), 70–71.

28. In July 1947, the minister of agriculture and forestry gave the following explanation to the Diet: "In the agricultural year [Showa] 22, that is from November 1 of the last year until October 31 of the next [*sic*] year, the Japanese government cannot help but having twenty-eight days, almost a month, of delay in its distribution [of rice]." *Asahi shinbun*, July 3, 1947, quoted in Matsudaira Makoto, *Yamiichi maboroshi no gaidobukku* (Tokyo: Chikuma shobō, 1995), 88.

29. From the time this news was first reported in newspapers, it has been rumored that the judge's heroic death was a fabrication of the news media. Iwanami shoten henshūbu, *Kindai Nihon sōgō nenpyō*, 362.

30. For the repercussions of his death in postwar society, see Yamaguchi Yoshiomi, "Yamaguchi hanji no tsuma—sono sei to shi," *Bungeishunjū*, July 1982, 342–47.

31. Sakata Minoru, "Nihongata kindai seikatsu yōshiki no seiritsu," in *Zoku Shōwa bunka, 1945–1989*, ed. Minami Hiroshi and Shakai shinri kenkyūjo (Tokyo: Keisō shobō, 1990), 13.

32. This edict replaced the 1939 edict on controlling prices. This regulation took the form of an edict since the government was still operating under the Meiji Constitution. Masamura Kimihiro, "Bukka tōseirei," in *Sengoshi daijiten*, ed. Sasaki Tsuyoshi et al. (Tokyo: Sanseidō, 1991), 801.

33. Matsudaira, *Yamiichi maboroshi no gaido bukku*, 122–24.

34. Matsudaira, *Yamiichi maboroshi no gaido bukku*, 91–94.

35. Nosaka Akiyuki, "Yamiichi to sukurīn," in *Sakka no jiden*, vol. 19 (Tokyo: Nihon toshosentā, 1994), 207.

36. Nosaka, "Yamiichi to sukurīn," 211.

37. Kurumizawa Kōshi, *Kuropan horyoki* (Tokyo: Bungeishunjū, 1983), 39.

38. Kurumizawa, *Kuropan horyoki*, 121.

39. Sexually charged scenes in short-lived magazines in the immediate postwar period were often accompanied by the description of food. Yamaoka Akira, *Kasutori zasshi ni miru sengoshi* (Tokyo: Orion shuppansha, 1970), 199–203.

40. Tamura Taijirō, *Waga bundan seishunki* (Tokyo: Shinchōsha, 1963), 219.

41. The rubric of "literature of the flesh" also included the works of such writers as Sakaguchi Ango, Funabashi Seiichi, Niwa Fumio, Kitahara Takeo, and Inoue Tomoichirō. Ishikawa Hiroyoshi et al., eds., *Taishū bunka jiten* (Tokyo: Kōbundō, 1994), 579.

42. Tamura Taijirō, *Nikutai no bungaku* (Tokyo: Kusano shobō, 1948), 11–13.

43. Tamura, *Nikutai no bungaku*, 13.

44. Tamura, *Nikutai no bungaku*, 17.

45. Tamura, *Nikutai no bungaku*, 18.

46. Tamura, *Nikutai no bungaku*, 18.

47. Sakaguchi Ango, "Zoku darakuron," *Sakaguchi Ango zenshū*, vol. 14 (Tokyo: Chikuma shobō, 1990), 589–90.

48. Sakaguchi Ango, "Nikutai jitai ga shikōsuru," *Sakaguchi Ango zenshū*, 14:577.

49. Sakaguchi, "Nikutai jitai ga shikōsuru," 578.

50. These magazines were called *kasutori zasshi*. *Kasutori* was the name of an alcoholic beverage made out of potatoes and grains. The alcohol content of *kasutori* was high, and it was said that anybody who drank three cups (*sangō*: 540 cc) collapsed (*tsubureru*); most *kasutori zasshi* went under (*tsubureru*) by their third issue (*sangō*). For discussions of relatively well known *kasutori zasshi*, see Yamaoka, *Kasutori zasshi ni miru sengoshi*, and Yamamoto Akira, *Kasutori zasshi kenkyū* (Tokyo: Chūōkōronsha, 1998).

51. Striptease reportedly began in a modest form in 1947—naked women stood still in a frame—at Teitoza Theater in Tokyo. Sakaguchi Ango was among the men who frequented the theater while the show was on. Shimokawa, *Dansei no mita seisōshi*, 46–47.

52. Tamura Taijirō, "Nikutai no mon," in *Tamura Taijirō senshū*, vol. 1 (Tokyo: Kusano shobō, 1948), 303.

53. Tamura, *Tamura Taijirō senshū*, 324.

54. Tamura, *Tamura Taijirō senshū*, 325.

55. Tamura, *Tamura Taijirō senshū*, 329.

56. Another writer, Ishikawa Jun, found Christ among the ruins of Tokyo, too. In his 1946 story, "Yakeato no Iesu," a boy covered in "rags, abscesses, pus, and probably lice" tackles the protagonist for the bread he is carrying. When the protagonist sees the boy's face, it becomes clear to him that the boy is Jesus of Nazareth. Ishikawa Jun, *Ishikawa Jun senshū*, vol. 1 (Tokyo: Iwanami shoten, 1979), 322–37.

57. Tamura, *Waga bundan seishunki*, 219.

58. "Nikutai no mon" was made into a film five times. The fifth version (1988) distinguishes itself from the earlier ones with its clear anti-American tone. Americans appear only as male members of the American occupation forces: many of them as sexually overcharged GIs. Borneo Maya's sexual encounter with Ibuki recedes as a minor subplot, while a newly added subplot of a vendetta against an American receives more attention: in retaliation for the rape of herself and her mother, one of the prostitutes kills an American sergeant. She fails to kill the man with a gun but succeeds in her second attempt with a short sword—a Japanese weapon. This film is an early example of the blatant anti-Americanism that became more prevalent in 1990s Japan. For further discussion of anti-Americanism, see this book's conclusion.

59. Maruyama Masao, *Maruyama Masao shū*, 17 vols. (Tokyo: Iwanami shoten, 1995), 4:207–27.

60. *Maruyama Masao shū*, 4:226.

61. *Maruyama Masao shū*, 4:212–13.

62. *Maruyama Masao shū*, 4:212.

63. *Maruyama Masao shū*, 4:225.

64. *Maruyama Masao shū*, 4:226–27. Kanō Masanao lists the bodily references in Maruyama's early writings (*Momotarō sagashi*, 50–51).

65. *Maruyama Masao shū*, 3:143.

66. *Maruyama Masao shū*, 3:93, 109.

67. See Maruyama Masao, *Nihon seiji shisōshi kenkyū*, in *Maruyama Masao shū*, vols. 1 and 2, and *Studies in the Intellectual History of Tokugawa Japan*, trans. Mikiso Hane (Tokyo: University of Tokyo Press, 1974). In the 1970s, Maruyama pushed this loss out of historical time altogether and posited it as the ur-loss of Japanese history. See Maruyama Masao, "Rekishi ishiki no 'kosō' " in *Maruyama Masao shū*, vol. 10, and "Genkei, kosō, shitsuyōteion" in *Maruyama Masao shū*, vol. 12.

68. Maruyama Masao et al., "Sensō to dōjidai," *Dōjidai* 8 (1958): 23.

69. Kristin Ross locates France's desire after World War II to distance itself from, and simultaneously to naturalize, its colonial legacies in its obsession with cleanliness and functionality. See *Fast Cars, Clean Bodies: Decolonization and the Reordering of French Culture* (Cambridge: MIT Press, 1995), 71–122. On the contrary, postwar Japan, as I argued in chapter 1, paid little attention to its past as a colonial power.

70. Crawford F. Sams, *"Medic"* (Armonk, N.Y.: M. E. Sharpe, 1998), 188.

71. On August 22, 1945, the Department of the Army communicated the summary of SWNCC 150/3, "U.S. Initial Post Surrender Policy for Japan," to Douglas MacArthur as a guideline before his landing on Japan's shores. The Department transmitted its entire text to MacArthur on August 29. On September 6, Truman officially approved as official policy a slightly modified version of SWNCC 150/3 (SWNCC 150/4). Iokibe Makoto, *Beikoku no Nihon senryōseisaku*, vol. 2 (Tokyo: Chūōkōronsha, 1985), 253–54.

72. Public Services, General Headquarters, United States Army Forces, Pacific, Military Government Section, "Basic Plan for Operations," August 30, 1945. The National Archive file, Declassified E.O. 12065—Section 3–402/NNDC, No. 775024. National Diet Library, Modern Japanese Political History Material Room, GHQ/SCAP Records, PHW 01948.

73. Sams, *"Medic,"* 59.

74. In 1946 in Japan, 32,366 people contracted typhus fever and 28,210 suffered from malaria. Murakami Yōichirō, *Iryō—kōreishakai e mukatte*, 20 seiki no Nippon, vol. 9 (Tokyo: Yomiuri shinbunsha, 1996), 71–73.

75. In January 1946, GHQ made the first of its numerous releases of military provisions. See Crawford F. Sams, *DDT Kakumei*, trans. and ed. Takemae Eiji (Tokyo: Iwanami shoten, 1986), 113n. In 1947, the U.S. government began relief efforts through its GARIOA (Government and Relief in Occupied Areas) fund. See Sasaki et al., *Sengoshi daijiten*, 572–73.

76. Sams, *"Medic,"* 81.

77. Numerous Army documents attest to the United States' extensive use of DDT toward the end of the Pacific War. For example, a letter from the Office of the Quartermaster General, Army Service Forces, to the Surgeon General, Army Service Forces, dated November 4, 1944, shows that the U.S. Army shipped

176,235 lbs. of DDT to the Southwest Pacific Area and 176,000 lbs. to China, Burma, and India through September 15, 1944. An Additional 38,550 lbs. were shipped to the Southwest Pacific Area in September and October 1944 alone. Furthermore, when the letter was written, 189,895 lbs. of DDT were at the pier to be shipped to the Southwest Pacific Area. SPQSG QM 444.2 SWPA. National Archives, Box 85, Entry 30, Record Group 112. In May 2, 1944, the Military Planning Division within the Army Service Forces, Office of the Quartermaster General, predicted that the U.S. Army and related agencies would need 8,735,322 lbs. of pure DDT in 1945. National Archives, Box 86, Entry 30, Record Group 112. See also Sams, *"Medic,"* 14.

78. Sams, *DDT Kakumei*, 18n.

79. Sams, *DDT Kakumei*, 19n.

80. Internal memoranda of PHWS show that airplane spraying of DDT was conducted in 1946. According to the PHWS memorandum dated May 1, 1946, the areas subjected to the airplane spraying were as follows: Otaru, Sapporo, Sendai, Tokyo-Yokohama, Kyoto, Osaka-Kobe, Tatsuno, and Okayama. Spraying was also conducted in Korea in the same year. See the memoranda included in the National Archive file, Declassified E.O. 12065—Section 3–402, No. 775024, "Airplane Spraying of DDT," National Diet Library, Modern Japanese Political History Material Room, GHQ/SCAP Records, PHW-04539.

81. Sams, *"Medic,"* 93–94. GHQ sent memoranda to the Japanese government directing specific use of DDT. See Memorandum for the Ministry of Welfare from GHQ, PHMJG 3, dated December 13, 1946, subject "Rickettsicidal (Typhus Control) Spray Program," and Memorandum for Japanese government, SCAPIN 2011, dated May 28, 1949, subject "Prevention and Control of the Typhus Fever Group of Diseases in Japan."

82. Sams, *"Medic,"* 85.

83. Murakami, *Iryō—kōreiskakai e mukatte*, 59. Dispensing of DDT was done even though U.S. Army authorities suspected DDT's carcinogenic effects. In a memo, dated August 26, 1944, James S. Simmons, from the Office of the Surgeon General, Army Service Forces, sent the following explanation to Captain Ludwid Cross, who had earlier (August 17, 1944) inquired about DDT research opportunities. It reads: "The possibility that DDT may have carcinogenic action has been in the minds of responsible authorities ever since its use in the Army was contemplated. Observations are available on the results of prolonged application of DDT to the skin of animals, and numerous long time observations have been made on the organs and tissues of animals to which DDT has been fed and to which DDT preparations have been injected. Thus far no carcinogenic effects have been produced. Investigations of the subject will be continued." SPMCE 441 (DDT), A.S.F., S.G.O., 26 August 1944, National Archives, Box 85, Entry 30, Record Group 112. Although the initial research in 1944–45 detected no carcinogenic effects of DDT in subject mice, the National Institute of Health continued experiments in the postwar era. "Memorandum for the Quarter General, 17 May 1946: DDT for Experimental Purposes," National Archives, Box 641, Entry 29, Record Group 112. The Army used methyl bromide to delouse its own men. Field chambers were set up for the application of methyl bromide. A November 23, 1945,

memo from John W. Regan, Medical Corps Chief, explains the application method in detail. SPMDY, JWR/mw/79051. National Archives, Box 684, Entry 29, Record Group 112.

84. Nosaka, "Yamiichi to sukurīn," 213. In one of Nosaka's short stories, the protagonist even eats DDT mixed with corn meal to fill his empty stomach. Nosaka Akiyuki, "La Cumparsita," *Amerika hijiki, Hotaru no haka* (Tokyo: Shinchōsha, 1988), 178.

85. Mainichi shinbunsha, *Iwanami shoten to Bungeishunjū*, 46–47.

86. Watanabe Naoko, "DDT no uta," in Sams, *DDT Kakumei*, 134n–135n.

87. Sakurai Tsunao, "Haisen zengo no seishinbyōin," in Tsukazaki, *Koenaki Gyakusatsu*, 141.

88. Murakami's father was an army doctor who opened a small clinic in Tokyo after the war. Murakami recalls that GHQ annually delivered DDT powder and a dispenser between 1947 and around 1950 even to his father's small clinic. He also remembers that GHQ distributed some items whose use he was not sure about. One of the items was undiluted Coca-Cola formula. Murakami's father was at a loss since the formula came with no specifications for its use. It was more than ironic that this American object par excellence was distributed along with DDT powder to Japanese medical facilities. Murakami, *Iryō—kōreishakai e mukatte*, 60–64.

89. Murakami, *Iryō—kōreishakai e mukatte*, 65.

90. Murakami, *Iryō—kōreishakai e mukatte*, 65. Actually, this information was not accurate: a sulfa drug was used for Churchill's illness.

91. For the effects of this misinformation on the Japanese development of penicillin, see Hirata Akitaka, "Penishirin: Jimaede kanseisaseta 'kiseki no kusuri,' " *Sengo 50 nen Nippon no kiseki*, vol. 1, ed. Yomiuri shinbun henshūkyoku—"sengoshi han" (Tokyo: Yomiuri shinbunsha, 1995), 105–6.

92. Murakami, *Iryō—kōreishakai e mukatte*, 65–66.

93. *Yomiuri Hōchi Shinbun*, August 20, 1945, 2, quoted in Sasamoto Yukio, *Beigunsenryōka no genbaku chōsa: genbaku kagaikoku ninatta Nihon* (Tokyo: Shinkansha, 1995), 235.

94. According to one of the contributors to *8 gatsu 15 nichi no kodomotachi*, after the emperor's radio announcement, her sixth-grade teacher claimed: "The war is over. The loser is the winner" [Makeruga kachi desu]. Anohi o kirokusurukai, ed., *8 gatsu 15 nichi*, 90. The defeat could be explained as a victory only by assuming the future resolution of the conflict. The scientific basis of Japan's defeat was one way to explain the losers as the future winners.

95. Murakami, *Iryō—kōreishakai e mukatte*, 69.

96. Sams, *"Medic,"* 106.

97. Sams, *"Medic,"* 107.

98. The Japanese pharmacological industry succeeded in manufacturing penicillin during the war. Some Japanese-produced penicillin was used in Hiroshima and Nagasaki after the atomic attacks. However, Japan still lacked the technology for mass production and managed to produce large quantities of penicillin only with U.S. assistance after the war. Hirata, "Penishirin," 106–9.

99. Hirata, "Penishirin," 108.

100. Sams, *"Medic,"* 107.

101. The Japanese government's wartime regulatory practices actually did not disappear in the postwar period. GHQ decided to maintain the Ministry of Health, which had been responsible for the wartime hygienic policies, as the organization through which it implemented its hygiene policies. Sugiyama Akiko, *Senryōki no iryōkaikaku* (Tokyo: Keisōshobō, 1995), 58–61. The number of sterilization cases drastically increased under the new postwar eugenic legislation. In the decade between 1952 and 1961, a total of 10,017 cases of sterilization were carried out by doctors. Ichinokawa Yasutaka and Tateiwa Shinya, "Shōgaishaundō kara mietekurumono," *Gendai shisō* 26, no. 2 (1998): 260; Ichinokawa Yasutaka, "Yūsei shujutsu (= funin shujutsu) ni tsuite," in *Seishoku gijutsu to jendā*, ed. Ehara Yumiko (Tokyo: Keiseishobō, 1996), 384.

Chapter 3

1. Yoshida Shigeru, *The Yoshida Memoirs*, trans. Yoshida Ken'ichi (Westport, Conn.: Greenwood Press, 1973), 263.

2. Foreign Affairs Association of Japan, *Japan Year Book, 1949–52* (Tokyo: Foreign Affairs Association of Japan, 1952), 463; emphasis added.

3. Foreign Affairs Association of Japan, *Japan Year Book, 1949–52*, 478.

4. Shibagaki Kazuo, *Kōwa kara kōdoseichōe*, Shōwa no rekishi, vol. 9 (Tokyo: Shōgakkan, 1989), 31.

5. Martin E. Weinstein, *Japan's Postwar Defense Policy, 1947–68* (New York: Columbia University Press, 1971), 87–90.

6. Foreign Affairs Association of Japan, *Japan Year Book, 1949–52*, 482; and Ara Takashi, "Saigunbi to zainichi Beigun," in *Iwanami kōza: Nihon tsūshi*, vol. 20, ed. Asao Naohiro et al. (Tokyo: Iwanami shoten, 1995), 169–70.

7. Weinstein, *Japan's Postwar Defense Policy*, 111.

8. The Liberal Democratic Party's various attempts to increase the regulatory power of the government and the police were frustrated by a strong liberal opposition in the 1950s. In the following decade, the party shifted its focus away from political issues and toward economic development. For a discussion of this shift, see Watanabe Osamu, "Sengo hoshushihai no kōzō," in Asao et al., *Iwanami kōza: Nihon tsūshi*, 20:90–93.

9. Avoiding reference to the war in "special procurements" was consistent with the fact that Japan's Self-Defense Forces were initially called the National Police Reserve. The National Police Reserve was established in 1950 to make up for the deployment to Korea of American military divisions based in Japan. War-related references in the language of the National Police Reserve were replaced with more neutral terms. For instance, tanks were called "special vehicles," infantrymen "normal course," and artillerymen "special course." We see at work a logic reminiscent of *1984*: a military is not a military insofar as it is not designated as such. Kanda Fumihito, *Senryō to Minshushugi*, Shōwa no rekishi, vol. 8 (Tokyo: Shōgakkan, 1989), 385–86.

10. Sasaki et al., *Sengoshi daijiten*, 611.

11. Although Joseph Dodge recommended a rate of 330 yen to the dollar, Washington set the rate at 360 yen to the dollar. Nakamura, *Shōwashi*, 2:431. Shigeto Tsuru characterizes the positive effects that the yen-dollar exchange ratio

had on the Japanese economy: "It may be recalled that the single exchange rate of 360 yen to the dollar was established in April 1949 while Japan was still under the Occupation and also that this rate was judged by many experts then as similar to a handicap given to a convalescent golfer. Quite soon after, the 360-yen rate turned out to be yen-cheap as Japanese manufacturing industries recovered their potential efficiency and further caught up with the front-ranking countries of the West." Shigeto Tsuru, *Japan's Capitalism* (Cambridge: Cambridge University Press, 1993), 179; Shibagaki, *Kōwa kara kōdoseichōe*, 220–26.

12. Nakaoka Tetsurō, "Gijyutsu kakushin," in Asao et al., *Iwanami kōza: Nihon tsūshi*, 20:219.

13. Asahi shinbunsha, ed., *"Nichibei kaiwa techō" wa naze uretaka* (Tokyo: Asahi shinbunsha, 1995), 16–17.

14. In 1946, *Shūkan asahi* and, in January 1949, *Asahi shinbun* began carrying Chic Young's comic strip *Blondie*.

15. For instance, the Civil Information and Education Section in General Mac-Arthur's headquarters actively circulated and screened films promoting American values throughout Japan during the occupation. See Asahi shinbun gakugeibu, *Daidokoro kara sengo ga mieru* (Tokyo: Asahi shinbunsha, 1995), 30–34.

16. Yamaguchi Masatomo, "Dōgu," in *Kōdoseichō to Nihonjin*, part 2: *Kazoku no seikatsu no monogatari*, ed. Kōdoseichō o kangaerukai (Tokyo: Nihon editā sukūru shuppanbu, 1986), 69.

17. The radio program *Amerika dayori* began in February 1948. Although the program offered very straightforward reportage about American lifestyles (an announcer read reports by a Japanese journalist in the United States), it soon became extremely popular. Ishikawa Hiroyoshi, *Yokubō no sengoshi* (Tokyo: Kōsaidō, 1989), 33–34.

18. In the initial development stage of appliances after the war, developers more or less concentrated their efforts in copying European and American models. However, for some, the rice cooker became a symbol of national pride for its uniquely Japanese features. Akatsuka Chiemi recalled her first impressions of the rice cooker her family bought: the quality of the cooked rice may not have been as good as before, but "as a uniquely Japanese appliance entering a Japanese household," it luminously radiated "a light that was similar to that of the swimmer Furuhashi Hironoshin when he established world records in the postwar years." Akatsuka's mother kept saying that "this invention is a hope for Japan's tomorrow." Asahi shinbun gakugeibu, *Daidokoro kara sengo ga mieru*, 64–65, 67. In the late 1980s, this sentiment reappeared as a more blatant form of nationalism in Ishihara Shintarō's controversial *The Japan That Can Say No*, trans. Baldwin Frank (the Japanese original first appeared in 1989). Ishihara claims that Japan occupies a strategically advantageous position in the U.S.-Soviet conflict, thanks to its advanced computer chips. Ultimately, Japan has the key bargaining "chip," since neither the United States nor the Soviet Union will be able to guide its nuclear missiles without the next generation of chips from Japan. Ishihara then insists that "unlike Japan, the United States lacks a market for the wide variety of products that use semiconductors, such as rice cookers." Ishihara in effect makes a postmodern claim that the rice cookers will save Japan. Ishihara Shintarō, *The Japan That Can Say No*, trans. Frank Baldwin (New York: Simon and Schuster, 1991), 22–23.

19. The average ratio of the number of applications to each vacancy was fifty-three to one in 1964. Asahi shinbun gakugeibu, *Daidokoro kara sengo ga mieru*, 58.

20. The trope of in-betweenness was not peculiar to postwar Japan. For instance, in the 1893 Columbian Exposition in Chicago, Japan was spatially represented "in between" in the exposition's hierarchical representation of progress. This evidence attests to a nineteenth-century American view that regarded Japan as a country between the developed West and other geopolitical areas of the world on the scale of universal progress. Yoshimi Shunya, *Hakurankai no seijigaku* (Tokyo: Chūōkōronsha, 1992), 211.

21. Katō Norihiro compiled a list of such tropes from the comprehensive index of *Chūōkōron*. They include *mushisōjin, zasshubunka, higashi to nisni no aida, senchūha, chūnen joyū, chūkan bunka, chūkansei, chūritsu kokka, daisan no shinjin*, and *chūkan shōsetsu*. Katō Norihiro, *Nihon to iu shintai* (Tokyo: Kōdansha, 1994), 252–54.

22. These four articles were later published as a book, Maruyama Masao, *Nihon no shisō* (Tokyo: Iwanami shoten, 1961).

23. Nakamura Masanori, "1950–60 nendai no Nihon: Kōdo keizaiseichō," in Asao et al., *Iwanami kōza: Nihon tsūshi*, 23:25–26.

24. Katō Shūichi, "Nihon bunka no zasshusei," *Zasshubunka* (Tokyo: Kōdansha, 1974), 28–32.

25. Katō, *Zasshubunka*, 47.

26. Katō, *Zasshubunka*, 48.

27. Maruyama, *Maruyama Masao shū*, 7:242–44. All four articles included in *Nihon no shisō* first appeared in the second half of the 1950s.

28. Maruyama Masao, *Nihon seiji shisōshi kenkyū* (Tokyo: Tokyo daigaku suppankai, 1952), *Studies in the Intellectual History of Tokugawa Japan*, trans. Mikiso Hane (Tokyo: University of Tokyo Press, 1974), *Maruyama Masao shū*, 1:125–307, and 2:3–125, 225–68.

29. Maruyama, "Rekishi ishiki no 'kosō,' " 10:3–66.

30. Ōe Kenzaburō, *Mirumae ni tobe* (Tokyo: Shinchōsha, 1958). See particularly his afterword, 251–52.

31. Kojima Nobuo, "Enkei Daigaku Butai," *Amerikan sukūru* (Tokyo: Shinchōsha, 1967). Subsequent references are given in the text.

32. Kojima Nobuo's desire to problematize the character's relation to language can be contrasted to another Japanese writer's treatment of this issue. In his 1974 biography of a Japanese American navy officer, Yoshida Mitsuru contrasts the relative ease of deciphering Japanese codes with the practical impossibility of decoding the random coding system of the U.S. Navy. This crucial difference, according to Yoshida, lay in the peculiarities of the Japanese language. Yoshida claims that "Ōta, who was beginning to like the subtlety of expressions in written Japanese, felt tragic destiny in its limitation as a language of coding." For Yoshida, the Japanese language is burdened with subtleties that defy simple mechanical coding, and, in turn, mastery of these subtleties assured the Japanese American, Ōta, a place within the hermeneutic circle of the Japanese society. Yoshida Mitsuru, *Chinkon senkan Yamato* (Tokyo: Kōdansha, 1974), 193.

33. Kojima Nobuo, "Hoshi," in *Amerikan sukūru*. Translated by Van C. Gessel as "Stars," in *The Shōwa Anthology*, edited by Van C. Gessel and Tomone

Matsumoto (Tokyo: Kodansha International, 1989). Subsequent page references, for the Japanese and the English editions, are given in the text. I have modified the translation in some passages.

34. "Where am I?" is my translation. The original Japanese is "Jibun wa do-koni irunoda."

35. American military power did not exactly displace the order and hierarchy of stars. The United States rather sought to legitimate its military presence through the emperor, who ultimately supported the order and hierarchy of stars, in postwar Japan.

36. This case is listed in almost all popular chronologies published in the postwar period. See Sasaki et al., *Sengoshi daijiten*, 14, 88, 761; Uno Shun'ichi et al., eds., *Nihon zenshi: Japan Chronik* (Tokyo: Kōdansha, 1991), 1098; Ishikawa Hiroyoshi et al., eds., *[Shukusatu ban] Taishūbunka jiten* (Tokyo: Kōbundō, 1994), 24, 111; Nishii Kazuo, ed., *Sengo 50 nen: Post war 50 years* (Tokyo: Mainichi shinbunsha, 1995), 40; and Iwanami shoten henshūbu, *Kindai Nihon sōgō nenpyō*, 3d ed., 380.

37. The man was thrown from Sukiya Bridge into the outer moat in the Ginza district by three GIs on November 24, 1953. *Asahi shinbun*, November 25, 1953, 7. Another Japanese man was also thrown into the water from Sukiya Bridge by two GIs four weeks later. *Asahi shinbun*, December 19, 1953, 7.

38. Ōe, *Mirumae ni tobe*, 251. Subsequent references are given in the text.

39. Benedict Anderson, *Imagined Communities* (London: Verso, 1991), 9–12.

40. For a critical discussion of the case, see Ide Magoroku, "W. S. Girard no hanzai," in *Sengoshi*, vol. 1 (Tokyo: Iwanami shoten, 1991), 287–304.

41. *Asahi shinbun*, September 28, 1971, 1.

42. The next day's *Asahi shinbun* printed the entire text of the emperor's speech with the comment that "the voice of his majesty resonated high to the last word in the ceremony hall." *Asahi shinbun*, September 28, 1971, 1, 3.

43. *Irie Aimasa nikki*, vol. 4 (Tokyo: Asahi shinbunsha, 1991), 229, 306, quoted in Yoshida, *Showa tennō no shūsenshi*, 243–44.

44. Nakamura Takafusa, *Shōwashi*, vol. 1 (Tokyo: Tōyōkeizai shinpōsha, 1993), 342–43.

Chapter 4

1. In order to fuel the excitement further, Noguchi Tsurukichi, the head of the publicity section at Shōchiku Cinema, circulated the rumor that the women's sections of public bathhouses were empty when the show was on air. This rumor was later believed by many to be the truth. I received this information from Professor Ishikawa Hiroyoshi, who interviewed Noguchi Tsurukichi. For rankings of gross earnings, see Kinema junpō, ed., *Sengo Kinema junpō best ten zenshi: 1946–1992* (Tokyo: Kinema junpōsha, 1993), 42. In the fiscal year between April 1953 and March 1954, *Kimi no nawa* parts 1 and 2 together earned 550 million yen. The next most commercially successful Japanese film of the year was *Taiheiyō no washi*, which earned 163 million yen.

2. The film was directed by Ōba Hideo. Part 1 appeared in 1953, and parts 2 and 3 came out in the following year. The Nihon Hōsō Kyōkai Broadcast Museum Library holds ninety-seven of the ninety-eight scenarios of the radio episodes. The scenario for episode 60 is missing. The radio broadcast version and the book version are fairly close to each other in structure, with a few notable differences. The radio version tends to make more commentary on current political issues early in the series. For instance, in the June 21, 1952, episode, Kikuta makes critical comments on the Communist Party's role in the May Day Incident (the bloody confrontation between six thousand demonstrators and five thousand police on May 1, 1952, in a square in front of the Imperial Palace); however, this is not included in the book. Furthermore, the radio series does not end with the protagonists' reunion, as does the book version. All in all, the narrative of the book is more self-contained, whereas that of the radio series is more disjunctive and less developed, particularly toward its end; it appears that Kikuta was working under great time pressure to produce the scenario. The film version reproduces the narrative line of the book, in a more condensed form.

I mainly rely on the book version (Kikuta Kazuo, *Kimi no nawa*, 4 vols. [Tokyo: Kawade shobō, 1991]; references are given in the text) in this section because it shows a more developed plot than do the radio scenarios and provides more detailed information than both the film and radio versions. I make occasional reference to the radio and film versions when variations affect my reading of the story.

3. Isoda Kōichi, *Sengoshi no kūkan* (Tokyo: Shinchōsha, 1993), 239.

4. In the radio version, the ending is more abrupt and cynical. The final episode ends with Katsunori's second wedding with Yoshiko, a daughter of his superior. In the final scene, both Katsunori and Yoshiko acknowledge and accept the fact that their marriage does not stem from their love but from Katsunori's desire to advance in the bureaucratic system through the newly forged family ties.

5. Kikuta suggests that Katsunori works for the Home Ministry. Katsunori hopes to gain points by marrying Yoshiko, daughter of his powerful superior. However, Yoshiko's brother, who also works for the Home Ministry, is rather critical of Katsunori's vulgar determination to advance in the bureaucratic system. However, such a connection is impossible. The Home Ministry, which was in charge of domestic security in prewar and wartime Japan, was abolished in 1947 by the GHQ. The historical blunder of the author notwithstanding, Katsunori's link to the Home Ministry is revealing in terms of his function as the embodiment of the patriarchal system. See *Kimi no nawa*, 4:192–93.

6. This half-American child is also an embodiment of contradicting desires toward the memories of the war. One of the characters tries to sort out his feelings: "For the sake of Toshiki [the child], I wish it [the fact that he is an interracial child] forgotten. However, I do not think we should forget that such children were born because of the war" (4:310).

7. For instance, Katsunori's mother accuses Machiko of a fascination with foreign (European and American) men (3:289). This attests to the paranoid concerns of the patriarchy regarding the state of Japanese women's sexuality.

8. Two other characters suffer from illness or injury, and their subsequent recovery also signals the healing of social ties. For example, Katsunori's mother falls ill while she visits Machiko in Kyushu. Due to Machiko's dedicated care, she

recovers and establishes affectionate relations with Machiko. As another example, while Toshiki's injury in a car accident reveals a deep-seated prejudice against interracial children (the responsible party did not take the injury seriously because he is an interracial child), it also brings his doctor into the circle of his protectors. The story further suggests that the doctor will marry the child's mother.

9. As I mentioned earlier, the radio series ends rather abruptly without this denouement.

10. These two scenes that make reference to *Madame Butterfly* were not incorporated into the film version.

11. Tokyo kōsoku dōro kabushiki gaisha, *Tokyo kōsoku dōro 30 nenno ayumi* (Tokyo: Tokyo kōsoku dōro kabushiki gaisha, 1981), 95.

12. Asahi shinbunsha, *Asahi shinbun no uchi soto* (Tokyo: Asahi shinbunsha, 1984), 114.

13. Asahi shinbunsha, *Asahi shinbun no uchi soto*, 85.

14. Mainichi shinbunsha, *Iwanami shoten to Bungeishunjū*, 56–57.

15. Iwanami shoten henshūbu, 3rd ed. *Kindai Nihon sōgō nenpyō*, 366.

16. Even the figure who embodied loss for Machiko disappeared: Sata Keiji, the actor who played Haruki in the film, died in a car accident in 1964, the year of the Tokyo Olympics. I discuss the link between Japan's motorization and the disappearing signs of wartime destruction in the next chapter. For the details of his accident, see *Asahi shinbun*, evening version, August 17, 1964, 7, and "Shinchōsa ga maneita furyo no shi," *Sandei Mainichi*, August 30, 1964, 114–15.

17. The film producers consciously referred to the Sukiya Bridge. In the ritual prayer offered to the monster during a Godzilla festival held in a Tōhō studio celebrating the completion of the film, the name of the bridge and *Kimi no nawa* are mentioned: "stamping the Sukiya Bridge with dirty splash; even though your name is called, it cannot be heard." Takeuchi Hiroshi, " 'Gojira' no tanjō," in *Tsuburaya Eiji no eizōsekai*, ed. Yamamoto Shingo (Tokyo: Jitsugyō no Nihon sha, 1983), 88.

18. The voice of Godzilla was produced by pulling a string of a contrabass with a resined leather glove: the string was attached to the tail piece and released from a peg. Takeuchi, " 'Gojira' no tanjō," 88.

19. For American censorship in Japan regarding information on atomic weapons and their effects, see Monica Braw, *The Atomic Bomb Suppressed: American Censorship in Occupied Japan* (Armonk, N.Y.: M. E. Sharpe, 1991); and Horiba Kiyoko, *Kinjirareta genbaku taiken* (Tokyo: Iwanami shoten, 1995).

20. The original scenario of the film begins with the *Lucky Dragon V* returning to its base port in Japan and creating a panic in Japan. Takeuchi, " 'Gojira' no tanjō," 71. Although this scene was cut in the end, other signs anchor the return of Godzilla to this specific historical event. For instance, the ship destroyed at the beginning of the film was named *Eikōmaru*, the same as the boat also exposed in the radioactive fallout of March 1954. Kobayashi Toyoaki, *Gojira no ronri: A Study of the Godzilla Era* (Tokyo: Chūkyō shuppan, 1992), 22. In addition, before the ship is destroyed, the surface of the ocean wells up as if it were the outcome of an explosion; a surviving man claims that "the sea suddenly exploded." Furthermore, the paleontologist Dr. Yamane testifies to a Diet committee that the

hydrogen bomb testings were responsible for the return of the monster. Neither Yamane nor the ensuing heated discussion among the committee members directly raises the name of the United States. "The difficult international situation" (in the phrase of one Diet member) is the only extent to which the United States is identified in the film.

21. U.S. government policy played an indirect role in the Tōhō Cinema Company's production of *Godzilla*. Tōhō had been involved in a joint project with the Indonesia National Film Company for a film based on an episode in the Indonesian independence movement. The Indonesian government suddenly withdrew its support, and the project was subsequently canceled. The change in the Indonesian government's attitude toward the project was due partly to American intervention: the American government was not happy about a joint film project between Japan and Indonesia, because these countries had not reestablished official relations. The two companies were planning to have Yamaguchi Yoshiko (Ri Kō-ran) as the film's heroine. Takeuchi, " 'Gojira' no tanjō," 68.

22. Takeuchi, " 'Gojira' no tanjō," 69.

23. Ono Kōsei, *Chikyūgi ni notta neko* (Tokyo: Tōjusha, 1982), quoted in Tsurumi Shunshuke, "Sengo no taishū bunka," in *Kōza Nihon eiga, 4: Sensōto Nihon eiga* (Tokyo: Iwanami shoten, 1986), 350.

24. Kobayashi, *Gojira no ronri*, 25–28.

25. The actual size of the Self-Defense Forces was 146,285 in 1954. Weinstein, *Japan's Postwar Defense Policy*, 111.

26. For instance, all the F-86 fighter jets that attack Godzilla are emblazoned with the rising sun. However, the Self-Defense Forces did not deploy F-86s until 1955. Kobayashi, *Gojira no ronri*, 27.

27. In contrast to the ineffectiveness of Japanese forces, American counterparts manage to kill Godzilla in the 1998 version of *Godzilla*.

28. The titles of the films are *Taiheiyō no Washi* (Eagle in the Pacific) (1953) and *Saraba Rabauru* (Goodbye, Rabaul) (1954). *Taiheiyō no Washi* grossed 163 million yen, the third highest total in 1953, beaten only by parts 1 and 2 of *Kimi no nawa*. Kinema junpō, *Sengo Kinema junpō best ten zenshi*, 42. For a discussion of these films, see Higuchi Naofumi, *Guddo mōningu Gojira: kantoku Honda Toshirō to satsueisho no jidai* (Tokyo: Chikuma shobō, 1992), 157–67.

29. Jinbo Tadahiro, "Kisha no me," in *Mainichi shinbun*, March 25, 1993, quoted in Kawamoto Saburō, *Imahitotabi no sengo Nihon eiga* (Tokyo: Iwanami shoten, 1994), 82.

30. "10 no danshō o tōshite mietekuru sengo 50 nen, soshite konokuni no 'rinkaku,' " *SPA*, February 1, 1995, 5.

31. Contrary to Kawamoto's claim, Godzilla does not directly return to the sea. According to the radio reports, Godzilla moves to Asakusa and Ueno and then returns to the sea via the Sumida River. Nonetheless, the absence of reference in the film to the Imperial Palace is notable.

32. Kawamoto, *Imahitotabi no sengo Nihon eiga*, 86.

33. The way in which the "Oxygen Destroyer" works also attests to a desire to contain the nuclear threat that the monster represents. The Oxygen Destroyer itself is shaped like and is about the size of a softball. It is encased in a glass cylinder and separated into two half-spheres when it operates. The process is thus

a complete reversal of the detonation of the Hiroshima-type atomic bomb in which two half spheres of uranium were collided by the conventional explosives.

34. *Godzilla* had the eighth largest earnings, 154 million yen, in the fiscal year 1954. *Kimi no nawa*, part 3, grossed highest, with 330 million yen. Kinema junpō, *Sengo Kinema junpō best ten zenshi*, 48.

35. Between 1954 and 1995, twenty-two Godzilla movies were produced in Japan. For a synopsis of each episode, see Kawakita Kōichi, ed., *Bokutachi no aishita kaijū Gojira* (Tokyo: Gakushu kenkyūsha, 1996).

36. Chon A. Noriega, "Godzilla and the Japanese Nightmare: When *Them!* is U.S.," *Cinema Journal* 27, no. 1 (1987): 63–75. Although Noriega offers astute readings both of the relationship between the monstrosity of Godzilla and U.S. nuclear policies, and of the Japanese audience's identification with the monster, he resorts to an ahistorical position in presenting his readings. Accepting Suzuki Takao's dubious linguistic explanation of the Japanese sense of self and other, Noriega explains the audience's identification as "cultural."

37. Takeuchi, " 'Gojira' no tanjō," 76–78. Also, the actor could not wear the costume more than a few minutes at a time because it trapped his body heat inside. Takeuchi, " 'Gojira' no tanjō," 86.

38. Takeuchi, " 'Gojira' no tanjō, 84.

39. For exemplary criticism of the 1960s Godzilla films, see Higuchi, *Guddo mōningu Gojira*, 266. Furthermore, Kobayashi Toyoaki claims that the way in which his generation encountered Godzilla bespeaks life under the regime of a high-growth economy. The "real" Godzilla was long gone when the generation to which he (b. 1959) belongs became aware of its existence. They discovered and were moved by Godzilla only retrospectively. Kobayashi, *Gojira no ronri*, 48.

40. Fukuda Kazuya, *Rikidōzan wa erakatta* (Tokyo: Bēsubōru magajinsha, 1996), 10.

41. Yoshinosato, whom Rikidōzan trained as a pro-wrestler, recalls gruesome drinking sessions with Rikidōzan. Rikidōzan forced him not only to empty a bottle of whisky but also to eat the glass out of which he was drinking. Rikidōzan led the way by finishing a bottle and eating a glass himself. Lee Sunil, *Mōhitori no Rikidōzan* (Tokyo: Shōgakkan, 1996), 163.

42. Muramatsu Tomomi, *Watakushi puroresu no mikatadesu* (Tokyo: Chikuma shobō, 1994), 310.

43. Lee, *Mōhitori no Rikidōzan*, 125.

44. "Karate chops"—beating the opponent with the side of one's hand—were nothing new in professional wrestling. When Japanese American wrestlers used the technique in the United States, it was called a "judo chop." When Native American wrestlers used the same technique, it was called a "tomahawk chop." "Rikidōzan," *Asahi shinbun*, nichiyōban, satellite edition, December 6, 1998, 3.

45. Muramatsu, *Watakushi proresu no mikatadesu*, 103.

46. Japanese television stations began color broadcasts on a regular basis in 1960. Iyoda Yasuhiro et al., *Terebishi handobukku* (Tokyo: Jiyūkokuminsha, 1996), 34.

47. One can see the pinnacle of such propaganda in the 1943 film *Anohata o ute* (Dawn of freedom), the first joint production between Japan and the Philip-

pines. One of the fundamental messages of the film is that other Asian people eventually come to understand Japan's sincere intentions to rescue them from the hands of the evil American conquerors. Japan's use of its forces is justified as a necessary means to grant the Philippine people independence. For a detailed discussion of the film, see Markus Nornes, "Dawn of Feedom," in *Media Wars: Then and Now* (Pāruhābā 50 shūnen: Nichibei eigasen), ed. Fukushima Yukio and Markus Nornes (Tokyo: Sōjinsha, 1991), 256–63.

48. However, there was one element that Rikidōzan's matches did not replicate in wartime propaganda. What Rikidōzan rescued with his karate chops was not Asia but traditional Japan: Kimura's status as a former judo champion was significant in the construction of the narrative in the matches against the Sharpe brothers. The spatial relation between Japan and other Asian countries was displaced by a temporal relation between a new (postwar) Japan and traditional Japan.

49. Seto Masato, "Waga seishun no hīrō in 1961—Rikidōzan," *Asahi shinbun*, satellite edition, June 23, 1997, 11.

50. Seto, "Waga seishun no hīrō in 1961—Rikidōzan," 11.

51. Seto, "Waga seishun no hīrō in 1961—Rikidōzan," 11.

52. Lee, *Mōhitori no Rikidōzan*, 92–93.

53. For instance, one biography claims that Rikidōzan ran one hundred meters in thirteen seconds flat when he was nine, at an elementary school where he was never registered. Supōtsu Nippon shinbunsha, ed., *Rikidōzan hana no shōgai* (Tokyo: Supōtsu Nippon shinbunsha, 1964), 73. Ushijima Hidehiko accounts his futile attempt to trace Rikidōzan's childhood in Japan in his *Rikidōzan: ōzumō, puroresu, urashakai* (Tokyo: Daisan shokan, 1995), 6.

54. Muramatsu, *Watakushi puroresu no mikatadesu*, 292.

55. Ushijima, *Rikidōzan*, 152; *Mainichi shinbun*, November 4, 1954, 6.

56. *Mainichi shinbun*, November 27, 1954, 6.

57. Inose Naoki, *Yokubō no media* (Tokyo: Shinchōsha, 1994), 308–10. See also Kimura Masahiko, "Watashi to Rikidōzan no shinsō," *Bungeishinjū ni miru supōtsu Shōwashi* (Tokyo: Bungeishinjūsha, 1988), 628–37.

58. One month later, Rikidōzan defeated Yamaguchi Toshio, the leading wrestler of a rival wrestling association, and consolidated his monopoly on wrestling promotion. Lee, *Mōhitori no Rikidōzan*, 144.

59. Anzai Mizumaru witnessed the match as a child. In an interview, he mentions his astonishment at seeing the legendary Japanese martial arts champion being defeated by a Western-style wrestler. *Bunshū nonfikushon bideo, Rikidōzan to sono jidai* (Tokyo: Bungeishunjū sha, 1995).

60. Lee, *Mōhitori no Rikidōzan*, 132. For Kimura's reputation as a legendary judo champion, see Kajiwara Ikki, *Rikidōzan to Nihon puroresushi* (Tokyo: Yudachisha, 1996), 227–31.

61. Lee, *Mōhitori no Rikidōzan*, 146–49.

62. Yoshimura Yoshio, personal secretary to Rikidōzan, confirms Rikidōzan's dissatisfaction with his financial compensation. Yoshimura Yoshio, *Kimiwa Rikidōzan o mitaka* (Tokyo: Asuka shinsha, 1988), 111–12.

63. For a dramatized account of the first match in which Azumafuji teamed up with Rikidōzan in Hawaii, see Kajiwara, *Rikidōzan to Nihon puroresu*, 252–53.

64. Lee, *Mōhitori no Rikidōzan*, 149; and Kajiwara, *Rikidōzan to Nihon puroresu*, 266–68.

65. Muramatsu, *Watakushi puroresu no mikatadesu*, 303.

66. For instance, the professional baseball player Yamanouchi Kazuhiro was voted the most valuable player in the all-star games in 1954. The prizes he received for this honor were two electric fans, a motorcycle, and a bicycle. *Supōtsu Nippon*, July 5, 1954, 2.

67. For Rikidōzan's business operations, see Yoshimura, *Kimiwa Rikidōzan o mitaka*, 192–201; and Ushijima, *Rikidōzan*, 243.

68. For a list of dirty tricks introduced to Japan each year, see Muramatsu, *Watakushi puroresu no mikatadesu*, 102–3.

69. Muramatsu, *Watakushi puroresu no mikatadesu*, 104–5.

70. The idea of a league tournament came from Katō Akira, who worked for Japan Pro-Wrestling Enterprises, the company that promoted Rikidōzan's matches. Previously, Katō was also successful in organizing a *naniwa-bushi* all-star show during the occupation, thereby contributing to the revitalization of the art. Yoshimura, *Kimiwa Rikidōzan o mitaka*, 184–86.

71. This was his age according to the household registry created in 1951 on the basis of Rikidōzan's own application. However, from other circumstantial evidence, Lee Sunil surmises that Rikidōzan was two years older than his official age. Lee, *Mōhitori no Rikidōzan*, 96–98.

72. Tanaka Yonetarō, who gave up the career as a sumo wrestler and joined Rididōzan in professional wrestling in 1950s, attested to Rikidōzan's substance abuse around the time of Rikidōzan's wedding in 1963: "Probably he was too stressed because of his business and what not. He had been using sleeping pills. At the beginning, he used one or two pills. But, toward the end [of his life, he was using] ten and then twenty. Then he could not wake up in the morning: he took a drug to wake himself up. That was a strong drug. I myself have taken one, but I could not fall sleep all night long. He took about three doses when he woke up in the morning. Perhaps because he kept taking these drugs, he was a bit abnormal toward the end. He began yelling for nothing, and the way he beat [young wrestlers under his tutelage]. It got so bad that I stayed away from him toward the end." Ide Kōya, "Tsuiseki! Rikidōzan," *Number*, March 1983, reprinted in *"Bungeishunjū" nimiru supōtsu Shōwashi* (Tokyo: Bungeishunjū, 1988), 627; Ushijima, *Rikidōzan*, 242.

73. Muramatsu Tomomi's insistence in the epigraph that one has to see professional wrestling "dead seriously" is hence a demand for taking its function as the producer of myth seriously.

74. For instance, Satō Tadao sees *Kimi no nawa* as a drama that reflects the old traditional family values that disappeared in postwar Japan. He dismisses the film as simply "a clichéd tragic love melodrama." Satō Tadao, " Hyūmanizumu no jidai—Nihon eigashi 5," in *Sengo eiga no tenkai*, Kōza Nihon eiga, vol. 5 (Tokyo: Iwanami shoten, 1987), 49. Satō also dismisses *Godzilla* as a "horror movie filmed with the cheap and easy special effects of a body-suit monster" (18).

75. Contemporary reviews of *Godzilla* dismissed it condescendingly as a mere copy of American science fiction films. For such reviews see "Chakusō to doryoku o kau," *Supōtsu Nippon*, November 6, 1954, 4; and "Kikaku dake no omoshirosa," *Asahi shinbun*, evening edition, November 5, 1954, 2.

Chapter 5

1. The average number of applications in 1964 for each vacancy was fifty-three. Asahi shinbun gakugeibu, *Daidokoro kara sengo ga mieru*, 58.

2. Shibagaki Kazuo reports that when washing machines first appeared on the market they were called *yome namake dōgu* (the tool for goof-off housewives). Shibagaki, *Kōwa kara kōdoseichōe*, 246.

3. Even within companies that developed rice cookers, there were some who were opposed to marketing them on the ground that they would make women lazy. Asahi shinbun gakugeibu, *Daidokoro kara sengo ga mieru*, 62–63.

4. Bureau of Statistics, Office of Prime Minister, *Japan Statistical Yearbook, 1965* (Tokyo: Japan Statistical Association and Mainichi shinbun, 1966), 446–47.

5. Ueno Kōshi, *Nikutai no jidai* (Tokyo: Gendai shokan, 1989), 478–81.

6. Kōdoseichō o kangaerukai, *Kōdoseichō to Nihonjin*, quoted in Ueno, *Nikutai no jidai*, 480.

7. Kishi himself later admitted to an interviewer that his goal was the return of the wartime dream of the ideal of Great Asianism that promoted Japan as the leader of Asia. Hara Yoshihisa, *Kishi Nobusuke* (Tokyo: Iwanami shoten, 1995), 190.

8. NHK Shuzaihan, *Kokusan jōyōsha/60 nen Anpo to Kishi Nobusuke*, Sengo 50 nen sonotoki Nihon wa, vol. 1 (Tokyo: Nihon hōsō shuppan kyōkai, 1995), 251–53.

9. *The Japanese Annual of International Law, 1961* (Tokyo: Japan Branch of the International Law Association, 1961), 274–75.

10. The observation was made by Marshall Green, who served as regional planning adviser for the Far East in the Department of State from 1956 to 1959. An NHK research team conducted interviews with him; the excerpts are included in NHK Shuzaihan, *Kokusan jōyōsha/60 nen Anpo to Kishi Nobusuke*. For his particular discussion on Article II, see 274.

11. *Japanese Annual of International Law, 1961*, 275.

12. Not all LDP members supported renewal of the Security Treaty. There were debates within the party even before the new treaty met the opposition of the Communist Party and the Socialist Party. For the early factional conflicts within the LDP, see Shinobu Seizaburō, *Anpo tōsōshi—35 nichi seikyoku shiron* (Tokyo: Sekaishoin, 1961), 8–46.

13. Watanabe Osamu, *Seiji kaikaku to kenpōkaisei: Nakasone Yasuhiro kara Ozawa Ichirō e* (Tokyo: Aoki shoten, 1994), 237–39.

14. Hidaka Rokurō, ed., *1960 nen 5 gatsu 19 nichi* (Tokyo: Iwanami shoten, 1960), 151.

15. NHK Shuzaihan, *Kokusan jōyōsha/60 nen Anpo to Kishi Nobusuke*, 278–81.

16. Matsuo Takayoshi, *Kokusai kokka eno shuppatsu*, Nihon no rekishi, vol. 21 (Tokyo: Shūeisha, 1993), 237. A minority within the JCP dissented from the majority assessment by identifying Japanese monopoly capital—the driving force of Japanese imperialism—as the target of their political struggle.

17. *Japanese Annual of International Law, 1961*, 277; Hara, *Kishi Nobusuke*, 216.

18. Hidaka, *1960 nen 5 gatsu 19 nichi*, 46–49.

19. Hosaka Masayasu, *60 nen Anpo tōsō* (Tokyo: Kōdansha, 1986), 37–38.

20. Hosaka Masayasu quotes a survey conducted by the *Asahi shinbun* on the occasion of the signing of the revised treaty by the two countries. As many as 34 percent of the people who responded to the survey said they were not aware of the revision issue, while 17 percent were opposed to the revision. Hosaka, *60 nen Anpo tōsō*, 73.

21. Hosaka, *60 nen Anpo tōsō*, 157–58.

22. For the conflicts within the GHQ and their potential effects on Kishi's acquittal, see Hara, *Kishi Nobusuke*, 139–41.

23. In 1953, Kishi joined the Liberal Party, which merged with Democratic Party two years later to create the Liberal Democratic Party.

24. The struggles against American bases at Uchinada and Sunagawa seemed to Shimizu a battle. The anti-Security Treaty movement was itself a culmination of the antibase movement; hence, the struggle against the treaty revision was a war. Shimizu Ikutarō, *Shimizu Ikutarō chosakushū*, vol. 14 (Tokyo: Kōdansha, 1993), 484.

25. Unofficial discussions between Kishi and MacArthur had begun as early as the summer of 1958. NHK Shuzaihan, *Kokusan jōyōsha/60 nen Anpo to Kishi Nobusuke*, 259–60

26. Discussing the Police Bill, Kishi maintained that "the revision of the Police Duties Performance Law was an important bill within my administrative policy. I expected a great degree of opposition to the revision of the Security Treaty. But I had a strong determination to override the opposition to realize the revision. I was determined to even risk my life for it and believed the revision of the Police Duties Performance Law was indispensable to maintain the social order [while forcing the revision of the Security Treaty]." Kishi Nobusuke, Yatsugi Kazuo, and Itō Takashi, *Kishi Nobusuke no kaisō* (Tokyo: Bungeishunjū, 1981), 196.

27. Maruyama Masao, "Sentaku no toki," in *Maruyama Masao shū*, 8:347–48.

28. Takeuchi Yoshimi, "Minshu ka dokusaika," *Takeuchi Yoshimi zenshū*, vol. 9 (Tokyo: Chikuma shobō, 1981), 109–14.

29. Mitani Taichirō argues that the wartime mobilization system prepared the conditions conducive to the postwar reforms. Mitani Taichirō, "Senji taisei to sengo taisei," in *Ajia no reisen to datsu-shokuminchika*, edited by Ōe Shinobu et al., Kindai Nihon to shokuminchi, vol. 8 (Tokyo: Iwanami shoten, 1993), 329–30. Mitani also points out that the efforts to expand the tax revenue for the Sino-Japanese and Russo-Japanese Wars expanded the number of eligible voters, and

this expansion was crucial for the universal male suffrage movement. Mitani, "Senji taisei to sengo taisei," 329–30.

30. George R. Packard, *Protest in Tokyo: The Security Treaty Crisis of 1960* (Princeton: Princeton University Press, 1966), 337–38.

31. The wartime past returned to some in a more direct form. Journalists of Kyōdō News Service reported that, after the Security Treaty's passage in the Diet on May 19, some one hundred female members of the All Japan Telecommunication Union (Zendentsū) rushed to the prime minister's residence with two thousand *senninbari* (thousand-stitch cloths). Ide Busaburō, ed., *Anpo tōsō* (Tokyo: San'ichi shobō, 1960), 151. *Senninbari* was a common practice during the Asia Pacific War; women sent off their husbands and sons with *senninbari* for their protection. They stood on street corners asking other women passers-by to stitch their cloths (one stitch per woman) until they collected a thousand stitches. (Tigers were regarded as auspicious animals for their perceived survival ability. Therefore, women who were born in the Year of the Tiger were asked to stitch the numbers of their ages.) Through their *senninbari* making, these union members, consciously or unconsciously, demonstrated the connections between the anti–Security Treaty movement of 1960 and their wartime experiences.

32. Shimizu, *Shimizu Ikutarō Chosakushū*, 482.

33. Shimizu, *Shimizu Ikutarō Chosakushū*, 482.

34. *Asahi journal*, July 10, 1960, 74, quoted in Hidaka, *1960 nen 5 gatsu 19 nichi*, 200.

35. On June 16, 1960, the *Asahi shinbun, Yomiuri shinbun, Maichini shinbun, Sankei shinbun, Tokyo shinbun, Tokyo taimusu shinbun*, and *Nihon keizai shinbun* carried the joint statement on their front pages.

36. NHK Shuzaihan, *Kokusan jōyōsha/60 nen Anpo to Kishi Nobusuke*, 334–38.

37. NHK Shuzaihan, *Kokusan jōyōsha/60 nen Anpo to Kishi Nobusuke*, 304–5.

38. Although the administration projected a 7.2 percent annual increase in income, Ikeda promised an annual growth rate of 9 percent over the next ten years. Yoshikawa Hiroshi, *Kōdoseichō—Nippon o kaeta 6,000 nichi*, 20 seiki no Nippon, vol. 6 (Tokyo: Yomiuri shinbunsha, 1997), 180.

39. Hosaka Masayasu, "Sengo Nihon no tsūkagirei—ano nekki wa nandattanoka," in Mainichi shinbunsha, *Iwanami shoten to Bungeishunjū*, 19.

40. The portion of defense-related expenses in the general account steadily declined from the inception of the Self-Defense Forces until the early 1980s (14 percent in 1954, 9.9 percent in 1960, 7.2 percent in 1970, and 5.2 percent in 1980). The trend was reversed in the 1980s under the Nakasone administration, and the figure crept up to 6.5 percent in 1988. *Bōei Handbook* (Tokyo: Asagumo shinbun, 1990), 229, quoted in Watanabe, *Seiji kaikaku to kenpōkaisei*, 266.

41. Although the LDP gained fewer votes than in the 1958 general election, it managed to capture nine more seats in the House of Representatives. The LDP's share in the total vote declined by 0.2 percent, yet the downturn was not significant enough to demonstrate general disapproval of LDP policies. In the 1958 election, the LDP had 57.8 percent of the entire vote and received 287 out of 467 seats, while the Socialist Party attracted 32.9 percent of the votes and filled 166

seats. Two years later, the LDP secured 57.6 percent of the votes and 296 seats. Reflecting the split in 1959, the share of the votes for the Socialist Party fell to 27.6 percent and the number of its seats dropped to 145. The Democratic Socialist Party (which had split off from the Socialist Party) gained 8.8 percent of the votes and 17 seats. The JCP slightly increased its share of the votes, from 2.6 percent to 2.9 percent, and the number of its seats grew from 1 to 3. Sasaki et al., *Sengoshi daijiten*, 981.

42. Hosaka, *60 nen Anpo tōsō*, 162–63.

43. Fujita Shōzō also used a corporeal metaphor to characterize the revised Security Treaty. He claimed that the revised Security Treaty willingly offered "the body [*shintai*] of Japan [to the United States]." Hidaka, *1960 nen 5 gatsu 19 nichi*, 12.

44. NHK Shuzaihan, *Kokusan jōyōsha/60 nen Anpo to Kishi Nobusuke*, 370.

45. This repetition was not an isolated case in the history of the modern Olympic games. All three Axis countries held Olympic games in the postwar period, as if to complete their incomplete prewar projects. After the 1936 Berlin Olympics, Rome bid for the 1940 spot. However, the delegates from Tokyo persuaded Mussolini to apply political pressure on the Italian Olympic committee to withdraw Rome from the competition. Agreements were made between Rome and Tokyo that Rome would host the 1944 Olympics, although the actual power to make this decision belonged to the International Olympic Committee. If the war had not intervened, the Olympics would have been held successively in three fascist countries. Although the order was reversed, these same three countries managed to have the Olympic games in the postwar period. Rome and Tokyo had their Olympic games in 1960 and 1964, respectively, while Munich hosted the 1972 games (the Berlin Olympics would have been highly impractical before Germany's unification).

46. "Icchōen no Orinpikku seisen," *Shūkan yomiuri*, October 11, 1964, 34–41; and Fujitake Akira, *Tokyo Orinpikku sono 5 nenkan no ayumi* (Tokyo: Nihon hōsō kyōkai hōsō yoron chōsajo, 1967), 91.

47. Satō Akira, ed., *"Nippon kabushiki gaisha" shuppansu*, Shōgen no Shōwashi, vol. 9 (Tokyo: Gakushū kenkyūsha, 1982), 65.

48. *Yomiuri shinbun*, September 19, 1964, quoted in Fujitake Akira, *Tokyo Orinpikku: sono 5 nenkan no ayumi*, 90.

49. Even thirty-three years after the Tokyo Olympics, Anno Mitsumasa wrote: "I, who stood at the leveled field of Tokyo after the war, am filled with deep emotions. Who could have predicted these spectacular Tokyo Olympics games twenty years prior?" Anno Mitsumasa, "Eno mayoimichi," *Shūkan asahi*, June 13, 1997, 74.

50. Sugimoto Sonoko, "Asueno kinen," in *Tokyo Orinpikku: bungakusha no mita seikino saiten* (Tokyo: Kōdansha, 1964), 30–31.

51. Sugimoto, "Asueno kinen," 31.

52. Etō Jun, " 'Heiwa no saiten' no hikari to kage: gen'ei no 'Nihon teikoku,' " *Bungeishunjū*, December 1964, 174.

53. Etō, " 'Heiwa no saiten' no hikari to kage," 174.

54. Hashimoto Osamu, "Shōwa 39 nen, Tokyo ni sensō ga atta: kiroku eiga "Tokyo Orinpikku, sono 1," *Esquire Japan*, August 1988, 124.

55. Ichikawa used a telephoto lens and faced the direction of Shin-Sukiyabashi when he shot the Ginza 4 chōme junction. Ichikawa Kon and Mori Yūki, *Ichikawa Kon no eigatachi—Films of Kon Ichikawa* (Tokyo: Waizu shuppan, 1994), 308.

56. Hashimoto, "Shōwa 39 nen, Tokyo ni sensō ga atta," 121.

57. Tokyo hyakunenshi henshū iinkai, *Tokyo hyakunenshi*, vol. 6 (Tokyo: Teikoku chihō gyōsei gakkai, 1972), 298.

58. Japanese railway tracks were standardized to a narrow gauge (three feet six inches) in 1900. Harada Katsumasa, *Nihon no tetsudō* (Tokyo: Yoshikawa kōbunkan, 1991), 40.

59. Inoue Shōichi, *Senjika Nihon no kenchikuka: āto, kicchu, Japanesuku* (Tokyo: Asahi shinbunsha, 1995), 105–18.

60. In contrast to the original stadium plan, which required a thousand tons of steel, the new plan only needed six hundred tons of steel. The grim prospect of failing to construct the stadium was one of the major factors in canceling the 1940 Olympics. Hashimoto Kazuo, *Maboroshi no Tokyo Orinpikku* (Tokyo: Nihon hōsō kyōkai shuppan, 1994), 209–10.

61. Shiota Ushio, *Tokyo wa moetaka* (Tokyo: PHP kenkyūsho, 1985), 187.

62. Ueno, *Sengo saikō*, 170.

63. Fujisawa Kikuo et al., " 'Sekai ichi Hikarigō' eno michi—kiteki issei kara chōtokkyū made," *Toki*, November 1964, 178.

64. Sankei shinbun "Sengoshi kaifū" shuzaihan, *Sengoshi kaifū* (Tokyo: Sankei shinbunsha, 1995), 213.

65. Uno et al., *Japan Chronik: Nihon zenshi*, 1059; Harada, *Nihon no tetsudō*, 105.

66. The Tōkaidō Shinkainsen is only 322 miles long; on average, one life was lost for every one and half miles. Fujisawa et al., " 'Sekai ichi Hikarigō' eno michi," 179.

67. Maema Takanori, *Ajia shinkansen: maboroshi no Tokyo hatsu Pekin iki chōtokkyū* (Tokyo: Kōdansha, 1998), 462–63.

68. Maema, *Ajia shinkansen*, 446, 467–68.

69. Maema, *Ajia shinkansen*, 384, 468

70. Sankei shinbun "Sengoshi kaifū" shuzaihan, *Sengoshi kaifū*, 216.

71. Sankei shinbun "Sengoshi kaifū" shuzaihan, *Sengoshi kaifū*, 217.

72. Satō Noriko, "Orinpikku ga yattekita," in *Kōdoseichō no jidai, onnatachi wa*, ed. Onna tachi no ima o toukai, Jūgoshi nōto sengohen, vol. 6 (Tokyo: Inpakuto shuppankai, 1992), 51.

73. *Yomiuri shinbun*, April 3, 1964, 1.

74. *Yomiuri shinbun*, April 3, 1964, 1.

75. Sakurai Tetsuo, *Shisō toshiteno 60 nendai* (Tokyo: Chikuma shobō, 1993), 35–36.

76. Nakano Tsuya, "Fujinbuchō no yūutsu: Tokyoto no Orinpikku taisaku," in Onna tachi no ima o toukai, *Kōdoseichō no jidai, onnatachi wa* (Tokyo: Inpakuto shuppankai, 1992), 58–59.

77. Nakano, "Fujinbuchō no yūutsu," 59.

78. Popular magazines warned against the potential harm that encounters with "foreigners" could inflict on young Japanese women. A writer for *Shūkan taishū*

foresaw the "tragedies of the immediate postwar period" revisiting them. "Tatta gorinde yorumo nemurarezu," *Shūkan taishū*, October 15, 1964, 95. The October 1964 issue of *Fujin kōron* carried a special collection of essays that both described and warned against sexual encounters between Japanese women and foreign males. One essay in the collection was entitled "Dangerous Foreigners."

79. *Asahi shinbun*, March 27, 1964, 14.

80. The May 11, 1964, issue of *Shūkan shinchō* reports the reactions of hotel managers as well as of those who worked at drinking establishments. Many expressed varying degrees of disapproval of the plan, while a few accepted its premise. *Shūkan shinchō*, May 11, 1964, 114–19.

81. Tokyoto eisekyoku, *Tokyoto eisei nenpō*, vol. 17 (Tokyo: Tokyoto eiseikyoku gyōmubu fukyūka, 1966), 130–31.

82. The Tokyo ward area is highly urbanized. There are twenty-three wards *(ku)* in this area. This datum designated the ratio of the area that had the sewer system. Tokyoto gesuidōkyoku, *Jigyōgaiyō: Heisei 6 nenban* (Tokyo: Tokyoto gesuidōkyoku, 1994), 3.

83. Ōtake Akiko, "Doromichi to dobugawa no Tokyo ga nakunatta hi," *Tokyojin*, August 1994, 41. For the development of this night soil recycling system during the Edo period, see Susan B. Hanley, *Everyday Things in Premodern Japan* (Berkeley and Los Angeles: University of California Press, 1997), 113–16.

84. The amount of feces that the Tokyo Metropolitan Government collected kept growing until 1963, and more than half of the collected feces ended up being dumped in the Pacific. For instance, in 1963, the Tokyo Metropolitan Government collected 2,304,320 kl of feces, of which it dumped 1,251,088 kl into the sea. Tokyo Metropolitan Government, *Tokyo Statistical Yearbook, 1964* (Tokyo: Tokyo Metropolitan Government, 1965), 480–81. Until 1957, the majority of feces was used on farmland. Tokyo Metropolitan Government, *Tokyo Statistical Yearbook, 1960* (Tokyo Metropolitan Government, 1961), 548–49.

85. Murano Masayoshi, *Bakyūmukā wa erakatta* (Tokyo: Bungeishunjyū, 1996), 158.

86. Gesuidō Tokyo 100 nenshi hensan iinkai, *Gesuidō Tokyo 100 nenshi* (Tokyo: Tokyoto gesuidōkyoku, 1989), 193.

87. Gesuidō Tokyo 100 nenshi hensan iinkai, *Gesuidō Tokyo 100 nenshi*, 508–9.

88. In 1960, the Tokyo Metropolitan Government organized the Tokyo Urban Planning River and Sewer System Special Research Committee. In the following year, this committee produced a report recommending the conversion of either parts or all of the fourteen polluted rivers into main sewage lines. The metropolitan government followed the committee's recommendation; in fact, the government was already converting the Momozono River and the Shibuya River into sewer lines when the committee published the report. Gesuidō Tokyo 100 nenshi hensan iinkai, *Gesuidō Tokyo 100 nenshi*, 196–97.

89. Ōtake, "Doromichi to dobugawa no Tokyo ga nakunatta hi," 42.

90. Gesuidō Tokyo 100 nenshi hensan iinkai, *Gesuidō Tokyo 100 nenshi*, 512–13. The book lists other psychological, physical, and economic damages caused by the polluted river.

91. Keishichō, *Orinpikku Tokyo Taikai no Keisatsu kiroku* (Tokyo: Keishichō, 1964), 140.

92. The new ordinance came into effect on August 1, 1964.

93. One finds a similar example in the physical and discursive production of "bright" Hiroshima as a countersymbol against the dark memories of the war. See Lisa Yoneyama's *Hiroshima Traces*, 43–65.

94. Keishichō, *Orinpikku Tokyo Taikai no Keisatsu kiroku*, 140–41. In addition, 42,290 street lights were added to the neighborhood surrounding the Olympic facilities between January and September of 1964. Keishichō, *Orinpikku Tokyo Taikai no Keisatsu kiroku*, 150.

95. These newly produced material conditions brought bodies under a new regime of management. Washing machines simplified household work, and notions of bodily hygiene changed accordingly in 1960s Japan. Ueno Chizuko, for instance, reports that it became customary to change one's underwear every day in the mid-1960s, whereas before the decade, most people changed their undergarments only when they took a bath, which occurred only two to three times a week. Ueno Chizuko, *Kindai kazoku no seiritsu* (Tokyo: Iwanami shoten, 1994), 191.

96. Keishichō, *Orinpikku Tokyo Taikai no Keisatsu kiroku*, 145.

97. Keishichō, *Orinpikku Tokyo Taikai no Keisatsu kiroku*, 145.

98. *Asahi shinbun*, August 10, 1964, 1, 14; August 11, 1964, 6, 7.

99. "Monku tsukerareta saishūsōsha: 'genbakukko' ga ataeru kaigai e no shokku," *Shūkan shinchō*, September 7, 1964, 34.

100. *Asahi shinbun*, August 11, 1964, 6.

101. "Rippa na genbakkuko—Seika rirē saishū rannā Sakai Yoshinori," *Toki*, October 1964, 115.

102. "Monku tsukerareta saishūsōsha," 33.

103. "Monku tsukerareta saishūsōsha," 34–35.

104. The coach of the team, Daimatsu Hirobumi, explained that a Soviet newspaper gave them the nickname. Initially, they were called "the Typhoon of the Orient"; the implication was that their strength was temporary. When the team was proven invincible, they began being called "the Witches of the Orient." Thereafter, journalists replicated Daimatsu's explanation. Yet, other instances strongly indicate various connections between their nickname and collective memories of the Asia Pacific War: Japanese soldiers were called *dongyanggui* (devils of the Orient) in China, and a former Japanese military policeman recalled that he was called *Tōyō no maō* (the devil of the Orient) in postwar China. Daimatsu Hirobumi, *Oreni tsuitekoi* (Tokyo: Kōdansha, 1963), 187; and Miyazaki Kiyotaka, "Tōyō no maō to yobarete," *Chūōkōron*, February 1954, 256.

105. Mushiake Aromu, "Sengo besutoserā monogatari: Daimatsu Hirobumi, Oreni tsuitekoi," *Asahi journal*, January 8, 1967, 44.

106. Daimatsu, *Oreni tsuitekoi*, 29–30.

107. Daimatsu, *Oreni tsuitekoi*, 154.

108. Ōsumi Hideo, "Sutā no za, 2: Eikō ka kekkon kano wakaremichi," *Fujin gahō*, February 1, 1963, 225–26.

109. Daimatsu Hirobumi and Kaga Mariko, "Mariko no binantanken: danseiteki miryoku kajōna Daimatsu Hirobumi shi," *Fujin kōron*, March 1965, 249; and Daimatsu Hirobumi et al., "Rekishi shōgen—Shiberia no Nihonhei

horyo: Zadankai shūyōsho guntō no saigetsu," *Shūkan yomiuri*, September 4, 1976, 47. Aida Yūji also relates a similar account in his 1962 book on his experiences in the Ahlone POW Camp:

> One day, however, this sergeant [who conscientiously worked on his chores] came back from the women's quarters hopping mad. He told us that when he was doing laundry, an auxiliary came, took off her knickers, and made him wash them.
> "She came in naked, I tell you, and just threw her pants at me."

Aida Yūji, *Āron shūyōjo* (Tokyo: Chūōkōronsha, 1973), 49; Aida Yūji, *Prisoner of the British: A Japanese Soldier's Experiences in Burma*, trans. Hide Ishiguro and Louis Allen (London: Cresset Press, 1966), 33.

110. Daimatsu Hirobumi, *Nasebanaru* (Tokyo: Kōdansha, 1964), 115

111. Daimatsu offers a revealing anecdote regarding the gender issues in an interview. After witnessing a training session for the team, one of the leaders of Tenrikyō church wondered if such hard training would actually transform women into men. Daimatsu Hirobumi and Ichimura Kiyoshi, "Konjō, tōkon, shidōryoku: kukyō nitateba tatsuhodo tsuyokunaru," *Bungeishunjū*, November 1964, 102.

112. It is noteworthy that some Japanese women called menstruation *hinomaru*, "the rising-sun flag," even during the war period. Amano Masako and Sakurai Atsushi, *"Mono to onna" no sengoshi: shintaisei, kateisei, shakaisei o jikuni* (Tokyo: Yūshindō, 1992), 73.

113. Of the twelve players of the Olympic team, ten were Nichibō players. The company changed its name to Nichibō in April 1964. Nichibō shashi hensan iinkai, *Nichibō 75 nenshi* (Osaka: Nichibō kabushikigaisha, 1966), 561.

114. Daimatsu, *Nasebanaru*, 108.

115. Daimatsu, *Oreni tsuitekoi*, 61.

116. Daimatsu, *Oreni tsuitekoi*, 84.

117. Daimatsu, *Oreni tsuitekoi*, 59.

118. Daimatsu, *Oreni tsuitekoi*, 88.

119. Daimatsu, *Oreni tsuitekoi*, 167–68, and "Tōyō no majo: shōri no namida," *Shūkan Yomiuri*, November 8, 1964, 17.

120. Okuno Takeo, "Daimatsu kantoku ni miru otoko no kenkyū," *Fujin kōron*, December, 1964, 118.

121. Daimatsu and Ichimura, "Konjō, tōkon, shidōryoku," 104.

122. Daimatsu, *Oreni tsuitekoi*, 205.

123. Daimatsu, *Nasebanaru*, 44–45.

124. Daimatsu, *Nasebanaru*, 72–73.

125. Daimatsu, *Nasebanaru*, 83.

126. Daimatsu, *Oreni tsuitekoi*, 31.

127. Daimatsu, *Oreni tsuitekoi*, 80.

128. Ten years after Daimatsu's success at the Olympics, Nakauchi Isao, the founder of the Daiei supermarket conglomerate, similarly articulated his sense of guilt for surviving the war: "I feel guilty [*ushirometai*] when I think about my war buddies who rotted to death in that jungle [in the Philippines]. We have to "pay" [English in the original] them back. I have always felt that I would like to return what I owe [to them]." However, the way Nakauchi acted out his guilty con-

science was extremely ironic: he was driven to create the embodiment of American material culture—supermarket chains—in Japan. Sano Shin'ichi, *Karisuma: Nakauchi Isao to Daiei no "Sengo"* (Tokyo: Nikkei BP, 1998), 260.

129. "Tōyō no majo," 19.

130. For instance, in a survey conducted by the NHK (Japan Broadcasting Service) Broadcast Poll Research Institute in June 1964, 36 percent of 1,132 people in Tokyo and 35 percent of 762 in Kanazawa answered that they disliked Russians, while 35 percent and 26 percent of each group replied they liked Russians. On the other hand, 70 percent and 59 percent of the same groups said that they liked Americans. The only nation that fared worse than Russia was Korea: 54 percent and 47 percent disliked Koreans. Fujitake, *Tokyo Orinpikku: sono 5 nenkan no ayumi*, 143.

131. Telecasts of gymnastics, diving, wrestling, track and field, and weight lifting also received high ratings (70 to 80 percent). Fujitake, *Tokyo Orinpikku: sono 5 nenkan no ayumi*, 236, 246. In August 1964, 91 percent of the households in Japan had a television set. Bureau of Statistics, *Japan Statistical Yearbook, 1965*, 446.

132. The NHK (Japan Broadcasting Service) Broadcast Poll Research Institute conducted the survey November 4 through November 6, 1964. Fujitake, *Tokyo Orinpikku: sono 5 nenkan no ayumi*, 195.

133. Daimatsu, *Oreni tsuitekoi*, 62–63, 141.

134. Shimizu Tetsuo, "Ganso Tōyō no majo 12 mei, eikōno Tokyo Gorin karano 'onnano shiawase,' " *Shūkan gendai*, October 7, 1976, 95.

Chapter 6

1. Bureau of Statistics, Office of Prime Minister, *Japan Statistical Yearbook, 1975* (Tokyo: Nihon Statistical Association and Mainichi shinbun, 1976), 485.

2. The average annual working hours for Japanese workers were above 2,300 throughout most of the 1960s; they were 2,424.5 in 1960. By 1991, the number of average hours had decreased to 2,016. Rōdōshō, *Rōdō hakusho 1992* (Tokyo: Rōdōshō, 1992), 191–92.

3. In February 1965, 90 percent of Japanese households owned television sets, 73 percent owned washing machines, and 62 percent owned refrigerators. Bureau of Statistics Office of the Prime Minister, *Japan Statistical Yearbook, 1965*, 446–47. In 1966, the number of color television sets was included in the government statistical data for the first time: 0.3 percent of Japanese households owned color television sets. The number increased to 25 percent in 1969. Bureau of Statistics, Office of the Prime Minister, *Japan Statistical Yearbook, 1970*, 421.

4. Sasaki et al., *Sengoshi daijiten*, 352.

5. Former prime minister Fukuda Takeo reportedly created the term in 1964. Takahashi Nobuo, "Shōwa Genroku," in Ishikawa et al., *Taishūbunka jiten*, 375.

6. These dramas were called *supokon mono* (sports guts stories). Serialized in *Shōnen magajin* from 1966 to 1971, *Kyojin no hoshi* (Star of the Giants) was not the first *manga* to feature sport heroes, but, the protagonist's relentless training in pursuit of glory separated this story from its predecessors in the genre and served as an icon of the period. In *Kyojin no hoshi*, the protagonist, Hoshi Hyūma,

overcomes his physical handicap of being too small to be a professional baseball pitcher through outrageously strenuous training and devising pitches with magical effects. Hoshi's loyalty to the team, the Yomiuri Giants, is never shaken under any circumstances: he can attain glory only as a member of the team, as an ace pitcher of the Giants. Following the success of *Kyojin no hoshi*, many similar works were serialized in comic magazines. For a discussion of the emergence of *supokon mono*, see Ishiko Junzō, *Sengo mangashi nōto* (Tokyo: Kinokuniya shoten, 1994), 144–47. Representative works serialized in comic books include the following: Nagashima Shinji, *Jūdō icchokusen*, 1967; Tsuji Naoki, *Taigā masuku*, 1968–71; Chiba Tetsuya, *Ashita no Jō*, 1968–73; Uraga Chikako, *Attaku No. 1*, 1968–70; and Mochizuki Akira, *Sain wa V*, 1968. Though possessing wide appeal in the 1960s, *supokon mono* were reduced to objects of parody in the popular media of the second half of the 1970s.

7. *Asahi shinbun*, March 14, 1970, evening edition, 10. The Japanese government also objected to the selection of pavilion photograph exhibits on Hiroshima and Nagasaki. The government claimed that some photos were "too graphic." Yoshimi, *Hakurankai no seijigaku*, 226.

8. The discussion was aired as part of NHK's "Sutajio 102" in August 1945. Participants in the discussion included ten college students, two women who had been mobilized to work in factories during the war, and the social critic Yasuda Takeshi, who had served as a student soldier. Satō Takeshi, "Kōdo seichō to terebi bunka," in Minami and Shakai shinri kenkyūjo, *Zoku Shōwa bunka, 1945–1989*, 175.

9. For instance, Yoshida Yutaka finds a perspective that was critical of Japan's aggression in China within a collection of letters recounting individual war experiences (Shūkan asahi, ed., *Chichi no senki* [Tokyo: Asahi shinbunsha, 1965]). However, Yoshida also points out the lack of concern for other Asian peoples' experiences, which explains the overall sentimental tone of the collection. Yoshida Yutaka, *Nihonjin no sensōkan* (Tokyo: Iwanami shoten, 1995), 116–18.

10. *Kurashi no techō*, August 1968. The publisher of the magazine printed nine hundred thousand copies of the issue in total, one hundred thousand more than the magazine's normal circulation. The issue sold out completely. Kurashi no techō-sha later reprinted the issue in book form. Kurashi no techō henshūbu, ed., *Sensōchū no kurashi no kiroku* (Tokyo: Kurashi no techō-sha, 1980).

11. Kurashi no techō henshūbu, *Sensōchū no kurashi no kiroku*, 53.

12. Kurashi no techō henshūbu, *Sensōchū no kurashi no kiroku*, 250.

13. Satō, "Kōdo seichō to terebi bunka," 175.

14. An objection also came from a rather conservative position as well. One of the students who participated in the discussion categorically rejected discussion of war experiences on the grounds that "once [our] country started the war, it had to be won: some sacrifices could not be helped." Satō Takeshi saw this student's response as representative and collapsed the distance that separated this statement from the other questions. Satō then expressed surprise over what he perceived as the younger generation's rejection of history, not recognizing the fundamental challenge the other students posed to his generation (he was born in 1932). His hasty dismissal testified to the extent to which Satō himself reified the war experiences of his generation. Satō, "Kōdo seichō to terebi bunka," 176.

15. Yoshida Yutaka argues that the heroic war stories that filled such comic books as *Shōnen Sandē* and *Shōnen magagin* in the first half of the 1960s demonstrate that critical perspectives toward the Asia Pacific War were fast disappearing. Yoshida also quotes Takahashi Saburō to support his observation. Takahashi maintains that the war stories of the Shōwa forties (1965–74) lost a "kind of 'ghastliness' [*sugomi*]." Takahashi continues: " 'Ghastliness' is something very vague and subjective. But, it may be explained as something that transcends [the question of] what is war and forces us to contemplate the nature of humanity. In many cases, readers sense it in authors' narration of their harsh experiences as individuals." Takahashi Saburō, *"Senki mono" o yomu* (Tokyo: Akademia shuppan, 1988), quoted in Yoshida, *Nihonjin no sensōkan*, 114–15.

16. In his earlier fragmentary recollections of the war years, Nosaka was silent about or fictionalized parts particularly traumatic to him. However, in more recent writings, he has begun to describe the life he has hitherto concealed from the readers. The accounts of Nosaka's war experiences in this chapter rely on his own recent work. Nosaka Akiyuki, *Adoribu jijoden*, in *Nosaka Akiyuki*, Sakka no jiden, vol. 19, ed. Tōmaru Tatsu (Tokyo: Nihon tosho sent, 1994); *Kakuyaku taru gyakkō: shisetsu Mishima Yuko*, (Tokyo: Bungeishunjū, 1987); *Waga shikkoku no hi* (Tokyo: Kōbunsha, 1992); and *Hitodenashi* (Tokyo: Chūōkōronsha, 1997). For a critical discussion of Nosaka's autobiographical accounts, see Shimizu Setsuji, *Sensai koji no shinwa: Nosaka Akiyuki + Sengo no sakkatachi* (Tokyo: Kyōiku shuppan sentā, 1995), 52–71.

17. Mishima Yukio, "Kyokugen to riaritī," in *Mishima Yukio Hyōron zenshū*, vol. 1 (Tokyo: Shinchōsha, 1989), 1012–15.

18. They were published only a month apart: "Amerika hijiki" appeared in the September issue of *Bessatsu Bungeishunjū*, and "Hotaru no haka" appeared in the October issue of *Ōru Yomimono*.

19. Nosaka, *Nosaka Akiyuki*, 222.

20. Nosaka Akiyuki, *Amerika hijiki, Hotaru no haka* (Tokyo: Shinchōsha, 1972), and "American *Hijiki*."

21. Nosaka, *Nosaka Akiyuki*, 195.

22. Nosaka Akiyuki, "Hotaru no haka," in *Amerika hijiki, Hotaru no haka*, 35.

23. Nosaka, *Waga shikkoku no hi*, 95.

24. Nosaka, *Waga shikkoku no hi*, 15.

25. Nosaka, *Nosaka Akiyuki*, 196.

26. For instance, when his own daughter approached the age of sixteen months, Nosaka could simply not bear to stay at home, being afraid that she would die at any moment. For this reason, he traveled around Japan for three months. Nosaka, *Waga shikkoku no hi*, 93.

27. Nosaka, *Waga shikkoku no hi*, 111–14.

28. Nosaka, *Waga shikkoku no hi*, 134.

29. Nosaka, *Waga shikkoku no hi*, 222.

30. Nosaka claimed in 1992 that he had never reread the story. *Waga shikkoku no hi*, 11.

31. In 1988, an animated film version of *Hotaru no haka* was produced by Shinchōsha. Takabatake Isao served as the director.

32. The motif of impossible encounters with loss and repetition of the past seems to have gained popular circulation in cultural expressions of late 1960s Japan. Besides Nosaka's short stories and Mishima's novel, Tsuge Yoshiharu's 1968 cartoon, "The Master of Gensenkan" (Gensenkan shujin) and Ōshima Nagisa's 1970 film, *A Man Who Left His Will on Film* (Tokyo sensō sengo hiwa) are exemplary cases. For a critical reading of "The Master of Gensenkan," see Shimizu Masashi, *Tsuge Yoshiharu o yomu* (Tokyo: Gendaishokan, 1995), 61–102. Ōshima provides a brief self-commentary on the film in Oshima Nagisa, *Cinema, Censorship, and the State: The Writings of Nagisa Oshima* (Cambridge: MIT Press, 1992), 187–92.

33. Mishima Yukio, "*Hōjō no umi* nōto," *Shinchō*, January 1971, 85.

34. Mishima, "*Hōjō no umi* nōto," 86.

35. Even his name, Tōru, suggests the transparency of his existence.

36. Walter Benjamin's often quoted passage reads as follows: "The angel would like to stay, awaken the dead, and make whole what has been smashed. But a storm is blowing from Paradise; it has got caught in his wings with such violence that the angel can no longer close them. This storm irresistibly propels him into the future to which his back is turned, while the pile of debris before him grows skywards. This storm is what we call progress." "Theses on the Philosophy of History," *Illuminations* (New York: Schocken, 1969), 257–58.

37. Andō Takeshi, *Mishima Yukio "nichiroku"* (Tokyo: Michiya, 1996), 308.

38. Isoda Kōichi, "Junkyō no bigaku," in *Isoda Kōichi chosakushū*, vol. 1 (Tokyo: Ozawa shoten, 1990), 17–18, and Isoda Kōichi, "Onchō to shiteno sensō," in *Hihyō to kenkyū Mishima Yukio*, ed. Shirakawa Masayoshi (Tokyo: Haga shoten, 1974), 70–86..

39. Maruyama et al., "Sensō to dōjidai," 23.

40. Etō Jun, "Mishima Yukio no ie," in *Etō Jun chosakushū*, vol. 2 (Tokyo: Kōdansha, 1967), 124.

41. The English translation is from Mishima Yukio, *The Temple of the Golden Pavilion*, trans. Ivan Morris (New York: Perigee Books, 1980).

42. My own translation. The original reads: "Haisen no shōgeki, minzokuteki hiai nadoto iumonokara, kinkakuwa chōzetsu shiteita. Moshiku wa chōzetsu o yosootteita."

43. The English translation is from Mishima Yukio, *Confession of a Mask*, trans. Meredith Weatherby (New York: New Directions, 1958).

44. Unlike Nosaka, Mishima resisted autobiographical writing throughout his career. *Confession of a Mask*, however, was the exception that deeply reflected Mishima's actual life. Mishima later confided to one of his close friends the story of how he dodged military services. See Inose Naoki, *Persona: Mishima Yukio den* (Tokyo: Bungeishunjū, 1995), 107.

45. Recollections by Mishima's father corroborate this account. See Hiraoka Azusa, *Segare Mishima Yukio* (Tokyo: Bungeishunjū, 1996), 69–70.

46. On this point, I rely on insights offered by Matsumoto Ken'ichi. See *Mishima Yukio bōmei densetsu* (Tokyo: Kawadeshobō shinsha, 1987), 79.

47. The widely acknowledged failure of *Kyōko no ie* (The House of Kyōko) (1959) probably stems from this fundamental transformation of postwar Japanese society. Mishima's writing had already prefigured the problems he encountered in

the third and fourth volumes of *The Sea of Fertility*: his critical descriptions of nonevents in postwar society were simply not enough to sustain the drama in his writing.

48. Mishima Yukio and Furubayashi Takashi, "Mishima Yukio wa kataru—saigo no intabyū," In *Mishima Yukio*, ed. Ōoka Shin et al., Gunzō Nihon no sakka, vol. 18 (Tokyo: Shōgakukan, 1990), 214.

49. Friedrich Nietzsche, *On the Genealogy of Morals and Ecce Homo*, trans. Walter Kaufmann (New York: Vintage Books, 1989), 36–37.

50. In 1968, Mishima inaugurated Tatenokai, whose purpose was the defense of the nation. The organization was solely funded by Mishima. He also arranged short-term training sessions in the Self-Defense Forces for himself and Tatenokai members. Andō, *Mishima Yukio "nichiroku,"* 359, 380–81, 385.

51. My description of November 25 is based on Andō, *Mishima Yukio "nichiroku,"* 412–22.

52. Masao Miyoshi, *Accomplices of Silence* (Berkeley and Los Angeles: University of California Press, 1974), 180. Murakami Haruki also provides an account of Mishima's speech in his novel, *A Wild Sheep Chase*. The protagonist and his girlfriend just happen to notice something happening on television: "We walked through the woods to the ICU [International Christian University] campus, sat down in the student lounge, and munched on hot dogs. It was two in the afternoon, and Yukio Mishima's picture kept flashing on the lounge television. The volume control was broken so we could hardly make out what was being said, but it didn't matter to us one way or the other. A student got up on a chair and tried fooling with the volume, but eventually he gave up and wandered off." Mishima's message neither reached his intended audience nor society at large. Everyday life simply turned a deaf ear to his pleas. This scene, which appears in an early section of Murakami's book, also announces that Murakami began his fiction at the very point when Mishima ended his. Murakami chooses to create his fiction in the sphere of everyday life that Mishima so detested. Haruki Murakami, *A Wild Sheep Chase* (New York: Plume, 1990), 8.

53. Tokuoka Takao, *Gosui no hito* (Tokyo: Bungeishunjū, 1996), 247.

54. Mishima implicated the United States in the creation and maintenance of the postwar paradigm. His choice of location for his suicide is indicative of this: the building at the Ichigaya headquarters of the Self-Defense Forces had housed the sessions of the International Military Tribunal for the Far East. However, Mishima never publicly denounced the United States as an enemy country. Even in the manifesto he prepared for his suicide, he is more critical of Japan's complacency with the postwar paradigm than the U.S. role in maintaining it. Only in private conversations with Henry Stokes did Mishima express his deep resentment toward the United States through an enigmatic metaphor of "the curse of the green snake." Perhaps, the "curse" of the United States was so strong that he could not even name it as such in his public discourse. Mishima Yukio, "Geki," in *Mishima Yukio hyōron zenshū*, vol. 2, 531–34; and Henry Scott Stokes, *The Life and Death of Yukio Mishima* (New York: Noonday Press, 1995), 282.

55. The song climbed as high as number 71 on the pop charts in mid-December 1970. However, its ranking fell soon afterward. See *Confidence Hot 100*, vol. 193 (December 21, 1970) and vol. 194 (December 28, 1970).

56. For instance, according to a 1980 survey conducted by TBS (Tokyo Broadcasting System), a Japanese television station, "Sensō o shiranai kodomotachi" was selected as the fiftieth most representative song from the popular songs of the Meiji, Taishō, and Shōwa periods. Three thousand subjects were asked to select as many as they liked from 1003 preselected songs. 27 percent of them identified "Sensō o shiranai kodomotachi." Suzuki Akira, *Kayōkyoku besuto 100 no kenkyū* (Tokyo: TBS Britanica, 1982), quoted in Komoda Nobuo et al., eds. *Shinpan Nihon ryūkōkashi,* vol. 2 (Tokyo: Shakaishisōsa, 1995), 78–81.

57. Melody by Sugita Jīrō. Lyrics by Kitayama Osamu.

Conclusion

1. For a history of Japanese biological warfare, see Seldon H. Harris, *Factory of Death: Japanese Biological Warfare, 1932–45, and the American Cover-Up* (London: Routledge, 1994), and Tsuneishi Keiichi, *731 butai: seibutsu heiki hanzai no shinjitsu* (Tokyo: Kōdansha, 1995).

2. Hara Akira, "Sensō baishō mondai to Ajia," in *Ajia no Reisen to datsu-shokuminchika,* ed. Ōe Shinobu et al., Kindai Nihon to Shokuminchi, vol. 8 (Tokyo: Iwanami shoten, 1993), 275–82.

3. For a list of payments made by Japan to the twenty-eight countries, see Tanaka Hiroshi, "Nihon no sengo sekinin to Ajia—sengo hoshō to rekishi ninshiki," in Ōe et al., *Ajia no Reisen to datsu-shokuminchika,* 199.

4. Tanaka Hiroshi, "Nihon no sengo sekinin to Ajia," 200; Prime Minister Yoshida claimed, "The Japanese government designated the monetary payment to Burma [in 1954] as reparation because the Burmese government resented the term *investment.* From our perspective, it was an investment." Toyoshita Narahiko, *Anpojōyaku no seiritsu—Yoshida gaikō to tennō gaikō* (Tokyo: Iwanami shoten, 1996), 232.

5. "Ano haikyū jidai o omoidasu kami kikin no nazo," *Shūkan asahi,* November 23, 1973, 159. Another weekly reports a housewife who bought six hundred rolls in Osaka. See "Aa naki warai toireshi kaishime shimatsuki," *Josei jishin,* November 24, 1973, 180.

6. "Aa naki warai," 180.

7. "Zaiko jūbun no nichiyōhin made kaidame," *Asahi shinbun,* November 17, 1973, 23.

8. "Kano bōdō de yūmei na Nishi Ageo Danchi o ossotta 'mono busoku' jōhō to 6,000 setai no kaidame sakusen," *Shūkan Shinchō,* vol. 18, no. 49 (December 6, 1973): 47.

9. Kakuei Tanaka, *Building a New Japan* (Tokyo: Simul, 1973), 142.

10. "Kami busoku de kyūni shinpai sare dashita genrontōsei," *Shūkan gendai,* vol. 15, no. 45 (October 18, 1973): 38.

11. The production of toilet paper in 1973 actually increased by 16 percent from the same period in 1972 . *Asahi shinbun,* November 23, 1973, 23.

12. See "Zaiko jūbun": 23; "Ano haikyū jidai": 159; and, "Kano bōdō": 50.

13. For detailed accounts of how the Japanese government responded to the Middle East crisis, see NHK shuzaihan, *Sekiyu shokku/Kokutetsu rōshi funsō,*

Sengo 50 nen sonotoki Nihon wa, vol. 5 (Tokyo: Nihon hōsō shuppan kyōkai, 1996), 1–206.

14. Honda Katsuichi, Chūgoku no tabi (Tokyo: Asahi shinbunsha, 1981), 298–300.

15. Morimura Sei'ichi, Akuma no hōshoku (Tokyo: Kōbundō, 1981) and Akuma no hōshoku, zoku (Tokyo: Kōbundō, 1982).

16. Suzuki Yūko, Sensō sekinin to jendā (Tokyo: Miraisha, 1997), 52–53.

17. Kimura Shōichi, " 'Jōi' eno senzo gaeri," Asahi shinbun, satellite edition, August 15, 1998, 17.

18. Kobayashi Yoshinori, Sensōron (Tokyo: Gentōsha, 1998). For his denial of the comfort women issue, see his Shin gōmanizumu sengen, vol. 4 (Tokyo: Shōgakukan, 1998). Journals Sekai and Ronza carried critical responses to Sensōron in their special sections. See Sekai, no. 656 (December 1998) and Ronza, no. 44 (December 1998).

19. Kobyashi Yoshinori, Sensōron, 150.

20. Mishima Yukio, "Bunka bōeiron," in Mishima Yukio Hyōron zenshū, vol. 3, 223–28.

21. In the 1960s, Hayashi Fusao articulated the position that Japan's "Great East Asia War" was a just war. Kobayashi's reasoning replicates many of Hayashi's points. However, there are crucial differences between their writings. Hayashi's text has had a relatively small audience since the 1960s; and Hayashi did not demonize the United States as the counterpoint against which to articulate Japan's nationhood. For instance, Hayashi claims he has no memories of August 6, 1945, the day when the atomic bomb was used on Hiroshima. See Hayashi Fusao, Daitōa sensō kōteiron (Tokyo: Banchōshobō, 1970), 631. The popularity of Kobayashi's manga and his anti-Americanism, hence, attests to the condition particular to post–Cold War Japanese social conditions.

22. These articles were later published in book form. See Katō Norihiro, Haisengo ron (Tokyo: Kōdansha, 1997).

23. Kishida Shū, Monogusa seishinbunseki (Tokyo: Seidosha, 1977), 10–12.

24. Katō Norihiro, Sengo o sengoigo kangaeru (Tokyo: Iwanami shoten, 1998), 2–13.

25. For such criticisms, see Ōkoshi Aiko, "Mōhitotsu no 'Katarikuchi no mondai'—Donoyōni rekishiteki jijitsu to deauka," Sōbun, April 1997, 21–26; Tessa Morris-Suzuki, "Unquiet Graves: Katō Norihiro and the Politics of Mourning," Japanese Studies 18, no. 1 (1998): 21–30; Takahashi Tetsuya, "Ojoku no kioku o megutte," Gunzō 50, no. 3 (1995): 176–82, and "Shōgen to jendā no seiji," Shisō, no. 874 (April 1997): 2–4; Minato Michitaka, "Kaisetsu," in ed. Jean-Luc Nancy, trans. Minato Michitaka, et al. Shutai no ato ni darega kurunoka (Tokyo: Gendaikikakushitsu, 1996), 327–37; Karatani Kōjin, Asada Akira, Nishitani Osamu, and Takahashi Tetsuya, "Sekinin to shutai o megutte," Hihyō kūkan 2, no. 13 (1997): 6–40; Ueno Chizuko, Nashonarizumu to jendā (Tokyo: Seidosha, 1998), 187–90.

26. For example, Ueno Chizuko discusses a participant's strong emotional response to her presentation in a 1995 workshop. In the workshop, Ueno insisted that feminism in Korea and Japan should overcome the national boundaries "out

of the concern that the 'comfort women' issue [was] used as a political tool by the Japanese and Korean governments to negotiate their national interests." A Korean American participant strongly objected to Ueno's urging, claiming: "Our national boundaries were violated by the soldiers of your country. You cannot tell us to forget the national boundaries that easily." One needs to be mindful that such strong resentment posits the collective subjectivity of Japanese from the exterior. However, Ueno Chizuko does not address the content of this Korean American's remark—the emotional undercurrent of nationalism in feminism. She simply uses it to reiterate the difficulty and importance of overcoming national divisions in feminist thought. *Nashonarizumu to jend*, 194–99, 226.

27. Katō is not uninterested in problematizing the concept of "the Japanese" through its historicization. His 1988 article, "Nihonjin no seiritsu," is an example of such an effort;, in it, he claims that one needs to transform the concept of "the Japanese" by learning that it is changeable. However, his focus is almost exclusively on the origins of the concept in the ancient period, as if the way the concept was produced somehow defines the later history. After positing a close relationship between "the Japanese" and the "emperor," the article abruptly ends by asking what can be done to transform the concept of "Japanese." As a response to his question, I emphasize the importance of the history of the recent past as a site to contemplate possible transformations of the concept. Katō, "Nihonjin no seiritsu," in *Kanōsei to shiteno sengo igo* (Tokyo: Iwanami shoten, 1999), 3–108.

Bibliography

"10 no danshō o tōshite mietekuru sengo 50 nen, soshite konokuni no 'rinkaku.' " *SPA*, February 1, 1995, 5.

Adorno, Theodor W. *Negative Dialectics*. New York: Continuum, 1973.

Aida Yūji. *Āron shūyōjo*. Tokyo: Chūōkōronsha, 1973.

———. *Prisoner of the British: A Japanese Soldier's Experiences in Burma*. Translated by Hide Ishiguro and Louis Allen. London: Cresset Press, 1966.

Akagi Munenori. "60 nen to watshi: chian shutsudō yōkyūsareta." *This Is Yomiuri*, May 1990, 176–78.

Akiyama Josui. *Tokyo Orinpikku no uchi to soto*. Tokyo: Baseball magaginsha, 1965.

Alperovitz, Gar. *The Decision to Use the Atomic Bomb: And the Architecture of an American Myth*. New York: Knopf, 1995.

Althusser, Louis. *Lenin and Philosophy and Other Essays*. Translated by Ben Brewster. New York: Monthly Review Press, 1971.

Amano Masako and Sakurai Atsushi. *"Mono to onna" no sengoshi: shintaisei, kateisei, shakaisei o jikuni*. Tokyo: Yūshindō, 1992.

Anderson, Benedict. *Imagined Communities*. London: Verso, 1991.

Andō Takeshi. *Mishima Yukio "nichiroku."* Tokyo: Michiya, 1996.

———. *Mishima Yukio no shōgai*. Tokyo: Natsume shobō, 1998.

" 'Ankēto' Orinpikku watashi no shinpai." *Fujin kōron*, October 1964, 76–82.

Anohi o kirokusurukai. *8 gatsu 15 nichi no kodomotachi*. Tokyo: Shōbunsha, 1987.

Aoki Tamotsu. *"Nihon bunkaron" no henyō: sengo Nihon no bunka to aidentitī*. Tokyo: Chūōkōronsha, 1990.

Ara Takashi. "Saigunbi to zainichi Beigun." In *Iwanami kōza: Nihon tsūshi*, vol. 20, edited by Asao Naohiro et al., 147–81. Tokyo: Iwanami shoten, 1995.

Arai Shin'ichi. *Sensō sekininron*. Tokyo: Iwanami shoten, 1995.

Arakawa Shōji. "Kyōben nisuginu 'monogatari' ni dokusha o sasoikoku shikake." *Ronza*, December 1998, 192–97.

Aramata Hiroshi. *Daitōa kagaku kitan*. Tokyo: Chikuma shobō, 1996.

———. *Kessenka no yūtopia*. Tokyo: Bungenshunjū, 1996.

———, ed. *Chishikijin 99 nin no shinikata: mōhitotsu no sengoshi*. Tokyo: Kadokawa shoten, 1994.

Asaba Michiaki. *Shibusawa Tatsuhiko no jidai: yōnen kōtei to Shōwa no seishinshi*. Tokyo: Seikyūsha, 1993.

Asagumo shinbunsha, ed. *Tokyo Orinpikku—shien ni sankashita jieitaiin no shuki*. Tokyo: Asagumo shinbunsha, 1965.

Asahi shinbun gakugeibu. *Daidokoro kara sengo ga mieru*. Tokyo: Asahi shinbunsha, 1995.

Asahi shinbunsha, ed. *Asahi shinbun no uchi soto*. Tokyo: Asahi shinbunsha, 1984.

Asahi shinbunsha, ed. *Chichi no senki*. Tokyo: Asahi shinbunsha, 1965.

———, ed. *"Nichibei kaiwa techō" wa naze uretaka*. Tokyo: Asahi shinbunsha, 1995.

———, ed. *Onnatachi no Taiheiyōsensō*. Tokyo: Asahi shinbunsha, 1996.

Asahi shinbun Yamagata shikyoku, ed. *Aru kenpei no kiroku*. Tokyo: Asahi shinbunsha, 1991.

Asakura Setsu. "Yoyogi kichi—okāsantachi wa tatakatteiru." *Kaizō*, July 1954, 146–50.

Asao Naohiro et al., eds. *Iwanami kōza: Nihon tsūshi*, vol. 20. Tokyo: Iwanami shoten, 1995.

Awaya Kentarō. "Report 4." In Fujiwara Akira et al., *Tetteikenshō: Shōwa tennō "Dokuhakuroku."* Tokyo: Ōtsuki shoten, 1991.

———. "Tokyo saiban ni miru sengo shori." In Awaya Kentarō et al., *Sensō sekinin—sengo sekinin*. Tokyo: Asahi shinbunsha, 1994.

Awaya Kentarō et al. *Sensō sekinin—sengo sekinin*. Tokyo: Asahi shinbunsha, 1994.

Barthes, Roland. *Mythologies*. Translated by Annette Lavers. New York: Newday Press, 1972.

Benjamin, Walter. *Illuminations*. Edited by Hannah Arendt. Translated by Harry F. Zohn. New York: Schocken Books, 1969.

Bernstein, Barton J. "The Struggle over History: Defining the Hiroshima Narrative." In *Judgement at Smithsonian*, edited by Philip Noble, 127–256. New York: Marlow, 1995.

———. "Understanding the Atomic Bomb and the Japanese Surrender." *Diplomatic History* 19, no. 2 (1995): 227–73.

Bhabha, Homi K. "Interrogating Identity." In *The Location of Culture*. London: Routledge, 1994.

Bix, Herbert. "The Showa Emperor's 'Monologue' and the Problem of War Responsibility." *Journal of Japanese Studies* 18, no. 2 (1992): 292–363.

Boyer, Paul. *By the Bomb's Early Light: American Thought and Culture at the Dawn of the Atomic Age*. New York: Pantheon, 1985.

Braw, Monica. *The Atomic Bomb Suppressed: American Censorship in Occupied Japan*. Armonk, N.Y.: M. E. Sharpe, 1991.

Bret, Corinne. "Heiwa no nakano 'ko.' " *Sekai*, December 1998, 127–29.

Brooks, Peter. *The Melodramatic Imagination: Balzac, Henry James, Melodrama, and the Mode of Excess*. New Haven: Yale University Press, 1995.

Bungeishunjū, ed. *"Bungeishunjū" nimiru supōtsu Shōwashi*. Tokyo: Bungeishunjū, 1988.

———, ed. *Bunshū nonfikushon bideo, Rikidōzan to sono jidai*. Tokyo: Bungeishunjū, 1995.

Cho Kyengtal. "Yūtopia nakisedai no kokkashugi." *Sekai*, December 1998, 86–93.

Confina, Alon. "Collective Memory and Cultural History: Problem of Method." *American Historical Review* 102, no. 5 (1997): 1386–1403.

Cook, Haruko T., and Theodore F. Cook. *Japan at War: An Oral History*. New York: New Press, 1992.

Craig, William. *The Fall of Japan*. New York: Dial Press, 1967.

Crane, Susan A. "Writing the Individual Back into Collective Memory." *American Historical Review* 102, no. 5 (1997): 1372–85.

Crichton, Michael. *Rising Sun.* New York: Ballantine Books, 1993.

Daimatsu Hirobumi. *Daimatsu, Chūgoku o kitaeru.* Tokyo: Kōdansha, 1965.

———. *Moyase! kokoroni yūki.* Tokyo: Kōdansha, 1968.

———. *Nasebanaru.* Tokyo: Kōdansha, 1964.

———. *Oreni tsuitekoi.* Tokyo: Kōdansha, 1963.

Daimatsu Hirobumi and Ichimura Kiyoshi. "Konjō, tōkon, shidōryoku: kukyō nitateba tatsuhodo tsuyokunaru." *Bungeishunjū,* November 1964, 100–106.

Daimatsu Hirobumi and Kaga Mariko. "Mariko no binantanken: danseiteki miryoku kajōna Daimatsu Hirobumi shi." *Fujin kōron,* March 1965, 246–51.

Daimatsu Hirobumi et al. "Rekishi shōgen—Shiberia no Nihonhei horyo: Zadankai shūyōsho guntō no saigetsu." *Shūkan yomiurim,* September 4, 1976, 2–47.

Daimatsu Michiyo. "Watashi wa Orinpikku o nikumu." *Maihōmu,* April 1963, 152–54.

Dower, John W. "Japan Addresses." *Journal of the International Institute,* fall 1995, 8–11.

———. *War without Mercy: Race and Power in the Pacific War.* New York: Pantheon, 1986.

Eguchi Keiichi. *Nicchū ahen sensō.* Tokyo: Iwanami shoten, 1988.

Ehara Yumiko, ed. *Seishoku gijutsu to jendā.* Feminizumu no shuchō, vol. 3. Tokyo: Keisō shobō, 1996.

Etō Jun. *Etō Jun chosakushū.* Vol. 2. Tokyo: Kōdansha, 1967.

———. " 'Heiwa no saiten' no hikari to kage: gen'ei no 'Nihon teikoku.' " *Bungeishunjū,* December 1964, 174–81.

———. "Nihon to watashi, 1–9." *Asahi journal,* January 1–February 26, 1967.

Fallows, James. "Containing Japan." *Atlantic,* May 1989, 40–54.

Field, Norma. "The Stakes of Apology." *Japan Quarterly,* October 1995, 405–18.

Figal, Gerald. "Historical Sense and Commemorative Sensibility at Okinawa's Cornerstone of Peace." *Positions* 5, no. 3 (1997): 745–78.

Foreign Affairs Association of Japan. *Japan Year Book, 1949–52.* Tokyo: Foreign Affairs Association of Japan, 1952.

Foucault, Michel. "Theatrum Philosophicum." In *Language, Counter-Memory, Practice,* edited by Donald F. Bouchard, translated by Donald F. Bouchard and Sherry Simon, 165–96. Ithaca: Cornell University Press, 1977.

Fujii Tadatoshi. *Kokubō fujinkai—Hinomaru to kappōgi.* Tokyo: Iwanami shoten, 1985.

Fujino Yutaka. *Nihon fashizumu to iryō.* Tokyo: Iwanami shoten, 1993.

———. *Nihon fashizumu to yūseishisō.* Kyoto: Kamogawa shuppan, 1998.

Fujisawa Kikuo. " 'Sekai ichi Hikarigō' eno michi—kiteki issei kara chōtokkyū made." *Toki,* November 1964, 174–79.

Fujita Kōichirō. *Seiketsu wa byōkida.* Tokyo: Asahi shinbunsha, 1999.

Fujitake Akira. *Tokyo Orinpikku: sono 5 nenkan no ayumi.* Tokyo: Nihon hōsō kyōkai hōsō yoron chōsajo, 1967.

Fujiwara Akira. *Shōwa tennō no 15 nen sensō.* Tokyo: Aoki shoten, 1991.

Fujiwara Akira et al. *Tetteikenshō: Shōwa tennō "Dokuhakuroku."* Tokyo: Ōtsuki shoten, 1991.

Fujiwara Hirotatsu. "Shijōkūzen no kutsujyoku jōyaku." *Bungeishunjū*, April 1960, 62–68.

Fujiwara Yoshie. "Abunai gaijin." *Fujin kōron*, October 1964, 88–93.

Fujiyama Ai'ichirō and Yamamoto Mitsuru. "Shōgen, 1960 nen Anpo kaitei: Senryō gyōsei kara no dakkyaku." *Chūōkōron*, July 1977, 196–204.

Fukatsu Masumi. "The Eclipse of Shōwa Taboos and the Apology Resolution." *Japan Quarterly*, October 1995, 419–25.

Fukuda Kazuya. *Rikidōzan wa erakatta*. Tokyo: Bēsubōru magajinsha, 1996.

Fukushima Jirō. *Mishima Yukio—ken to kanbeni*. Tokyo: Bungeishunjū, 1998.

Fukushima Kikujirō. *Sensō ga hajimaru*. Tokyo: Shakaihyōronsha, 1987.

Furukawa Takahisa. *Kōki, Banpaku, Orinpikku: Kōshitsu burando to keizai hatten*. Tokyo: Chūōkōronsha, 1998.

Gayn, Mark. *Japan Diary*. Tokyo: Charles E. Tuttle, 1981.

Gendai fūzoku kenkyūkai. "Tokyo Orinpikku marason kōsu no hakkutsu." In *Gendai fūzoku, gendai iseki*, edited by Gendai fūzoku kenkyūkai, 229–98. Tokyo: Ribopurōto, 1991.

Gerrow, Arron. "Consuming Asia, Consuming Japan: The New Nationalist Revisionism in Japan." *Bulletin of Concerned Asian Scholars* 30, no. 2 (1998): 30–36.

———. "Zushō toshiteno *Sensōron*." *Sekai*, December 1998, 118–23.

Gesuidō Tokyo 100 nenshi hensan iinkai, ed. *Gesuidō Tokyo 100 nenshi*. Tokyo: Tokyoto Gesuidōkyoku, 1989.

Gibney, Frank, ed. *Senso: The Japanese Remember the Pacific War*. Translated by Beth Cary. Armonk, N.Y.: M. E. Sharpe, 1995.

Gluck, Carol. "The 'End' of the Postwar: Japan at the Turn of the Millennium." *Public Culture* 10, no. 1 (1997): 1–23.

Gomi Mitsuo. "Anpo sōdōka no shushō kantei." *Bungeishunjū*, December 1964, 206–13.

Gotō Masaharu. "Nihonjin wa Orinpikku ni nanio kaketaka." *Ushio*, October 1994, 142–56.

Hachiya Michihiko. *Hiroshima Diary: The Journal of a Japanese Physician, August 6–September 30, 1945*. Chapel Hill: University of North Carolina Press, 1955.

Handō Kazutoshi. *Seidan*. Tokyo: Bungeishunjū, 1985.

Hanley, Susan B. *Everyday Things in Premodern Japan: The Hidden Legacy of Material Culture*. Berkeley and Los Angeles: University of California Press, 1997.

Hara Akira. "Sensō baishō mondai to Ajia." In *Ajia no Reisen to datsu-shokuminchika*, edited by Ōe Shinobu et al., 69–89. Kindai Nihon to shokuminchi, vol. 8. Tokyo: Iwanami shoten, 1993.

Hara Yoshihisa. *Kishi Nobusuke*. Tokyo: Iwanami shoten, 1995.

Harada Katsumasa. *Nihon no rekishi: Bekkan Shōwa no sesō*. Tokyo: Shōgakukan, 1983.

———. *Nihon no tetsudō*. Tokyo: Yoshikawa kōbunkan, 1991.

Harris, Sheldon H. *Factories of Death: Japanese Biological Warfare, 1932–45, and the American Cover-Up.* London: Routledge, 1994.

Harwit, Martin. *An Exhibit Denied: Lobbying the History of "Enola Gay."* New York: Copernicus, 1996.

Hasegawa Takuya. *Kasutori bunka kō.* Tokyo: San'ichi Shobō, 1969.

Hashikawa Bunzō. "Chūkansha no me." In *Hihyō to kenkyū Mishima Yukio,* edited by Shirakawa Masayoshi, 132–45. Tokyo: Haga shoten, 1974.

Hashimoto Kazuo. *Maboroshi no Tokyo Orinpikku.* Tokyo: Nihon Hōsō Kyōkai Shuppan Kyōkai, 1994.

Hashimoto Osamu. "Shōwa 39 nen, Tokyo ni sensō ga atta: kiroku eiga *Tokyo Orinpikku,* sono 1." *Esquire Japan,* August 1988, 121–24.

———. "Yabanna nikutai: kiroku eiga *Tokyo Orinpikku,* sono 2." *Esquire Japan,* September 1988, 96–100.

Hata Ikuhiko. *Nankinjiken: "gyakusatsu" no kōzō.* Tokyo: Chūōkōronsha, 1986.

Haver, William. *The Body of This Death: Historicity and Sociality in the Time of AIDS.* Stanford: Stanford University Press, 1996.

Hayashi Fusao. *Daitōasensō kōteiron.* Tokyo: Banchō shobō, 1970.

Hayashi Shigeru et al., eds. *Nihon shūsenshi: maboroshi no wahei kōsaku,* vol. 2. *chūkan.* Tokyo: Yomiuri shinbunsha, 1962.

Henson, Maria R. *Comfort Woman: A Filipina's Story of Prostitution and Slavery under the Japanese Military.* Lanham, Md.: Rowman and Littlefield, 1999.

Hidaka Rokurō, ed. *1960 nen 5 gatsu 19 nichi.* Tokyo: Iwanami shoten, 1960.

Hidaka Rokurō et al. "Anpo kaitei to Minshushugi." *Fujin kōron,* June 1960, 112–20.

Higashino Makoto. *Shōwa tennō futatsu no "Dokuhakuroku."* Tokyo: Nihon hōsō kyōkai shuppankai, 1998.

Higuchi Keiko. *Watashi wa 13 sai datta.* Tokyo: Chikuma shobō, 1996.

Higuchi Naofumi. *Guddo mōningu Gojira: kantoku Honda Toshirō to satsueisho no jidai.* Tokyo: Chikuma shobō, 1992.

Hiraiwa Yumie. "Yoru no Orinpikku urakaidō." *Fujin kōron,* October 1964, 100–106.

Hiraoka Azusa. *Segare Mishima Yukio.* Tokyo: Bungeishunjū, 1996.

Hiraoka Shizue. "Bōryū no gotoku." *Shinchō,* December 1976, 96–120.

Hirata Akitaka. "Penishirin: Jimaede kanseisaseta 'kiseki no kusuri.' " *Sengo 50 nen Nippon no kiseki,* jō. Edited by Yomiuri shinbun henshūkyoku—sengoshi han. Tokyo: Yomiuri shinbunsha, 1995.

Honda Katsuichi. *Chūgoku no tabi.* Tokyo: Asashi shinbunsha, 1981.

———. *Nankin eno michi.* Tokyo: Asashi shinbunsha, 1989.

Horiba Kiyoko. *Kinjirareta genbaku taiken.* Tokyo: Iwanami shoten, 1995.

Horie Kō. "Tokyo no kansendōro keisei ni kansuru shiteki kenkyū." Ph.D. diss., Tokyo Institute of Technology, 1990.

Hosaka Masayasu. *60 nen Anpo tōsō.* Tokyo: Kōdansha, 1986.

———. *Samazama naru sengo.* Tokyo: Bungeishunjū, 1995.

———. "Tennō amakudaruhi—senryōka, hatsu no Kanagawa junkō." *Bessatsu bungeishunjū,* winter 1989, 268–315.

Hosokawa Morisada. *Hosokawa nikki.* 2 vols. Tokyo: Chūōkōronsha, 1989.

Ichikawa Kon and Mori Yūki. *Ichikawa Kon no eigatachi—Films of Kon Ichikawa*. Tokyo: Waizu shuppan, 1994.

Ichinokawa Yasutaka. "Yūsei shujutsu (= funin shujutsu) ni tsuite." In *Seishoku gijutsu to jendā*, edited by Ehara Yumiko. Tokyo: Keiseishobō, 1996.

Ichinokawa Yasutaka and Tateiwa Shinya. "Shōgaishaundō kara mietekurumono." *Gendai shisō* 26, no. 2 (1998): 258–85.

Ide Busaburō, ed. *Anpo tōsō*. Tokyo: San'ichi shobō, 1960.

Ide Kōya. "Tsuiseki! Rikidōzan." In *"Bungeishunjū" nimiru supōtsu Shōwashi*, edited by Bungeishunjū. Tokyo: Bungeishunjū, 1988.

Ide Magoroku. *Sengoshi*. 2 vols. Tokyo: Iwanami shoten, 1991.

Ienaga Saburō. *The Pacific War, 1931–1945*. Translated by Frank Baldwin. New York: Random House, 1978.

———. *Sensō sekinin*. Tokyo: Iwanami shoten, 1985.

Igarashi Takeshi. *Sengo Nichibei kankei no keisei: Kōwa, Anpo to reisengo no shisenni tatte*. Tokyo: Kōdansha, 1995.

Igarashi Yoshikuni. "Imagining History: Discourses of Cultural Politics in Japan, 1930's and 1960's." Ph.D. diss., University of Chicago, 1994.

Iida Momo. *Sengoshi no hakken*, vol. 2. Tokyo: Sanpō, 1975.

Iida Susumu. *Tamashizume eno michi: muimina shikara tou sensō sekinin*. Tokyo: Fujishuppan, 1997.

Iizuka Kōji. *Nihon no guntai*. Tokyo: Heibonsha, 1991.

Ikeda Kiyohiko. "Ōbei to Nihon no shokuminchi taiken no uketomekata no chigai wa naze shōjitanoka." In *Bokura no "shinryaku" sensō: mukashi atta anosensō o dōkangaetara yoinoka*, edited by Miyazaki Tetsuya, 204–17. Tokyo: Senyōsha, 1995.

Inose Naoki. *Persona: Mishima Yukio den*. Tokyo: Bungeishunjū, 1995.

———. *Yokubō no media*. Tokyo: Shinchōsha, 1994.

Inoue Hisashi. *Besuto serā no sengoshi*. 2 vols. Tokyo: Bungeishunjū, 1995.

Inoue Shōichi. *Senjika Nihon no kenchikuka: āto, kicchu, Japanesuku*. Tokyo: Asahi shinbunsha, 1995.

International Public Hearing 1993, Executive Committee, ed. *War Victimization and Japan: International Public Hearing Report*. Osaka: Tōhō shuppan, 1993.

Iokibe Makoto. *Beikoku no Nihon senryōseisaku*. 2 vols. Tokyo: Chūōkōronsha, 1985.

Irie Arimasa. *Irie Arimasa nikki*. Vol. 4. Tokyo: Asahi shinbunsha, 1991.

Irie Katsumi. *Nihon fashizumuka no taiikushisō*. Tokyo: Fumaidō shuppan, 1986.

Irokawa Daikichi. *The Age of Hirohito: In Search of Modern Japan*. Translated by Mikiso Hane and John K. Urda. New York: Free Press, 1995.

———. *Jibunshi*. Tokyo: Kōdansha, 1992.

———. *Shōwashi no tennō*. Tokyo: Iwanami shoten, 1991.

Ishibashi Takehiko and Satō Tomohisa. *Nihon no taisō—hyakunen no ayumi to jitsugi*. Tokyo: Fumaidō, 1966.

Ishida Yorifusa. *Mikan no Tokyo keikaku*. Tokyo: Chikuma shobō, 1992.

Ishihara Shintarō. *The Japan That Can Say No*. Translated by Baldwin Frank. New York: Simon and Schuster, 1991.

———. *Mishima Yukio no nisshoku*. Tokyo: Shinchōsha, 1991.

Ishihara Shintarō and Nosaka Akiyuki. "Mishima Yukio no eikō to zasetsu—nikutai o meguru kiyo to hōhen." *Subaru*, December 1995, 84–99.

Ishii Michiko. "Yūsei Hogohō niyoru dataigōhōka no mondaiten." *Shakaikagaku kenkyū* 34, no. 4 (1982): 113–73.

Ishikawa Hiroyoshi. *Yokubō no sengoshi*. Tokyo: Kōsaidō, 1989.

Ishikawa Hiroyoshi et al., eds. *Taishūbunka jiten*. Tokyo: Kōbundō, 1994.

Ishikawa Jun. *Ishikawa Jun senshū*. Vol. 1. Tokyo: Iwanami shoten, 1979.

Ishiko Junzō. *Sengo mangashi nōto*. Tokyo: Kinokuniya shoten, 1994.

Ishizuka Hiromichi and Ishida Yorifusa. *Tokyo: seichō to keikaku, 1868–1988*. Tokyo: Tokyo Toritsu Daigaku Toshikenkyū sentā, 1988.

Isoda Kōichi. *Isoda Kōichi chosakushū*. Vol. 1. Tokyo: Ozawa shoten, 1990.

———. "Onchō to shiteno sensō." In *Hihyō to kenkyū Mishima Yukio*, edited by Shirakawa Masayoshi, 70–86. Tokyo: Haga shoten, 1974.

———. *Sengoshi no kūkan*. Tokyo: Shinchōsha, 1993.

Itō Sei. "Kishi Nobusuke shi niokeru ningen no kenkyū." *Chūōkōron*, August 1960, 169–78.

Itō Takashi and Satō Seizaburō. "Ano sensō towa nandattanoka." *Chūōkōron*, January 1995, 26–43.

Iwanami shoten henshūbu, ed. *Kindai Nihon sōgō nenpyō*. 3d ed. Tokyo: Iwanami shoten, 1996.

Iyoda Yasuhiro et al., eds. *Terebishi handobukku*. Tokyo: Jiyūkokuminsha. 1996.

James, Daniel. "Meatpackers, Peronists, and Collective Memory: A View from the South." *American Historical Review* 102, no. 5 (1997): 1404–12.

Japan Branch of the International Law. *The Japanese Annual of International Law, 1961*. Tokyo: Japan Branch of the International Law, 1961.

Japanese Society for History Textbook Reform. *The Restoration of a National History: Why Was the Japanese Society for History Textbook Reform Established, and What Are Its Goals?* Tokyo: Japanese Society for History Textbook Reform, 1999.

Kaikō Ken. *Zubari Tokyo*. Tokyo: Bungeishunjyū, 1982.

Kajiwara Ikki. *Rikidōzan to Nihon puroresu*. Tokyo: Yudachisha, 1996.

Kakei Katsuhiko. *Yamato bataraki*. Tokyo: Kakei hakase chosakubutsu kankō-kai, 1929.

Kamei Hideo. *Shintai, kono fushiginaru monono bungaku*. Tokyo: Renga shobō shinsha, 1984.

Kamisaka Fuyuko. " 'Anohi' ga hitobito no mune ni nokoshita mono—Anpo tōsō 1 nenmeni." *Fujin kōron*, June 1961, 102–8.

Kan Takayuki and Kaibara Hiroshi. *Zengakuren: For biginners*. Tokyo: Gendaishikan, 1982.

Kanda Fumihito. *Senryō to Minshushugi*. Shōwa no rekishi, vol. 8. Tokyo: Shōgakukan, 1989.

Kaneko Mitsuharu. *Zetsubō no Shōwashi*. Tokyo: Kōdansha, 1996.

Kanō Masanao. *Momotarō sagashi—kenkōkan no kindai*. Rekishi o yominaosu, vol. 23. Tokyo: Asahi shinbunsha, 1995.

Kanzaki Kiyoshi. "Tokyo kichi." *Kaizō*, January 1954, 130–38.

Karatani Kōjin, Asada Akira, Nishitani Osamu, and Takahashi Tetsuya. "Sekinin to shutai o megutte." *Hihyō kūkan* 2, no. 13 (1997): 6–40.

Karino Kenji. *Tokyo yamiichi kōbōshi*. Tokyo: Sōfūsha, 1987.

Kasahara Tokushi. *Ajia no nakano Nihongun: Sensō sekinin to rekishigaku, rekishikyōiku*. Tokyo: Ōtsukishoten, 1994.

———. *Nankin jiken*. Tokyo: Iwanami shoten, 1997.

Kasza Gregory. *The State and the Mass Media in Japan, 1918–1945*. Berkeley and Los Angeles: University of California Press, 1988.

Katō Norihiro. *Haisengo ron*. Tokyo: Kōdansha, 1997.

———. "Nihon fūkeiron (2): 1959 nen no kekkon." *Gunzō*, September 1988, 296–318.

———. *Nihon to iu shintai: "dai, shin, kō" no seishinshi*. Tokyo: Kōdansha, 1994.

———. *Kanōsei to shiteno sengo igo*. Tokyo: Iwanami shoten, 1999.

———. *Katō Norihiro no hatsugen, 2: Sengo o koeru shikō*. Tokyo: Kaichōsha, 1996.

———. *Sengo o sengo igo kangaeru*. Tokyo: Iwanami shoten, 1998.

Katō Norihiro and Takeda Seiji. *Futatsu no sengokara*. Tokyo: Chikuma shobō, 1998.

Katō Shūichi. *Zasshu bunka: Niho no chiisana kibō*. Tokyo: Kōdansha, 1974.

Kawabata Yasunari and Mishima Yukio. *Kawabata Yasunari, Mishima Yukio ōfuku shokan*. Tokyo: Shinchōsha, 1997.

Kawakita Kōichi, ed. *Bokutachi no aishita kaijū Gojira*. Tokyo: Gakushū kenkyūsha, 1996.

Kawamoto Saburō. *Imahitotabi no sengo Nihon eiga*. Tokyo: Iwnami shoten, 1994.

Kawamoto Takeshi. " 'Chokkan to rikutsu' ni kinkō o torudoryoku o hōkishita gōmanizumu no hōhōteki hatan." *Ronza*, December 1998, 198–203.

Kawamura Minato. *Sengo bungaku otou—sono taiken to rinen*. Tokyo: Iwanami shoten, 1995.

Kawamura Minato, Narita Ryūichi, and Ueno Chizuko. " 'Sensō' wa donoyōni katararete kitaka." *Shūkan asahi bessatsu: shōsetsu Tripper*, June 25, 1998, 12–27.

Keishichō. *Orinpikku Tokyo Taikai no keisatsu kiroku*. Tokyo: Keishichō, 1964.

Kikuta Kazuo. *Kimino na wa*. 4 vols. Tokyo: Kawadeshobō shinsha, 1991.

Kimura Kazuaki. *Mōhitotsu no bungakushi—"sensō" eno manazashi*. Shizuoka: Zōshinkai shuppansha, 1996.

Kimura Masahiko. "Watashi to Rikidōzan no shinsō." In *Bungeishunjū ni miru supōtsu Shōwashi*, edited by Bungeishunjū, 628–37. Tokyo: Bungeishunjū, 1988.

Kinema junpō, ed. *Sengo Kinema junpō best ten zenshi: 1946–1992*. Tokyo: Kinema junpōsha, 1993.

Kiritōshi Risaku. "Kobayashi Yoshinori *Sensōron* gatoku 'ōyake no michi.' " *Shokun*, October 1998, 178–87.

Kisaka Jun'ichirō. "Ajia Taiheiyō sensō no koshō to seikaku." *Ryūkoku hōgaku* 25, no. 4 (1993): 386–434.

Kishi Nobusuke. " 'Tokubetsu shiryō' Kishi Nobusuke Sugamo gokuchū nikki." *Chūōkōron*, November 1979, 338–49.

Kishi Nobusuke and Yamamoto Mitsuru. "Shōgen—1960 nen Anpo kaitei: Dokuritu eno kodokuna ketsudan." *Chūōkōron*, July 1977, 185–96.

Kishi Nobusuke, Yatsuki Kazuo, and Itō Takashi. *Kishi Nobusuke no kaisō.* Tokyo: Bungeishunjū, 1981.

Kishida Shū. *Monogusa seishinbunseki.* Tokyo: Seidosha, 1977.

Kitaoka Shin'ichi. *Jimintō—seikentō no 38 nen.* 20 seiki no Nippon, vol. 1. Tokyo: Yomiuri shinbunsa, 1995.

———. "Rekishi no kenshō to kojin no sekinin." *Chūōkōron,* August 1995, 30–41.

Kobayashi Nobuhiko. *Ichishōnen no mita "seisen."* Tokyo: Chikuma shobō, 1998.

Kobayashi Toyoaki. *Gojira no ronri: A Study of the Godzilla Era.* Tokyo: Chūkyō shuppan, 1992.

Kobayashi Yoshinori. *Shin gōmanizumu sengen.* Vol. 4. Tokyo: Shōgakukan, 1998.

———. *Sensōron.* Tokyo: Tōgensha, 1998.

Kobayashi Yoshinori, Takeda Seiji, and Hashizume Daisaburō. *Gōmanizumu shisōkōza: seigi, sensō, kokkaron—jibun to shakai o tsunagu kairo.* Tokyo: Komichishobō, 1997.

Kōdoseichō o kangaerukai, ed. *Kazoku no seikatsu no monogatari.* Kōdoseichō to Nihonjin, part 2. Tokyo: Nihon editā sukūru shuppanbu, 1986.

Koenaki koe no kai. *Fukkokuban, Koenaki koe no tayori.* 2 vols. Tokyo: Shisō no kagakusha, 1996.

Kojima Nobuo. *Amerikan sukūru.* Tokyo: Shinchōsha, 1967.

———. "Stars." In *The Shōwa Anthology,* edited by Van C. Gessel and Tomone Matsumoto, 115–44.

Komoda Nobuo et al. *Shinpan Nihon ryūkōkashi,* vol. 2. Tokyo: Shakaishisōsha, 1995.

Kosaka Shūhei. *Hizai no umi—Mishima Yukio to sengo shakai no nihirizumu.* Tokyo: Kawade Shobō Shinsha, 1988.

Kōseishō mondai kenkyūkai. *Kōseishō 50 nen: Kijitsuhen, shiryōhen.* Tokyo: Kōseishō, 1988.

Koshizawa Akira. *Tokyo no toshikeikaku.* Tokyo: Iwanami shoten, 1991.

Kosuge Nobuko. "Puropaganda ni riyōsareta tsuitō no naratibu." *Sekai,* December 1998, 124–27.

Kubokawa Tsujirō. "Washinton haitsu." *Chūōkōron,* January 1953, 169–85.

Kuboshima Seiichirō. *Kaiga hōrō.* Tokyo: Ozawa shoten, 1996.

———. *Mugonkan.* Tokyo: Kōdansha, 1997.

———. *"Mugonkan" eno tabi.* Tokyo: Ozawa shoten, 1997.

Kurashi no techō henshūbu, ed. *Sensōchū no kurashi no kiroku.* Tokyo: Kurashi no techōsha, 1980.

Kurumizawa Kōshi. *Kuropan furyoki.* Tokyo: Bungeishunjyū, 1983.

Kusakabe Kushirō. "Daijin ga kechi o tsuketa Ichikawa Kon no Gorin eiga." *Hōseki,* August 1982, 190–95.

Kyōya Hideo. *1961 nen fuyu "Fūryū mutan" jiken.* Tokyo: Heibonsha, 1996.

LaCapra, Dominick. *History and Memory after Auschwitz.* Ithaca: Cornell University Press, 1998.

Laclau, Ernesto, and Chantal Mouffe. *Hegemony and Socialist Strategy: Towards a Radical Democratic Politics.* London: Verso, 1985.

Lee Sunil. *Mōhitori no Rikidōzan.* Tokyo: Shōgakukan, 1996.

Lindee, M. Susan. *Suffering Made Real: American Science and the Survivors at Hiroshima*. Chicago: University of Chicago Press, 1994.

Linenthal, Edward, and Tom Engelhardt, eds. *History Wars: The "Enola Gay" and Other Battles for the American Past*. New York: Henry Holt, 1996.

Lummis, Douglas. "Genshitekina nikkō no nakadeno hinatabokko." *Shisō no kagaku*, June 1981, 16–20.

MacArthur, Douglas. *Reminiscences*. New York: McGraw-Hill, 1964.

Machida Shinobu. *Makkāsā to Seirogan—Nippon dentōyaku monogatari*. Tokyo: Geibunsha, 1997.

Machimura Takashi. *"Sekaitoshi" Tokyo no kōzōtenkan*. Tokyo: Tokyo daigaku shuppankyoku, 1994.

Maema Takanori. *Ajia shinkansen: maboshoshi no Tokyo hatsu Pekin yuki chō-tokkyū*. Tokyo: Kōdansha, 1998.

Magajin hausu, ed. *Heibon panchi no jidai: ushinawareta 60 nendai o motomete*. Tokyo: Magajin hause, 1996.

Maier, Charles S. *The Unmasterable Past: History, Holocaust, and German National Identity*. Cambridge: Harvard University Press, 1997.

Mainichi shinbunsha, ed. *Iwanami shoten to Bungeishunjyū*. Tokyo: Mainichi shinbunsha, 1996.

Marchetti, Gena. *Romance and the "Yellow Peril."* Berkeley and Los Angeles: University of California Press, 1993.

Maruya Saiichi. "Abunai Eigo." *Fujin kōron*, October 1964, 83–87.

Maruyama Kunio and Murakami Hyōe. "5 gatsu 19 nichi igo—Anpotōsō arashi no 1 kagetsu." *Fujin kōron*, August 1960, 62–75.

Maruyama Masao. *Maruyama Masao shū*. 17 vols. Tokyo: Iwanami shoten, 1995–97.

———. *Nihon no shisō*. Tokyo: Iwanami shoten, 1961.

———. *Nihon seiji shisōshi kenkyū*. Tokyo: Tokyo daigaku shuppankai, 1952.

———. *Studies in the Intellectual History of Tokugawa Japan*. Translated by Mikiso Hane. Tokyo: University of Tokyo Press, 1974.

———. *Thought and Behaviour in Modern Japanese Politics*. Edited by Ivan Morris. Oxford: Oxford University Press, 1969.

Maruyama Masao et al. "Sensō to dōjidai." *Dōjidai*, 1958, 20–41.

Marx, Karl. *The Eighteenth Brumaire of Louis Bonaparte*. In *The Marx-Engels Reader*, 2d ed., edited by Robert C. Tucker, 594–617. New York: W. W. Norton, 1978.

Masamura Kimihiro. "Bukka tōseirei." In *Sengoshi daijiten*, edited by Sakai Tsuyoshi et al., 801. Tokyo: Sanseidō, 1991.

Masumi Junnosuke. *Shōwa tennō to sono jidai*. Tokyo: Yamakawa shuppan, 1998.

Matsubara Yōko. " 'Bunka kokka' no yūseihō." *Gendai shisō* 25, no. 4 (1997): 8–21.

———. "Minzoku Yūsei Hogo Hōan to Nihon no Yūseihō no keifu." *Kagakushi kenkyū II*, no. 36 (1997): 42–50.

———. "Senjika no Danshuhō ronsō: Seishinkai no Kokumin Yūseihō hihan." *Gendai shisō* 26, no. 2 (1998): 286–303.

Matsuda, Matt K. *The Memory of the Modern.* Oxford: Oxford University Press, 1996.

Matsudaira Makoto. *Yamiichi maboroshi no gaidobukku.* Tokyo: Chikuma shobō, 1995.

Matsumoto Hiroshi. "Genbaku o otoshitakuni Amerika." *Shisō no kagaku,* April 1996, 10–14.

Matsumoto Ken'ichi. "Kibun wa mō Nichibei sensō." *Chūōkōron,* February 1990, 122–27.

———. *Mishima Yukio bōmei densetsu.* Tokyo: Kawadeshobō shinsha, 1987.

Matsumura Kenzō. *Sandai kaikoroku.* Tokyo: Toyō keizai shinpōsha, 1964.

Matsuo Takayoshi. "The First Meeting of Showa Tennō with General MacArthur: A Documentation." *Kyoto Daigaku Bungakubu kenkyū kiyō* 29 (March 1990): 37–94.

———. *Kokusai kokka eno shuppatsu.* Nihon no rekishi, vol. 21. Tokyo: Shūeisha, 1993.

Matsuyama Iwao. *Gunshū—Kikai no nakano nanmin.* 20 seiki no Nippon, vol. 12. Tokyo: Yomiuri shinbunsha, 1996.

Minami Hiroshi. *Nihonjinron: Meiji kara konnichimade.* Tokyo: Iwanami shoten, 1994.

Minato Michitaka. "Kaisetsu." In *Shutai no ato ni darega kurunoka,* edited by Jean-Luc Nancy, translated by Minato Michitaka et al., 327–37. Tokyo: Gendaikikakushitsu, 1996.

Ministry of Foreign Affairs, ed. *Nihon no sentaku: Dainiji Sekaitaisen shūsenshi roku.* Tokyo: Ministry of Foreign Affairs, 1990.

Mishima Yukio. *Confession of a Mask.* Translated by Meredith Weatherby. New York: New Directions, 1958.

———. "Hōjō no umi nōto." *Shinchō,* January 1971, 70–89.

———. *Mishima Yukio Hyōron zenshū.* 4 vols. Tokyo: Shinchōsha, 1989.

———. *Mishima Yukio zenshū.* 36 vols. Tokyo: Shinchōsha, 1973–76.

———. *The Temple of the Golden Pavilion.* Translated by Ivan Morris. New York: Perigee Books, 1980.

Mishima Yukio and Furubayashi Takashi. "Mishima Yukio wa kataru—saigo no intabyū." In *Mishima Yukio,* edited by Ōoka Shin et al., 205–28. Gunzō Nihon no sakka, vol. 18. Tokyo: Shōgakukan, 1990.

Mita Masahiro. *Bokutte nani.* Tokyo: Kawadeshobō shinsha, 1997.

Mitani Taichirō. "Seiji taisei to sengo taisei." In *Ajia no reisen to datsu-shokuminchika,* edited by Ōe Shinobu et al., 315–60. Kindai Nihon to shokuminchi, vol. 8. Tokyo: Iwanami shoten, 1993.

Miyake, Yoshiko. "Doubling Expectations: Motherhood and Women's Factory Work under State Management in Japan in the 1930s and 1940s." In *Recreating Japanese Women, 1600–1946,* edited by Gail Bernstein, 267–95. Berkeley and Los Angeles: University of California Press, 1991.

Miyazaki Kiyotaka. "Tōyō no maō to yobarete." *Chūōkōron,* February 1954, 242–56.

Miyazaki Tetsuya. "Mizuki manga de hiteisareteita rojikku 'igiarushi koso seio imizukeru.' " *Ronza,* December 1998, 204–9.

Miyoshi, Masao. *Accomplices of Silence*. Berkeley and Los Angeles: University of California Press, 1974.

Mizuki Shigeru. *Mizuiki Shigeru no Rabauru senki*. Tokyo: Chikuma shobō, 1994.

———. *Sōin gyokusaiseyo*. Tokyo: Kōdansha, 1995.

Mohan, Uday, and Sanho Tree. "Hiroshima, the American Media, and the Construction of Conventional Wisdom." *Journal of American–East Asia Relations* 4, no. 2 (1995): 141–60.

Moon, Katharine H. S. *Sex among Allies: Military Prostitution in U.S.-Korea Relations*. New York: Columbia University Press, 1997.

Mori Akihide and Yamada Shōgo. *Kaden konjyaku monogatari*. Tokyo: Sanseidō, 1983.

Mori Takemaro. *Ajia Taiheiyō sensō*. Nihon no rekishi, vol. 20. Tokyo: Shūeisha, 1993.

Morimura Seiichi. *Akuma no hōshoku*. Tokyo: Kōbundō, 1981.

———. *Akuma no hōshoku, zoku*. Tokyo: Kōbundō, 1982.

Morioka Kiyomi. *Wakai tokkōtaiin to Taiheiyōsensō: sono shuki to gunzō*. Tokyo: Yoshikawa kōbunkan, 1995.

Moritan Akio et al. "Daigakusei wa *Sensōron* o kōyonda." *Sekai*, December 1998, 130–45.

Morris-Suzuki, Tessa. "Unquiet Graves: Katō Norihiro and the Politics of Mourning." *Japanese Studies* 18, no. 1 (1998): 21–30.

Murakami, Haruki. *A Wild Sheep Chase*. Translated by Alfred Birnbaum. New York: Plume, 1990.

Murakami, Ryū. *Almost Transparent Blue*. Translated by Nancy Andrew. Tokyo: Kodansha International, 1977.

Murakami Yōichirō. *Iryō—Kōreishakai e mukatte*. 20 seiki no Nippon, vol. 9. Tokyo: Yomiuri shinbunsha, 1996.

Murakami Yumiko. *Yellow Face*. Tokyo: Asahi shinbunsha, 1993.

Muramatsu Takeshi. *Mishima Yukio no sekai*. Tokyo: Shinchōsha, 1990.

Muramatsu Tomomi. *Shōwa seikatsu bunka kuronikuru*. Tokyo: Toto shuppan, 1991.

———. *Watakushi puroresu no mikatadesu*. Tokyo: Chikuma shobō, 1994.

Murano Masayoshi. *Bakyūmukā wa erakatta*. Tokyo: Bungeishunjyū, 1996.

Muro Kenji. "Pāruhābā kara Hiroshima made." *Shisō no kagaku*, April 1996, 4–9.

Mushiake Aromu. "Sengo besutoserā monogatari: Daimatsu Hirobumi, *Oreni tsuitekoi*." *Asahi journal*, January 8, 1967, 43–47.

Musolf, Peter. *Gojira towa nanika*. Translated by Ono Kōsei. Tokyo: Kōdansha, 1998.

Nagai Katsuichi. *"Garo" henshūchō*. Tokyo: Chikuma shobō, 1987.

Nagao Goichi. *Sensō to eiyō*. Tokyo: Nishida shoten, 1994.

Nakamura Masanori. "1950–60 nendai no Nihon: Kōdo keizaiseichō." In *Iwanami kōza: Nihon tsūshi*, vol. 20, edited by Asao Naohiro et al., 1–67. Tokyo: Iwanami shoten, 1995.

———. *The Japanese Monarchy*. Armonk, N.Y.: M. E. Sharpe, 1992.

Nakamura Masanori. "Sengo kaikaku to gendai." In *Senryō to sengo kaikaku*, edited by Nakamura Masanori, 1–27. Kindai Nihon no kiseki, vol. 6. Tokyo: Yoshikawa kōbunkan, 1994.

Nakamura Masanori et al. *Rekishi to shinjitsu: ima Nihon no rekishi o kangaeru.* Tokyo: Chikuma shobō, 1997.

Nakamura Takafusa. *Shōwashi.* 2 vols. Tokyo: Tōyō keizai shinpō sha, 1993.

Nakano Tsuya. "Fujinbuchō no yūutsu: Tokyoto no Orinpikku taisaku." In *Kōdoseichō no jidai, onnatachi wa*, jūgoshi nōto sengohen, edited by Onna tachi no ima o toukai. Tokyo: Inpakuto shuppankai, 1992.

Nakano Yoshio. "Saikin no hanbei kanjō—ichibu no sendō to katazukeruna." *Bungeishunjū*, November 1953, 56–63.

Nakaoka Tetsurō. "Gijyutsu kakushin." In *Iwanami kōza: Nihon tsūshi*, vol. 20, edited by Asao Naohiro et al., 183–225. Tokyo: Iwanami shoten, 1995.

Nakanishi Shintarō. " 'Kobayashi Yoshinori' to iu media." *Sekai*, December 1998, 106–11.

Nankin daigyakusatsu no shinsō o akiraka nisuru zenkoku renrakukai, ed. *Nankin daigyakusatsu: Nihonjin eno kokuhatsu.* Tokyo: Tōhō shuppan, 1992.

Narita Tōru. *Tokusatsu to kaijū: waga zōkei bijutsu.* Tokyo: Firumu āto, 1996.

Nathan, John. *Mishima: A Biography.* Boston: Little, Brown, 1974.

Natsume Fusanosuke. *Manga to "sensō."* Tokyo: Kōdansha, 1997.

NHK hōsō yoron chōsasho, ed. *Tokyō Orinpikku.* Tokyo: Nihon hōsō kyōkai, 1967.

NHK Shuzaihan. *Kokusan jōyōsha/60 nen Anpo to Kishi Nobusuke.* Sengo 50 nen sonotoki Nihon wa, vol. 1. Tokyo: Nihon hōsō kyōkai shuppan kyōkai, 1995.

———. *Sekiyu shokku/Kokutetsu rōshi funsō.* Sengo 50 nen sonotoki Nihon wa, vol. 5. Tokyo: Nihon Hōsō kyōkai shuppan kyōkai, 1996.

Nichibō shashi hensan iinkai, ed. *Nichibō 75 nenshi.* Osaka: Nichibō kabushiki-gaisha, 1966.

Nietzsche, Friedrich. *On the Genealogy of Morals and Ecce Homo.* Translated by Walter Kaufmann. New York: Vintage Books, 1989.

Nihon senbotsu gakusei kinenkai, ed. *Shinpan, Kike wadatsumi no koe: Nihon senbotsu gakusei no koe.* Tokyo: Iwanami shoten, 1995.

Nihon taiiku kyōkai, ed. *Tokyo Orinpikku senshu kyōkataisaku honbu hōkokusho.* Tokyo: Nihon taiiku kyōkai, 1965.

———, ed. *Tokyo Orinpiiku supōtsu kagaku kenkyū hōkoku.* Tokyo: Nihon taiiku kyōkai, 1965.

Nishibe Susumu. *60 nen Anpo: senchimentaru jānī.* Tokyo: Bungeishunjū, 1986.

Nishii Kazuo, ed. *Sengo 50 nen: Post war 50 years.* Tokyo: Mainichi shinbunsha, 1995.

Nishikawa Nagao. *Nihon no sengoshōsetsu—haikyo no hikari.* Tokyo: Iwanami shoten, 1988.

Nishitani Osamu. "Mirai eno shikinseki toshiteno Soren, soshite Roshia." *Shisō no kagaku*, March 1996, 4–15.

———. *Sensō ron.* Tokyo: Iwanami shoten, 1992.

———. *Yoru no kodō ni fureru: sensōron kōgi.* Tokyo: Tokyo daigaku shuppankai, 1995.

Nobile, Philip, ed. *Judgement at the Smithsonian*. New York: Marlowe, 1995.

Noda Masaaki. "Kajōdaishō to kōgekisei." *Sekai*, December 1998, 112–17.

———. *Sensōto zaiseki*. Tokyo: Iwanami shoten, 1998.

Nomiyama Gyōji. *Shomei no nai fūkei*. Tokyo: Heibonsha, 1997.

Nomiyama Gyōji et al. *Inori no gashū*. Tokyo: Nihon hōsōkyōkai shuppan, 1977.

Nomura Taku. *Iryō to kokumin seikatsu*. Tokyo: Aoki shoten, 1981.

Noriega, Chon A. "Godzilla and the Japanese Nightmare: When *Them!* Is U.S." *Cinema Journal* 27, no. 1 (1987): 63–75.

Nornes, Abé Mark. "The Body at the Center—*The Effect of the Atomic Bomb on Hiroshima and Nagasaki*." In *Hibakusha Cinema: Hiroshima, Nagasaki, and the Nuclear Image in Japanese Film*, edited by Mick Broderick, 120–59.. London: Kegan Paul International, 1996.

———. "Dawn of Feedom." In *Media Wars: Then and Now* (Pāruhābā 50 shūnen: Nichibei eigasen), ed. Fukushima Yukio and Markus Nornes, 256–63. Tokyo: Sōjinsha, 1991.

Nosaka Akiyuki. *Adoribu jijoden*. In *Nosaka Akiyuki*, edited by Tōmaru Tatsu, 1–247. Sakka no jiden, vol. 19. Tokyo: Nihon toshosentā, 1994.

———. "American *Hijiki*." In *Contemporary Japanese Literature*, edited by Howard Hibbet, 436–68. New York: Knopf, 1977.

———. *Amerika hijiki, Hotaru no haka*. Tokyo: Shinchōsha, 1972.

———. *Hitodenashi*. Tokyo: Chūōkōronsha, 1997.

———. *Kakuyaku taru gyakkō: shisetu Mishima Yukio*. Tokyo: Bungeishunjū, 1987.

———. *Sensō dōwashū*. Tokyo: Chūōkōron sha, 1980.

———. *Waga shikkoku no hi*. Tokyo: Kōbunsha, 1992.

———. "Yamiichi to sukurīn." In *Nosaka Akiyuki*, edited by Tōmaru Tatsu. Sakka no jiden, vol. 19. Tokyo: Nihon toshosentā, 1994.

O'Brien, David M. *To Dream of Dreams: Religious Freedom and Constitutional Politics in Postwar Japan*. Honolulu: University of Hawai'i Press, 1996.

Oda Mitsuo. *"Kōgai" no tanjō to shi*. Tokyo: Seikyūsha, 1997.

Ōe Kenzaburō. *Mirumae ni tobe*. Tokyo: Shinchōsha, 1958.

Office of the Prime Minister, Statistics Bureau. *Japan Statistical Yearbook, 1950*. Tokyo: Nihon Statistical Association and Mainichi shinbunsha, 1951.

———. *Japan Statistical Yearbook, 1965*. Tokyo: Nihon Statistical Association and Mainishi shinbunsha, 1966.

———. *Japan Statistical Yearbook, 1970*. Tokyo: Nihon Statistical Association and Mainishi shinbunsha, 1971.

———. *Japan Statistical Yearbook, 1975*. Tokyo: Nihon Statistical Association and Mainishi shinbunsha, 1975.

Ōgai Haruko. *Ōgai Yatarō isakushū*. Fukuoka, 1994.

Oguma Eiji. " 'Hidari' o kihisuru popyurizum." *Sekai*, December 1998, 94–105.

———. *Tan'itsu minzoku shinwa no kigen: Nihonjin no jigazō no keifu*. Tokyo: Shin'yōsha, 1995.

Oka Yuriko. *Shiroi michi o iku tabi: Watashi no sengoshi*. Kyoto: Jinbun shoin, 1993.

Okada Yasuo. *Shisetsu Matsuzawa byōinshi*. Tokyo: Miyazaki gakujutsu shuppansha, 1981.

Ōkoshi Aiko. "Mōhitotsu no 'Katarikuchi no mondai'—donoyōni rekishiteki jiji-tsu to deauka." *Sōbun*, April 1997, 21–26.

Okuno Takeo. "Daimatsu kantoku niokeru otoko no kenkyū." *Fujin kōron*, December 1964, 116–21.

———. *Sakaguchi Ango*. Tokyo: Bungeishunjū, 1996.

Okuyama Makoto. *Tokyo Orinpikku joshi senshumura*. Tokyo: Kokusho kankō-kai, 1988.

Onnatachi no ima o toukai, ed. *Kōdoseichō no jidai onnatachi wa*. Jūgoshi nōto sengohen, vol. 6. Tokyo: Inpakuto shuppankai, 1992.

———, ed. *Onnatachi no 60 nen Ampo*. Jūgoshi nōto sengohen, vol. 5. Tokyo: Inpakuto shuppankai, 1990.

Ono Kōsei. *Chikyūgi ni notta neko*. Tokyo: Tōjusha, 1982.

Orinpikku Tokyo taikai soshiki iinkai, ed. *Dai 18 kai Orinpikku kyōgitaikai kōshiki hōkokusho*. Tokyo: Orinpikku Tokyo taikai soshiki iinkai, 1966.

———, ed. *Orinpikku Tokyo taikai shiryōshū*. Tokyo: Orinpikku Tokyo taikai soshiki iinkai, 1965.

Orwell, George. *1984*. San Diego: Harcourt Brace Jovanovich, 1949.

Ōshima Nagisa. *Cinema, Censorship, and the State: The Writings of Nagisa Oshima*. Cambridge: MIT Press, 1992.

———. *Ōshima Nagisa 1960*. Tokyo: Seidosha, 1993.

Ōsumi Hideo. "Sutā no za, 2: eikō ka kekkon kano wakaremichi." *Fujin gahō*, February 1, 1963, 223–27.

Ōtake Akiko. "Doromichi to dobugawa no Tokyo ga nakunattahi." *Tokyōjin*, August 1994, 39–45.

Ōtsuki Takahiro. "Bokuga 'Atarashii rekishi kyōkasho o tsukurukai' o sukedachi-suru wake." *Seiron*, April 1997, 46–57.

———. "Watashi no *Sensōron*." *Ronza*, December 1998, 216–19.

Pacific War Research Society. *Japan's Longest Day*. Tokyo: Kodansha International, 1968.

Packard, George R. *Protest in Tokyo: The Security Treaty Crisis of 1960*. Princeton: Princeton University Press, 1966.

Pile, Steve. *The Body and the City: Psychoanalysis, Space, and Subjectivity*. London: Routledge, 1996.

Rajio taisō 50 shūnenkinenshi henshū iinkai. *Atarashii asa ga kita—rajio taisō 50 nen no ayumi*. Tokyo: Kan'ihokensha kan'yūshakyōkai, 1979.

Rōdōshō. *Rōdō hakusho 1992*. Tokyo: Rōdōshō, 1992.

Ross, Kristin. *Fast Cars, Clean Bodies: Decolonization and the Reordering of French Culture*. Cambridge: MIT Press, 1995.

Rousso, Henry. *The Vichy Syndrome: History and Memory in France since 1944*. Cambridge: Harvard University Press, 1991.

Ryū Shintarō. "Anpo kaitei o dōshitara yoika—hakai chokuzen no kikikara kok-kai o sukue." *Bungeishunjū*, June 1960, 64–72.

Saeki Shōichi. "Menohito no henreki: Mishima Yukio no kokusaisei." In *Hihyō to kenkyū: Mishima Yukio*, edited by Shirakawa Masayoshi, 314–24. Tokyo: Haga shoten, 1974.

———. *Nichibei kankei no naka no bungaku*. Tokyo: Bungeishunjū, 1984.

Saitō Michio. *Genbaku shinwa no 50 nen*. Tokyo: Chūōkōronsha, 1995.

Sakaguchi Ango. *Sakaguchi Ango zenshū*. Vol. 14. Tokyo: Chikuma shobō, 1990.
Sakai Naoki. *Shizansareru Nihongo, Nihonjin*. Tokyo: Shin'yōsha, 1996.
Sakamoto Kōjirō. *Shōchō tennōsei eno pafōmansu*. Tokyo: Yamakawa shuppansha, 1989.
Sakata Minoru. "Nihongata kindai seikatsu yōshiki no seiritsu." In *Zoku, Shōwa bunka, 1945–1989*, edited by Minami Hiroshi and Shakai shinri kenkyūjo, 7–32. Tokyo: Keisō shobō, 1990.
Sakuma Tetsuo. "Tennō o mita Nihonjin—gojunkō hiwa." *Shokun*, March 1989, 194–207.
Sakurai Tetsuo. *Kanōsei toshiteno "sengo."* Tokyo: Kōdansha, 1994.
———. *Shisō to shite no 60 nendai*. Tokyo: Chikuma shobō, 1993.
Sams, Crawford F. *DDT kakumei*. Edited and translated by Takemae Eiji. Tokyo: Iwanami shoten, 1986.
———. *"Medic."* Armonk, N.Y.: M. E. Sharpe, 1998.
Sankei shinbun "Sengoshi kaifū" shuzaihan. *Sengoshi kaifū*. 3 vols. Tokyo: Sankei shinbunsha, 1995.
Sano Shin'ichi. *Karisuma: Nakauchi Isao to Daiei no "sengo."* Tokyo: Nikkei BP sha, 1998.
Saotome Katsumoto. *Sensō o kataritsugu—onna tachi no shōgen*. Tokyo: Iwanami shoten, 1998.
———. *Tokyo daikūshū—Shōwa 20 nen 3 gatsu 10 ka no kiroku*. Tokyo: Iwanami shoten, 1971.
Sasaki Takeshi et al., eds. *Sengoshi daijiten*. Tokyo: Sanseidō, 1991.
Sasamoto Yukio. *Beigunsenryōka no genbaku chōsa: genbaku kagaikoku ninatta Nihon*. Tokyo: Shinkansha, 1995.
Sasamoto Yukio and Yoshioka Hitoshi. "Kakujidai to wa nanika." *Gendai shisō* 24, no. 6 (1996): 70–96
Satō Akira, ed. *"Nippon kabushiki gaisha" shuppansu*. Shōgen no Shōwashi, vol. 9. Tokyo: Gakushū kenkyūsha, 1982.
Satō Noriko. "Orinpikku ga yattekita." In *Kōdoseichō no jidai, onnatachi wa* edited by Onna tachi no ima o toukai, 44–55. Jūgoshi nōto sengohen, vol. 6. Tokyo: Inpakuto shuppankai, 1992.
Satō Tadao. "Hyūmanizumu no jidai—Nihon eigashi 5." In *Sengo eigano tenkai*, edited by Imamura Shōhei et al., 2–71. Kōza Nihon eiga, vol. 5. Tokyo: Iwanami shoten, 1987.
———. *Nihon eiga 300*. Tokyo: Asahi shinbunsha, 1995.
———. *Nihon eigashi*. Vol. 4. Tokyo: Iwanami shoten, 1995.
Satō Takeshi. "Kōdo seichō to terebi bunka." In *Zoku, Shōwa bunka*, edited by Minami Hiroshi, 145–79. Tokyo: Keisō shobō, 1990.
Sawano Masaki. *Raisha no sei: bunmei kaika no jōken to shiteno*. Tokyo: Seikyūsha, 1994.
Sawawatari Kazuo. "Washinton haitsu no 24 jikan." *Nihon*, January 1962, 46–49.
Schaller, Michael. *Altered States: The United States and Japan since the Occupation*. Oxford: Oxford University Press, 1997.
Seki Harunami. *Sengo Nihon no supōtsu seisaku—sono kōzō to tenkai*. Tokyo: Daishūkan Shoten, 1997.

Senō Kappa. *Shōnen H*, 2 vols. Tokyo: Kōdansha, 1997.

Sensō giseisha o kokoro ni kizamukai, ed. *Watashi wa "ianfu" dewa nai: Nihon no shinraku to seidorei*. Osaka: Tōhō shuppan, 1997.

Seo Ikuo. "Ningen no utsukushii shūyōjo." *Shisō no kagaku*, March 1996, 64–77.

Sherry, Michael. "Guilty Knowledge." *New York Times Book Review*, July 30, 1995, 11–13.

Shiba Ryōtarō and Handō Kazutoshi. "Shiba Ryōtarō sengo 50 nen o kataru." In *Iwanami shoten to Bungeishunjū*, edited by Mainichi shinbunsha, 7–17. Tokyo: Mainichi shinbunsha, 1996.

Shibagaki Kazuo. *Kōwa kara kōdoseichōe*. Shōwa no rekishi, vol. 9. Tokyo: Shōgakukan, 1989.

Shibata Shō. *Saredo wareraga hibi*. Tokyo: Bungeishunjū, 1964.

Shima Shigeo. *Bunto shishi*. Tokyo: Hihyōsha, 1999.

Shimizu Hiroshi. "Dainiji Sekai Taisen to shōgaisha, 1—Taiheiyō Sensō kano seishinshōgaisha, hansenbyōsha no seizon to jinken." *Saitama daigaku kiyō, kyōikugakubu (kyōikukagaku)* 39, no. 1 (1990): 19–45.

———. *Shōgaisha to sensō—shuki, shōgenshū*. Tokyo: Shin Nihon Shuppansha, 1987.

Shimizu Ikutarō. "Anpo tōsō 1 nengo no shisō—seiji no nakano chishikijin." *Chūōkōron*, July 1961, 45–57.

———. "Senryōka no tennō." *Shisō* 348 (June 1953): 626–44.

———. *Shimizu Ikutarō chosakushū*. Vol. 14. Tokyo: Kōdansha, 1993.

Shimizu Isao. *Manga ni miru 1945 nen*. Tokyo: Yoshikawa kōbunkan, 1995.

Shimizu Masashi. *Tsuge Yoshiharu o yomu*. Tokyo: Gendai shokan, 1995.

Shimizu Setsuji. *Sensai koji no shinwa: Nosaka Akiyuki + Sengo no sakkatachi*. Tokyo: Kyōiku shuppan sentā, 1995.

Shimizu Yasuko. *Mori to sakana to gekisenchi*. Tokyo: Hokuto shuppan, 1997.

Shimokawa Kōshi. *Dansei no mita Shōwa seisōshi*. Tokyo: Daisan shokan, 1992.

Shindō Eiichi. "Bunkatsu sareta ryōdo." *Sekai*, April 1979, 31–51.

Shinobu Seizaburō. *Seidan no rekishigaku*. Tokyo: Keisō shobō, 1992.

———. *Anpo tōsōshi—35 nichi seikyoku shiron*. Tokyo: Sekai shoin, 1961.

Shiota Ushio. *Tokyo wa moetaka*. Tokyo: PHP kenkyūsho, 1985.

Shirakawa Masayoshi, ed. *Hihyō to kenkyū Mishima Yukio*. Tokyo: Haga shoten, 1974.

Shūkan asahi, ed., *Chichi no senki*. Tokyo: Asahi shinbunsha, 1965.

Shuto kōsoku dōro kōdan. *Shuto kōsoku dōro kōdan 20 nenshi*. Tokyo: Shuto kōsoku dōro kōdan, 1979.

Silverberg, Miriam. "Remembering Pearl Harbor, Forgetting Charlie Chaplin, and the Case of the Disappearing Western Woman: A Picture Story." *Positions* 1, no. 1 (1993): 24–76.

Silverman, Kaja. *The Subject of Semiotics*. Oxford: Oxford University Press, 1983.

Sodei Rinjirō. *Haikei Makkāsā Gensuisama*. Tokyo: Chūōkōronsha, 1991.

———. *Watashitachi wa tekidattanoka*. Tokyo: Iwanami shoten, 1995.

Stimson, Henry L. "The Decision to Use the Atomic Bomb." *Harper's*, February 1947, 97–107.

Stimson, Henry L., and McGeorge Bundy. *On Active Service in Peace and War.* New York: Harper and Brothers, 1948.

Stokes, Henry Scott. *The Life and Death of Yukio Mishima.* New York: Noonday Press, 1995.

Sturken, Maria. *Tangled Memories: The Vietnam War, the AIDS Epidemic, and the Politics of Remembering.* Berkeley and Los Angeles: University of California Press, 1997.

Sugimoto Sonoko. "Asueno kinen." In *Tokyo Orinpikku: bungakusha no mita seikino saiten.* Tokyo: Kōdansha, 1964.

Sugiyama Akiko. *Senryōki no iryōkaikaku.* Tokyo: Keisōshobō, 1995.

Supōtsu Nippon shinbunsha, ed. *Rikidōzan hana no shōgai.* Tokyo: Supōtsu Nippon shinbunsha, 1964.

Suzuki Akira. *Kayōkyoku besuto 100 no kenkyū.* Tokyo: TBS Britanica, 1982.

———. *"Nankin daigyakusatsu" no maboroshi.* Tokyo: Bungeishunjū, 1973.

Suzuki Shizuko. "Tennō gyōkō to shōchō tennōsei no kakuritsu." *Rekishi hyōron,* February 1975, 53–66.

Suzuki Yūko. *Sensō sekinin to jendā.* Tokyo: Miraisha, 1997.

Tachibana Takashi. "60 nen Anpo eiyū no eikō to hisan." *Bungeishunjū,* February 1969, 244–54.

Takahashi Gen'ichirō. *Bungaku nanka kowakunai.* Tokyo: Asahi shinbunsha, 1998.

Takahashi Hidemine. *Subarashiki rajio taisō.* Tokyo: Shōgakukan, 1998.

Takahashi Hiroshi. *Heika, otazune mōshiagemasu.* Tokyo: Bungeishunjū, 1988.

———. *Shōchō tennō.* Tokyo: Iwanami shoten, 1987.

———. *Tennōke no shigoto: yomu "kōshitsu jiten."* Tokyo: Bungeishunjū, 1996.

Takahashi Saburō. *"Senki mono" o yomu.* Tokyo: Akademia shuppan, 1988.

Takahashi Tetsuya. *Kioku no echika: sensō, tetsugaku, Aushubittsu.* Tokyo: Iwanami shoten, 1995.

———. "Ojoku no kioku o megutte." *Gunzō* 50, no. 3 (1995): 176–82.

———. "Shōgen to jendā no seiji." *Shisō,* April 1997, 2–4.

Takahashi Toshio. *Gojira no nazo.* Tokyo: Kōdansha, 1998.

Takarada Akira. *Nippon Gojira ōgondensetsu.* Tokyo: Fusōsha, 1998.

Takasugi Ichirō. *Ikite kaerishi heino kioku.* Tokyo: Iwanami shoten, 1996.

Takayanagi Kenzō, Ōtomo Ichirō, and Tanaka Hideo, eds. *Nihonkoku Kenpō seitei no katei.* Tokyo: Yūhikaku, 1972.

Takeuchi Hiroshi. " 'Gojira' no tanjō." In *Tsuburaya Eiji no eizōsekai,* edited by Yamamoto Shingo, 66–93. Tokyo: Jitsugyō no Nihon sha, 1983.

Takeuchi Yoshimi. "Minshu ka dokusai ka." In *Takeuchi Yoshimi zenshū.* Vol. 9. Tokyo: Chikuma shobō, 1981.

Takeyama, Akiko. *Gyokuon hōsō.* Tokyo: Banseisha, 1989.

Tamura Taijirō. *Nikutai no bungaku.* Tokyo: Kusano shobō, 1948.

———. *Tamura Taijirō senshū.* Vol. 1. Tokyo: Kusano shobō, 1948.

———. *Waga bundan seishunki.* Tokyo: Shinchōsha, 1963.

Tanaka Hiroshi. "Nihon no sengo sekinin to Ajia—sengo hoshō to rekishi ninshiki." In *Ajia no reisen to datsu-shokuminchika,* edited by Ōe Shinobu et al., 183–216. Kindai Nihon to shokuminchi, vol. 8. Tokyo: Iwanami shoten, 1993.

Tanaka Kakuei. *Building a New Japan*. Translated by Simul International. Tokyo: Simul Press, 1973.

Tanaka Nobumasa. *Dokyumento Shōwa tennō*. Vol. 6. Tokyo: Ryokufū shuppan, 1990.

———. *"Sensō no kioku": sono inpei no kōzō*. Tokyo: Ryokufū shuppan, 1997.

Tanaka Nobumasa, Tanaka Hiroshi, and Hata Nagami. *Izoku to sengo*. Tokyo: Iwanami shoten, 1995.

Tanaka Satoshi. *Eisei tenrankai no yokubō*. Tokyo: Seikyūsha, 1994.

Taniguchi Gentarō. *Hinomaru to Orinpikku*. Tokyo: Bungeishunjū, 1997.

Tanimoto Kiyoshi. *Hiroshima no jūjikao idaite*. Tokyo: Kōdansha, 1950.

Tanuma Takeyoshi. *Tokyo no sengo: Tanuma Takeyoshi shashinshū*. Tokyo: Chikuma shobō, 1993.

Terasaki Hidenari and Mariko Terasaki Miller, eds. *Shōwa tennō dokuhakuroku: Terasaki Hidenari goyōgakari nikki*. Tokyo: Bungeishunjū, 1991.

Tezuka Osamu. *Boku no manga jinsei*. Tokyo: Iwanami shoten, 1997.

———. "Manga baka no ben." *Bungeishunjū*, August 1975, 85–87.

Toda Arinobu. "Sengo junkō no seishin—Shōwa denkō Kawasaki kōjō kara." *Seiron*, March 1989, 334–45.

Tōhō kabushikigaisha haikyūbu. *"Tokyo Orinpikku" haikyū hakusho*. Tokyo: Tōhō, 1965.

Tokuoka Takao. *Gosui no hito*. Tokyo: Bungeishunjū, 1996.

Tokyo hyakunenshi henshū iinkai. *Tokyo hyakunenshi*. Vol. 6. Tokyo: Teikoku chihō gyōsei gakkai, 1972.

Tokyo kensetsukyoku. *Kensetsukyoku jigyō gaiyō, 1965*. Tokyo: Tokyo kensetsukyoku, 1965.

Tokyo kōsoku dōro kabushiki gaisha. *Tokyo kōsoku dōro 30 nenno ayumi*. Tokyo: Tokyo kōsoku dōro kabushiki gaisha, 1981.

Tokyo Metropolitan Government. *Tokyo Statistical Yearbook, 1960*. Tokyo: Tokyo Metropolitan Government, 1961.

———. *Tokyo Statistical Yearbook, 1964*. Tokyo: Tokyo Metropolitan Government, 1965.

Tokyoto eiseikyoku. *Eisei jigyō gaiyō, 1965*. Tokyo: Eiseikyoku gyōmubu fukyūka, 1966.

———. *Tokyoto eisei nenpō*, no. 17 (1964). Tokyo: Eiseikyoku gyōmubu fukyūka, 1966.

Tokyoto gesuidōkyoku. *Jigyōgaiyō: Heisei 6 nenban*. Tokyo: Tokyoto gesuidōkyoku, 1994.

———. *Tokyoto gesuidō jigyō nenpō*, Shōwa 36 (1961) nendoban. Tokyo: Tokyoto gesuidōkyoku, 1963.

Toland, John. *The Rising Sun: The Decline and Fall of the Japanese Empire, 1936–1945*. New York: Random House, 1970.

Tomiyama Ichirō. *Senjō no kioku*. Tokyo: Nihon keizai hyōronsha, 1995.

Toyoshita Narahiko. *Anpojōyaku no seiritsu—Yoshida gaikō to tennō gaikō*. Tokyo: Iwanami shoten, 1996.

———. " 'Kūhaku' no sengoshi." *Sekai*, March 1990, 105–17.

———. "Tennō wa nanio kattataka." *Sekai*, February 1990, 232–51.

Treat, John W. *Writing Ground Zero*. Chicago: University of Chicago Press, 1995.

Truman, Harry S. *Memoirs of Harry S. Truman: Year of Decisions*. Garden City, N.Y.: Doubleday, 1955.

Tsuge Yoshiharu. *Tsuge Yoshiharu sakuhinshū: Gensenkan shujin*. Tokyo: Futabasha, 1984.

Tsukasa Osamu. *Sensō to bijutsu*. Tokyo: Iwanami shoten, 1992.

Tsukazaki Naoki, ed. *Koenaki gyakusatsu*. Tokyo: BOC shuppanbu, 1983.

Tsuneishi Keiichi. *731 butai: Seibutsu heiki hanzai no shinjitsu*. Tokyo: Kōdansha, 1995.

Tsuru Shigeto. *Japan's Capitalism: Creative Defeat and Beyond*. Cambridge: Cambridge University Press, 1993.

Tsurumi Shunsuke. "Sengo no taishū bunka." In *Sensō to Nihon eiga*, edited by Imamura Shōhei et al., 340–53. Kōza Nihon eiga, vol. 4. Tokyo: Iwanami shoten, 1986.

Ubuki Satoru. "Hibakutaiken to heiwaundō." In *Sengo minshushugi*, edited by Nakamura Masanori et al., 97–130. Sengo Nihon—Senryō to sengo kaikaku, vol. 4. Tokyo: Iwanami shoten, 1995.

Uchida Masatoshi. *"Sengo hoshō" o kangaeru*. Tokyo: Kōdansha, 1994.

Uchimura Gōsuke et al. " 'Sutārin shūyōjo rettō' no Nihonjin." *Bungeishunjū*, September 1982, 184–211.

Ueno Chizuko. *Kindai kazoku no seiritu to shūen*. Tokyo: Iwanami shoten, 1994.

———. *Nashonarizumu to jendā*. Tokyo: Seidosha, 1998.

Ueno Kōshi. *Nikutai no jidai: taikenteki 60 nendai bunkaron*. Tokyo: Gendaishokan, 1989.

———. *Sengo saikō*. Tokyo: Asahi shinbunsha, 1995.

Uesugi Satoshi. *Datsu gōmanizumu sengen*. Osaka: Tōhō shuppan, 1997.

United States Senate. Senate Resolution 257. *Congressional Record*, vol. 140, no. 134, September 22, 1994: S13315–16.

United States Strategic Bombing Survey. *The Effect of Strategic Bombing on Japanese Morale*. Washington, D.C.: United States Government Printing Office, 1947.

———. *Japan's Struggle to End the War*. Washington, D.C.: United States Government Printing Office, 1946.

Uno Shun'ichi et al. *Nihon zenshi: Japan Chronik*. Tokyo: Kōdansha, 1991.

"Uriwatasareta shin'iki—torihikidaikin 1 oku 6 senmanen nari." *Shinsō*, September 1954, 4–7.

Ushijima Hidehiko. *Rikidōzan: ōzumō, puroresu, urashakai*. Tokyo: Daisan shokan, 1995.

Wada Haruki. "Nigitta teo hanasazuni—Nichibei Anpo taisei o kangaeru." *Shisō no kagaku*, April 1996, 31–34.

Washida Koyata. *Tennō ron*. Tokyo: San'ichi shobō, 1989.

Watanabe Osamu. *Seiji kaikaku to kenpōkaisei: Nakasone Yasuhiro kara Ozawa Ichirō e*. Tokyo: Aoki shoten, 1994.

———. "Sengo hoshushihai no kōzō." In *Iwanami kōza: Nihon tsūshi*, vol. 20, edited by Asao Naohiro et al., 69–112. Tokyo: Iwanami shoten, 1995.

Weinstein, Martin E. *Japan's Postwar Defense Policy, 1947–1968*. New York: Columbia University Press, 1971.

Yamada Fūtarō. *Senchūha fusen nikki*. Tokyo: Kōdansha, 1985.

Yamada Masami. *Zettai Gojira shugi.* Tokyo: Kadokawa shoten, 1995.

Yamada Shōgo and Mori Akihide. *Kaden konjaku monogatari.* Tokyo: Sanseidō, 1983.

Yamaguchi Hitomi. "Taishū o bakani shuruna." *Bungeishunjū,* May 1965, 224–30.

Yamaguchi Masatomo. "Dōgu." In *Kazoku no seikatsu no monogatari,* Kōdoseichō to Nihonjin, part 2, ed. Kōdoseichō o kangaerukai, 60–104. Tokyo: Nihon editā sukūru shuppanbu, 1986.

Yamaguchi Yoshiko and Fujiwara Sakuya. *Ri Kō-ran: Watakushi no hansei.* Tokyo: Shinchōsha, 1987.

Yamaguchi Yoshiomi. "Yamaguchi hanji no tsuma—sono sei to shi." *Bungeishunjū,* July 1982, 342–47.

Yamamoto Akira. *Kasutori zasshi kenkyū—shinboru ni miru fūzokushi.* Tokyo: Chūōkōronsha, 1998.

Yamaoka Akira. *Kasutori zasshi ni miru sengoshi.* Tokyo: Orion shuppansha, 1970.

Yang, Daqing. "Review Essay: Convergence or Divergence? Recent Historical Writings on the Rape of Nanjing." *American Historical Review* 104, no. 3 (1999): 842–65.

Yasuoka Shōtarō. "Orinpikku eiga zukuri funsenki." *Fujin kōron,* December 1964, 122–28.

———. *A View by the Sea.* Translated by Kären Wigen. New York: Columbia University Press, 1984.

Yomiuri shinbun henshūkyoku "sengoshi han," ed. *Sengo 50 nen Nippon no kiseki,* vol. 1. Tokyo: Yomiuri shinbunsha, 1995.

Yonahara Kei. " 'Tasōde fukuzatsuna jūsōsei' shimeshite iruka: heiwaundō no gawanimo hoshii 'sensōron.' " *Ronza,* December 1998, 210–15.

Yoneyama, Lisa. "Critical Warps: Facticity, Transformative Knowledge, and Postnationalist Criticism in the Smithsonian Controversy." *Positions 5,* no. 3 (1997): 779–809.

———. *Hiroshima Traces: Time, Space, and Dialectics of Memory.* Berkeley and Los Angeles: University of California Press, 1999.

Yōrō Takeshi. *Shintai no bungakushi.* Tokyo: Shinchōsha, 1997.

Yoshida Ken'ichi. "Tokyo kyanpu kansatsuki—tachiiri kinshi chitai o manposuru." *Bungeishunjū,* February 1954, 113–19.

Yoshida Mitsuru. *Chinkon senkan Yamato.* Tokyo: Kōdansha, 1974.

———. *Senkan Yamato.* Tokyo: Kadokawa shoten, 1968.

Yoshida Morio. *Kyoto ni gengaku o tōkaseyo: Waner densetsu no shinjitsu.* Tokyo: Kadokawa shoten, 1995.

Yoshida Shigeru. *The Yoshida Memoirs.* Translated by Yoshida Ken'ichi. Westport, Conn.: Greenwood Press, 1961.

Yoshida Yutaka. *Gendai rekishigaku to sensōsekinin.* Tokyo: Aoki shoten, 1997.

———. *Nihonjin no sensōkan: sengoshi no naka no henyō.* Tokyo: Iwanami shoten, 1995.

———. *Shōwa tennō no shūsenshi.* Tokyo: Iwanami shoten, 1992.

Yoshikawa Hiroshi. *Kōdoseichō—Nippon o kaeta 6,000 nichi.* 20 sekiki no Nippon, vol. 6. Tokyo: Yomiuri shinbunsha, 1997.

Yoshimi Shunya. *Hakurankai no seijigaku*. Tokyo: Chūōkōronsha, 1992.

Yoshimi Yoshiaki. *Jūgun ianfu*. Tokyo: Iwanami shoten, 1995.

Yoshimi Yoshiaki and Kawata Fumiko, eds. *"Jūgun ianfu" o meguru 30 no uso to shinjitsu*. Tokyo: Ōtsuki shoten, 1997.

Yoshimura Yoshio. *Kimiwa Rikidōzan o mitaka*. Tokyo: Asuka shinsha, 1988.

Yoshinaga Haruko. *Nazo no dokuyaku: suikyū Tekigin jiken*. Tokyo: Kōdansha, 1996.

———. *Sasurai no "mifukuin"*. Tokyo: Chikumashobō, 1987.

Yui Daizaburō. *Nichibei sensōkan no sōkoku: masatsu no shinsōshinri*. Tokyo: Iwanami shoten, 1995.

Žižek, Slavoj. *Tarrying with the Negative: Kant, Hegel, and the Critique of Ideology*. Durham: Duke University Press, 1993.

Index